SACRAMENTO PUBLIC LIBRARY

D0149320

WITHDRAWN

AMERICAN QUEENMAKER

OTHER TITLES BY JULIE DES JARDINS:

Women and the Historical Enterprise in America: Gender, Race, and the Politics of Memory (2003)

The Madame Curie Complex: The Hidden History of Women in Science (2010)

Lillian Gilbreth: Redefining Domesticity (2012)

Walter Camp: Football and the Modern Man (2015)

AMERICAN QUEENMAKER

HOW **MISSY MELONEY** BROUGHT **WOMEN** INTO **POLITICS**

JULIE DES JARDINS

BASIC BOOKS
NEW YORK

Copyright © 2020 by Julie Des Jardins

Cover design by Ann Kirchner
Cover image: Library of Congress, Prints & Photographs Divison, LC-DIG-GGBAIN-32254, The Delineator. V.98 (1921), © indiovetorepurodotcom/Shutterstock.com; © Daboost/Shutterstock.com
Cover copyright © 2020 Hachette Book Group, Inc.

Hachette Book Group supports the right to free expression and the value of copyright. The purpose of copyright is to encourage writers and artists to produce the creative works that enrich our culture.

The scanning, uploading, and distribution of this book without permission is a theft of the author's intellectual property. If you would like permission to use material from the book (other than for review purposes), please contact permissions@hbgusa.com. Thank you for your support of the author's rights.

Basic Books
Hachette Book Group
1290 Avenue of the Americas, New York, NY 10104
www.basicbooks.com
Printed in the United States of America

First Edition: January 2020

Published by Basic Books, an imprint of Perseus Books, LLC, a subsidiary of Hachette Book Group, Inc. The Basic Books name and logo is a trademark of the Hachette Book Group.

The Hachette Speakers Bureau provides a wide range of authors for speaking events. To find out more, go to www.hachettespeakersbureau.com or call (866) 376-6591.

The publisher is not responsible for websites (or their content) that are not owned by the publisher.

Print book interior design by Six Red Marbles.

Library of Congress Cataloging-in-Publication Data
Names: Des Jardins, Julie, author.
Title: American queenmaker: how Missy Meloney brought women into politics / Julie Des Jardins.
Description: First edition. | New York: Basic Books, 2019. | Includes bibliographical references and index
Identifiers: LCCN 2019018614 (print) | LCCN 2019980687 (ebook) | ISBN 9781541645493 (hardcover) | ISBN 9781541645479 (ebook)
Subjects: LCSH: Meloney, Marie Mattingly, 1883–1943. | Women journalists—United States—Biography. | Women—Political activity—United States—History—20th century.
Classification: LCC PN4874.M4856 D47 2019 (print) | LCC PN4874.M4856 (ebook) | DDC 070.92 [B]—dc23
LC record available at https://lccn.loc.gov/2019018614
LC ebook record available at https://lccn.loc.gov/2019980687

ISBNs: 978-1-5416-4549-3 (hardcover), 978-1-5416-4547-9 (ebook)

LSC-C

10 9 8 7 6 5 4 3 2 1

To my mom,
Joy Des Jardins,
and the women who remain unsung.

CONTENTS

Contents

PREFACE

AMERICAN QUEENMAKER takes us back to the turn of the twentieth century to reimagine power and influence in female form. On the surface, one might not envision our heroine as influential at all: Marie Mattingly Meloney (1878–1943) was physically feeble, lacked college credentials, and was a "stay-at-home mom" for nearly a decade. She couldn't vote in a presidential election until her forties, and she never lived to see a television, let alone appear on one. And yet perhaps only now can the full impact of her feminine power be appreciated.

When female editors-in-chief were practically unheard of, Meloney held the reins of three major periodicals—*The Delineator* (1920–1926), the *New York Herald Tribune Sunday Magazine* (1926–1935), and *This Week* (1935–1943)—and elevated the readership, revenues, and literary quality of all three. But to understand the full scope of her influence, we also need to observe her life and work when she wore other hats. She was a journalist, publicist, social reformer, mother, rainmaker, diplomat, political operative, and patron of women, the arts, and sciences—all rolled into one small, inconspicuous package.

There is no single term to categorize who or what Meloney was, though maybe there should be. For now, perhaps the best way to encapsulate her is to call her a liaison, a connector, a facilitator, a human cultural antenna, or a matchmaker of sorts, who mastered the art and science of bringing politics, media, and culture to American women while bringing American women to politics, media, and culture. We've seen women perform facets of her work at other times in history on a smaller scale. There were the *salonnières* of the Enlightenment and later, for instance, who created a space for women to be intellectually engaged and politically minded in salons they held in their drawing rooms, and occasionally in publications they collated afterward. But these women, however smart or well intentioned, performed within the more limited upper echelons of society. As sophisticated as they were, they didn't manipulate the mechanisms of mass media the way Meloney did; her public impact reverberated broadly. Certainly there are women today who are considered highly effective networkers or influencers, but we'd be hard-pressed to name any among them who share Meloney's far-ranging social or civic purposefulness. Indeed, Meloney followed in no mold, and no one has filled hers since, though being aware of the contours of that mold is more important than ever before.

One of the first women reporters allowed in the Senate press gallery, Meloney became a political portraitist in Washington before moving on to magazine work in New York, where she bolstered the literary careers of Willa Cather, Edna Ferber, and Fannie Hurst, to name a reputable few. More so than male New York editors, she was equally influential in Washington politics—and well before the Nineteenth Amendment allowed American women to vote. A friend to ambassadors, cabinet secretaries, and US senators, she also served as an unofficial advisor to Calvin Coolidge, Herbert Hoover, Bill Donovan, and even the Democrat FDR after his first presidential campaign. Though she was a Republican operative, party affiliation proved immaterial to her pan-partisan relationships; presidents trusted her, and so did their wives. Hosted at chancelleries throughout Europe, she landed interviews with world leaders not known to schmoose with journalists; it was Meloney to whom the Italian prime minister Benito Mussolini first confided his intentions to invade Ethiopia in 1935. When the sculptor Gutzon Borglum needed federal funding to complete Mount Rushmore, he asked Meloney to do his bidding in Washington. For a decade, she ran the most influential forum on political affairs in the country, convincing celebrities and presidential candidates to participate in the sessions she hosted at the Waldorf Astoria Hotel and broadcasted across the country. Although she never held a political title, she used her public platforms to inform the citizenry in ways no politician ever could.

It was not any formal position, but rather her inherent understanding of the mechanisms of influence, that gave Meloney her power. And rather than self-aggrandizing, she used that power to reveal that women writers, readers, voters, and consumers were significant cohorts worth reckoning with. She brought women and their concerns into mainstream consciousness and proved that women could be savvy shapers of political issues and images both before and after they could vote. Understanding the purchasing power of women as well as their potential to sway public discourse and political tides, she filled a void in the market for publications that spoke to women directly in a serious way. As she brought women into American media and political culture, she taught marketers and politicians that the female demographic was one they were foolish to ignore; she was the first to prove, in fact, that women could make public campaigns, or break them. Meloney truly understood *women* as an American force.

On the one hand, she ran "feminine" features in her magazines and operated a domestic institute that promoted scientific housekeeping, lending prestige to women's work in the home. On the other, she made it increasingly acceptable for women to engage with politics, paid work, and world war as consumers, experts, authors, and journalists outside the home. Her success in speaking to women and promoting their efforts was obvious not only in soaring magazine subscriptions but also in the resonance of her PR campaigns and the popularity of her annual forums, which were initially intended for clubwomen but then were broadcasted across the nation as Meloney thrust her woman-centered agenda into the American mainstream.

Meloney's accomplishments are historically noteworthy in their own right, but their lessons about gender and power make them more instructive now than ever before. There are clear parallels between her story and those of more prominent women: Nearly everyone who has written about Eleanor Roosevelt, for instance, thought her exceptional because her leadership style was appropriately feminine for the times, yet also subversive of gender norms. Recent treatments of Madame Curie tell of the scientist's single-minded perseverance in a field hostile to her, while profiles of Grace Coolidge explore how a woman without a formal title held influence in political life. Profiles of the foreign correspondent Dorothy Thompson suggest that she opened gates for more women to enter her field. Meloney knew all these women intimately and could be recognized for all the same reasons. That she isn't is largely her own doing: a master at creating publicity for others, she eschewed exposure for herself. Hers was a humble sort of power that yielded rewards beyond recognition. Here we acknowledge its efficacy and call it what it is.

IN THE 1980s, historian Margaret Rossiter tried to introduce Meloney to the reading public as the American benefactress of the great Madame Curie, and I embellished on this portrait in *The Madame Curie Complex* (2010). That Meloney remains best known, if known at all, as a footnote in the life of a Nobel-winning scientist is ironic. This is a woman whose social-service campaigns and follow-through were second to none, and not just for Curie. Decorated by the governments of Belgium and France for spearheading relief efforts in World War I, she also organized the national Better Homes in America campaign and popularized the Tomb of the Unknown Soldier. She championed working women and freedom of the press through the Carroll Club, PEN, and the New York Newspaper Women's Club. Less driven to air her own opinions than to ensure that the public hear multiple points of view, she facilitated debate through her magazines and forums that enabled Americans to better participate in their democracy. Perhaps the time has come for her radium campaign to become the footnote in a story about her own extraordinarily useful life.[1]

But she hasn't made it easy to bring her story to the surface. Tucked away in her papers at Columbia University (donated not by her, but posthumously by her son) is a note jotted on loose-leaf paper in a hurried scrawl that's hard to read. Parts of it are missing altogether: "In a drawer in my desk there is a little pad on which I have noted seven books I have planned to write—twenty birthdays have come and passed since I first began planning. . . . But leisure for fine work does not come." In the end, Meloney never did write a book, and the closest she got to telling her own story was during one of her illnesses, when she passed along anecdotes of her early career to a secretary. "This was dictated when I was in a hospital strapped to a board—It shows it," she confessed to her friend and fellow editor Mary Day. Nevertheless, those seventy-four dictated pages are the most comprehensive source we have on her experience as a cub reporter. She died in 1943, in the midst of war, compiling the writings of others in her magazine *This Week*. But anyone who has looked through her papers recognizes the makings of a remarkable life. From outpourings of US presidents to invitations from monarchs to thank-you notes from a young Shirley Temple in a loopy, cursive script, her precious relics contain a story—perhaps some five or six—that would resonate with a modern audience, if teasing them out weren't such a daunting task.[2]

My introduction to Meloney came in 2005. I was researching women in American science, and Meloney—an American, but no scientist—cropped up unexpectedly as one of the most important figures in the story as fundraiser and publicist to Madame Curie. She was a curiosity. I wondered what would motivate someone to take on Herculean tasks for a female scientist in an age when people perceived the idea of a "woman scientist" as an oxymoron. And how could she be so successful at those tasks? I moved on to a project about the industrial engineer Lillian Gilbreth—a fascinating woman in her own right—only to discover in her papers yet another fertile collaboration with Meloney, one resulting in a lasting impact on the design of American kitchens. Meloney's influence in American society looked to run both high and broad: even as she convinced presidents to honor an exceptional woman scientist, she was shaping the domestic life of thousands of average American homemakers. She brushed elbows with the powerful while appealing to the masses.[3]

I found it interesting, too, that Meloney used her connection to Marie Curie to try to get Lillian Gilbreth nominated for a Nobel Prize—and that she took on time-consuming projects to ameliorate the ills of women at nearly every twist and turn. Was I observing a woman's woman of the modern sort, or did she intuitively detect the power in bonds like the ones historians have observed among Victorian women in their all-female domestic worlds of "love and ritual," only revamped in professional contexts for the modern age? As I personally struggled to balance my own home and work life, I wondered if Meloney had a thing or two to teach today's careerists feeling emotionally adrift and without female allies. Still, it wasn't until I had moved on to another book project, about Walter Camp, the "Father of American Football," and discovered that, yes, she corresponded with him too, that I was actually stunned. Who didn't this woman know? And how did she operate so deftly in spheres both dominated by men and populated by women?[4]

I spent the next three years digging into her papers and those of all the people I could find with whom she interacted. As I sit here writing, I haven't exhausted my search. After many years studying the lives of American women, I thought I had pretty good instincts about which rocks to look under, and yet Meloney has defied my expectations. Most of the tried-and-true formulas for structuring biographies don't apply to her, because she occupied so many spheres of influence at once. Nor does she fit many of the tidy tropes used to convey meaning in women's lives. I could see that it wouldn't be enough to itemize her public works and professional accomplishments, which are numerous. She was a powerful woman who never announced herself as such—a modern success story never formally declared, so we have to employ ways of seeing that reveal more than the expected angles and surface details. I'd have to tell her story through a specially gendered lens that, like a sort of ultraviolet light, finds uniquely feminine places and contexts where power looms, expands, and makes change, yet is rarely acknowledged. Only in those underexamined crevices of experience do we see more fully how Meloney operated like an influencer for modern times.

To understand the depths of Meloney's power, I zoom out to see her in relation to other editors and women of her generation, but I also zoom in to gain more granular views of her relationships, personal and professional, which I have to believe weren't typical. Take this handwritten note to Meloney from the Lebanese poet Kahlil Gibran: "Blessed and beloved Missy.—You do know in your heart how dear you are to us who in heaven's grace are allowed to walk your path and breathe the fragrant air you breathe. And surely you know also that to you, born rich-hearted and full-handed, we can offer no gifts. The little things we bring to your door are but faint expressions of our love and not of your loveliness, and we bring them in shyness." Or these words from the State Department's Stanley Hornbeck in 1938: "Your keenness, your courage, and your sense of humor, your smile and your gracious charm are truly extraordinary, each item in its own right and all of them together in a superb combination. I appreciate more than I can possibly tell you the fact of being within the circle, wide and ever wider though that circle is, of your friends."[5]

Such outpourings might be typical in eulogies written about people at the end of their lives, but the sheer number and sincerity of epithets expressed *when Meloney lived* left me wondering. What was her special power? No doubt, friends were effusive because she was effusive with them—and generous, and attentive. To more fully reveal her people skills (which were more like people instincts), her adroitness at making connections, her cultural clairvoyance, and her perceptiveness about the potential of people and ideas, I had to let *her* talk. Her voice is distinctive, prescient, and often more compelling than mine as a narrator, so I quote her liberally. I also quote her friends and associates to give a sense of the reactions to her way of being and relating to people. Harriet Eager Davis, an assistant and travel companion, described her as "maternally concerned with everybody's happiness." Ruth Pratt, the first congresswoman elected in New York, was grateful that Meloney took the time to send notes of encouragement, rather than only reaching out to register complaints, as the majority of her constituents did. Evidently, Meloney was exquisitely tuned in to people's emotional needs. She is a great case study in efficacy that doesn't shirk the human element. She disproves modern presumptions that high success is only achievable through a renunciation of vulnerability, or that it necessarily leaves human casualties in its wake.[6]

Another dynamic that came into view as I observed her relationships up close was a seamlessness in her private and public personas that left me intrigued. The woman at home was the woman at work, perhaps because "home" and "work" often occupied the same physical and psychic space in her case. As a consequence, she loved and was loved by those with whom she conducted business. To truly understand Meloney is to know her as "Missy" and to account for her obsessive giving of flowers (tulips preferably, sometimes roses), of books (usually first editions, specially bound and inscribed by their authors), and art (including exotic-looking masks and prints by Gutzon Borglum). She never forgot birthdays, spouses' names, whether people loved animals, or the meaning of Christmas. She made a celebration of exchanging gifts and a ritual of sending specially designed holiday cards that turned into treasured keepsakes. And there was her habitual closing of letters to friends and business associates with some variation of "Blessings On You," blurring any distinction between them.[7]

Missy was tender, maternal—and busy, by any standard. This fact posed challenges for me when I was sequencing her full and multifaceted story, but it wasn't an unconquerable hurdle. What proved harder was figuring out how to narrate a life that seemed impossibly useful and stifled at once, for Missy was a woman with substantial physical limitations. I didn't realize the extent of them until I stumbled on a note in which she confessed to spending nearly two consecutive years in the Hospital for the Ruptured and Crippled on East 42nd Street in New York. I'm embarrassed to say that even after three years of poring over her papers and charting her work, I hadn't suspected she had been incapacitated to this extent. My guess is that she wouldn't have mentioned this fact about herself at all had she not been divulging it to inspire hope in someone else who felt despondent because of illness.[8]

After finding that note, I started reading more carefully between the lines Missy wrote to others and grew resourceful in figuring out when she was ill and for how long. Her son kept a folder of dozens of prescriptions for tonics and painkillers she had been prescribed over the years, which gave me a glimpse of how debilitating her illnesses could be. I've concluded that she was miraculously productive through chronic suffering; my rough estimation is that some half of her adult days were "sick days"—not in the sense of days taken off for illness, but rather days of illness when she worked anyway. Illness and productivity were simultaneous in her experience, which forced me to be mindful of a different kind of accounting. Accomplishment can happen in recesses of time that history discounts as insignificant. I have brought to the surface many of Missy's private moments of bed rest and bodily malfunction, which she might not have wanted made public. Nevertheless, in these not-noteworthy moments an incredible life was lived. Her physical limitations often became a point of connection with others and drove her to employ strategies for interacting with people on her turf and terms. They also provided a perspective on social problems and made her sensitive to the plights of others. She might have been fragile, sometimes incapacitated, but her illness was not necessarily her weakness.[9]

In telling Missy's story, I have avoided the temptation to create a female form of hagiography. Here we look closely at what made her effective in her endeavors, without forgetting that she internalized some cultural prejudices of her time and place. Although more tolerant of nonwhites, non-Christians, and non-Westerners than many white Americans at the turn of the century, she nonetheless presumed the superiority of middle-class norms. And when she catered to the "average" reader or homemaker, no doubt it was a white woman who came to mind. To my ears, her lectures on immigration have a patronizing tone and oversell the idea of American exceptionalism; implicitly, she suggested that as an Anglo woman, she was best qualified to proclaim the ideals of American citizenship. Although she acted benevolently toward African Americans and treated a few like family, she had been raised in a household that accepted social hierarchies defined by race. And although largely silent on questions of sexuality, during World War II she expressed reservations about her daughter-in-law's choice to write plays with homosexual characters—albeit less because it offended her personally than because it sounded alarms in her as a publicist who had her finger on the pulse of the times.[10]

Missy was a person of her time and place, as are we all, and thus depicting her as progressive in twenty-first-century terms, or labeling her a prude, a racist, or a homophobe, is to set her in a contextual vacuum. Here, she is revealed as a stay-at-home mother who continued to preach the merits of that choice well after she went back to work full-time and advanced the careers of other women. We will also see how she introduced Americans to Madame Curie as a sort of Mother of the Year, even as she gave Curie the economic means to thwart that role. Missy's seeming contradictions and human inconsistencies reveal both her personal evolution and the complexities of her era. But she understood her professional milieu well enough to avoid pitfalls and gain acceptance as she reinvented roles for women in politics and media. She walked a fine gendered tightrope, and once she mastered it she restrung it in new directions and transformed it into a runway for feminine assets and female feet. In this, she was an unheralded mentor, an influencer, and a modern kind of leader from whom we can learn a great deal.

Chapter One

THE MAKINGS OF A SOB STORY

BACK IN 1907, IRVIN COBB of the New York *World* had noted the presence of women reporters—four of Missy's contemporaries—in front-row seats at the notorious Henry Thaw murder trial in New York City, and he warned that these "sob sisters" would pull on the heartstrings of readers rather than dispassionately report the news. The name stuck, likely because it fed into an existing stereotype of female reporters being unable to handle "real" news without letting their emotions get in the way. Cobb came to respect Missy's work in journalism, and yet she would have told him that she had felt the stigma of his judgments years before he coined the term "sob sister" and that overcoming them had been the challenge of her professional life. "I had been told by a journalist, a great journalist...that being sentimental, emotional and artistic, I would become a great sob sister," she recalled with resentment. Playing the conversation back in her mind, she realized how much, even then, she saw this as an insult. She knew what men like Cobb were thinking: that sob stories were "sentimental slush...sex stuff done by women for women"— the schlock that legitimate reporters "held in contempt." It infuriated her that men assumed that women were emotional at the expense of being factual.[1]

It wasn't easy to portray oneself as a "hard" newswoman in years when male editors saw profit in stories of the "soft" or "sob" variety. After the Civil War, improvements to the mechanisms of mass

1

printing had caused the number of dailies published in the country to grow exponentially. Newspaper and magazine editors had discovered the female reader, and recognizing her as the primary consumer of household goods, marketers placed more ads to appeal to women. The size of the women's page of major newspapers grew, and so did the number of domestic magazines devoted to "women's" issues. Thanks to female readers, newspapers spawned evening and Sunday editions. Now fiction, fashion, romance, recipes, social advice, domestic tips—the soft stuff that presumably appealed to homemakers— had a place in American journalism, albeit separate and distinct from the hard, disinterested news that men presumably reported.[2]

In 1880, only 288 of 12,308 journalists listed in the national census were women, and a mere 6 of those held full-time positions on daily newspaper staffs. By 1900, women numbered 2,193 of 30,098 journalists nationwide, hired in ever greater numbers to appeal to female readers. Advice columnists like Beatrice Fairfax and Dorothy Dix were paid generously by the column inch to help female readers cope with love lost. Their articles and matronly images found their way into papers across the nation once the two writers were put into syndication, but they never made their way to the front page. Pieces by and for women landed on society and women's pages, where, popular though they were, they announced themselves as trivia, light fare, "puff pieces"—non-news.[3]

To make a newsier impact some women turned to stunt reporting and won rare celebrity as "front-page girls." Nellie Bly's seventy-two-day around-the-world adventure in the late 1880s was the impetus for the trend. William Randolph Hearst and Joseph Pulitzer, publishers of the New York Journal and World respectively, seized on the appetite for sensationalized, unsubstantiated, often faked stories that came to be known as "yellow" or tabloid fare, and women stunters were their main attraction. With their growing reputations for colorful, emotional, questionably accurate first-person copy, women were hired more readily at the tabloids than at the reputable New York Sun or Times. Missy's contemporary Elizabeth Banks "entered into the Kingdom of the Yellow" when she couldn't get a reporter job any other way, allowing herself to be arrested and sent to lockup as a disreputable woman. She slummed it in tenements and sweat shops on Manhattan's Lower East Side and carried smelling salts to stave off the foul odors that assailed her while she worked undercover. She didn't mind, since the tabloids provided both higher wages and camaraderie with male reporters in the city room. But she couldn't say that she was respected as a serious journalist.[4]

And so Missy entered the newspaper business when the few women in it were at a crossroads. In the words of her soon-to-be colleague Ishbel Ross, "It was either clothes or cookery or the stunt girl.... The one class had little respect for the other...there was a sharp division between the sober and the sensational press." Female journalists were either feminine and not serious, or serious but not ladylike—and thus damned one way or the other. Reluctantly, Missy insinuated herself into a few unsavory situations for the sake of a getting a front-page story, but not without losing some self-respect. Her foray into yellow journalism was, looking back, "a low ebb" in her career and in the profession generally. She preferred a spot on the front page as a political reporter, but her first editors typically assigned such stories to seasoned men. They had more knowledge of the goings-on behind the scenes, the rationale went, which might have been true, because they had access to the press galleries, smoking rooms, and drinking holes where men of power convened to discuss the politically newsworthy.[5]

It took time for editors to stop trying to mold her into a stunt woman or sob sister and to view her stories as human-interest pieces, political profiles, and serious journalism. Missy would come to recognize that reshaping editors' presumptions about her work required recasting herself as one who figuratively walked and talked like a male journalist, without losing her femininity. This meant taking on political assignments, but also reshaping her personal narrative. Sometimes it was a Horatio Alger tale of manly success. At other times it read like a sob story.

In other words, she had to control her public image and remain an enigma to some degree. As much as she reveled in uncovering truths, she found it necessary to obscure them when they revealed too much. Even when she presented herself as an open book, there were significant chapters missing. Take the explanation she gave for her obvious limp: she spun it as a tale of a childhood horse-riding accident that left her lame and foiled her dream of becoming a concert pianist, but in fact her physical frailties were more complicated. Sometime before or shortly after the accident that she claimed had left her lame, she had already been exhibiting symptoms that caused her mother to send her away to rehabilitate her lungs, not her legs. It is hard to know when she contracted tuberculosis, because Missy spoke of her relapses in euphemism, but she had them episodically for the rest of her life. At the turn of the century, TB infected people across class lines, and yet it carried stigma as the malady of the great unwashed. When it ravaged households like hers, it was discreetly managed, not publicly announced. Although her limp was conspicuous, her lung ailment, which sometimes could be concealed or called something else, was more incapacitating. Sometimes it was an inconvenient truth that she excised from both the public record and the personal narrative she shared with others. And yet, she also carefully spun the narrative to her advantage. Her physical fragility created a vulnerability that drew people in. Rather than isolating her professionally, it conveniently spawned connection.[6]

Illness was not the only thing about her that she obscured; there was also her age. The people who met her in adulthood knew her as younger than she actually was, and she took that secret to the grave—literally: her tombstone in Woodlawn Cemetery is inscribed with a birth date in 1882, four years later than census records indicate. With her large, childlike black eyes, pale skin, curls, and petite frame, she pulled off looking younger until it didn't much matter. In the late Victorian era a ten-year difference in age between a bride and a groom was respectable, even preferable, and as her own parents attested, a forty-year spread was not out of the question. Missy might have felt social pressure to appear younger than her husband, who was born in 1878, and hence started lying about her age after marrying him in 1904. Whether she saw social or professional advantage in presenting younger, she was hardly the only woman to do similar math during that era. Rather than seeing it as being untruthful, we might view it as an indication of her ability to know deeper truths. She applied a shrewdness about subtext and optics to her own narrative and to those she created about other people. She observed closely and trusted her intuition about people's perceptions, ulterior motives, and self-deceptions. She noticed details that male journalists missed— a hand gesture, an uncomfortable grin—and cast them as germane to the political story. Indeed, many of the things that she couldn't glean about men from their words or the public record she came to understand about them anyway. Her power was uncovering human truths, though for a long time men didn't see them as truths at all.[7]

———————

THIS PENCHANT FOR FINDING TRUTH was evident early, much to the irritation of Missy's childhood friends in Bardstown, Kentucky. Her closest playmate had also been her niece, Josephine, her half brother's daughter, who couldn't understand why Missy didn't see herself as one of the luckiest girls alive: not only was she Grandfather's pet, but she could also boast that Bardstown—not Louisville, or Lebanon, or Lexington—was home. Indeed, Missy didn't understand why she should brag about a town whose abundance of horses and whiskey made it indistinguishable from the others surrounding it. "It's the Athens of the West," Josephine asserted. Missy remembered wondering whether or not there was an Athens of the East to compare it to.[8]

Missy grew up learning that the town's founding fathers were not gunslingers but lawyers, scholars, and churchmen, several of whose descendants went on to challenge the Know-Nothings in the years leading up to the Civil War. Many residents had a bent toward religious tolerance, because it was intolerance that had forced their Catholic forebears to settle there in the first place. In years when Catholics were violently attacked in nearby Louisville, Missy's father had run for the state senate and was a delegate to the Democratic National

Convention, with a primary aim of defending his faith. Bardstown was home to the first Catholic cathedral west of the Alleghenies. Its diocese had been founded in 1808, the same year of the founding of the dioceses of New York, Boston, and Philadelphia. And yet Missy was pretty sure that people in those cities knew nothing of the "Athens of the West." Josephine reminded her of the local lore—that the king of France, Louis Philippe, had lived in Bardstown for a time during the late eighteenth century and had taught their grandfathers in the old stone schoolhouse. Maybe this was true, but young Missy was skeptical, asking incredulously why a king would be teaching their grandfathers instead of ruling France. Josephine explained that there had been something like a civil war that had forced the king to flee Paris and, naturally, to spend his exile in the Athens of the West.[9]

Missy remained unconvinced that her hometown was the residence of an exiled king or that it was the cultural mecca that Josephine said it was, and she was probably right, since, to our knowledge, Louis Philippe had never set foot in Bardstown. Even as a young girl Missy had the good judgment to take the matter up with her father, a learned man whose opinion was second only to God's in her eyes. Cyprian Peter Mattingly (1812–1886) had studied medicine under a local doctor until he attended the University of Pennsylvania Medical School, where he graduated at nineteen. Locals heralded him as the hero of the cholera epidemic of 1831, for allegedly he was the only doctor who stayed at his post during the outbreak. By the 1850s he was president of the Kentucky Medical Society, an esteemed member of the American Medical Association, and a recipient of honorary degrees. European governments decorated him for research on yellow fever and tetanus, and his papers were translated around the world. Already as a young girl Missy had accompanied him to Paris, Edinburgh, and Washington. He would know if Bardstown were the Athens of anything, she figured, because, unlike most of their neighbors, he had actually left town long enough to form a basis of comparison.[10]

Cyprian's response to his daughter's query was to pull books from his library that were filled with photographs and drawings of reconstructed temples and arches of Athens. They spent many nights talking about the civilizations of ancient Greece. As an older woman, Missy recalled those conversations and wrote them down in unpublished vignettes; she remembered asking her father if the people of "that" Athens in Greece were proud, and Cyprian told her "very."

"Then why didn't they save Athens?" she wanted to know.

"Athens and her people had crumbled because they had lost the truth," Cyprian told her, and added a caveat: "I would not call [Bardstown] the Athens of the West, but I would not laugh at any one who called it that. The thought comforts some of them who have so little left."

Born after the immediate devastation of the Civil War, young Missy still lacked the lived experience or perspective to feel so sympathetic. And even at that tender age, she was not one to fuel delusions, so she challenged her father: "But they are losing the truth—and isn't that why Athens fell?"

Yes, Cyprian agreed, but he also advised her not to interfere with what other people believed or hoped. "Just be sure that *you* do not lose the truth," he qualified.[11]

It was a lesson that served her well—as a journalist, in politics, and in everything else.

MISSY REMEMBERED HER FATHER as a man of great physical strength and character. Many people and records corroborate her accounts, though her memories of Cyprian were also flawed and incomplete. She spoke of having seven brothers, all but one of them grown and with children by the time she was born, but Cyprian likely fathered more children than those Missy knew about, several having died in childhood and others having fought for the Confederacy. As far as she could discern, Missy was her father's favorite. She grew up presuming that his doting attention was the kind a father reserved for his one and only daughter.[12]

Missy's mother, Sarah Irwin (1852–1934), was Cyprian's much younger second or third wife. When they married in 1874, she was younger than her husband's children. She bore a son, Francis Carroll, and Missy a few years later. According to family lore, she had been promised to Cyprian's eldest son, but Sarah loved Cyprian more. Relatives speculated that she must have been after the older man's money, an idea Missy dismissed as irreconcilable with both her father's charms and the bookish mother she knew. They welcomed the needy into their home and dressed respectably plain. Their house, a combination of Georgian and Greek Revival, was large and tastefully appointed, but not ostentatious. Although they lived comfortably, they suffered losses during the economic downturns of the 1870s and '90s. Sarah's response was not to lament the losses, but rather to see them as opportunities to assert more independence. "My Mother was an intellectual and most of the other women were not," Missy later reflected of the female universe of Bardstown. "Father was a man of great mental power and they found an intellectual companionship which was very precious."[13]

Sarah's Carolinian roots were traceable to a Scotsman who first settled in Pennsylvania and fathered a member of General Washington's staff in the Revolutionary War. After the Battle of Lexington, three of her male forebears allegedly signed the Mecklenburg Declaration of Independence, further solidifying her eligibility for membership in the exclusive hereditary society the Daughters of the American Revolution. Missy also knew vaguely of a distant cousin who had been governor of South Carolina, of slaves who had traveled with the family west to Mississippi, and of a family fortune to which her mother had claims that she did not pursue. Sarah was a woman of privilege, but hardly one of complaisance. She spoke little about her past, though she shared with her daughter the story of a traumatic childhood trip to New Orleans, where she witnessed children being torn from their parents at a slave market. Her mammy begged her to say nothing of the incident, but when her father asked her what she wanted for her eighth birthday, Sarah asked him to free one of their slaves. That morning the enslaved men and women of the household lined up, and Sarah took the hand of the eldest, for he had likely suffered bondage the longest. At this tender age, she had already questioned the social absolutes and racial hierarchies of the patriarchal South, and she eventually encouraged her daughter to cultivate a compass of her own.[14]

Sarah's birthday ritual was carried out another five times, through the Emancipation Proclamation, until the Union had won freedom for all the slaves. By then, her father had died of pneumonia, several of her siblings had succumbed to disease, and one sister had been killed—a neighbor boy on a soldier's furlough accidentally discharged his pistol. The remaining three siblings became the charge of an uncle, who searched for a boarding school that had stayed open through the chaos of war. Sarah and her sisters found their way to Nazareth Academy near Bardstown and received a rigorous education. That is where Missy's parents first met, as student and resident doctor. More exceptional than marrying the academy physician, perhaps, was Sarah's graduation from Union Female College in Oxford, which eventually became part of the University of Mississippi. She chose marriage and motherhood, but Sarah was not seduced by the social trappings of the typical Southern belle, nor was she a Catholic for whom the Virgin Mary was a role model. She endured chronic pain, but never succeeded in being the sacrificial or silent sufferer of her religious teachings. Requiring constant care from nursemaids and doctors, she turned physically and emotionally unavailable as a parent. A woman of letters who engaged in cerebral, rather than social or maternal, pursuits, Sarah started a school for blacks in Bardstown (1876–1886), and, with Cyprian's blessing and financial backing, founded the *Kentucky Literary Magazine,* a monthly published in Louisville.[15]

As an older woman looking back, Missy acknowledged her mother's influence on her, but she was unconscious perhaps of the full or conflicting extent of it. On the one hand, she idolized her mother as the independent spirit who encouraged her intellectual pursuits, for few Southern mothers of privilege would have done so at the time. But Missy may have lacked full understanding of the emotional impact of her mother's invalidism, for her earliest inclination had not been to see her mother as a mentor, but rather to resent her physical and emotional deficits. Although her intellectual life was far ranging, Sarah's physical world shrank to a single room of the house. Young Missy lamented that her mother "lived her pained existence on a couch," the shades perpetually drawn. Perhaps this partly explains why an older Missy was driven to erase any semblance of limitation brought about by her own chronic illness. Sarah's invalidism helped to mold a daughter who worked obsessively despite her physical challenges, and who remained in a perpetual state of movement, often against doctors' orders. Her mother's example, in other words, was one she emulated and rejected at once. She wanted Sarah's intellectual life, not her physical one.[16]

Indeed, in her child's mind, the brightness of Missy's younger years had been her physically robust father. He was the one who accompanied her piano playing with strings and reserved corners in the greenhouse for her potted plants. The time he spent tending to patients seemed to collapse in Missy's recollections, for she claimed to spend nearly every hour of every day with Cyprian as a young child, accompanying him as he made his home visits and sleeping in his room (Sarah slept in the sickroom upstairs). Cyprian gathered the household every night to read passages from the Bible and to pray on the rosary for his children, the nation, his friends, his ever-ailing wife, the nursemaids, the cook, the horse groom, the gardener, Missy's mammy, and all the children of the former slaves. "I was the baby of the house and I came last but it was always the best prayer," she fondly reminisced.[17]

Missy was sure that her father had won her special favor with God. So perhaps it's no surprise that the nuns at the local convent thought her spoiled. When her father left on a hunting trip and dropped her off at the convent to stay with the orphans, Missy wouldn't eat or play nicely with the others. Praying in the chapel seemed unnecessary to a girl used to featuring prominently in others' prayers, and Mother Superior found Missy insufferable. When Cyprian returned from hunting two days early, the nuns implored him to leave Missy with them for a year to be righted. "It was sinful for him to cater his life to mine," she heard the nuns tell him. But he paid them no mind, vowing never to leave Missy again.[18]

Through the filter of a child's innocence, there was no animosity or sense of social caste in Missy's Bardstown home, just mutual affection and loyalty. Her memory was of black and white, young and old, rich and poor being equal, because that was what her father had willed. There was the time the horse groom, Dockery, caught a white neighbor stealing bacon from the smokehouse and Cyprian forgave him. He took Missy aside to make her understand. "The war played havoc with a lot of families—people just as decent and fine as we think we are," she remembered him telling her. "We haven't done our part when such people are actually hungry." There was the time he gave a carriage ride to Nellie Cotton, a local girl whom Mammy called "poor white trash." Missy couldn't believe that her father would take Nellie driving without her, and she pitched a small fit. Cyprian gently reminded her that it was wrong to be selfish, or snobbish, or to hold others in contempt for their poverty. Do not let jealousy take you over, he further beseeched. "It will eventually eat out your heart, and you will never know happiness." Missy believed that the two most important lessons Cyprian taught her were not to be jealous, and not to fear. By internalizing both, she would later come to terms with her illnesses, and closer to truth than most people.[19]

Decades later, Missy told a college audience, "There is nothing in life more courageous than a good father, not even a good mother." Such were the conclusions of a reverent daughter, but perhaps also one who mythologized her father over time. Cyprian died when she was too young to perceive him as anything other than unflawed, unwaveringly principled, and physically and spiritually larger than life. She recalled him as younger, stronger, more present than could have been the case. Although his lessons of kindness and mutual respect stayed with her, he was nonetheless a Confederate sympathizer who believed that racial hierarchy, if not the natural order of things, was at least more tolerable than religious persecution. A nephew once

confronted her about her father's excessive drinking and even suggested that Cyprian bought whiskey barrels at a time. Missy defen-
sively snapped back, "I don't think he did any more than the rest of
the family.... Every Kentuckian did that and had ten barrels in the
cellar.... Everybody of any importance worshipped Father." Coming
into adulthood in years when white men suffered a diminished sense
of political, economic, and social dominion in American life, Missy
gloried in a father whose manhood, in her childhood memories of
him, was left very much intact.[20]

———

WHEN CYPRIAN DIED, Sarah saw no need to stay in Bardstown.
She divvied up most of her husband's property among his children
and set out with her children, Missy and Carroll, and her spinster sister to find a new place to settle. It would have been easier to remain
where her family had status and servants. For an independent-minded
woman there might also have been the allure of adventure—and the
vote—in the West, where several states had granted formal political
rights to women. Yet in the end Sarah moved to where she thought
she could best write, teach, and influence: the nation's capital, to a
brownstone right in the center of the city on Massachusetts Avenue.[21]

Washington's social rules were unlike any other American city's
because of its hybrid culture. Its new wealth made it Northern, while
its aristocratic residues felt Southern. Because of the presence of
embassies and legations, there was also a foreign tinge to the social
customs. If one dressed less ostentatiously here than in foreign courts,
one's jewels were no less flawless. Menus were a mix of the best of
Southern and French cuisines, served on fine china, with European
wines. Elite women followed a strict calling schedule, hosting men of
the Supreme Court on Mondays, congressmen on Tuesdays, cabinet
members on Wednesdays, senators on Thursdays, and ladies of the
missions or diplomatic corps at the end of the week. When throw-
ing dinner parties, they seated guests according to rank or office, and
when one's standing was ambiguous a hostess turned to the State

Department for clarity. Such decisions were eventually left to social secretaries who developed an expert knowledge of the rules, as well as of the personalities who called for exceptions.[22]

Missy developed a reputation for making the right impression, perhaps to some degree because of the social knowledge her mother passed on to her. Washington's culture of calling cards hearkened back to the genteel experience of Sarah's childhood, and soon she inserted herself into a tradition of hobnobbing at Washington state dinners, as well as in congressional press galleries, where political wives, lobbyists, reporters, and dilettantes vied to bend a senator's ear. Missy would see that women with a gift for banter and a mind for the issues had an indirect hand in greasing the political machine. Sex scandals, temperance, women's suffrage—issues that mattered to these women—eventually permeated the consciousness of the political men to whom they found themselves in proximity. The cosmopolitan air of the capital city also gave Sarah license to be the literary critic she could only partly embody in Bardstown. Missy remembered her mother's careful preparations for a salon she hosted after reviewing Lew Wallace's *Ben-Hur* for *Harper's* magazine. Dressed in her best gown, the then-incapacitated Sarah was carried to her couch in the library, where she charmed Kentucky congressman Henry Watterson and Mark Twain, who Missy grew up knowing simply as Sam.[23]

To her observant daughter, Sarah seemed invigorated by the new life she had chosen. Other Washington women had chosen it too and had cleared a path before her. Even before the Civil War, Mrs. A. S. Colvin edited the *Weekly Messenger*, and Anne Royall edited *Paul Pry* and *The Huntress*. Mary Abigail Dodge (pen name Gail Hamilton) wrote for the abolitionist paper *National Era* in the 1850s, as did Sara Jane Clarke (pen name Grace Greenwood), who also wrote congressional character sketches and feminist essays. It was not coincidence that Washington's women journalists and literary critics were often single, widowed, or estranged from husbands; their political engagement and literary practices were part of their rebellion from traditional domesticity, even if not explicitly couched that way. Sarah associated with unconventional types like Kate Field, who never married yet traveled the country as a lecturer before starting, in 1889, the publication *Kate Field's Washington,* which covered the social, cultural, and political news of the capital. Sarah contributed to the weekly, following in a tradition of Washington women whose book and theater reviews evolved into social, then political, commentaries.[24]

To Missy, the mother who had once seemed the perpetual invalid had morphed into a sophisticate who was in her element around statesmen and men of letters. From the age of ten, she heard her mother's refrains before guests arrived for dinner: "He's only a Congressman," or "just a politician." "The background of my canvass had on it world characters, men like Lord Pauncefote, that true statesman of the British empire," Missy later mused. "Distinguished authors, artists, engineers, and a few statesmen were the scale by which I measured the men who came to Washington." Few other girls could boast of rolling Easter eggs on the White House lawn with the Cleveland children. As Missy grew older, visits to the private quarters of the White House to see the First Family became commonplace.[25]

Eventually the Mattinglys moved to the Woodmont, on 13th and Iowa Circle, likely in an effort to consolidate resources. Sarah was preparing to open a French-American school, Washington College for Girls, also known as Irwin Hall, and eventually she found a respectable location for cultivating genteel girls in Adams Morgan, at an address once belonging to the Greek legation and the first secretary of the British embassy. "Make your daughter a worthwhile woman," she advertised in the *Confederate Veteran.* "[Our] aim is the highest moral, mental, and physical development of Christian women to meet and manage the problems of real life." In the first year of operation the school graduated one student at a small ceremony at the Church of Our Father. Missy's Aunt Mary, vice president of the school, crowned the graduate with a wreath of laurel, and younger girls received medals in art, Latin, and reading. Missy, now a teenager, performed a recitation and piano solo that displayed a talent for music that her mother encouraged. Music was an acceptably cultured activity for a young lady, and admittedly the family needed any income that it might have yielded. Most of the items Sarah had brought with her from Bard-stown had gone up in flames in a storage warehouse in 1894, and running a school had its costs. Before long, Missy was playing public concerts and won a scholarship to study music in Leipzig.[26]

On the eve of the new century, the family relocated to a townhouse on 18th Street. Here, Missy had occasional sightings of a neighbor who lived on 19th—the assistant secretary of the navy, a man named Theodore Roosevelt. Missy took notice of how much he enjoyed the horse trails at Rock Creek Park, a public space newly created by an act of Congress. Bridges had not yet been built over the streams, so they had to be jumped. One afternoon when Colonel Roosevelt was riding nearby, Missy approached a pass and thrust herself forward as her horse stayed behind. She was propelled into a puddle of mud as Roosevelt looked on; when he saw that she wasn't hurt, his response was to laugh. Missy got back on the horse and attempted to cross again, only this time the horse turned and threw her off the saddle. Exasperated, she remounted her mare and finally jumped her over the brook multiple times to convince herself that she could. By then, it was Missy's recollection that the colonel had ridden away; it wasn't the impression she wanted to leave him.[27]

In that instance, she recovered quickly and got back on her horse, but in the coming weeks or months she suffered a fall from her horse that bruised far more than her ego. For all the times she referenced this accident to friends and reporters in later years, she provided few details about exactly where and when it occurred. All she stated about it in her autobiographical notes is that Dr. Virgil Gibney, a friend of her father's, broke the news that she would never walk again—a crucial detail to the story, because she would ultimately prove him wrong. In her adult years, friends even claimed that she walked with such brisk determination that it was hard to keep up with her. Missy had a slight limp for the rest of her life, it was true, but the emotional residues of the accident may have burrowed more deeply. Although her injury ultimately failed to slow her down, it made her invalidism outwardly apparent. Her lungs plagued her far more profoundly for the rest of her life, and yet the horse-riding accident seemed to flick a switch. From that day on, she vowed never to be the unavailable convalescent her mother had been. She developed especially strong emotional bonds with those around her, as well as an uncommonly rigorous work ethic to compensate for her handicaps. She fought intensely to live and work as though she were able-bodied, not realizing that in the fight, she lived and worked harder than most able-bodied people would think reasonable.[28]

The Christmas following her accident, she had asked for a pair of blue dance slippers, but Gibney gave her something else—a diary. Perhaps it was time to think less about riding or making music, he suggested. Her mother's invalidism hadn't prevented her from having an intellectual life; writing had given her freedom and purpose. Perhaps, he told Missy, it could do the same for her. It was not advice that Missy was ready to hear, but eventually she opened the diary to write her first line: "I shall try to be useful."[29]

And then a moment came to pass that she went on to mythologize, one when her life's work as a journalist supposedly came to her as a sort of ordained mission. She had gone to the chapel at St. Paul's to practice her playing, and there at the altar was a chalice of wedding rings and baby lockets, all sacrifices to the Savior for the altar service. In a quest for more trinkets, the rector asked young Missy not to practice piano, but instead to write an appeal for donations to be printed in the local paper. "If the gods of music had been on the job I would never have written the letter," she later joked, for she sent an appeal not just anywhere, but to the *Washington Post*. Surprisingly, her mother's response was apprehension. "More attention in my life had been paid to manners and graces, to music and history, than to the rule of three and the spelling book," Missy admitted. Sarah had always edited Missy's schoolwork, and yet in this instance her daughter circumvented her completely to submit her first piece of journalism to professional newspapermen who were likely to be less forgiving of her bad spelling. But the following morning, when Missy went to the door to retrieve the milk delivery, there was the *Post;* inside, on the editorial page, with proper spelling, was the letter she had submitted the day before. She received $4.60 for the piece, making it, she later joked, her best paid piece of writing for actual value.[30]

So began her career in journalism. So began a brand-new century. And so began a chance to rewrite her sob story into a tale of another kind.

Chapter Two

A CUB REPORTER IN 1900

COMING OF AGE AT THE TURN of the century, Missy belonged to a generation who felt the tug of old and new ideals of American womanhood. A few female renegades of her mother's generation had broken with traditional domesticity to pursue passions outside the home, making it easier, though not easy, for Missy to consider the same. Still, the pressures for a genteel lady to keep out of politics and paid work largely prevailed, and it would be another twenty years before the Nineteenth Amendment allowed women so much as a vote in national elections. In fact, white, middle-class women who had not already been forced by necessity to take paid work outside the home were often held up as the best justification for denying women suffrage. Unsullied by the corruption of politics or the unsavory atmosphere of the factory or the marketplace, such women were the moral influence in society, the argument went, and thus it was best to keep them in the safe haven of the home, above the fray of the outside world, where they could be principled mothers and untainted exemplars to the next generation of citizens.[1]

It was perhaps rhetorical then, when Edward Bok, editor of the *Ladies' Home Journal,* asked in 1901, "Is the Newspaper Office the Place for a Girl?" Most newsmen surveyed said that their daughters should not be exposed to their workplace conditions. Helen Winslow, an ex-reporter, was inclined to agree, confessing in the *Atlantic Monthly* that the field of journalism had been "too hard and too hardening" for her. One female editor warned young women to expect none of the courtesies of the drawing room in the city room. "Reserve and dignity form the armor of the successful newspaper woman," she declared. The key to survival was to blend in, stay quiet, and maintain a "perfectly cool, professional manner." Reporter Elizabeth Banks put it differently: "I have heard some women of my profession described as icicles, heartless, knowing not what it means to suffer, caring only for their work, their ambition, becoming almost sexless." Life as a woman reporter, in other words, was thought to require a renouncement of femininity.[2]

It had become fashionable for women to mail in prose to the local paper, but showing up to the downtown city room in person, where male reporters frantically milled about swearing, smoking, and hawking into spittoons, was a different proposition altogether. And yet young Missy showed up at the *Washington Post* anyway—unannounced, unchaperoned, and asking for a permanent job. To be taken seriously, she did not hide her femaleness, though she aged it a bit, combing out her curls, tying up her hair, and donning a long frock and bustle borrowed from her matronly aunt. She asked to see the managing editor, Scott Bone, whose initial response was surprised, yet fatherly. Did she know that reporters kept late hours? And had deadlines? And had no time to walk her home at night? He thought it cruel to encourage the girl, but Missy was politely persistent. With reticence, he agreed to pay her fifteen dollars a week to cover stories he chose for her—no crime or vice, just society events and interviews with local personages.[3]

Bone was a rare editor who gave a few female reporters a break. Helen Rowland was another teenager he paid three dollars to write her first story, money that her father apologetically returned. But Bone insisted that anything he considered printing deserved to be paid for, including first pieces by green reporters who were girls. That said, he sometimes regretted his decisions—as when he sent Missy out on her first assignment to interview New York senator Chauncey Depew, and she came back empty-handed. Having arrived to the Capitol early, she had stepped into the congressional library to pass the time and became so engrossed with the music collections there that she missed the senator altogether. Bone thought Missy lacked focus and sent her home.[4]

An exclusive scoop gave Missy renewed purpose, however. Washington reporters were obsessed with the Spanish-American War hero George Dewey, but all they had on him were rumors—rumors that he was in debt, rumors of his lady friends—nothing they could verify. Luckily, Missy's mother had a contact, the first assistant postmaster general Perry Sanford Heath, who had information about Dewey that had yet to break. Heath sat on a committee that raised donations to buy a home on the war hero's behalf, and he knew the address of the house chosen for Dewey. Missy asked if she could have the story, to which Heath initially squealed with laughter. But he came around to giving her the scoop, so long as she got a big price for it—nothing less than $200, he told her. The dailies paid up to $25 apiece for exclusive photographs, so Missy borrowed her brother's Kodak and met Heath at the future home of Dewey on Rhode Island Avenue. She photographed everything inside and out, even the cat hiding in the kitchen, and then went to market with her wares.[5]

Her first stop was the Washington office of the *World*, where editor Sam Blythe listened to her pitch with skepticism. He asked for the address of the house, but Missy wouldn't tell him; Heath had advised her not to. She did tell him that she had already written for the *Post*, where the city editor would undoubtedly want her story when he heard about it. Fine, Blythe told her, then sit here and write out everything you can remember, and she did, from the yard, to the wallpaper, to the look of the mid-Victorian furniture. She squeezed out four lackluster paragraphs, but Blythe wanted more. The *World* had come to expect real color and spice from its women reporters, he told her, several of whom even embellished their stories with personal accounts. It dawned on her that she could supplement details about the house with snippets about the personalities Dewey would likely encounter in his new neighborhood. Various ambassadors, Teddy Roosevelt, Madame Bonaparte—all of them were neighbors who Missy and her family knew personally.[6]

By the time she submitted her copy, it was well after dark, much to the obliviousness of the male reporters frantically clacking at their typewriters. Unlike their male colleagues, newspaperwomen didn't have the luxury of forgetting the time. Reporting on balls that went on past midnight, female society reporters faced the problem of getting home after hours unchaperoned. Missy was able to safely board a street-car, but her mother had been worried sick. Sarah's impulse was to forbid more journalistic ventures, until she saw that her daughter was paid $200 for the Dewey story and another $110 for the isochromatic plates in Carroll's camera. Blythe offered Missy a regular job, if she wanted it. Her mother decided that the offer was acceptable, so long as Missy focused on "Church News," the one savory beat in the city room.[7]

As luck would have it, it was the beat with the scoop that launched Missy's career. She had gone to choir practice at St. Paul's one morning, when the priest told her that she was about to bear witness to a famous wedding secretly taking place. On November 9, 1899, a chapel house-keeper, a choirmaster, and Missy watched Admiral Dewey wed the social-ite Mildred McLean Hazen. She knew she had stumbled upon big news. Not only was the couple well known in Washington society, but the unannounced service at St. Paul's was not officially sanctioned: Dewey was not a Catholic. Amidst the excitement of the newlyweds' departure from the church, Missy remembered her editors' previous appeals for details and began collecting evidence. She gathered the prayer book used in the ceremony and the marriage license left for the rector to file with the Department of Vital Statistics and taxied to the *World*'s office to photograph the items before returning them promptly. Her editor was impressed: "You'll make a great reporter some day. . . . I don't know a man who would have had the nerve to steal the marriage license of Admiral Dewey!" Missy took it as affirmation of her reporter's chops. Now she had ins at the *Post* and the *World* and tried to land more scoops for both.[8]

———

BUT PERHAPS the Dewey stories came too easily. Initially eluding the daily grind, poverty, and self-doubt of other cub reporters, Missy settled into their catch-as-catch-can existence soon enough. The next several months felt like an endless grind of chasing down false leads, without the companionship of women friends in the newsroom. Almost all her peers were young men, typically eighteen to twenty-five years in age. Older reporters had moved on, either rising into editorial or other staff positions, or opting out of the news altogether, unable to cope with the lack of security, the grueling pace, or the disappointment of stories leading to dead ends. She had been told that the newspaper game was for more strapping types and, increasingly, strapping types with college degrees; to an ever greater extent, lacking such credentials made it difficult for a blue-collar reporter to advance into the white-collar ranks of the newspaper business. Missy's liabilities in this line of work were obvious, and yet remarkably, she remained determined "to make good in the game."[9]

She found American newspapers woefully provincial, so she looked for stories that other reporters weren't covering. By the summer of 1900, people were dying in the Boxer Rebellion in China, but most Americans were unaware of it. Interest had picked up in the situation in Peking when American missionaries began relaying tales of retaliation against them, but communications from Asia were unreliable. A few of Missy's colleagues were dispatched to the legations for news, but they returned with meager accounts. Washington city editors wanted more sources, and Missy took up the challenge of finding them, knowing that she already had an advantage: Wu Tingfang, the Oxford-trained Chinese foreign minister, was her mother's chess opponent. Having refused to grant any interviews to the press, he agreed to speak with Missy for the sake of her breaking a story. He greeted her at the Chinese legation in silken robes and directed her to a chair across from his. "This is China," he pointed out, running his fingers over the onyx tabletop, veins in the stone representing various provinces, rivers, and boundaries. He talked of the first Christian missionaries and how they brought "the shadow of the cross" to his countrymen. Missy thought she understood. The Boxer uprising was, from the standpoint of many Chinese peasants, a struggle for religious freedom, much like her ancestors' in Bardstown. Whereas other reporters struggled to obtain updates coming in from China, she heard straight from the minister about the cable he had received that morning assuring him that measures were being taken to protect Americans in Peking. The minister gave Missy the cablegram and signed her notes to verify the authenticity of her story. It was an exclusive for which Missy earned double rates.[10]

Around the same time she submitted her Boxer Rebellion story, the 1900 presidential race was heating up domestically. Admiral Dewey had decided to run, and William Jennings Bryan was, in Missy's words, "making silver tongued and silver coined talk across the country." Theodore Roosevelt, now the governor of New York, was yet another Spanish-American war hero whom Republicans considered a possible candidate for president, though William McKinley remained the clear favorite for reelection. Any reporter with front-page ambitions had to attend the national conventions—for the Republicans in Philadelphia, and for the Democrats in Kansas City—and Missy was sent to cover both, for the *Post* as a "correspondent" and for the *World* as a "specialist." With travel expenses covered and double rates on stories, the compensation was unheard of for a woman her age— unfortunately, so was going to a large city unchaperoned. Sarah told Missy that she could go to Philadelphia if accompanied by her aunt and a maid, but Missy thought this too humiliating an arrangement for a cub reporter trying to prove herself to her male peers. She convinced her mother to let her travel less conspicuously with two of the wives of other Washington correspondents. As soon as she arrived in town, she planned to politely depart their company.[11]

In the days prior to the first convention, Missy whetted readers' appetites with a story about Wu Tingfang's journey to Philadelphia to witness American party politics in action, and once again the minister obliged her with an exclusive interview, graciously pausing between sentences to allow Missy time to scribble in her notepad. Her editor was amused as he dictated her notes to a stenographer. It was not just her creative spelling but her unorthodox questions that made her story unlike anything he had ever seen. He ran the piece the next morning as the lead: a political convention through Chinese eyes. Missy was rewarded with a $200 bonus, a momentous start to a promising week of political scoops. There was the drama of her birth state of Kentucky unfolding on the national stage, as William S. Taylor, the former governor turned fugitive, appeared at the convention in defiance after his indictment as an accessory in the murder of his Democratic successor. Missy saw another potential headline when McKinley won the presidential nomination and Teddy Roosevelt looked as though he might bolt from the hall, if not from the Republican Party. Roosevelt received 925 votes for his vice presidential nomination, with his being the only abstention.[12]

So many political dramas to cover—and yet Missy experienced the disenchantment of not being assigned to any of them. Though she proved capable of conducting intriguing interviews, her editor felt she was still too green to cover the main events of the week. Some topics were frankly too scandalous for female ears, he also reasoned. "God defend [you] against ever knowing enough politics to write a leader," he joked, assigning Missy instead a story he thought more befitting: an exclusive on one of the two female alternate delegates at the convention. Not coincidentally, they were from Western states, where women had the franchise and had started filling party positions.[13]

No doubt the assignment was her editor's way of making a "political" story appropriate for a woman reporter, but Missy decided that it was a vote of nonconfidence, hence tainting any assessment she might have had of the woman delegate she interviewed that afternoon. Her first impression of her interviewee, she later recalled, was of a "tall, aggressive, militant" person, "all that was meant by 'new woman,'" and any goodwill that she might have shown dissipated as their conversation wore on. "I wanted her to talk about the forces and the influences which had brought her to Philadelphia. And instead she scolded me for wearing a dainty dress and a curl on the nape of my neck. I came partly to agree with her in the years that followed. But on the 17th day of June [1900], this 'new woman' with her resentment of all things feminine, and her businesslike, aggressive manner, stirred resentment and animous [*sic*] in me." Missy was a cub reporter eager to please and to be accepted among male peers, so she embraced the conventional negative opinion of a woman unfeminine enough to call herself a feminist. In hindsight, she recalled the interview with great regret. "I went back to the office and wrote what I believe today to be the only unfair piece of reporting of which in my many years of journalism I have been guilty. The fact that my criticism pleased the men in the office, that they chuckled over my jibes, commended me for it, did little the next day to salve my conscience. I had done a mean, petty piece of work and I knew it."[14]

Later, when Missy worked for the New York *Sun,* she still felt the resentment that piece had provoked in suffragists whom she came to admire, including the formidable Carrie Chapman Catt of the National American Woman Suffrage Association. Missy's feminism, which she never named, took time and experience to cultivate. In the moment, however, she only knew intuitively that making it as a political reporter required not looking disgruntled, unfeminine, or intentional in her success. She would have to quietly surprise men with her reporting, cover politics without appearing political, advance in the journalistic ranks by not letting on that she wanted to. Her editor expected stories on what senators' wives were wearing to evening socials, and for now she would have to appear willing to write them until she had the chance to exceed expectations with a story written as a man would have written it. She pined for that opportunity.[15]

As male colleagues covered the Republican National Convention well into the night, she walked back to the hotel with nothing in her notebook but observations from afar. Any run-ins with the major players in the week's unfolding dramas were accidental. Waiting for an elevator on the eighth floor of the Hotel Walton, for instance, she encountered a group of senators that included National Committee Chair Mark Hanna and Teddy Roosevelt. The elevator hadn't been working properly, and guards stood on each floor monitoring the number of people getting into the car. The party that collected on the eighth floor was too large, and an argument ensued: who would get off the elevator? One of the senators summoned Missy to volunteer, and she refused. Roosevelt intervened, swearing the ridiculousness of the situation and insisting that everyone remain in the elevator, including Missy, who was far too petite to cause a problem anyway.[16]

In an elevator car of important men, Missy had stood her ground. Still, she wondered if Roosevelt even recognized her as the girl on the horse from Rock Creek Park. So ended her stint as a correspondent at the Republican National Convention. Any dreams of glory she had for its Democratic counterpart had already been greatly diminished.

───────────

AFTER MISSY RETURNED TO WASHINGTON, Scott Bone gave her another chance to land a story in the *Post*. It was an interview of yet another family friend—Julian Pauncefote, the British ambassador. Bone figured that Pauncefote, like Wu Tingfang, might shed light on diplomatic relations in China, where he had been previously posted. Instead, when Missy got to the British embassy something unexpected was clearly afoot. Suddenly the entire staff was convened in the parlor and Pauncefote was bowing before one of the granddaughters of Queen Victoria. She had left Europe for Canada and had just arrived in Washington undetected. Missy couldn't hide her excitement, for she was witnessing a runaway royal! Was the princess seduced by rebelliousness or romance, she asked Pauncefote. She was committing political, not emotional rebellion, he later confided, but he implored Missy not to write about it. He gave her a statement on China and then sent her on her way.[17]

In Bone's office, Missy conjured up a hypothetical situation: Suppose one had stumbled upon a stunning piece of news—could one be forbidden from printing the facts? Or what if one just happened to be in a public place, like a foreign embassy, for instance, when one heard something of great importance but was asked not to print it? Bone asked if this said person had made promises not to. As much as he wanted an exclusive, he was a man with impeccable professional ethics. Missy stopped talking in hypotheticals. "I had given no promise, but I felt as bound as though I had," she confessed. With that, Bone told her that he would leave it to her sense of honor. "We have to develop a code for ourselves in this game," he reminded her. Although he believed journalism to be the noblest of professions, he thought it easily corrupted. If someone entrusted Missy with a confidence, he hoped that she might feel obliged to keep it.[18]

Missy did keep it—and one week later she watched a rival reporter publish her scoop. It was a sad fact about journalism, Bone told her. More often than not the best stories did not make it to print, but they formed building blocks of trust that eventually paid off. "Make notes as you go along, and see how many you have in a few years, the great stories that can never be told," he said, and then he left her with some final advice: "Never pass through a door that will not open for you again." It was wisdom that Missy repeated to young journalists through the years. The list of stories she never wrote went with her to the grave, but many others were written because she had laid solid foundations of trust. Two decades later, Calvin Coolidge, who went on to become the thirtieth president of the United States, would feel that Missy was one of the few reporters he truly trusted with a confidence. When the time came to give her the big interview that he had refused everyone else, the wisdom of Bone's advice was manifest. "Silent Cal" could be downright chatty whenever Missy was in the room, because he trusted her implicitly.[19]

––––––––

IN THE WEEKS between the Republican and Democratic National Conventions of 1900, Missy felt a relapse in her lungs. She said nothing about it, hoping that her editor couldn't detect it from the flush in her cheeks. Although her first political convention had been disappointing, she knew that anyone with ambitions in political reporting couldn't miss the one coming up the week of Independence Day in Kansas City. A family physician advised that she not leave town for it, but Missy offered an ultimatum: if she could cover the convention, she would spend the rest of the summer in Denver, where her editor had given her the names of contacts at the *Denver Post* and the mountain air would help her lungs to recover. Sarah was all too familiar with rehabilitating out west, but again she worried about her daughter traveling alone. Missy appeased her by arranging once more to travel with journalists' wives as far as Kansas City and to contact a Jesuit priest her mother knew once she made her way to Denver.[20]

Sarah would never know that her daughter broke from her chaperones the moment she arrived in Kansas City. "They were doing the city, and I was doing the convention," she justified to herself. Once again, Missy was dispatched immediately to get an interview, this time with the fifteen-year-old daughter of soon-to-be Democratic nominee William Jennings Bryan. Missy found young Ruth sitting in a box in the convention audience gossiping about party leaders. Most of what she said Missy found "drab and uninteresting," that is, except for the part about a prominent Tammany man's allegiance to her father. Blythe assured her that this was news and urged Missy to write up the story, which was reprinted all over the country the next morning. Apparently a teenaged girl could be a vital source of front-page political news.[21]

But Missy couldn't gloat for long. The evening papers of July 5 carried an Associated Press statement issued by Bryan denying that his daughter had ever given an interview to a reporter named Mattingly. Missy was stunned. "I had grown up in a little world where truth was godliness and also good breeding. . . . Yet the whole country had been told on the front pages of the press by William Jennings Bryan that what I had written over my own signature was an untruth. My heart was full of bitterness. I was physically ill." Colleagues thought her thin-skinned. They insisted that she was overreacting and that she should accept Bryan's denials "as part of the game." But she couldn't, especially because she knew that the falsehoods she was accused of were expected of a female reporter. That night she walked aimlessly in the streets of Kansas City, eventually settling on the steps of a Baptist church. The thought of returning to the *World* headquarters the next morning to read the political pages repulsed her. Yet when she arrived there, a telegrapher showed her an unexpected front-page story: backed by eyewitnesses, Sam Blythe had personally refuted Bryan's claims. A stickler for the facts, this newspaperman had also grown fiercely protective of his girl reporter.[22]

Missy felt vindicated—but also pretty weak. Her overnight bender had exhausted her more than she'd already been, and before the morning was over she found herself in a local hospital. She later dismissed the episode as a mere "hemorrhage," her preferred way to refer to a tubercular relapse. On this occasion, she needed all of twenty-six days to recover. Her stint as a convention reporter came, yet again, to an abrupt and disheartening end.[23]

Although the *World* supplied Missy with a stipend for living expenses, it was significantly smaller than the allowance given her male colleagues, who could afford hotels near the convention hall while she boarded on the outskirts of town. Any money saved on lodging went toward hiring a nurse in the weeks after the convention. An editor at the *Kansas City Star* took mercy and offered her a press pass to Denver when she was well enough to travel, but by then the pass had expired, and she had only eleven dollars left in her purse. Thanks to a generous couple traveling from the East Coast, she managed to reach Denver by September, but she had nothing more than a trunk, a handbag, and sixty cents to her name when she arrived. In her luggage were letters of introduction from Eastern newspapermen and clippings of her stories, which she planned to use to find work. Storing her trunk at the train station, she checked her bag and wrote immediately to the local Jesuit priest she promised her mother she'd contact, trusting that he'd find her a family to board with for free.[24]

Missy paid a nickel fare and found her way to the office of the *Denver Post*—a paper "yellow from the first to the last page," she had been told, yet run by a crack city editor, according to Blythe. She climbed up a dingy stairwell to find reporters typing in a ramshackle newsroom. A stout, middle-aged, blond woman sat at a partition away from the others; Missy recognized her immediately from photographs as Winifred Black, the columnist known by most across the country as Annie

Laurie. Starting from her days at the *San Francisco Examiner,* when she first covered murder trials, Black faked accidents and snuck into leper colonies, polygamous communities, and prizefights to get inside exposés. To see the devastation of a historic flood in Galveston, she had dressed as a boy doing the work of recovery. To interview President Harrison, she had stowed away on a train until she could confront him alone. Her escapades were legendary, and her vivid writing style created a winning formula that other women reporters tried to emulate, though Missy, an aspiring political correspondent, had not been one of them.[25]

City editor Joe Ward occupied a sparse office up a level from Black. He offered Missy a job on the spot for twenty-five dollars a week, ten dollars more than the going rate for most Denver reporters. Missy was grateful, but presumed naively that she'd be paid up front; she had forty-five cents left, and her bag was still at the train station. Nevertheless, she seemed to forget her predicament immediately once Ward handed her her first assignment. Colorado was in the throes of a heated senatorial race between Republican incumbent Edward Wolcott and the former senator turned pro-silver candidate Henry Teller. Wolcott was campaigning in town, and Ward wanted his new reporter to write a profile.[26]

Missy had actually known Wolcott in Washington, though apparently a very different version of him. In the cosmopolitan atmosphere of the capital, he had become something of a dandy—"Waistcoat Wolcott," he was frequently called. Rumor had it that he kept half a dozen suits in his office, changing at least once a day between legislative sessions. It amused Missy to see an entirely new iteration of Wolcott campaigning in the poor mining districts of Colorado. He donned a Stetson, baggy trousers, and an old Abe Lincoln collar, his tie unevenly arranged. He was compelled to be someone else entirely in the West, she observed, and it moved her to write about "Farmer" versus "Waistcoat" Wolcott. "There was a certain smug political sophistication about that story," she admitted. It was obvious to Ward, too, that she had a gift for political portraiture.[27]

Theodore Roosevelt was also in town campaigning for Wolcott, so Ward sent Missy to interview him before he left. Coloradans had not been kind to the New York governor that September. At stump speeches in the mining towns of Leadville and Canon City, resentment brewed over his defense of the gold standard. Roosevelt had hoped to win over crowds in the town of Victor with his Rough Rider image, but he was egged and assaulted with the broken end of a flagpole before being whisked onto a train. Missy assured Ward that she would get the interview, so long as she could find her way around town. She hadn't been in Denver a full day, and she only had thirty cents to last until payday.[28]

Finally, she took a cab to see the Jesuit priest. "He asked if I was fixed for funds. And I heard myself assuring him that I was quite all right and that I had a good job," she recollected. He sent her to a landlady, who offered a room for two dollars a week. Again, Missy's lack of life experience was evident, because she assumed that she wouldn't have to pay up front. The landlady took pity on her, offering her a cramped space in the attic temporarily. Because Missy couldn't afford to retrieve her bag at the train station, she made do with her smaller handbag and left the boardinghouse to buy bread and a bottle of milk. Only twenty cents remained, half of which went toward getting to the Brown Palace Hotel the next morning. She had agreed to meet reporter Joe Kerr there and to approach Roosevelt with him for the interview. Reminiscing in later years about that morning in Denver, Missy recalled feeling "weak as a cat, but still exhilarated and happy." It was the charge that she would get used to feeling every time she pursued a big story.[29]

Roosevelt approached the reporters with outstretched hands and a grin: "Dee-lighted to see you!" Missy thought his affability remarkable given the circumstances. He was the consummate politician, despite being, as she described him, "the only man in history who resented being nominated vice president of the United States." But as Missy also recollected, Joe Kerr was less impressed. "The last time I met you, Colonel Roosevelt, was when you were Police Commissioner of

New York, and I was a reporter for *The Sun*. You ordered me thrown out of the building," he said, scowling. The colonel's smile dissipated, and his face turned cold. But before he could respond, Missy quickly intervened: "The last time I saw you, Colonel Roosevelt[,] was in the elevator of the Hotel Walton. Somebody tried to throw me out and you swore." With that, his face brightened, and he chuckled. Having diffused tensions, Missy pulled out her notebook and started asking questions. It's hard to know if her notes give an accurate portrayal of the incident or if she was spinning her own myth, but Missy maintained that when she finished her questions and stood to depart from the room, Roosevelt called to her from behind. "Good luck to you in your new work," he allegedly said. "And always remember that if you stick to it, you can make the horse jump the gap."[30]

IT WAS WEDNESDAY. Payday was Saturday. Missy had ten cents, and the only trinkets she could pawn remained in the trunk that she could not yet afford to retrieve from the train station. She walked to the telegraph office to cable Washington, but she couldn't send a wire without a deposit. She wanted to buy a bottle of milk, but there was no place nearby where a woman could acceptably sit alone to drink it. So she returned to the office and worked on rewrites until it was time to go home. On the walk back to her room, she bought a loaf of bread that would have to last. The next morning, she spent her last five cents riding into the office. Standing on the street corner, she wondered if she should write a story about what it felt like to be broke. Panic should have set in, yet strangely, it didn't.[31]

Decades later, she recalled the day vividly. Ward had called her into his office, because he had been tipped off about a story taking shape in Boulder and wanted Missy to cover it. She was obviously hesitant. Had he been able to read her mind, he would have known that she couldn't afford the fare to get to Boulder, for it had never occurred to her, nor had anyone ever explained, that the office would front her the money. It would take time to get to know male colleagues well enough to discover that they asked for advances all the time, some-times to pay off gambling loans, rent, or unexpected medical bills. But right now, Ward was confused by his new reporter's body language. "Anything ever happen to you in Boulder?" he asked, but Missy couldn't respond. Ward took a few seconds to scrutinize her, and then suddenly it seemed to hit him. "By God, when have you had something to eat?" he asked her. The questioned so startled Missy that she blurted out honestly, "Yesterday." "What d'you have?" he pressed. "A loaf of bread," she told him. It was half past eleven in the morning, the busiest hour at an afternoon newspaper, but Ward left the room, returned with a roll of bills, picked up Missy's shabby purse, put the money inside, grabbed his hat from the hook, and led her out of the office. The clicking of typewriters stopped as he and Missy walked to the stairwell. The boss was taking the new reporter to lunch.[32]

As Missy remembered it, Ward ordered a steak, sliced tomatoes, fried potatoes, celery, olives, and a big cup of coffee and cream—"all the things a man would order for a he-meal," but Ward didn't stay. When the feast came, he excused himself. "I won't want you anymore today," he told her, "but come in in the morning." He promised Missy that her job was secure so that she wouldn't feel bad about sitting for a proper meal. Unfortunately, that generous meal overtaxed her empty stomach. She felt nauseous as she went to retrieve her trunk from the station, and back at her room she fell into fits of coughing. By supper time, she had brought on another hemorrhage, as she called it. The landlady put her in a cab and sent her to the hospital. Missy guessed that she probably looked like just another "T. B. stranger" in the emergency ward that evening, for Denver was teeming with them. The locals increasingly resented their presence, passing laws that jailed visitors who expectorated on public streets. "I was not afraid to be broke and alone in Denver, but I was terrified to be ill and helpless there," she recalled. Rather than coming clean to Ward about her condition, she sent a note stating that she would be out until Tuesday and gave no further explanation. She was not completely recovered when Tuesday came, but already she had become habituated to working while ill. She established a work schedule of eight to four, returning to a new, sunnier room at her boardinghouse on Franklin Street to recover her strength for the following day. She put on weight and appeared eager to work. No one seemed to suspect a problem.[33]

One morning, Ward gave her the address of a ten-year-old orphan who had committed suicide by ingesting a bottle of Lysol. A note the boy left revealed how much it had weighed on him to be contagious with TB and another mouth to feed in a house full of hungry siblings. Ward decided that the story demanded the compassionate treatment of a woman reporter, but Missy worried about her barely established reputation. "Anything that touched the emotion, anything that revealed the raw side of life, if written by a woman, would be called sob sister stuff," she thought to herself. Men could write similar pieces, soon under the classification "human interest," without stigma, but would she be perceived as journalistically detached if she did the same? Ultimately, her conscience told her to take the assignment, so she did.[34]

If there was levity to be had, it was in Ward accidentally sending Missy to a brothel, rather than to the boy's home, to get the story. Joe Kerr was dispatched to retrieve her just before she entered the building. When Ward told her that she had almost walked into a house of prostitution, Missy looked confused. Did she know what that was? Ward asked her. Because she didn't, she decided that such things must not exist in Washington, and Ward could only laugh. Missy wrote up the boy's story and made a plea for the siblings he'd left behind. For the longer term, she also organized a public recital to be given by the boy's eldest sister, the organist at the local Lutheran church. Her reporting raised thousands of dollars for the family.[35]

Another worthwhile crusade presented itself when a court reporter phoned in a tip about a nineteen-year-old girl, recently widowed, who had been sent to the city prison for stealing a scarf pin and then pawning it for a fraction of its worth. Missy suspected that it was an act of desperation, since the woman had a baby to feed. When she went to the jail to interview the inmate, she could not get past the front lobby; access was restricted to family and social workers. But she saw a group of Salvation Army workers arriving for visitation, and she melded in with them; one worker even gave her a Salvation Army bonnet and pretended to know her. "I was so intent upon the job I was doing that the ethical point of my entering the prison under false pretenses never even occurred to me," she later admitted. But she regretted it the following Sunday morning when her story appeared next to a photograph of the Salvation Army workers. There she was, prominently featured alongside them in the borrowed bonnet, appearing to be someone else for the sake of a front-page story. Even then, she was hard on herself: "It was the evidence of a cheapness which I myself would have been the first to criticize." She mailed a letter of resignation to Ward, too ashamed to submit it in person.[36]

Ward thought that she was being ridiculous. Thanks to her, one of the best lawyers in Denver had taken the widow's case and had her freed from prison. Readers of Missy's story had taken mercy on the young mother and found her work. She had done some effective reporting, Ward insisted. And before she could object, he dispatched her to the mining town of Cripple Creek, where a political story was brewing. Nevada senator William M. Stewart, a Silver Republican, was scheduled to speak in the heart of miner territory, where the strikers had grown violent. Ward wanted Missy to cover what ensued, but he warned her that she was about to enter the real "Wild West," which, to this point, she had only read about in tales by Bret Harte. Indeed, Cripple Creek was so lawless that, unbeknownst to Ward, its women had been ordered out of town for their protection. Her first stop was a drinking hole where rough men played cards and roulette. Two barkeeps poured beer in front of a long stretch of mirror. Missy looked so out of place when she arrived that a customer asked if he could help her with something. She smiled and inquired about a hotel. "This is her," he told her. "The counter's down there. That's where you register."[37]

Missy approached a man and asked for a room with a bath. He looked at her perplexed, wondering how she had even gotten there when women had been given orders to leave. Because passenger trains weren't running, Missy had arrived in a freight car via Canon City. Another woman was with her and had gotten off at Victor, but Missy stayed on to Cripple Creek. No trains were leaving town until the next day, so the man gave Missy a room and told her to lock the door until morning. From her post, perched a story above the street, she opened her bedroom window and leaned out, only to hear gunshots and slam it closed. An hour later there was a knock at the door, but she was too frightened to answer. Through the door a voice told her that Senator Stewart and his wife had a private Pullman car at the train station and that Missy could stay with them. An unescorted woman in town was apparently news that traveled fast. She grabbed her bag and was escorted into a cart, but their journey to the train station was blocked by a mob gathering in front of the grandstand. The driver instructed Missy to lie down at the bottom of the rig to avoid gunfire, but she thought that plan no safer than keeping her head up to see where the fire was coming from. She pulled out her notebook and jotted down what she could observe of her chaotic surroundings. Eventually she arrived at the train station and dictated her story to the railroad telegrapher. Not only had Missy been the only woman in town to witness the event; as a reporter she had the exclusive story.[38]

Cripple Creek was a turning point, because after that Missy started hitting her stride. She got more political stories and earned regular pay and bonuses for exclusives. In the mountain air her health vastly improved, and yet it occurred to her that she hadn't heard her Christian name uttered since she had left Washington. She had kind colleagues, but no real friends. There was no fraternizing after hours, just going back to her room to recover for the next day. Although it was hard to admit that she was homesick, she found herself dropping subtle hints about returning to Washington.[39]

Ward was sympathetic. But because he didn't want to relinquish his talented reporter, he proposed a way for Missy to go home and yet still write for him: he offered her a promotion as the *Denver Post's* Washington correspondent. He even raised her salary to one hundred dollars a week to sweeten the deal. All he asked was that en route back east, Missy cover one more human-interest story at Fort Leavenworth in Kansas: an interview with a military prisoner whose story Missy had remembered from her childhood. The man's arrest had been the talk of Washington society, for he had been a revered army captain charged with fraudulently obtaining funds for government use. Some of her neighbors had considered him a hero; others shunned him as the Benedict Arnold of their time. Now he seemed a shell of the man he had been. Ward thought that Missy could breathe life into his forgotten story more successfully than anyone, shaping it into a narrative of both intrigue and human interest.[40]

Fort Leavenworth, Kans., Oct. 27 [1900]—

"I am innocent, and some day I shall prove it." These confident words were spoken by a numbered but unnamed convict in the military prison. Hollow, meaningless words! Despair was betrayed in the manner, tones and expression of the speaker. In the height of his glory, when men and women, soldier and citizen, natives of every land worshipped at his shrine, he was known as Oberlin M. Carter, captain Engineer Corps, United States Army. But his name has been blotted from the record.[41]

When Missy had arrived at the prison to interview Carter, he was tending asters in a walled-in garden on the grounds. Over the side of the wall she could see in the distance the cottage where he had honeymooned as a younger man, and she highlighted for readers the irony of his being the architect who had designed the very prison that now confined him. She claimed to have no opinion as to his innocence. The torture she wanted to convey was of his mental isolation, and she concluded her piece with a flourish: "How long will it be before the warden will write on the prison record '1924 dead,' or, far worse than that fate, his name will be changed from the present register to the hospital list in the insane ward?"[42]

A psychological portrait of a shamed war hero—Missy thought it noble work to bring the man back into public consciousness, though she also worried that the story could pigeonhole her in the future. "I shared the contempt of other journalists for cheap, sentimental stuff, but I felt regret at the thought that my future work would be purely mechanical, impersonal," she reflected at this professional crossroads. She struggled with a small crisis of identity, trying to shed lingering impressions as a sob sister so that she could be perceived as a hard-nosed political journalist. But admittedly, she fell somewhere in between.[43]

———

HAVING STARTED OUT in Washington and knowing something of the game, Missy wondered if Ward understood what she was up against as a female political reporter. No women currently sat in the Senate press gallery, where Ward had assigned her, though this hadn't always been the case. The abolitionist Jane Grey Swisshelm was approved as a press gallery reporter in 1850, and Mary Windle sat in the gallery under the Buchanan and Lincoln administrations until imprisoned as a Confederate spy. Unfortunately, Windle and Swisshelm seemed to confirm men's already formed prejudices about women: that they couldn't help but be sentimentalists or firebrands, too emotionally charged to cover politics objectively. Emily Edson Briggs of the *Chronicle* managed a longer tenure in the gallery after 1861, becoming the first woman to wire stories through the Capitol telegraph office. And yet, although some twenty women had been admitted to Capitol press galleries by 1879, often under assumed names so that readers didn't suspect a female doing the reporting, access was halted the following year. Women were casualties of efforts to tamp down on the sale of news that grew commonplace in the unregulated ranks of Washington journalism. The all-male Standing Committee of the Senate press gallery granted privileges only to primary representatives of newspapers who wired their stories, which didn't bode well for women who lacked access to the wires. The Senate gallery remained a male monopoly thereafter, excepting Isabel Worrell Ball of the *Star*. If Missy got approved, she would be the first woman to sit in the Senate gallery in the twentieth century.[44]

A new session of Congress convened as Missy arrived back in Washington. She went to Capitol Hill to present her credentials and to get permission to send copy over the wires. Sam Blythe and Ernie Walker of the *Washington Post* were there to greet her, but also to break it to her that her admission to the gallery was denied until taken up at a future meeting of the Standing Committee. She knew that if she had been a man, temporary privileges would have been granted. Blythe didn't disagree and was candid about the issues involved. The few women occasionally admitted to do special features had been perceived uniformly as sob sisters, and "Mrs. Ball" was considered a nuisance, with her complaints about drafts and cigar smoke in the gallery. Missy ignored her bad lungs when she told Blythe that none of it posed a problem for her, and Blythe assured her that no one took issue with her personally. But would opening the gallery doors to Missy open the floodgates to unwanted others? The Standing Committee didn't want to risk it.[45]

Her access was either denied or tabled at the next meeting of the Standing Committee; she didn't know which. Jimmy Preston, superintendent of the Senate press gallery, kindly offered to send her copy over the wires himself, but Missy believed there was more at stake than making deadlines—there was principle. "If the admission committee winked at this exception to the rule they would feel satisfied with having given me a chance," she supposed. "They would salve their conscience with the knowledge that they were making it possible for me to cover my job, or at least to hold on to it."[46]

So she continued to pursue her gallery seat, filling out the required applications and filing the requisite two thousand words a day to prove her serious intentions. This was no small feat, given her disadvantages. She paid a messenger boy out of her own salary to carry her copy to the *Post*'s offices to be telegraphed, and she sat in the visitors' gallery, rather than with other journalists. To interview a statesman, she could not approach him directly; she either intercepted him near the ladies' reception room, or she sent someone in to slip him a card as she waited in the visitors' gallery and hoped he would meet her there. The system prevented any incidental encounter, but she never complained. "When Mr. Blythe, Mr. Coolidge, or Mr. Patterson, or any of my friends would offer to help in some way, or would ask me how I was getting along, or would protest against the injustice of keeping me out, I would reply confidently that it wouldn't be very long." Missy didn't want Ball's reputation for being difficult, and her instincts paid off. When Congress reconvened after Christmas, the Standing Committee granted her a seat in the Senate press gallery.[47]

It was a sort of anointing really, for in the eyes of her male peers, the seat converted any sob sister who sat in it into a bona fide political reporter. In this male space of the Senate press gallery, Missy could write in the human-interest vein and not be shunned or belittled for her more personal perspective of politicians. In fact, she could be seen as an innovator of a rising genre written from the point of view of a political insider. Even after she left the Senate press gallery, this aura of legitimacy stayed with her and gave her an edge over other women trying to break into hard political news. Rather than use that advantage to widen the distance between her and other women, she ultimately carried women with her into the political realm, and into the public sphere generally. But for now she had more to prove, both as a reporter and as a semi-invalid desperate to fulfill what even Sarah Mattingly would have proclaimed her biological destiny: becoming a mother.

Chapter Three

MANHATTAN, MARRIAGE, MOTHERHOOD, MAGAZINES—AND MODERNITY

1901–1914

FOR THE NEXT THREE YEARS, Washington's political beat both energized Missy and took its physical toll. In that first winter of 1901, she borrowed $500 to go west. A cycle emerged: manic coverage of politics, followed by burnout and winters spent in the Arizona desert. She took on small reporting assignments for the Phoenix papers during her off-season, and sometimes she even became the story, as reporters followed her movements in and out of town. It's hard to know if locals thought her a celebrity or an abomination, but as a woman daring to be a reporter, she was nonetheless newsworthy. An editorialist for the *Arizona Republican* half resented and half pitied her when he told locals not to deal with this "unsophisticated eastern girl" "too harshly" for naively believing the tall tales of railroad porters and hackmen. Missy assuredly sensed people's ambivalence about her, and she tried to seize on Western life and stories as much as she could, writing profiles of local personalities as she boarded on a cattle ranch and even rented an alfalfa patch. But she never fully belonged to the West. Home was back east, though more and more she wondered if it had to be in Washington.[1]

In the Senate press gallery, Missy earned more ready acceptance than Isabel Ball, no doubt because she acculturated easily to the environment rather than complaining about it too much. But there was also something in Missy telling her that blending into the press-gallery walls wasn't enough. Her time in the Senate was a necessary experience for her to continue on in journalism, to be sure, but now that she had had her first real taste of acceptance in the male world of political reporting, she wanted more—not necessarily more acceptance, but more impact, and not just political impact, but cultural influence. From the perspective of a woman who had never had the vote, this felt more like real power in the modern age.

In the solitude of Arizona, Missy had begun her foray into magazine writing—first for *Harper's Weekly* and then for *Cosmopolitan,* both magazines with national readerships and editorial content extending beyond politics, and both headquartered in New York City, the center of the media universe for an American journalist. Although the Washington beat had rigor and energy, Missy's journalistic interests had expanded. Wanting to write about religion, immigration, and social and cultural trends, she wondered if she should seek a reporter job that would permit her to cover more than Washington politics. After one last sojourn west in 1904, she decided to relocate permanently to New York. With references and political portfolio in hand, she made her way to downtown Manhattan's Newspaper Row, where the stone edifices of the New York *World, Sun, Tribune,* and *Times* jutted to the sky.[2]

Even with her exceptional experience, Missy knew that landing a job on the Row was no given. At the time, only three hundred women worked as newspaper reporters nationwide, including at small-town papers, where their numbers were greater. What were the chances, she wondered, of working full-time in the city room of a major New York daily? No doubt, the city rooms of the Row fostered a culture no less bawdy or hostile to women than those in Washington. As a rule they were cluttered, and their occupants were disheveled, having come in from overnight stints at police stations, gory crime scenes, and red-light districts. Amidst piles of paper, old food, heaping ashtrays, and bottles of hard liquor, the ringing of phones and tapping at typewriters added to the chaos of these virile spaces. Smoke and dictation filled the air. Editors barked out assignments, as reporters shouted for the rewrite man. Neither patience, temperance, nor manners had currency in these deadline-driven dominions. Newsmen of the Row called the city-room library "the morgue" and the area where most of them congregated "the bullpen." Completely set apart was the less manic space where columnists assembled the women's page. Patronizingly, men in the city room referred to it as the "Hen Coop."[3]

With some beginner's luck, Missy found an editor willing to try her out at the New York *World*—and not in "the coop." But she didn't stay long. Despite her previous experience in the Senate press gallery, she was deployed essentially as a stunt reporter. When told that her first assignment would be to get arrested and sent to jail so that she could write about life inside a women's prison, she decided that this was not an assignment she particularly wanted to ace. Within forty-eight hours she was looking elsewhere, including at the *Herald,* but she still could not get assignments that allowed her to be the reporter she wanted to be. One editor seemed less interested in her investigative reporting than in her family's ties to Mark Twain, and after she wrote up that interview, her assignments fell exclusively under the rubric of "Church News." Her scoop on the nuns of Mount Carmel was hardly the stirring stuff of the US Senate, but her family in the South likely approved. A Nashville magazine heralded the cub reporter as "one of the cleverest women in New York journalism to-day...petite brunette, with large, soulful brown eyes, and so nun-like in appearance that she would never be accused of being a reporter." Indeed, few colleagues questioned her on the church beat, where they thought her demureness a fit, nor did they check her copy. In one story she mistakenly referred to "the Vatican at Vienna," and no one caught the error before it went to press. But her assignments were sporadic, and she wanted regular features. After three months, she tried to get a job at the more reputable New York *Sun.*[4]

Since its founding in 1833, the *Sun* had earned cachet with reporters and a reputation as a gentleman's shop. Its first woman reporter had been hired in 1868, followed by the fashion editor Eleanor Hoyt

Brainerd in the 1880s, but no women of note had broken into its ranks since. The paper was essential reading for artists, intellectuals, and elites. Under Charles Dana, storytelling became its specialty, at first about political figures, but eventually about ordinary people too. Dana shunned stock phrases and flamboyant language, encouraging staff writers to emphasize human interest and color in concise and easy prose. Not coincidentally the paper spawned some of the best novelists, essayists, and playwrights of the age—hence why Missy wanted her big break to be there.[5]

Her future employer, *The Delineator's* George Wilder, believed that the *Sun* was where Missy had truly "won her spurs." Certainly it was where she solidified many connections with the personages of New York and honed the art of character sketching. She also covered topics ranging from the suffrage movement to the juvenile courts, gathering knowledge of the sociological problems of the city along the way. Archie Fowler, a Princeton man with a seventeen-year run at the paper, admired her ability to stay positive as she bided her time. She didn't complain when she substituted for men on the church beat, or finished a story for a colleague too drunk to make his deadline. Because she paid her dues, no one balked when she became a salaried reporter—the first woman employed on the general staff of the *Sun*. Eventually, she was given her own lighthearted column, "Men About Town," albeit written largely anonymously. She was no household name, but colleagues regarded her as a talented member of the team.[6]

It would have nonetheless helped to have had a female mentor, a woman who had already drawn up blueprints for a successful career in reporting—not for the women's page, but as a bylined investigative journalist or political portraitist. The only woman Missy knew in New York who had shaped a career nearly in that mold was the magazine writer Ida Tarbell, whose serials on Napoleon and Lincoln increased *McClure's* subscriptions and served as proof that a woman could cover men without sentimentality. She was a shrewd muckraker and already renowned by the time she compiled her exposés into *The*

History of the Standard Oil Company in 1904. Her investigations prompted Congress to pass antitrust legislation and to establish a Department of Commerce. This was the impact that Missy wanted to have too, and she could also see that Tarbell's career had been shaped through careful posturing. Tarbell's political activities never included suffrage activism, for instance, perhaps because in the minds of male editors such radical agitation would have tainted her reputation as a disinterested journalist.[7]

Surprisingly, Missy didn't find this observation unnerving in the least. She found it comforting, in fact, to think that a journalist need not necessarily vote or rabble-rouse to get attention or accumulate influence. It was to Missy's advantage that mechanisms of power in political parties were changing in the new century. The overt woman activist had less access to powerful men than the political wife or widow, who demurely hosted her social events and whispered her impressions in a politician's ear. In the new century, a more understated yet effective style of politicking emerged that played to a well-read woman's strengths, since it required a nuanced knowledge of the issues and the subtle art of persuasion. Politicking moved out of the saloons and into the homes of female hostesses, where women presented themselves as decorous feminine types. More and more clubwomen, not necessarily suffragists, found party politics to be an outlet for their social acumen and organizational skills. Tarbell proved to Missy that if her journalism had integrity, she could hold sway through stories that found their way to important people and through publications that were read in the home, rather than through clamoring in the streets. It was a more discreet way of being heard, and in this, Missy found Tarbell to be a more successful model of influence than any suffragist could ever be.[8]

But Tarbell was the unicorn, the rare exception. For now, the more realistic role models for Missy's purposes were celebrity portraitists—"interviewers"—who used their feminine charms to make people talk. The best in this vein was Nixola Greeley-Smith, granddaughter of *Tribune* founder Horace Greeley, who had joined the *Evening World* in 1901. When she cross-examined a person, she looked as inscrutable as a sphinx, yet she molded uninteresting people into figures of substance, cultivating a niche of writing without resorting to stunts. Reporter Elizabeth Banks insisted that women were better at the "personal write-up" than were men; as natural students of human nature, they were "more apt at observing and taking account of the little things of life, and more capable of making 'much ado about nothing,'" as she put it. *Herald Tribune* reporter Ishbel Ross agreed that there was "no better outlet for the paper woman's skill," and indeed, Missy's stock increased as she popularized the interview and made it a valued feature of the city paper.[9]

AT THE SAME TIME that Missy was rising steadily on the Row, a reporter named William Brown Meloney IV was making inroads into the respected ranks of New York journalism. Remarkably, for all the admiring words Missy ever wrote about her eventual husband, she didn't leave a record of when and where they met and fell in love. But given the timing of their marriage in June of 1904, it's possible that she met Bill on assignment—perhaps for the *Herald* or *World,* but likely for the *Sun*—or had been introduced to him by other reporters. They had people and places in common; if he hadn't been the impetus that drew Missy to New York City in the first place, he became the most compelling reason for her to stay.

Bill had started out working the crime beat at the *San Francisco Chronicle* (1896–1897), the *Examiner* (1897–1899), and the *Bulletin* (1899–1901) before joining the staff of the New York *World* and the *Sun*. "Wild Bill," as he was affectionately called, scoured the corners of the city, covering the underworld of the city docks, police corruption, the practice of slumming in Chinatown, and "Strikebreaking as a Profession." Crusading in the same muckraking spirit as Tarbell, Ray Stannard Baker, and Lincoln Steffens, he also contributed exposés to the publication they founded, *American Magazine*. Blending into the seedier aspects of city life was not difficult for him, because, despite his stuffy name, Bill had been less pampered than most Eastern journalists. He had studied at Berkeley until the death of his father, a fire engine driver, forced him into reporting to support his widowed mother. At eighteen, he started covering the shipping news, probably because he had spent his adolescence away at sea, crewing on the tallest clipper in the world and even commanding a ship in the fleet of the Hawaiian queen Liliuokalani. He shared with Missy harrowing stories of his cub reporter days—such as when he testified against the police lieutenant he had been investigating and was beaten by two men after the trial. Or the time when a competing reporter confronted him in a hotel lobby and called him a liar. Bill ended the disagreement swiftly by striking him in the face.[10]

. No, there were no traces of frippery, aristocracy, or effeminacy in Bill Meloney, which was probably why Missy was smitten. His truth seeking, along with his heightened sense of daring and physical courage, made editors of the *World* call him a "modern on-the-spot newspaperman," and Missy confirmed the characterization when a train they were riding together derailed outside Atlantic City. One man was dead, and thirty people were injured, including Missy, mildly. Bill's leg had been crushed, yet he grabbed his notepad and started investigating the cause of the crash. Within a half hour, he had dragged himself an eighth of a mile to a phone, where he called in the exclusive story. Missy admired his physical brand of reporting and his crusading style of heroism. He was, in her estimation, the best kind of modern man.[11]

"He was young and had only a reporter's salary. We were poor in material things, but the world was ours," Missy romantically reminisced decades later. Their wedding at St. Patrick's Cathedral made the society pages of the major Washington and New York papers. Missy wore a gown of white chiffon over liberty silk and walked with a bouquet of her favorite daisies. Her dress, like her hat, was trimmed with old point lace passed down from her mother—an ironic choice given the extent to which she would break with tradition in this marriage. Her mother and brother were the only members of her family at the ceremony, and Missy thought it just as well. Her Aunt Mary had passed away the year before, and the rest of her Southern kin hadn't abided her decision to leave pampered gentility to live in the city, marry a Westerner, and work for pay. "I am one member of the family who has never had time to look behind me, nor have I tried to live on the dead bones of my ancestors," she told a cousin. It was Virgil Gibney, her next-best father figure, who gave her away that day. Having no siblings, Bill made Missy's brother, Carroll, his best man. Missy's maid of honor was Cora Rigby, a political correspondent who went on to blaze trails for women reporters as founder of the National Women's Press Club. Cora was the sister Missy never had and part of the family she had chosen in her life outside the South.[12]

The newlyweds settled first in Westchester County, in a neighborhood of New Rochelle called Halcyon Park. Missy's mother had lived with her in New York for a time but now returned to Washington, replaced by Bill's mother, Adelaide, as the live-in in-law. However, the commute to Newspaper Row grew burdensome after the city reduced the number of trains servicing the commuter line. It wasn't long before the Meloneys moved back to the city, to a rented apartment on St. Nicholas Avenue in a neighborhood eventually recognized as part of Harlem.[13]

Professionally, Missy now went by Mrs. William B. Meloney, but she was far from a woman with her former identity subsumed. Izola Page, a rare female colleague of Bill's at the *World*, described the Meloneys in those early years as "symbols of happiness and love and togetherness," but that was only true because each afforded the other ample time and space to create on their own. Like the bond between her parents, Missy's relationship with Bill was affectionate and intellectual. They consulted and inspired each other as journalists, yet pursued career endeavors apart much of the time. They shared the same yearning for adventure and larger purpose. Facilitating each other's professional pursuits kept them emotionally fused, and thus their marriage was a mutual partnership of the modern kind.[14]

Bill didn't view women's influence in the world as inherently lesser, nor did he think it should be relegated to the domestic sphere. A full decade before the Nineteenth Amendment, he wrote a piece for *Munsey's* titled "What Women Have Accomplished Without the Ballot," which acknowledged women's public service across the country— from advocating for health initiatives, to lobbying in the Consumers League, to creating parks, to saving California's missions. He wrote, "A cynical French man once said that the biography of the average woman could be written in five words: 'She married and drank tea.' If he could be set the task of putting the biography of the typical American woman of to-day into one thousand words, the sex might be revenged."[15]

He was describing the rising American "New Woman," who increasingly left home to pursue higher education, paid work, and reform and service activities in the public sphere. Indeed, as much as Missy found her husband's physical courage and muckraking spirit alluring, Bill was charmed by the wife who embodied this modern woman, even if her ambitions were not yet fully realized. At the time he wrote these words, the US Census Bureau tallied four thousand women employed as full-time journalists throughout the country, and yet for the time being Missy was no longer one of them. In May of 1905 she had given birth to William Brown Meloney V and vowed to stay home to raise him. She was temporarily suppressing her tendencies as a New Woman to become the doting mother she'd always wished she'd had.[16]

"Little Bill," as she called him, was her greatest joy; at many low junctures in her life to come, Missy would tell people that her son was the most important motivation she ever found to will herself back to wellness. Although he had Missy's dark eyes and occasional lung ailments, Bill Jr. eventually took on his father's lankier stature. Missy felt blessed to have been able to birth a child, let alone to have the stamina to raise him with the attention her father had given her. That's not to say that the parenthood she desperately wanted didn't bring its insecurities or social isolation. Her mother-in-law was with her in their humble apartment, but her relationship with Adelaide, although cordial, felt strained. It's likely that the unpublished story Missy wrote around this time about a sickly first-time mother (named Missy) was both autobiographical and a way to blow off some steam. The fictional husband worries about his frail wife, and the unnamed mother-in-law criticizes her relentlessly, causing the fictional Missy to remain distant as she daydreams about other places. In those early years of motherhood, the real Missy probably found greater companionship and much-needed help in Queenie Betts, a young black woman from North Carolina who was employed by the Meloneys as a live-in nursemaid. It was a comfort to have a full-time caregiver for Little Bill, like Missy's mammy had been for her.[17]

WHILE MISSY'S JOURNALISM CAREER was on hold, Bill's was too, briefly, in 1910. Focused largely on New York corruption, his muckraking had earned him a reputation that caught the attention of the newly elected mayor, William Jay Gaynor. A different sort of Tammany man than most who had come before him, Gaynor, to the irritation of party bosses, sought to clean up municipal fraud and vice and actually uphold the Bill of Rights. Bill Meloney never fashioned himself a paper pusher, but Gaynor hired him as his executive secretary to take advantage of his powers of investigation. Upon hearing complaints that a Brooklyn alderman was obtaining illegal licenses for peddlers, the mayor handed the matter over to Bill to probe. In the first two months on the job, Bill accompanied Gaynor around Lower Manhattan to police precincts where rumors abounded of officers taking bogus shifts in front of gambling houses that had long gone out of business. But then Bill found himself investigating another crime— the attempted assassination of the mayor himself. Gaynor survived a bullet to the throat, though his recovery was slow. For those weeks Bill tended to clerical matters under the acting mayor, John Purroy Mitchel, also an Irish Catholic with reformist politics. The Meloneys admired Mitchel's principled running of municipal government. Bill was already a close friend, and Missy became one of Mitchel's staunchest supporters once he became the elected "boy Mayor" in 1913.[18]

Bill only stayed on as executive secretary until late May of 1911. "The Mayor said he was sorry to lose Meloney but realized that the drudgery of the office did not appeal to a man of his literary attainments," reported the *Tribune*. There was also the problem of making ends meet. One of Gaynor's first decisions as mayor had been to cut Bill's salary a third from what the executive secretary of the previous administration had made, forcing Bill to consider writing fiction for additional income. That October, the *Sun* announced production of his four-act play, *Graft*, but it only provided a hand-to-mouth existence. Bob Davis, editor of *Munsey's*, agreed to publish one of his novels serially for $1,000 but gave him only six weeks to write it, with no advance. In the meantime, Missy made eighty dollars stretch for forty-two days. The moment Bill finished the manuscript Missy ran it downtown to *Munsey's* office in the Flatiron Building. She got the payment, but it was a Sunday and there was nowhere to deposit the check until Monday. Walking in the sweltering heat up Fifth Avenue, she stopped into St. Patrick's Cathedral and entered the confessional, asking the priest for forgiveness—and a quarter for the fare home.[19]

Making the deadline came at a cost. Soon after, Bill suffered a nervous breakdown and rehabilitated at a friend's plantation in the West Indies. Missy was exceptionally understanding, since she, too, took time and trips away as her health required. Both accepted each other's occasional retreats as a natural consequence of succeeding in the modern world—the price exacted for burning the midnight oil yet loving the work. Bill left his wife and young son for months at a time when his research or state of mind required it. In 1913, after bearing down to write his first novel, *The Girl of the Golden Gate*, Bill left New York again, this time for Costa Rica.[20]

All the while, Missy claimed to have quit journalism entirely to raise Little Bill, shunning any suggestion that she sought distraction from contented motherhood. The truth, however, was that her break was briefer, less clear cut. She continued to report occasional tidbits of church news and to do editorial work for a magazine Bill contributed to called *Everybody's*. Indeed, it appears that from mental restlessness, sedentary illness, and domestic isolation, a literary career emerged. Claiming to need the supplemental income, she essentially justified parenting less to write and edit a little more, and in so doing sounded like authors Mary Roberts Rinehart and Kathleen Norris, mothers who, in due time, Missy helped turn into best-selling writers and better breadwinners than their husbands. Although Missy kept quiet about her income, it is likely that she, too, eclipsed her husband in this regard, for in 1914 she accepted a full-time position as managing editor of a journal called the *Woman's Magazine*.[21]

During the years that Missy described as ones of exclusive motherhood, she forged the connections that took her into the world of domestic magazines. The *Woman's Magazine* and *Everybody's* were publications of the Butterick Company and one of its subsidiaries. Since the 1870s, Butterick had been steadily seizing on the domestic market and the nation's growing female readership. By the time Missy was a full-time editor, the company had come to occupy a fifteen-story building on MacDougal Street in SoHo. Its flagship publication, *The Delineator*, which had started out as a mere forty-eight pages of dress patterns, had grown to dozens more pages of expanding content subscribed to by over half a million readers. Although it still contained fashion plates in the back, now they appeared in color and featured the waistcoats and updos of vigorous New Women, and its growing editorial pages included articles that reflected the increasing female presence in colleges, athletic arenas, and the workplace. By the turn of the century, *The Delineator* had joined *McCall's* (1873–2002), *Pictorial Review* (1899–1939), *Ladies' Home Journal* (1883—), *Woman's Home Companion* (1873–1957), and *Good Housekeeping* (1885—) as one of the "Big Six" domestic magazines in the country. Missy's timing had been propitious, for she had learned a great deal by acquiring pieces for Butterick that she could apply to its fledgling publication, the *Woman's*

Magazine. Although she had a small budget, management was willing to give her much latitude to experiment, reinvent, and apply what she learned to the *Woman's Magazine,* as well as to their more established publications.[22]

By now, it was not unusual for a woman to be editor of a domestic magazine. *McCall's* had had five women editors between 1884 and 1911, *Harper's Bazaar* had three before World War I, and Josephine Redding edited the fashion-forward *Vogue* and Kate Upton Clark, *The Housewife.* Most famously, Gertrude Battles Lane, a friend of Missy's, became editor-in-chief of *Woman's Home Companion* in 1911. No doubt the logic in hiring a female editor was that she best understood the domestic reader. Missy played up this angle, telling Butterick management that she had been a reader of women's magazines throughout her son's infancy, noting flaws in their advice columns along the way. There was an article, for instance, that recommended putting glue and a feather on baby's forefinger and thumb to keep him occupied, which hardly seemed sound. Another one showed how to make a bassinet out of a clothes basket and silk ribbons, which Missy found more inspiring but unsafe. It was accompanied by a picture of a baby sucking on a kidney-shaped bottle attached to tubing that lay next to him. Missy tried replicating the contraption, thinking that it could help soothe Little Bill to sleep if left in his crib; the result was a violently ill baby and a doctor excoriating her for thinking that a homemade mechanism designed for a baby to suck continuously overnight would be sanitary. From then on, she vowed never to perpetuate the advice of hacks in her publications, only that of medical professionals.[23]

It helped Missy that another woman, the future novelist Honoré Willsie, had become editor of *The Delineator* in 1914 and worked closely with her at the Butterick offices. Missy realized quickly that Willsie had to find a different editorial voice from those adopted by the men who had edited *The Delineator* before her. Charles Dwyer (1894–1906), Theodore Dreiser (1907–1910), and William Hard (1910–1913) were relatively progressive editors for the times, publishing pieces to coincide with campaigns for education, orphanage reform, pure-milk

reform, the rights of married women, and gun control. In 1913, Hard
had even tackled the bugaboo of women's suffrage. Willsie, however, chose to be less bold, deciding instead to revive *The Delineator*'s
emphasis on domestic advice. It was an indication to Missy that for a
female editor to succeed, she had to conform to traditional expectations. At a woman's magazine, more of her authority was expected
to come from her experience as a mother than as a hard-reporting
newswoman.[24]

Still, Missy also saw opportunities to fill a void that other editors
of women's magazines hadn't yet seized. Drastic changes in American
women's urban existence necessitated a magazine revamped to meet
the challenges of modern motherhood and homemaking. As homemakers spent less time producing than consuming, they had more
leisure but little information on how to incorporate new technologies into their daily living. And thus rather than dole out advice in a
tone reminiscent of her mother's or grandmother's generation, Missy
treated her magazine as a manual for work and consumption in the
modern home—and to some extent outside it. Although she forged
bonds with her audience through old-fashioned readers' bureaus and
essay contests, she did not glorify Victorian domesticity as much as
she proselytized scientific housekeeping and educated motherhood
for the modern age. Readers took comfort in her telling them that
they were capable, were keeping current, and were not alone.[25]

"The day of twaddle is past," Missy told her staff at the *Woman's
Magazine*. "The amateurish, impractical, fictionized housekeeping
articles, which a great many editors put over on women readers ten
years ago, no longer will be accepted by the reading public. Women
want, and I believe are entitled to, expert opinions on their household
problems." She revamped the Baby Department to include pieces
approved by Virgil Gibney, recently retired as president of the American Orthopaedic Association, and the Domestic Department featured
advice from home economists at Cornell University. A September
edition of the magazine included articles not by home cooks but by
world-famous chefs; in November, a panel of culinary professionals

discussed best methods for dressing the Thanksgiving turkey. "Food scientist" Edouard Panchard contributed a December piece on decorating cakes for the holidays. No more "letters to the lovelorn," Missy vowed, or beauty articles that physicians could not endorse.[26]

She pushed for masculine treatment of feminine subjects at a time when women readers were increasingly dividing their time between the home and public pursuits. As birthrates decreased among the white middle class, more conservative, Anglo elements of society worried that the homemaker seemed to have lost sight of her traditional duties. Rather than stoking fires, Missy proposed that paid work and domesticity need not be either/or propositions. The *Woman's Magazine*'s masthead read, "THE MAGAZINE WITH A DOUBLE MESSAGE—TO THE WOMAN IN THE WORLD—TO THE WOMAN IN THE HOME." "We are told that between seven and eight million women in this country are wage-earners," Missy pontificated to her staff. "That does not mean that eight million women are estranged from home interest any more than all the citizens in Switzerland who are receiving military instruction, are destined to be military men." Missy laid out her argument, and her editorial, in a way that encouraged a gradual acceptance of working women, insisting that paid work did not denature them.[27]

One of the most contested issues at the crux of her claims was education for women. Some experts continued to suggest that women should be discouraged from pursuing college degrees, because too much education would be detrimental to their female constitutions and maternal duties. Others, like Missy, countered claims that college learning necessarily detracted from women's functions in the home. After poring over articles published in *Century, Harper's, Atlantic Monthly, Scribner's,* and *McClure's,* reports of the Department of Education, and studies from abroad, she pointed out that educated mothers hadn't lost their maternal instincts, but rather were informed for the better. According to her research, not only were more American girls expected to earn wages as teenagers in the modern age, but their predicament was not necessarily alleviated by marriage. Education, she claimed, was necessary for their future lives. Missy critiqued fads in educational philosophy and evaluated the usefulness of public high school programs that prepared girls for their future endeavors. She recommended a combination of domestic-science classes and training in a trade. In her increasingly authoritative voice as editor, she wrote, "The Catholic Church says—'Give me the first seven years of a child's life—you may have the rest. I will have made a life-long Catholic of him.' ...My belief is—Give the first seven years of a girl's school life to the above training and we shall have made a *woman* out of her."[28]

Her educational philosophy resembled elements of her mother's pedagogy at the Irwin School: the latter prepared girls to be maternally minded and cultured, and the former for them to be maternally minded and self-sufficient. Missy's emphasis was a reaction to modern conditions, but also to an invalidism that made her more pensive than most about how women might help themselves.

————

MISSY ALSO DEVELOPED STRONG opinions about college education for women, but she didn't want it to look that way. She broached the subject carefully in the pages of the *Woman's Magazine*, letting esteemed men speak for her when she could. In 1915 she figured who better to weigh in than former Harvard University president Charles Eliot. Still a vibrant public intellectual at the age of eighty, Eliot didn't hide his long-held prejudices against women's magazines when Missy first approached him. She assured him, however, that her readers were worthy of his opinions as those primarily charged with raising up the nation's boys. All she wanted was five minutes of his time, face to face, on his own turf in Cambridge, to try to convince him to collaborate with her—not yet about articles on college women, but simply on the education of American boys, to start.[29]

When Eliot finally agreed to see her, Missy came to him exceedingly prepared, showing him an exhaustive pile of documents that included twenty-five years of his speeches, lectures, newspaper interviews, and comments on American education. "It is too valuable to be lost, and none of it has been put in any permanent form," she reminded him. "When you die these clippings will be destroyed. I think you owe it to yourself and to posterity to do something about this." As Missy recalled later, Eliot disappeared for a time to take the stack of papers to his office to reread. "You haven't missed anything," he marveled when he returned, and he agreed that perhaps it wasn't a bad idea to revise some old ideas. He appreciated that Missy had studied his lifelong body of work, and it mattered that she had taken the time to see him in person. He was so impressed by her, in fact, that he reworked some of his material and prepared an article that was in her hands by the following Monday.[30]

Missy booked trains to Boston and sometimes arranged to meet Eliot at his summer retreat in Maine if that's what it took to make him a regular contributor to her magazine. "You must not take the long journey with any assurance that I shall be able to write another article for you," he would warn, but Missy was never deterred, even when early morning trains and steamboat rides to Seal Harbor and Rockland were involved. The face-to-face meetings materialized into published pieces that she ever so adroitly coaxed Eliot into writing. It didn't take long before the very opinionated educator started deferring to her on matters of angle, style, and readability. Missy convinced him to write an unexpected piece about the advantage to American boys of growing up poor, and gave him suggestions for how he might better appeal to female readers. "The average woman's mind does not grasp a philosophy which is not illustrated with human experience," she explained. "If, looking back over the years, you recall other illuminating incidents of the character-making of certain poor men's sons, in contrast with the corroding influence which too much luxury has produced, we would be very grateful indeed if you would incorporate them in your article." Eliot adjusted his analytical style by adding a story about a fourteen-year-old farm boy that Missy, with a few flourishes, helped him to flesh out even more. Before long, Eliot felt comfortable writing for a female audience.[31]

Whether Eliot recognized it or not, Missy was laying the groundwork, building trust, planning for the day when she would steer the educator of men into the uncharted waters of writing not just *for* women but *about* them. Actually, the suggestion finally came from Eliot himself: "I hope you will have a chance in the *Woman's Magazine* to deal with the most important question for discussion among American women," he not so subtly hinted, "namely, the cause of the decline in strength and vitality which successive generations of women in America experience both in city and country. This decline seems to be experienced not only by women of English stock, but of many other European stocks. What causes this decline?"[32]

Missy agreed that the question deserved more than casual attention, and she suspected that his notions about women's education and their physical decline were intertwined. She considered asking Dr. Simon Flexner of the Rockefeller Institute and directors of physical education at the Seven Sisters colleges to weigh in on the health of women students on their campuses, and she encouraged Eliot to focus in on the higher-education debate, pressing him for his thoughts about whether women's increased college matriculation caused declining vitality, a postponement of marriage, or smaller families in the long term, as many conservatives feared. Was he opposed to extending college to a twenty-four- or twenty-five-year-old woman if it did not "materially affect her domestic life?" she queried further. Now she honed in on the controversial questions she had always wanted to raise for her readers. She had her own thoughts, ones supported by two years of research on the attitudes of college and working women toward motherhood and domesticity. But rather than disclose them as hers, she went once again to Maine to share her data with Eliot, for she had grown adept at persuading him to see her side when backed by evidence. Such was the patient and painstaking work of pushing envelopes on controversial topics covered in the *Woman's Magazine*.[33]

Eliot was one of the first of many reputable men who, won over by Missy's doggedness and editorial instincts, no longer dismissed women's magazines as trivial fare. Contributors to her pages soon included the New York superintendent of education, the president of Oberlin College, and the interior secretary, to name just a few. To judge a children's patriotic-essay contest, she called upon former president William Howard Taft. And who better than the first chief of the US Forest Service to judge essays on conservation? Franklin Lane, a long-time reporter friend of Bill's and a commissioner of the Interstate Commerce Commission under Presidents Roosevelt and Taft, praised the *Woman's Magazine* for its intellectual heft and agreed to weigh in on the political topics Missy increasingly covered. After Lane became Woodrow Wilson's interior secretary, she asked if he would approach the president about letting her interview him for the magazine. It was a bold request, one that many male editors had made to no avail. But Lane was sufficiently impressed with the operation Missy was running to make a special plea on her behalf.[34]

MISSY UNDERSTOOD THE CULTURAL milieu in which she had become a woman's editor. Although a good bit of her editorial authority came from her status as a wife and mother, she borrowed the rest from prestigious men, or at least let it appear that way when she broached topics beyond the typical scope of a domestic magazine. Proceeding this way, she perfected her special niche, drawing from culturally feminine and masculine sources to craft magazines that were hybrids of domestic advice and social- and civic-minded journalism, the quality of which critics soon heralded as rivaling the *Atlantic Monthly* and *Leslie's*. In the space of a domestic magazine, men didn't question her expertise on the home, even as she expanded the scope of that sphere to include topics of interest to men and women outside it. She was modernizing the woman's magazine, and doing it under the cover of her married name, Mrs. William Brown Meloney. It was not a liability that she looked to embody the physical delicacy reminiscent of a lady of the Victorian age. Her feminine accouterments created a shield of social acceptance, soothing men's anxieties as she maneuvered through the publishing world, advancing its social agenda and competing with male editors for readers without really seeming to.[35]

Charles Eliot nevertheless told her that he was concerned with how hard she worked, and in a fatherly way he recommended that she take a vacation now and again. It was advice Missy would grow accustomed to hearing, and her response to Eliot, as it was to most men, was charming and deferent, yet ultimately dismissive. "It is a sad commentary on the blindness of inexperience that I, who have for years considered your teaching philosophy as the highest authority, having been honored with advice from you, should have failed to follow it implicitly," she told him. She was perfecting the art of trading in ideas and reputations, without any man feeling as though he had lost the upper hand in the exchange.[36]

Eliot also could not help but mention that he had opened up the most recent edition of Who's Who in America and found Missy's accomplishments as a journalist listed ahead of her husband's. Missy casually passed it off as a clerical error, seeing no reason to draw more attention to it.[37]

Chapter Four

WHAT IT MEANS TO BE A PATRIOT
(THE SUFFRAGIST WHO WASN'T)

1915–1920

ISSY LEARNED MUCH ABOUT patriotic sacrifice from her brother, Carroll, who had done his share of military and civic service. In 1896 he had been appointed first lieutenant of Company D, Fifth Battalion Infantry, of the Washington National Guard, and three years later President William McKinley promoted him to first lieutenant of the Signal Corps. He stepped down from the guard to study law and become a justice of the peace, and when he finally turned to the family business of journalism, he covered the police and city hall beats like a citizen watchman would. Sadly, he died shortly afterward, in 1908, a newlywed and only thirty-two years of age. The *Washington Post* reported rheumatic fever as the cause of death, but Missy believed that an injury Carroll had sustained while playing football at Georgetown had set off his gradual decline. For sixteen years he had lived with chronic pain, much as his sister had, staving off signs of physical distress long enough to become an instructor of military tactics in the National Guard and to begin his career of service. He had stoically suffered for the higher cause of country. It gave a sister solace to believe that her brother, though untried in war, had still been an American hero.[1]

Women, too, could be American heroes, she believed—unsung ones, but ones who sacrificed no less. After his tenure as president of the United States, Teddy Roosevelt seemed to agree, praising Missy for having "the heart of a patriot and the spirit of a soldier" as the Great War loomed. They saw in each other opposite sides of the same patriotic coin: Missy's ideal male was the principled warrior, and certainly a former Rough Riding, Big Stick–toting type like Roosevelt filled his shoes. And Roosevelt's ideal female was a raiser of warriors, who, in her distinctive way, sacrificed equally for the national good. American women would not be enlisted to fight alongside their men in battle, but Roosevelt saw in Missy a woman willing to serve as a second line of defense. She agreed that although women's preparation for war differed from men's, they worked in parallel to build morale and to aid in the moral victory.[2]

Missy would prove that one need not declare war or fight in war to be of considerable consequence to it. Her patriotism would be manifest in the near sacrifice of a husband on the front lines, but also in the innovations brought to waging different kinds of battles—PR blitzes, humanitarian relief, and education campaigns that were modern in their method and scope and that included women in the work of war. And because she would prove effective and stalwart in these battles, she would enjoy great influence in the peace that followed. Once Americans formally joined the Allied cause in World War I, many felt that the fight for women's suffrage, which had been waged already for decades, was an unpatriotic distraction from the more important priority of winning the military fight. Missy would not doubt those optics, and thus like a good female patriot she kept focused on morale-building campaigns to prepare the military and to provide humanitarian relief to civilian casualties. And yet by taking this "patriotic" path, she might have been laying the groundwork for women's suffrage more effectively than many women who openly organized as suffragists. By the time women got the vote in 1920, she would have already anticipated its coming and planned accordingly. No one seized on the potential of the woman voter to shape party politics and the national agenda more quickly or effectively. World War I was devastating, yet strangely also proved an opportunity for a woman who was ready to seize it.

————

FOR A TIME, it looked as though that opportunity might never come. Isolationist sentiments ran deep in America after the assassination of Archduke Franz Ferdinand in Sarajevo, which had reverberated throughout Europe and sparked the beginnings of World War I. Woodrow Wilson won reelection in 1916 as the American president who "kept us out of war," and yet Missy sensed it was only a matter of time before Americans joined the Allied forces against the Germans. She knew women in New York who had taken to the streets to rally for peace, and she preferred peace, to be sure. But she was a realist who believed that it was her civic duty to support calls for heightened military preparation. Already in 1914 she was researching the efficacy of military training in American schools, sharing her findings with the steel magnate Andrew Carnegie. "The United States Army is reported to have in its ranks from Boston and six suburbs, where military instruction has been compulsory for fifty years, only one half of one percent enlistment; almost the lowest record," she reported, disheartened. "Militiamen complain that boys who have had military training in private and public schools will not join military organizations." Carnegie responded, "If that be the case, fysical [sic] training should be established...for the defence of the country.... Most American boys in the country kno[w] how to shoot. No nation in the world has so many guns distributed among the young men, and no nation has such good marksmen as the American. You could travel thru many of the European countries without finding one humble home even, which had a gun. America has, I think, some seventeen millions in its Militia, subject to call. The majority of these, at least, know how to shoot and have guns in the family."[3]

Missy had grown up knowing good marksmen, it was true, but she wasn't sure that being competent with a gun was enough in modern warfare. American males needed the psychological hardening of formal military training, she held. Hence why she acted nothing less than encouraging when her own husband volunteered to train up for war in the summers of 1915 and 1916 at Major General Leonard Wood's army officer-training camp upstate in Plattsburgh. Wood was the sort of man of service who Missy could believe in. He had been an army physician, Teddy Roosevelt's commanding officer in the Spanish-American War, the military governor of Cuba, and commander of the Philippines Division and the Department of the East. By 1910 he was chief of staff of the US Army and clamoring for the combining of arms divisions to prepare American forces for more war, since he was sure it was coming. Missy thought him a model of "vigor and efficiency" and predicted that future generations would proclaim him "the prophet of our times" as he tuned up untried American men for the battlefield. "Rich Young New Yorkers Drill in Rain to Learn How to Be Real Soldiers," announced the *Evening World*. Lawyers, doctors, mayors, and prominent Ivy League football players converged on Wood's camp, along with Roosevelt's sons, the New York police inspector, and Mayor John Purroy Mitchel, who, given his similarly long and slender frame, was paired with Bill Meloney as a tent mate at the camp.[4]

Wives like Missy who were left at home played their roles on the peripheries of the Preparedness Movement by joining wartime auxiliaries, such as the Woman's Section of the Movement for Preparedness, the Women's Department of the National Civic Federation, or the Woman's Section of the Navy League. But Missy took an even more direct path to usefulness. In an effort to offer more than moral support, she called for drilling and other preparedness measures on the pages of Butterick publications. Much the way she had asked Eliot to contribute to the *Woman's Magazine* to get her points across about women's higher education, she called on Cornell University president Jacob Schurman to write the article "What Colleges in the United States Should Do for the Military Strength of the Country" for *Everybody's,* paying him for research and writing that she largely did herself.

A year later she conducted a survey on the military state of the country and asked prominent friends to promote preparedness from multiple angles. One of them, of course, was the always influential Teddy Roosevelt, whom she asked to ruminate on "national consciousness as the woman's job." "You have said that until we plant this consciousness in the mothers we will not find it in the sons," she reminded him. "It seems trite to say that what our nation of tomorrow will depend upon is our women today. And yet, this fact among educators, and even among thinking men, seems to be receiving very little attention. It is time to preach Americanism—and to preach it to the women." It is worth reiterating that the Americanism Missy envisioned when she wrote those words apparently did not require women's right to vote.[5]

In 1914, Missy was behind *The Delineator*'s Woman's Preparedness Bureau, which advised readers on how to support the men of the Allied cause. Her pleas to the female citizenry intensified a year later, when the Germans sank the British passenger liner *Lusitania*. President Wilson admonished the aggressors, but Missy thought his words hollow at the time. Americans had been among the casualties, and yet Wilson was still vowing to keep America out of war. Already disenchanted with the president's position and tactics on a number of issues, for the 1916 presidential election Missy enthusiastically backed Republican candidate Charles Evans Hughes, a jurist of lofty civic service who promised to beef up army and naval forces and institute universal military training for men of fighting age. Needless to say, when Wilson won reelection, Missy was devastated, as were Republicans of all stripes, since they had put differences aside to unite around Hughes.[6]

The Allied powers had been engaged in warfare against the German and Austro-Hungarian Empires for nearly three years and were desperate for Americans to intervene in the fight. In April of 1917 Wilson finally declared war and called up American troops. Once war was at hand, Missy sprung into action, helping Willsie make over *The Delineator* into a war-propaganda machine, albeit for the woman reader. From the fiction to the fashion, all of it evoked life in the trenches. In the department Special War Subjects, anti-German articles abounded, along with advice columns to mothers and wives of men in battle. In the Children's Department, Missy enlisted silent-film star Charlie Chaplin to judge essays written to boost the morale of soldiers heading to the front. The Women's Preparedness Bureau shifted gears, encouraging housewives to conserve resources by using Butterick wartime dress patterns. A series on Julia Ward Howe, writer of "The Battle Hymn of the Republic," provided a model of female patriotism, and editorials condemned women suffragists whose clamoring for the vote appeared to be a distraction from the fight for freedom overseas. The magazine had become an unabashed mouthpiece for Missy's feminine brand of patriotism.[7]

Now using Butterick Company offices as a clearinghouse, Missy spearheaded grassroots campaigns like "Adopt a Town" and sent donations to civilians of devastated areas overseas. She secured housing for orphans, and fed and clothed babies of Belgium and France, appealing to American mothers to make and collect necessities that she personally delivered to war-torn towns. Carrying some ten thousand infant outfits with her to Belgium in 1918, her efforts were reminiscent of those of the Red Cross and the Sanitary Commission of Civil War times. But now she brought an updated set of organizational skills to benevolence work, allowing her to carry it out on a grander scale than had ever been seen before.[8]

It wasn't just women whom Missy brought into relief work; she wanted to educate American children about the plights of families around the world, and she partnered with Charles Eliot to propose a children's auxiliary of the American Red Cross War Council. From there, the Junior Red Cross (JRC) was born. Led by Vassar College president Henry MacCracken and advised by Julia Lathrop of the US Children's Bureau, the JRC was, in Missy's words, a "great international, impersonal, unembittered influence," spreading goodwill and civic-mindedness in wartime. Its short term goal was to provide humanitarian relief in Europe, its long-term aim to nurture international understanding in future generations of Americans. The JRC began mailing lesson plans to teachers across the country that encouraged students to run fund drives and outreach to orphans of war. By 1918, a staggering eleven million children belonged to the organization. In addition to Missy's humanitarian campaigns, being involved in the JRC was yet another way, without legislating, fighting, or voting, for her to be useful in wartime.[9]

––––––––––

BY ALL APPEARANCES, Missy was the sacrificial woman patriot incarnate. Very few at the time would have sensed a hint of opportunism in what she was doing, and yet she, like many American women, was taking advantage of the contingency of war to make new professional inroads. An estimated 1.5 to 2 million American women held jobs directly connected to the war effort that wouldn't have been available to them otherwise, nearly 25,000 of them in Europe as social workers, ambulance drivers, secretaries, and college relief workers ministering to civilians displaced by the war. And now, too, a few women journalists were able for the first time to travel overseas as war correspondents. *Herald Tribune* reporter Ishbel Ross noted that World War I, like the fight for women's suffrage, gave several women an opportunity to move their bylines to the front page. Even though female journalists were encouraged to cover the war from a "feminine" point of view, taking on human-interest stories and civilian crises away from the front lines, as more male journalists were recruited into the military, vacancies opened for women to cover the gritty, less genteel theaters of physical combat.[10]

Wearing the hats of both the "hard news" reporter and the "softer" woman's editor turned philanthropist, Missy, too, wanted to be central to the military action and humanitarian crises of the war. Before leaving for Europe, she had gathered letters of introduction from prominent men, which she used like admission tickets through parliaments, royal parlors, and war zones. "I beg to present Mrs. Meloney, Editor of the Women's Magazine, whom I have known for several years, and who is discretion itself," wrote Franklin Lane to Secretary of State Robert Lansing. "She wants to go to France, and I am in thorough sympathy with this desire of hers. She has a specific object; she wishes to write a series of articles on how American money is spent on improving the conditions over there; and she wants to know in general how the money that American women raise should be expended. . . . She can do this well, and all she needs is your consent to go. I will vouch for her Americanism and her loyalty."[11]

Missy had also arranged with Belgian officials to meet with Queen Elisabeth, a German by birth who was devoted to her adopted countrymen. The editor was eager for her readers to know the queen who nursed soldiers on the front lines—if only Missy's health didn't conspire to hinder her. The moment Missy arrived in Belgium, it was obvious that she had suffered a relapse in her lungs. She swore to an army doctor that it was just a mild flu, but he disagreed and instructed her to abandon her plans to meet with the queen and to stay in bed for the time being. Missy jotted down her recollections of that conversation; there was really nothing the exasperated physician could say to make her cancel her royal interview. "You will surely die if you leave that bed," he threatened her. "It is not serious," she assured him. "I have had that chest for more than twenty-five years." "Not *that* chest," he insisted. "The very same chest," she reiterated, "sometimes worse than this. . . . The left lung has been no good for a quarter of a century—but this cold—how can I protect the Queen from it?" The doctor was shocked that Her Highness was Missy's only concern. "You'll die!" he insisted again. "Of old age—some years from now," Missy assured him. Somehow, she convinced him to give her medicine for the cough and then let her proceed with her plans.[12]

The next day Missy appeared at Laeken Castle in remarkably good form. A lady-in-waiting took her to Queen Elisabeth's drawing room and curtsied: "Your Majesty—Mrs. Meloney." Elisabeth looked pleased to lay eyes on Missy. She asked after the Prince and Princess de Ligne and Baron de Cartier—all Belgians whom Missy knew in Washington. The women spoke at length of the human toll of war, which made Missy want all the more for her readers to know this queen who saved lives. So she came out and asked it: Would the queen write a biography for an American audience? Her Highness had already considered it but had given up on the idea of writing it herself. She could be persuaded to let someone else, an American, write it with Missy's guidance. Perhaps Ida Tarbell, she suggested. "Would you send me some of the books of several who might be interested and perhaps we can settle on one?" the queen requested, and Missy told her that she would happily oblige. The conversation then digressed to fine Belgian lace. Missy lamented that ladies no longer wore velvet gowns trimmed with it, and Elisabeth agreed that it was a custom she missed, as was the art of making it. Then she put in Missy's hand a fan exquisitely woven by a local artisan; it was one of several coveted gifts of lace Missy would receive from the Belgian queen. She took this generous gesture as a cue to express gratitude and then gracefully to depart. It was good manners to curtsy when leaving a royal, but Missy couldn't. "Your Majesty, I am lame and I cannot bow to you, but my soul does." With that, the queen clasped her hand affectionately, as if ending a visit with an old friend.[13]

Missy made her way to Verdun, the French town she had vowed to Butterick readers to help rebuild through their charity. It was rubble and ruins, "a ghost land—a world that was," she lamented. According to Missy's friend the *Herald Tribune* executive Helen Rogers Reid, Missy was so determined to avoid taking a bed away from anyone who had lost a home that she spent her nights in Verdun sleeping under overturned carts, refusing to consider her illness. She jotted down her impressions, not that she'd ever forget them. "Even nature's veil suggests the hell beneath," she wrote. "Shell holes and trenches filled with red, red poppies like the fresh blood of men—and the dark red clover staining the ground with yesterday's sacrifice.... These days have eaten into my heart and mind."[14]

Missy's access to the warfront ironically had come more easily than her husband's. Since Wilson declared war, Bill had been transferred to officer training at Camp Oglethorpe and commissioned a captain; he was to be stationed in Columbia, South Carolina, with the

156th Brigade Field Artillery. Ever the supportive patriot and spouse, Missy had traveled with her son to the South to present Bill's regiment with their unit flag, which she embroidered in crimson and gold. Bill's decision to go south had been a gesture of support for Leonard Wood, who had been overlooked for the more prestigious post as commander of the American Expeditionary Forces in Europe and instead was assigned to the Southeast Division. Republican leaders supported him for the overseas position, but President Wilson selected John J. Pershing instead. Wood was bitter, and Missy was bitter for him. "If I had permitted myself to write to you immediately after the news came of your transfer to Charleston, I should probably have been liable to imprisonment for treason or some lesser crime against the administration," she told him. "I felt just what all other loyal Americans felt—aside from my personal admiration for you, I believed that the interests of my country had been betrayed."[15]

Missy was sure that Wood had been underappreciated and underutilized. And come the summer of 1918, she felt the same about her husband, who still hadn't seen a battle overseas. Bill applied for a transfer with the 6th Division, and as a major he finally got his chance to go to France and show his mettle in the Meuse-Argonne campaign. In that first and only skirmish he suffered his first and only injury from gassing—the very week the Armistice ended the war. An order had been drawn for a regular army officer to replace him, but the order hadn't reached him until the damage had been done. Missy heard about the Armistice after Leonard Wood intercepted the wire and let her know; to her relief, Bill's injury didn't require his immediate evacuation. To keep up his morale, she sent her husband a calendar containing messages from friends. Teddy Roosevelt penned entries on the dates of his inauguration, the anniversary of the sinking of the Lusitania, and the official beginning of the war. But sadly, only days after New Year's Day 1919, Roosevelt died in his sleep. Although he had wanted to prove his manhood in war once again, his hope of taking another division to the front was never realized. Every time Missy had ever witnessed him in action—be it horse riding or stump speaking—she had marveled at his courage. She mourned this patriot deeply as she awaited her husband's return.[16]

Her contacts in the War Department encouraged her to apply for Bill's early release, but Missy refused to even consider it. As she reminded Leonard Wood, releases were for soldiers who worked in "essential industries" or had spouses who needed them because of illness or financial dependency. "Bill does not belong to an essential industry. He is a magazine writer, and while to us, who know the need of educating the public, this is an essential activity at least, the Administration does not put that interpretation upon it—particularly in view of the fact that Bill is known to be an anti-administration man." Like her husband, Missy had not been shy in expressing her disapproval of Wilson. As for claiming that she was ill or financially dependent, she told Wood that she would not "subject Bill to such a humiliation or myself to such a falsification." Instead, she waited until her husband was honorably discharged with the rank of lieutenant colonel in March of 1919. She reunited with him at Camp Meade, where he had been sent along with future president Dwight Eisenhower. He looked to be "in fine condition," she reported to Wood. "He wants to jump into the ring for you," she added. "He is very anxious to get in touch with you as soon as he can get into a plaid suit."[17]

———

INDEED, MISSY HAD ALREADY TURNED her attention to the 1920 presidential election. Other prominent Republicans, including Teddy Roosevelt's children, agreed that Wood was an ideal choice for the party ticket. "We are striving to make Everybody's Magazine and the other publications in this house strong backers of Leonard Wood for President," Missy assured Wood. "This is not a new impulse with me. Both Republican and Democratic leaders will tell you that I have been talking Leonard Wood as the one great American leader since the Plattsburg [sic] days. I feel that I have a right to claim to be, if not the original Wood man, at least the original Wood woman. And so I naturally desire, if possible, to get you into these magazines in a big way." Missy went through her files to find the letters she had kept in which Teddy Roosevelt had praised Wood over the years. In light of the former president's recent death and the tributes that poured forth, she figured there was no better endorsement of Wood than words straight from Roosevelt's pen, which could make him look like the next best thing to a handpicked successor.[18]

No one had asked Missy to take on the role of Wood's point person; she assumed it naturally, for it seemed an extension of the persuasive propaganda work she had already performed during the war. In her attempt to raise Wood's national profile, she thought of ways to upstage the nation's current media darling, the war hero General John Pershing, who, she believed, was getting the acclaim that should have been Wood's with the end of the war. Per Missy's request, Wood consented to being interviewed for Butterick magazines, though he worried that questions like the one about his favorite supper-time meal edged toward the line between the relevant and the ridiculous. Missy assured him that revealing his human side was how he was going to appeal to a female constituency that, given the political tides, would likely be allowed to vote in 1920.[19]

Indeed, she had an ulterior motive for handpicking her own horse for the upcoming presidential race. Who better to make the next champion of women voters than a man with a lifetime of virile service under his belt? His prestige in American life could legitimize newly minted women voters if Missy could establish Wood as their savior and advocate in the national press. It seems that Missy was one of the first to start thinking in these terms. "The woman vote in this country cannot be overlooked," she insisted to Wood. "In my opinion, it is not too soon for you to begin to talk to women." Finding her request awkward but ultimately trusting her instincts, Wood disclosed that his favorite meal was roast beef and potatoes, with corn pone on the side; Missy would print it as part of her unannounced publicity for his unannounced political campaign.[20]

Missy didn't plan to stop at shaping the image of this chivalrous candidate. She also wanted to put him on the record as supporting issues that she thought would poll well with women if women were polled (which of course they weren't). This was a bold move, considering that most of the positions were likely to make Wood lose favor with men. Take the issue of married women's property rights, for instance, which was complicated since the rights and support for them differed drastically from state to state. Missy brought Wood up to speed on the issue and molded him into a candidate who backed an expansion of these rights, particularly as they pertained to homestead claims, to reduce cases of female destitution throughout the country. "The Government should remedy this by allotting the land in joint ownership to husband and wife where they go on the land together," Wood agreed. "Where the man married after he has developed the land, nothing could be done without the broadest kind of legislation which would secure the property rights of wives....Women have come into politics to stay and suffrage is practically here, and we now must look the matter squarely in the face with open eyes."[21]

There, now Wood was on the record. It was hardly accidental that his statements, couched between an editor's endorsements, found their way onto the pages of *The Delineator* and the *Woman's Magazine*. And Missy's predictions about suffrage came to pass. On August 26, 1920, a federal amendment finally gave American women the right to vote in local, state, and national elections throughout the country. During the war, prominent suffragists like Carrie Chapman Catt of the National American Woman Suffrage Association (NAWSA) had changed their pacifist positions as a point of political strategy, and the calculation paid off; Wilson and male legislators viewed the Nineteenth Amendment as women's reward for dutifully supporting the troops. Given her very public campaigns to prepare the troops for battle and her avid support of a military man like Wood, Missy might have done more to secure women's suffrage than many women who marched, lobbied Congress, and identified themselves with the cause.[22]

But American women never got the chance to vote for Missy's military man for president, because his party nomination fell through.

Despite his winning the first four ballots at the Republican National Convention, party leadership decided that rather than a strict conservative or progressive, a compromise candidate, Warren Harding, should be on the 1920 ticket instead. Harding would win the presidency by disavowing Wilson while promising a return to prewar normalcy—just as Missy had advised Wood to do had he been elevated to a position to do it.

Nevertheless, though she no longer had a horse in the presidential race, Missy had gotten a taste of campaigning and proved that she had instincts and perspective not shared by even the most seasoned of party operatives. No one yet knew how women voters would shape the political landscape, but the leadership of the Republican Party recognized that perhaps they had a figure among them who understood, and could guide, the woman voter better than any of them knew how. As someone who gleaned women's opinions from her readers' bureaus and who editorialized to shape her readers' views of politicians and their issues, Missy had engaged women as political beings more than anyone else before her. By creating this relationship, she carved out a niche in American politics. She was fashioning herself as an unusual sort of operative, one positioned to do future battle in the trenches of party politics (as men did), and yet one heralded as a benevolent saint, given her feminine wartime service. Who else in American life enjoyed the privilege of being perceived as a political insider and yet above the political fray at the same time?

––––––––––

THE LONGER-TERM DAMAGE to Bill Meloney's lungs became apparent after the war. When he got back to New York he suffered an infection—not his last. Still, Missy considered herself lucky, knowing too many women whose loved ones had made the ultimate sacrifice. Teddy Roosevelt's wife, Edith, endured the loss of her husband as well as of her son Quentin, who died in aerial combat in France. Likewise, John Purroy Mitchel left behind a grieving wife and mother after he died in an accident late in the war. Mitchel had embarked on his final training run in a scout machine, circling the airfield at about five hundred feet, when his plane took an unexpected nosedive. Not fastened into his seat, Mitchel was catapulted out of the aircraft. Witnesses saw him in the air, grasping with his hands, trying to position his body to land on his feet, but he died upon impact.[23]

Missy joined the friends gathered on the lower level of Penn Station to collect Mitchel's casket as policemen kept the way clear for the cortege. New Yorkers stood on the streets, heads bowed, as Mitchel's hearse turned from 31st Street up Eighth Avenue, to 59th, to Broadway, to Mary Mitchel's home on West 162nd. She had a moment alone with her son before his body was taken to City Hall, where some six thousand filed past his coffin under the dome to pay respects.[24]

After the war, biographers approached the Mitchel family to write Mitchel's story, but his mother believed that only Bill Meloney could do it justice. "You know my boy and understood him and loved him and I feel that you will be as just to him as he would be to you were the task you are undertaking his," she told him. She gave Bill all the papers her son had given her, including those that had bearing on the various controversies brewed up by his political enemies when he was in office. His mother believed that they proved him a benevolent mayor and a model Catholic. Bill vowed to vindicate him beyond what his sacrifice in war had already achieved, and Missy vowed to help him.[25]

Mitchel was not the only soldier the Meloneys defended following the war, for their patriotic work extended well after the Armistice. Despite his ailments, Bill tried to help other veterans readjust to life back home by writing *Where Do We Go from Here? The Real Dope.* The War Department disbursed some five million copies of the manual to veterans and their families as a resource for finding work and navigating the red tape of the Veterans' Bureau. Friends implored Missy to take a break and let Bill do this work alone, but she couldn't help but feel protective of him, given his lingering lung trouble. She assisted him with his research of veterans' benefits and took advantage of her connections to Franklin Lane to push more congressional appropriations for housing for returned soldiers. Once again, it helped to be able to take her cause to the pages of the *Woman's Magazine*.[26]

Former police commissioner Arthur Woods, a family friend, had been tasked with finding jobs for discharged soldiers through the War Department, and he scolded both Meloneys for working too hard at the job he was being paid to do. He urged Missy to take stretches of time off at the farmhouse that she and Bill had purchased upstate in Dutchess County, appealing to her sense of maternal and wifely obligation. "The boy needs you up there in the country, [and] you'd be bait for Bill, who shouldn't haunt the library too intensely this winter," he scolded. But Missy had obligations that kept her in the city. She received word from the Belgian Consul that Her Majesty Queen Elisabeth wanted an audience with her at the Waldorf Astoria for reasons only disclosed two months later in the *Sun*:[27]

> Mrs. William Brown Meloney, editor of the *Woman's Magazine*, associate editor of *Everybody's* Magazine, and consulting editor of the *Delineator*, yesterday received the decoration of the Order of Queen Elisabeth from the Queen of the Belgians. The investiture was made by Baron de Cartier, the Belgian Ambassador, and the presentation took place at Mrs. Meloney's home, 33 West 12th St.
>
> The decoration was bestowed for distinguished service rendered the Belgian cause in the United States from the beginning of the German invasion in 1914. In 1917 Mrs. Meloney received the Medaille de Charleroi in recognition of her services in behalf of Belgian children. She was formerly on the staff of THE SUN.[28]

Missy seemed to have come full circle since her days hunting for a reporter's job. Editors once reticent to print her byline now made her a news story and proudly trumpeted their associations with her. Because she looked to be a sacrificing sort of patriot, reporters publicized the work ethic they always knew she had. Her boss at *The Delineator*, George Wilder, seconded the claim that no woman had been more patriotic in wartime: "During these tearful days the heart of the wife never faltered, or faltering, got new courage by more intensive work at times for the Federal Government without pay. . . . Only those associated with Mrs. Meloney in our offices have an idea of how much she gave of herself physically, spiritually, and mentally during the terrible war years. Still, one thing stands out, uniquely—never once did she serve on a committee or don a uniform."[29]

Wilder touched on the crux of Missy's power. Hers was not influence sanctioned by title or position. It was a feminine way of operating, an effective yet modest way of being. She had never engaged in war work to aggrandize herself. She did what she thought any female patriot would have done, had they her connections to prominent people and to a mouthpiece with national reach.

In 1920, Missy made one last patriotic gesture in an attempt to heal her readers, many of them mothers and wives who needed to know that their sacrifice of sons and husbands had not been in vain. She reached out to the War Department to propose erecting what she called a "Tomb of Unknown Soldiers" in Washington. Having seen the emotional effects of similar gestures in Europe, where unidentified men were entombed at Westminster Abbey and the Arc de Triomphe, she believed that an institutionalized paying of respects near the nation's capital would bring comfort to families who lacked the closure of burying loved ones after the war. Army Chief of Staff Peyton Conway March agreed on the merits of the idea, but he told Missy that the number of unidentified soldiers was small and getting smaller and hence that the psychological need for the tomb might be less dire than she assumed. Missy's own eyewitness account suggested otherwise. "It is not sob-sister stuff. It is not weak, sentimental hog wash," she assured March. "There are many unidentified. Long aisles of them I saw at Romagne. The very top of the hill in that beautiful, quiet spot of consecrated United States property is crowded with crosses marked 'Unknown.' One of these lying under the new monument would challenge the actual passerby. It brings patriotism home to men in a personal way. Nothing lures the mind so much as mystery. Nothing elevates it so much as justice." Missy didn't believe that the tomb would have meaning for her generation alone; it would cast shadows of heroism for the next one and forever after.[30]

Enough congressmen were convinced of her logic to approve the monument in March of 1921. The following November, eight veteran soldiers, handpicked by General Pershing, escorted their unknown comrade to Arlington National Cemetery. Three years to the day after the end of World War I, President Harding presided over an Armistice Day ceremony at which he dedicated the Tomb of the Unknowns. Few in attendance could have guessed at the role played by an editor of a woman's magazine in honoring military service and healing the nation for the long term. Nor would they have believed that this same editor, who grieved with her readers, would eventually urge sacrificing women to vote their economic interests as widows and self-sustaining breadwinners—but such was the work of the quiet patriot behind the scenes. When Teddy Roosevelt proclaimed that Missy had "the heart of a patriot and the spirit of a soldier," he did not know the full extent of his prescience.[31]

Chapter Five

CULTIVATING RELATIONSHIPS AND BEST SELLERS FOR AND BY WOMEN

1920S

B UTTERICK COMPANY PRESIDENT George Wilder finally made it official: his woman patriot, "Mrs. William Brown Meloney," former editor of the *Woman's Magazine* and associate editor of *Everybody's,* was now chief editor of *The Delineator.* He reserved the front page of an issue of his magazine to praise his woman in charge:

> When only 17, she first dipped her pen in the ink pot of American journalism, and except for lapses due to the care of a home, motherhood and occasional ill-health, she has continued dipping it ever since.... [She] cares not who gets credit for doing a thing so long as the thing gets done. She can work with people, but what is more, she can work herself. She has a genius for friendship and she has judgment. She must have judgment or she could not have had the friendship and confidence of such leaders among a host as Theodore Roosevelt, Leonard Wood, Franklin K. Lane, Lindley Garrison, Dr. Eliot of Harvard, Chester Lord, Dr. King of Oberlin College, and the late John Purroy Mitchel....
>
> She is as good a housewife as she is an editor; and withal, she is very human and very feminine.[1]

Apparently Wilder could only justify Missy's promotion over men by giving readers some assurances. His woman editor reasoned enough like men to be trusted by them, and yet her domesticity, her mother-hood, and her social graces kept her very much a lady. It was a mixed message that Missy internalized but also dismissed, as if nothing in her magazine or professional persona had ever been incompatible.

To be successful in her new role, Missy would need sensitive cultural antennae while she shaped the content of her magazine. Now that American women had the vote, she sensed that many readers felt more license to step out further into public contexts and that she should encourage them, but sometimes, too, women looked to be in retreat, pining nostalgically for domestic ideals that might never have existed in the first place. Some readers seemed eager to be politically engaged, yet there were also those who moralistically insisted on staying out of politics, refusing to use their vote or their voice in the marketplace of ideas. Whereas some ventured out of the home to earn money, others remained as entrenched in the home as ever, much to the approval of more conservative elements in society. And thus striking the right editorial balance was like shooting at multiple moving targets—all while moving yourself. Nevertheless, because she identified with women who considered themselves combinations of politicized, domestic, *and* working to some degree, Missy recognized that her messaging should speak to a broader, shifting readership than what had been tackled by previous editors of *The Delineator*. She listened and observed, creating a feedback loop with her writers and readers that helped her to calibrate just how far to push the envelope and air some new ideas.

Already intimately familiar with *The Delineator* and responsible for much of its content, Missy planned to take lessons learned in her other positions to create a hybrid publication that merged political sketch and maternalist reform, traditional domesticity and modern science, escapist fiction and social commentary. It would have masculine content and feminine purpose, but also feminine topics discussed with a masculine lack of sentimentality to bring legitimacy to women's issues and perspectives. She would take the woman reader seriously and avoid insulting her intelligence. "The authors that go into making the Delineator are the cream of the world today," she boasted. "No place is too far, too hard to reach, no person too difficult for us to approach, to gain them for the women who read the Delineator." It wasn't long before her readers discovered just how literally she meant what she wrote.[2]

INDEED, MISSY HAD A WAY of getting people to write for her whom other woman's editors would not have dared to even approach. She succeeded because she took the time to build relationships and then make the ask. Such was the case after befriending Calvin Coolidge in 1919, when he was still just a governor harboring national political ambitions. One night she and Bill were both up late working, he slogging away on a profile of the Massachusetts governor for *Everybody's,* and she fed up with her daunting task of cutting a manuscript by Arnold Bennett in half before sending it to print. Glancing over at Bill's desk, she saw Coolidge's speeches and writings collected there, picked up a few, and started to read. She sniffed out potential better than most. As she recollected in her personal notes, she couldn't help but to laugh out loud. "What's funny?" Bill asked. "I was just wishing that Calvin Coolidge had been Arnold Bennett's English teacher," she joked, and kept reading.[3]

To her pleasant surprise, Coolidge had a talent for the written word. Perhaps she had found her next contributor, she suggested to Bill, and this time it was Bill who laughed. He assured his wife that she wouldn't have much luck interesting a serious man like Coolidge in a woman's magazine, but Missy never saw the harm in asking. All she needed was a one-on-one audience to make her case. She wrote the governor that night, and her plea must have been as compelling as the one she had made to Charles Eliot a few years before, because Coolidge responded by inviting her to the State House in Boston to talk about what she had in mind. In time, Missy managed to become a rare female advisor to Coolidge by identifying ways they could mutually benefit each other—she as a sort of publicist and sounding board, especially about the mentality of this unknown constituency of women voters, and he as one of her big-name political writers.

Missy seized on opportunities when she got them. Much like she had when first meeting Eliot, she arrived at the State House prepared to pitch Coolidge with outlines of subjects she thought her readers would appreciate the governor weighing in on. Given recent criticism that he had not been "internationally-minded" and that this might be a sticking point given his political ambitions, she suggested that he write pieces on foreign relations—but she didn't get very far. The governor's secretary suddenly appeared in the doorway to announce his next appointment. Needing no further prompting, Missy stood to leave, but apparently Coolidge didn't want her to go. "Look around the State House a little while," he suggested, and Missy patiently obliged him.[4]

Twenty minutes later they picked up their discussion. Coolidge explained that he thought Americans had enough problems to solve at home and that he wanted to write about some of them—"problems of labor and capital, better understanding on both sides, wider education, preservation of the principles upon which this republic was built," Missy recalled him ranting. He was especially irked by what he called "organized propaganda from alien sources," which he alleged had spread into churches, colleges, and American businesses. He thought that Americans should be forewarned about "the inroads the Reds, especially from Russia, were making in our institutions." "Twenty years from now, we shall be reaping a bitter harvest from those seeds if we do nothing to correct it," he prophesized. Missy listened intently, the wheels in her mind in motion. She was thinking of how Coolidge could write about the topics that were stuck in his craw, tailored slightly to meet her editorial needs and angled to appeal to her female readers.[5]

The governor's secretary interrupted again to announce another appointment. Missy obliged another request to wait in the hallway, and this time when she returned to his office Coolidge had taken out files containing evidence of the spread of Bolshevik propaganda in schools and churches in the Midwest, as well as information about hired speakers who went to campuses to radicalize students. He worried about the infiltration of ideas by false prophets, particularly at women's colleges, where he thought students especially susceptible to radical suggestion. Missy finally intervened, proposing that perhaps Coolidge had found the purpose and topic for his next article. If he felt so strongly that college women needed to be less naive about the political messages bombarding them, then why not educate them to be more informed citizens? Missy assured him that women were interested in politics, but they had some catching up to do, as any newly minted electorate would. Help bring them up to political speed, she suggested. Don't simply write *about* women; write *to* them directly. Coolidge looked stunned. No editor had ever suggested such a thing.[6]

When Missy returned to New York and told Bill that Coolidge had spoken to her that morning for an hour and forty minutes, he was in utter disbelief. He joked that Coolidge didn't know enough words to speak to a woman for that long, and perhaps it was Missy who had done all the talking. Missy bit her tongue until the following week, when Coolidge was in New York and asked the Meloneys to breakfast. During the meal Missy pulled a stunt that left Bill nearly gasping. She wrote of the incident afterward: "Governor Coolidge," she began, "my husband and I have lived together for a number of years. He never doubted me until I met you. I realize that the next five minutes will be uncomfortable ones, but their discomfort is not so important as the restoration of my husband's faith in me. He doesn't think the Governor of Massachusetts knows enough words to talk to a woman for an hour and forty minutes. So will you please tell him what we talked about in your office?" Missy was conscious of Bill putting down his utensils, but she didn't dare look at him. The governor appeared startled for a few seconds, but then his eyes twinkled and his mouth turned up in a grin. He left out nothing, enumerating the subjects he had broached with Missy, one after the next. And in fact there was more to talk about, he told Bill, including the outline he had prepared of an article he had written at Missy's request.[7]

Coolidge's "Enemies of the Republic" came out in *The Delineator* in 1921; by the time he followed up with "The Reds in Women's Colleges," he had moved from the State House in Boston to the Capitol in Washington as vice president of the United States. His lady editor at *The Delineator* was the first recipient of a note on his new executive letterhead. He wanted to express his appreciation for her allowing him an outlet to speak to American women, and for her ability to make his words resonate and appeal to them.[8]

Missy's notes from that Saturday-morning meeting with Coolidge reveal a man who defied expectation in every way. He offered all sorts of unsolicited commentary on topics presumably verboten to a man who was notoriously tight-lipped, private, and limited in worldview. And yet it was Coolidge who brought up the fact that his wife read domestic magazines and that his grandmother had read *Godey's Lady's Book* in years past. There was something about Missy's demeanor as she listened to him that made him naturally drift to a tangent about this grandmother, who had ingrained in him the importance of universal education, as well as skills for handling argumentative men. Though he claimed to be irritated with the "professional woman agitator," he joked that "Pilgrim mothers" deserved more credit than "Pilgrim fathers," "because they not only had to endure all of the hardships the Pilgrim fathers had to endure, they had to put up with the Pilgrim fathers." He had voted for woman's suffrage when it was unpopular and fought to improve laws in Massachusetts for women who worked for a wage. Missy remarked at how glowingly he spoke of women who taught boys to be citizens and surmised that he approved of her because he thought her one of those. She indulged him when he pulled a photograph of his mother out of the desk drawer and reminisced. He confided that she had died when he was very young and that he had been practically raised by his stepmother. Missy just let him talk, storing these nuggets in her mental files. His latent respect for the wisdom of the women in his life was obvious to Missy, which made her conclude, contrary to the claims of nearly everyone she knew, that Coolidge had no prejudices against women and that he could write for them with a little guidance.[9]

This habit of listening and allowing the conversation to naturally drift led Missy to uncommonly astute insights about men who remained enigmatic to others. "I was never in a position to understand the cold reserve and restraint and the lack of friendliness which some of the Coolidge chroniclers have commented on," Missy wrote in later years. As Bill perceived it, his wife was simply able to access parts of people that the most accomplished of his reporter friends never could. He reminded his wife that Coolidge was a man who hadn't use for "cowards or dissemblers or make-believe people." "He is going to be President of the United States some day," he predicted. "If you understand him, you can be very useful." Indeed, she did become useful, because she took the time to listen, gain trust, and tell the truth as she saw it.[10]

———————

IN THE SPRING OF 1920, Missy left for Europe on a quest to bring fresh literary talent to her American readers. Actually the trip was intended as part business, part rehabilitation, which no one would have suspected by looking at her full calendar of appointments. Having been plagued by fatigue and lung ailments since the war, Missy was taking two months away from her New York office, albeit to work even more overseas. Worry not, she assured her secretaries. If she wore herself out, she would curtail her travel and transfer operations to the Butterick Company offices in London and Paris, or to the hotels where she convalesced. It had increasingly played to her advantage to conduct meetings away from official places of business anyway. Holding court informally, over lunch in her hotels, without any entourages present, allowed conversations to veer organically from business to vacation plans and other topics that stirred writers to be their most creative selves. The novelist William John Locke regretted that his writings were already contracted elsewhere, and yet he planned to meet with Missy to catch up just the same. Relationship building is how you foster trust until you acquire pieces from "the very top liners of the world," she told junior editors. Sometimes she acquired a chef d'oeuvre because she was not necessarily soliciting it.[11]

Sending Missy to Europe in search of material to print was like unleashing a child in a candy store. She needed no help in deciding what to buy, just time to sample the goods, which she did gleefully, and the budget to pay for what she liked. Wilder gave her permission to offer top dollar, trusting her instincts implicitly. It helped that she had already built a reputation with some of the most critically and commercially successful literary figures of the age. At Everybody's, she had established relationships with Booth Tarkington, Samuel Hopkins Adams, Owen Johnson, Robert Frost, John Erskine, Edgar Wallace, Arthur Train, and H. L. Mencken, to name a few. Fiction and nonfiction writers, mystery writers, satirists, adventurists, philosophers, domestic-advice columnists, and political commentators made up her list of devotees, which came also to include Willa Cather, Zona Gale, Edna Ferber, Kathleen Norris, Mary Roberts Rinehart, and Fannie Hurst—some of the most popular women authors to emerge in the 1920s.

Once she arrived at the Grosvenor Hotel in London in April of 1920, before meeting with potential contributors, Missy put pen to paper to let Bill know that she was off the ship and getting settled. It was hard to leave her husband behind, but his lungs still gave him trouble; he stayed in New York to rest, to write Mitchel's biography, and to make up for lost time with his son. Nevertheless, Missy painted him a picture in words of the view of Buckingham Palace from her window, of her cavernous bedroom ("like the rotunda of the Capitol"), and of her well-appointed sitting room full of Chippendale pieces and a piano that would have tempted her to play, had she not slotted appointments for nearly every hour of the day over the next six weeks. Wood burned in the fireplace, despite the postwar fuel shortage. Maids stepped in regularly to fan the flames and refresh the flowers, serve her tea, draw the curtains, and place hot water bottles in her bed. It embarrassed her that they curtseyed in her presence, so she engaged them in conversation to remind them that she saw them as social equals. She was not the typical guest they were accustomed to, just "Missy Meloney of Bardstown, Ky, U.S.A.," which stood for "You Sell Anything," she casually joked. Her class sensibilities remained hopelessly American.[12]

Even in the confines of her hotel suite she observed and took copious notes. Interviewing a maid, she discovered that despite her medical requirements she apparently gave the staff less grief than "the Duchess of something or other" who had occupied the room before her. Missy was effusive in her shows of appreciation; it felt wrong to luxuriate, as if no ill effects of the war had lingered. She noticed that even at the swank Grosvenor Hotel, the staff heated only one of her rooms. The grand clocks and armoires in the lounge belied the daily ration of a small pat of butter, two lumps of sugar, and no cream in her afternoon tea. The bustle of servants in and out contrasted with the shortage of laborers outside the hotel walls, particularly in the coal mines. Prewar normalcy had yet to be achieved, she reported to Bill. She continued to see military uniforms everywhere, as if England were still at war. These were the observations that formed the impressions she planned eventually to share with her readers in her column "From the Editor's Point of View."[13]

Before Missy left for Europe, Franklin Lane had sent her a list of topics that would make for intriguing stories in *Everybody's*, which she still occasionally acquired for: the world's choirs, American shoe styles, English labor leaders, the Child Health Organization, widow-burning in India, or, something racier yet, the rise of the Chinese "New Woman." As far-fetched as they were, his ideas didn't differ much from what Missy already had in mind for *The Delineator*. She didn't want to re-create a domestic rag of the prewar years, so she searched for fresh fiction and serious-minded editorials, believing that American women were ready for them. And thus the list of people she scheduled meetings with included the novelist Hugh Walpole, the suffragist turned author May Sinclair, the newspaper magnate Alfred

Charles Harmsworth, detective writer J. S. Fletcher, playwright Neil Lyons, humorist Jerome K. Jerome, and Henry De Vere Stacpoole, author of *The Blue Lagoon,* with whom Missy ended up spending a lovely Sunday in Essex. She planned lunches with novelists Joseph Conrad and Arthur Conan Doyle and to catch up with future Nobel Prize–winning author John Galsworthy in Devon. She booked tea with adventure writer Sir Anthony Hope Hawkins and made appointments with up-and-coming fictionists John Collis Snaith and F. Brett Young, as well as with literary agents who were trying to establish their clients as stars. And there was no leaving England without seeing Lady Astor, the American-born socialite and member of Parliament. Every time Missy went to London, Lady Astor was swamped, and yet she always managed to squeeze in lunch with her American editor between committee meetings at the House of Commons.[14]

Indeed, Missy went to Herculean lengths to meet with the people who intrigued her most. This meant taking boats, trains, and taxis in the wee hours to make breakfast meetings at offices and country estates. London literary agents warned her, with her bad lungs and American naiveté, to avoid the Underground, but she grew accustomed to riding it alone to the train station to make her out-of-town appointments. For longer trips she booked overnight berths, almost always unchaperoned, arriving at her destinations with gifts and memories of her last visits. Sometimes she found authors bedbound or suffering from bouts of writer's block, spouses primed to divulge the unfortunate details. They trusted that she would not judge, but would offer sympathy and advice.[15]

Such was the case when she visited A. S. M. Hutchinson that spring. He had piqued Missy's interest with novels that sold modestly before the war, so she had written him from London. Hutchinson was flattered by her interest in him, but the war had depressed him, quashing his inspiration to write. He threatened to return to making his living as an editor at the *Daily Graphic,* but Missy talked him out of it. She took one of his unfinished pieces back to her hotel, where she read it and wrote to him daily. Hutchinson had incorporated divorce, unwed motherhood, and suicide into a single manuscript—all racy themes that Missy sensed were a match for modern sensibilities. She helped him work through his problems with plot and characters until Hutchinson had the first half of the novel *If Winter Comes*. Published first in *Everybody's* and then in book form, it was not critically acclaimed. But it was clearly a book Americans were ready for, because the *New York Times* declared it the country's best-selling novel in 1922.[16]

Hutchinson was exactly the sort of success story Missy hoped to make more of while in Europe. She was cultivating the palates of her readers, opening their horizons to non-American authors, because she believed that shared stories would promote empathy and peace after the war. It pained her that so many of her countrymen had been isolationists until 1917, and she wondered how much their unseasoned literary tastes were to blame. She met with both the ambassador to England and Sir Eric Drummond, the secretary general of the newly established League of Nations, who promised to pass along works of novice British writers. "I have no fear of a real break between Britain and America," she told Drummond, "but I do feel that it is the duty of all of us...to counteract the breach which Mr. [William Randolph] Hearst is daily trying to create." She was referring to Hearst's sensational journalism, which she feared was fueling American provincialism. To counteract the trend, she sought pieces of international interest. The memoirs of the French prime minister Georges Clemenceau and the war prisoner E. H. Jones were high on her wish list, but so was adult-minded fiction. "Our standard is high," she assured J. S. Fletcher. "We are not looking for lurid fiction.... Conrad, Irving Batchelor [*sic*], Blas[co] Ibanez, Arnold Bennett, Mr. Galsworthy, and a long list of standard Authors, whose work we are publishing, bear testimony to this."[17]

In the postwar years, it was Missy's conviction that the American reading public was growing more rapidly than the number of quality authors writing for it. Belgians had been virtually untapped for the American market, so she looked for talent in Brussels. "There has been a tradition in the Publishing Profession for a great many years that only the Anglo-Saxons can write popular and successful fiction for the English reading public," she admitted to Belgian agents, but then assured them that she could change this outmoded impression. "My claim was justified last year when Blas[co] Ibanez was translated from the Spanish into English, published in America and sold more books than any two American or English Authors combined." But she prefaced that breaking into the American market required an under-standing of the American mind-set. "The great mass of our people are perhaps a little narrow and prejudiced by what in our country we call 'New England Conscience.' The psychology of this is very sim-ple, Latins write chiefly for mature minds. Americans and the English write for youth. Most of our current publications contain little fiction which cannot be put in the family sitting-room, and read by the boys and the girls of the family. This difference in the morals of literature is not so great as most critics would make us believe. It is not the story itself but the way in which it is told which makes it acceptable or not to the American mind."[18]

Missy had lined up appointments with up-and-coming Belgian authors but was forced to miss several when she was lured away from Brussels to return to a London court. She had been trying to get injunc-tions lifted that had been preventing her from publishing the third vol-ume of Otto von Bismarck's letters in *Everybody's*. Representatives of the family of the former German chancellor didn't want her to have them, but she thought it imperative to get the documents out of Europe and into her "impartial" American hands in light of ongoing discussions of German war reparations. From there, she pivoted swiftly, returning to acquiring pieces for *The Delineator*. She secured the proofs of comedian George Robey's "After Dinner Stories" and reconnected with Sir Gilbert Parker, who had generated war propaganda for the Allied coalition, as she had. After they met face to face, he gave her first dibs on his latest novel. Because she acquired pieces for all the Butterick publications, she had perhaps the most eclectic list of titles of any editor in the business.[19]

H. G. Wells checked in with Missy near the end of her trip to see if she had met with everyone she had hoped to while in London, and she told him that she had, with one bothersome exception: she never got to sit down with his friend Sir James Barrie, the famed author, playwright, and creator of Peter Pan. Missy had wanted to be his American editor since she first observed him on a train during the war. Returning to London from Paris, they had shared a passenger car with refugees, sick soldiers, and weary war correspondents. A few of the young reporters saw Barrie sitting with a book in the corner and asked what he did for a living. "I try to write, too," he said, and went on reading. He was as humble as Missy had heard that he was from his friends.[20]

Although Barrie's writings for children had made him famous, Missy was drawn to him because of a speech he had given to students at St. Andrews and printed in a little volume called *Courage.* "It came into my hands at a time when I needed courage," she confided to Barrie. She understood his moments of weakness, his temptation sometimes to accept a life of invalidism. But his inspirational writing kept her on her quest to be useful. He had lost two adopted sons, one in the war, as did any number of American mothers; his lessons would prove inspirational to her readers, since they, too, knew physical and emotional suffering. She wanted him to write an original piece for *The Delineator* and offered to pay handsomely for it. But Barrie gently turned her down, and it wasn't the first time. His author friends—and Missy knew many of them—confessed that this had become his pat response to editors. He had grown reclusive. According to his neighbor George Bernard Shaw, he was harder to see than kings and princes. His contention proved true when Missy wrote Barrie two more times and received two more polite rebuffs. "I endeavored to picture to Barrie how seriously the people who run the Delineator take their work and how important are the women who read this magazine. They are the real mothers and the real home makers. They are the stabilizing force in a very unsettled world. I tried to put that into a letter but it seemed so futile."[21]

Word on the street was that editors failed with Barrie so long as they made their appeals from on high. This was a man who became a favored storyteller and playmate to little Elizabeth, the future queen of England. Seize on his love of children, John Galsworthy advised, half joking that Missy might make the noises of a lonely child outside his door until he mercifully opened it. Missy looked more childlike than she acted, but her appearance actually gave her one last glimmer of hope. The novelist Frank Swinnerton revealed to her that Barrie had asked his friends about her, and they had turned his query into a game. She "is a tall, drugstore blond," H. G. Wells joked; Galsworthy added to the intrigue by describing her as "a small person with ears like a faun."[22] Missy took advantage of the lighthearted exchange:

> Dear Sir James: I hear you have asked Mr. Wells and Mr. Galsworthy for descriptions of me. Having no vanity and desiring to satisfy your curiosity, I inclose herewith my passport and my photograph:
>
> Age: 37
> Height: 5' 2"
> Forehead: high
> Nose: large
> Mouth: medium
> Chin: round
> Hair: black/gray
> Complexion: olive
> Face: oval
> Occupation: Editor
> ...Please return it to me as I must have it to go home with.[23]

Although she retrieved her passport, she failed to succeed with Barrie in 1920 and in the visits that followed. She wrote more letters pleading for him to reconsider, but tore them up for sounding too much like the others. Finally, she shamelessly asked the American ambassador in London to throw a party for Barrie's literary friends, and on cue at the party the ambassador spoke of *The Delineator*'s significance to American womanhood. If Barrie was unmoved by her personal pleas, Missy hoped that he at least could be moved by the gossip of his friends. It apparently worked, because Barrie finally asked her to come to his home at 3 Robert Street, Adelphi Terrace, in London—a historic spot, the past residence of Sir Walter Raleigh, and overlooking the spires of St. Paul's Cathedral. Missy was awestruck when she reached the top floor, where he kept his study. In the center of the room stood an old brick fireplace, and the bookshelves encircling it along the walls were narrow and uneven, seemingly custom fitted to the volumes they contained. This had been Barrie's retreat from the rest of the world after the sons for whom he had created Peter Pan had been killed. He evidently had been mourning them ever since.[24]

Like Missy, Barrie had been ill following the war. He confessed that after leaving a nursing home, chronic pain in his right arm had made it nearly impossible to write in longhand. His friend Lady Asquith tended to his correspondence, but he never was one for dictation. Finding himself at a crossroads, he had doubts about ever again conveying ideas for publication. After explaining all of this, he directed Missy to a table near the window. There sat a sewing box that had belonged to his mother, and in it, one of his most prized possessions—a tattered, yellowed letter from an old friend. Barrie let Missy hold it until she could make out its author: the Scottish explorer Sir Robert Scott. He had written Barrie from the South Pole during whiteout conditions; he knew that he was going to die. When his body was retrieved from the Antarctic months later, the letter was with it. Scott confessed to contemplating suicide rather than suffering the long agony of starvation and exposure. But as a Christian gentleman he endured until his body gave way on its own. The last sentence of the letter was hardly decipherable, but Missy could make out a single word—"COURAGE." Barrie then handed Missy a gift—a copy of his *Courage*, specially bound. The story of Barrie's gift was one Missy would tell many times, even to college students in commencement-like addresses, since she thought it would inspire others as much as it inspired her.[25]

The transition to other topics was awkward that afternoon, but Missy managed it for the sake of her readers. "Why won't you give something more to the world?" she asked Barrie. His response was not what she expected. "They don't want my work. If they want something from me, it is because they think it would be unique—an advertising value. 'Barrie, who has been silent so long, has at last turned out another Tommy or Peter or whatever it might be, and it will appear exclusively in this magazine.' A literary curiosity." "But that is not why I came to you," Missy assured him, and he seemed to know that this was true. "That is why I let you come here and talk to me," he conceded. "I believe you are sincere—that you honestly think my work will do some good, and you want the world to be better." He puffed at his pipe. "But I don't want to write. I *died* in the war. This is only the shell of me."[26]

Barrie walked over to his wall of pictures and fixed his eyes on his handsome boys. "This one came back. He's married and has taken hold of life. The others gave their lives. . . . Their Eaton caps, I like to keep them there." He returned to the mantel, stood in silence, and then turned to Missy again. He told her that although he wasn't writing much, he was reading voraciously. Missy asked him who, and he told her that his new favorite was the American woman who wrote *Showboat*. "That is art," he insisted. "I should like to know Miss Ferber." "She works very hard," Missy confirmed. Again, they sat in silence, until Barrie finally spoke. "So you think I ought to write?" It was as if he had only decided at that very moment to give Missy's reason for being there its proper consideration. "I am one of many who hope you will," she answered. "The war hurt you but it did not kill you. You did 'Courage' after that and it is probably your most beloved and useful book." Again, there was a long silence . . . and then an unexpected offer: "There are some characters of my own I am going to write about some day—great characters the world has passed by, and when I get the pieces done, I'll send them to you." The proposal was generous, but not knowing if she might have another, Missy seized on the moment to offer to buy his next novel—and this time, Barrie didn't refuse. It took patience, years of it, but what happened that afternoon proved to Missy that some things are worth the wait.[27]

———

COMPETING EDITORS DESPERATE TO know the science of Missy's successful acquisitions rarely recognized that she was not so much an astronomer discovering stars, but a horticulturist, patiently cultivating her diverse and bountiful garden. And her water was honesty. Take young Maynard Greville, the son of the Countess of Warwick, who submitted pieces that Missy thought not yet ready for publication. Rather than mail him rejection slips, she gave him advice. "You may not thank me for what I am going to say but it is honest," she prefaced.

> You are not writing for the public. Even great artists or especially great artists write for the public; else why write or publish. Poe, Guy de Maupassant, Dr. Johnson, Dickens, all of them cared what the public thought. Your contribution to life is measured exactly in proportion to the number of people you influence or to whom you give real pleasure. In your work you are dealing with atmosphere. Apparently it is going to be one of the strong elements in your work, but in order to produce a balanced art you must get your feet down on the ground. I should say you need to develop a sense of plot and interest in people....
>
> I think your work would profit by a year's roughing it on your own; such as W. Townend did in California.... He saw the rough and hard unpleasant side of life and the occasional streak of pure gold in human nature. When he sat down to write he had a background and a purpose and no longer made word music, which was more or less the reflection of other men's living and thinking. He had a contribution to make to life. The same is true of Henri Roche, who went out to America and worked his way up from the bottom. You will never be able to do this in England. People will always know who you are and drop the veil that falls between your class and exceedingly simple people.[28]

Once again, her insights were hopelessly American—but human. If it took years for the young writer to gain some life experience before writing for her publications, then so be it. High, inaccessible art was of no use to her; she looked for universal stories that lifted the barriers between people, and she made those who could tell them the next great thing in the American literary market.

Only because the satirist Channing Pollock asked for these details did Missy supply him quotes from an article cataloguing her impressive track record: "She set a new high for poetry, a dollar a word.... She bought Edna Millay and Rudyard Kipling, E. A. Robinson and Housman and Noyes at their best." And only when pressed to recall it did Missy concede that she was the first to pay $50,000 for a serial. "That was to Sinclair Lewis," she recalled, "about the time he won the Nobel Prize." But more remarkably, she also paid that much for the domestic fiction of Kathleen Norris at much the same time. By giving women editorial advice, publicity, and compensation that legitimized them to publishers and broader readerships, she helped to propagate their universal stories and propelled a few of them to literary fame.[29]

The key was in having never been conditioned to think that literary acumen was a male asset by definition. The "Lost Generation" of the 1920s—the F. Scott Fitzgeralds, T. S. Eliots, and Ernest Hemingways—seemed proof to other editors that only men achieved the angst of modern realism. Although they thought women could be the muses of highbrow literature, they tended to dismiss the notion that women could create it themselves. Even female editors, like Margaret Anderson of the *Little Review,* Marianne Moore of *Dial,* and Elinor Wylie of *Vanity Fair,* brought more male writers into prominence than female ones, highlighting how Missy's approach to women writers was a departure in the 1920s. She not only believed that female literary voices were essential in the modern age, she thought they *were* the modern age. And thus when the *World* solicited nominations for literary prizes for up-and-coming standouts, she nominated more women than most, including former *Delineator* editor Honoré Willsie Morrow. Future *Herald Tribune* books editor Isabel Paterson felt indebted to Missy for publishing her stories when no one else would and jump-starting her literary career.[30]

Missy had good reason to consider women writers and readers the harbingers of what was modern and new. The rising popularity of the book-review sections of major newspapers, Great Books groups, and Book of the Month Clubs indicated a sea change in American literature. More and more, publishers were appealing to the middlebrow, which, at the time, Missy's friend and contributing author Margaret Widdemer identified as a readership gapingly broad, somewhere between a "tiny group of intellectuals" and the "tabloid addict class." Though not erudite, this demographic was increasingly educated; Missy would know, since she was pretty sure that her readers made up a good bit of its bulk. It's also why she figured women writers would best appeal to it. She valued writers' ability to make meaning for the masses over their ability to achieve critical acclaim, and hence she never had to rid herself of the notion that supporting female writers was commending lesser literature. She saw herself as a facilitator, introducing female readers to a diversified range of writers and vice versa, broadening palates and best-seller lists ultimately for the advancement of women, but also for the social good.[31]

So Missy gave women their breaks and paid them like men. It was not always enough to eradicate women's deeply rooted insecurities as artists, but it was a start. She understood that it would take time to make them believe in their own voices and in their transcendent powers as shapers, communicators, and interpreters of the modern sensibility. Several of her most highly paid women contributors found critical acclaim elusive, which made them feel inadequate. "I was being labeled the 'highest-priced story writer in America,'" Fannie Hurst recalled of her career in the 1920s, yet she wondered if her "mass appeal prove[d] lack of stature?" Despite winning the Pulitzer Prize for *So Big* in 1925, Edna Ferber, too, was plagued by judgments of her work being too "commercial." Missy tried to make Ferber see herself as an artist by sharing her work with established literary men who publicly praised it. She did the same for Willa Cather, sending James Barrie an inscribed copy of *My Ántonia,* to which he generously responded, "Her Antonia is now my Antonia." Missy used men's endorsements to lend women prestige, a trick she had mastered when she enlisted Charles Eliot to bolster her own editorials in the *Woman's Magazine*—at least until women believed in themselves.[32]

Not surprisingly, Missy's ability to communicate and appeal to both men and women allowed her to carve out a niche managing literary couples. The loyalty of Charles and Kathleen Norris, for instance, was hard won, and she earned it by making Kathleen one of the highest-paid writers in the country, male or female. On the surface Kathleen looked, like Missy, to be the submissive wife in a traditional marriage, but she, too, benefited from a husband devoted to her career. Like Bill, Charles Norris was a San Francisco–born journalist, novelist, and member of the literary fraternity Dutch Treat Club, who settled into a role as his wife's hard-driving agent. Kathleen was no shrinking violet, but deploying her husband to do her bidding with editors allowed her to maintain the look of aloofness when it came to getting paid, thus thwarting any appearance unbecoming a domestic author. Missy played by Charles's strict ground rules when she bought Kathleen's serial "The Secret of Margaret Yorke" in 1922 and negotiated through Charles again to buy another of Kathleen's serials for $40,000, and another for $50,000 in 1926.[33]

Missy was also a close friend and editor to married writers Inez and Will Irwin; they worked with her at PEN, an international organization that promoted literary freedom, and flouting conventions they nominated Missy to be a member at large in the Authors' League of America. Obviously, Missy was not an author, but she was most definitely revered as an author's editor and a supporter of writers' creative efforts in every way. Which is why the novelist John Erskine also nominated her to be a member of the esteemed Author's Club as soon as it admitted women in 1930. She joined an inaugural class that included Ida Tarbell, Fanny Hurst, Alice Duer Miller, and Dorothy Canfield Fisher—"everybody that counts," Erskine told her.[34]

Missy made her role in the literary revolution of the 1920s look effortless. It wasn't. Authors stayed loyal because she was an all-service editor, poring over manuscripts, strategizing publicity, and managing careers. She booked lecture circuits, particularly for European authors trying to break into the States. And if she read exceptional pieces that she couldn't accept in her magazines, she found suitable homes for them elsewhere. Authors were grateful that she made the effort, and competing editors thought her generous, since it wasn't her practice to pass along uninspired work. When she lost bids for pieces she wanted, she was exceedingly gracious. "I sincerely regret that the Delineator will not have the honor of publishing your articles," she wrote British writer E. V. Lucas in 1925, "but I am delighted to know that the American public will have them through the excellent medium, The Ladies Home Journal." She never burned bridges, and in remaining civil became an ambassador for American periodicals and women's magazines broadly, which only enhanced her already unimpeached reputation with authors.[35]

Missy thoroughly researched potential contributors before meeting with them, which allowed her to "just happen" to propose innovative pieces that they hadn't yet considered but could be convinced were in their wheelhouse. Once she was face to face with writers, she observed them carefully, listened to what they had in mind, and amended her proposals accordingly. Or she planted seeds and patiently waited for her vision to germinate inside the author until it took root. After the meeting, she recorded detailed memos about what they discussed, as well as some of her thoughts. The following notes from a tea with Mary Roberts Rinehart in Washington reveal how well she listened and how shrewdly she strategized when she had an author in her sights:

> She has in mind an ambitious "big story," a novel which would begin in a crude community in the West and bring the product of Oklahoma's wealth to Washington and to national politics. It is a story of political intrigue, love and the new rich.
>
> She has a rough outline in four parts of the Prince of Wales serial, which I suggested to her last year...75,000 words. She wants $40,000 for it—$50,000 if it runs beyond that length. She never promises a date of delivery.

Concerning her own life story, she would not consider letting any one write it, since this, she says, would be stealing her thunder. She has kept a diary and intends to write her own biography, which will be a combination of Cellini's autobiography and the "Soul of Woman," by Gina Lombroso; in other words, a frank description of her own life and her philosophical observations.

Mrs. Rinehart is absorbed just now in spiritualism and would like to do one article on "The Strange Case of Mary X," being the experiences of a friend of hers and the study and research which Mrs. Rinehart has done as the result of these so-called messages from the spirit world.

McCall's offered Mrs. Rinehart $60,000 for a mystery serial, but she does not want that audience. Cosmopolitan and Collier's have each offered her fifty thousand dollars for her next serial....

As a matter of politics, I suggest that we win Mrs. Rinehart to us by giving her something she desires more than anything else in the world—a painting of herself done by one of the greatest portrait painters and to be handed down to her grandchildren. Dr. Rinehart does not see the wisdom of this investment. It is an investment. Any family with a John Singer Sargent could today get double its original cost. We would cash in on this in two ways—tying Mary to us and having a great picture to use in our advertisement and with the first installment of her story.[36]

Rinehart liked that Missy seemed old school, that she, too, looked the part of her husband's helpmeet, even though she was the better breadwinner of the two. Her lady editor demonstrated Victorian character and hadn't fallen prey to the modern cult of personality, though she seemed to understand how to manipulate it better than anyone. The poet Theodosia Faulks confided to Missy in the 1920s that as a middle-age person, she felt washed up. Missy was roughly the same age, and yet her proclivity as an editor was to look perpetually forward, often to younger writers. She won over several who, after the war, collectively departed from conservative themes, flouted

Prohibition, shirked parenthood, fought for the Equal Rights Amendment, favored socialism, experimented in trial marriages, and kept their maiden names. The iconic Edna St. Vincent Millay protested the execution of anarchists Nicola Sacco and Bartolomeo Vanzetti and enjoyed the bohemian lifestyle of Greenwich Village in every sense; Missy's acceptance of her eccentricities was rewarded with her inspired poetry for *The Delineator*.[37]

Although Missy was no radical or flapper, she understood both the established writer and the edgier set reshaping literary tastes in the twenties. In heart and mind, perhaps she was wedged between their generations, but that was likely what made her more open-minded. The wisdom of her years gave her the advantage of perspective over the fleeting fad, and yet when it came to embracing the fresh and enduring, much of it written by women, her instincts were second to none. Such was the positioning that made her one of the most important literary trendsetters of the 1920s—and all with larger agendas for women in mind. If her readers were not yet ready for what she was going to give them, she'd make them ready. She was calibrating their literary tastes but cultivating them too.

Chapter Six

THE PUBLICIST OF MADAME CURIE
1921

ALTHOUGH MOST OF THE PEOPLE Missy had gone to Europe to see were potential contributors to her magazine, one ended up becoming the story herself. It all came about when one of Missy's French contributors and the editor-in-chief of *Le Matin*, Stéphane Lauzanne, wanted to return her kindnesses. Having introduced Missy to the French president and arranged her interview with the new prime minister, Alexandre Millerand, Lauzanne asked if there was anyone else Missy wanted to see. Missy told him there was—the two-time Nobel Prize–winning co-discoverer of radium, the savior of injured soldiers, the widow, the mother, the most famous woman scientist in the world. For reasons personal and professional, Missy wanted to meet with the great Madame Curie, and she vowed to stay in Paris until Lauzanne could make it happen.[1]

Unlike at any other time in history, Missy was sure the scientist would be a draw for the readers of *The Delineator*, as both a curiosity and a role model. Curie had initially been introduced to the American reading public in 1904, on the heels of winning her first Nobel Prize with her husband, Pierre. *Vanity Fair* depicted her then as a troubling contradiction: part exceptional genius, part sacrificial woman standing behind her man. In a piece called "The Curies at Home," a journalist for the *World To-Day* made Curie known to Americans primarily as a wife and a mother of two daughters, not as a scientist. Before the war, *The Delineator* might have taken a similar tone, but now Missy had other things in mind. More of her readers were engaging in higher education, social reform, paid work, athletics, the professions—public endeavors marking them as New Women. Their transformation coincided with *The Delineator's* evolving editorial content and A-line dress patterns, which gave women the physical freedom of movement that reflected their freer mobility in the public sphere. As a woman's editor, Missy was both architect and archetype of this makeover of American womanhood.[2]

In Missy's hands, Curie's story would show readers that they, too, could combine intellectual and domestic pursuits, marriage, motherhood, and career. But for those not yet ready for unabashed New Womanhood, she would have to spin Curie's story carefully. Curie's success would have to be couched in terms of feminine sentimentality, rather than overt masculine ambition; her collaboration and widowhood emphasized over her solo career and single motherhood; her professional achievements cast as the unintended consequence of maternal sacrifice—much as Missy portrayed her own success so that no male editor would question her.

She knew, too, that Curie's discovery of radium piqued the interest of American readers as much as Curie did herself. Her friend Edward Bernays, often called the "Father of Public Relations," had been hired by the American chemical industry to kindle the nation's fascination with Curie's radium. Journalists seized on its luminous and therapeutic powers, namely its potential to cure cancer, the incidence of which had tripled over the last sixty years in the Western world. By the turn of the twentieth century, cancer was the eighth-leading cause of death in the United States, and doctors searched desperately for cures. Missy joined boards and raised money for cancer-treating hospitals and had come in contact with many of the nation's pioneers of radiotherapy. People referred to William J. Mayo's radium clinic in Minnesota as the "Curie Hospital," suggesting that connections between the famous scientist and cancer cures had already been drawn. Missy believed that the time was ripe for American women to seize Curie as their savior— an altruistic curer of cancer and a successful woman in a man's world.

Both images of womanhood appealed, so long as Missy's portrayal of Curie kept them in careful balance.[3]

But Lauzanne was skeptical about getting Missy her interview. "Curie will see no one," he warned. "She cannot understand why scientists, rather than science, should be discussed in the press." True enough, Curie hadn't made a public appearance in fifteen years. Life lessons had taught her that being a woman scientist required avoiding the limelight. Before she shared the Nobel Prize with her husband and Henri Becquerel in 1903, French scientists had lobbied for the prize to be awarded to the men only. Pierre Curie insisted that the selection committee reconsider, and it did, but it billed Marie as Pierre's help-meet, rather than the partner and principal investigator that she was. Rather than stir controversy, she declined the invitation to attend the Nobel ceremony in person. Even then, she knew that the only acceptable woman of the scientific establishment was an inconspicuous one.[4]

Pierre Curie encouraged his wife to publish separately from him when he cast too long a shadow over her, much as Bill encouraged Missy. But after his tragic death in 1906, Marie could no longer hide behind a husband's advocacy or practice science without suspicion. Whereas Pierre had been elected to the Académie des Sciences in 1905, Marie was rejected five years later; apparently, research good enough for a second Nobel Prize was insufficient for the country-men who voted to keep her out of their prestigious institution. She didn't care about the accolades, but without them it was hard to raise research funds, and the French press refused to let her do science without distraction. In 1911 the wife of a French physicist named Paul Langevin went public with allegations that Curie and her husband were lovers, creating a scandal for which the adulterous Langevin was forgiven in the court of public opinion, but the widow Curie was not. Journalists in the French press disowned the Polish émigré, maiden name Sklodowska, as a hussy who preyed on their countrymen for her unsavory ambitions. The public scorning taught Curie a valuable lesson: no publicity was good publicity for a woman scientist, because in the public mind a "woman scientist" was an oxymoron.[5]

Lauzanne explained what he could of this to Missy, but she would not be deterred. She had nothing but good intentions for Curie, she insisted. Rather than reveal her to American readers as a contradiction, she would show that Curie's science and womanhood were very much compatible. All she needed was an introduction, a face to face, woman to woman. She did not want to meet with Curie to judge, only to champion her science.

It's hard to know what about Missy's plea made the difference—that she was an American? A woman? Perhaps her reputation preceded her and Curie had heard enough about this charming editor to know that she was no sensationalist, but exceedingly critical of the yellow press, condemning the tawdriness of the French tabloids and Hearst's American equivalents. Whatever it was, Curie granted her an interview for the morning of June 20, 1920, at her laboratory in Paris, a humble building on a humble street renamed the Rue Pierre Curie.

When Missy arrived, she found a timid woman, pale and plain in her black cotton dress. Despite her outsized reputation in science, there was nothing particularly imposing about Curie. Even to Missy's untrained eye, her lab equipment looked antiquated. She was astonished to find the most famous woman scientist in the world looking so forlorn and frail; Curie's was the saddest face she had ever seen. And she repeatedly rubbed the tips of her fingers over the pads of her thumbs. This had become a habit, Missy learned, Curie's futile way of trying to regain nerve sensation that had been lost in her hands. Although Curie had yet to acknowledge that her physical ailments were the consequence of radium poisoning, Missy could see that the woman had sacrificed greatly for her science.[6] The journalist in her already saw the headline she wanted to print:

CURIE—NOBEL PRIZE–WINNING MOTHER; SCIENTIFIC SAINT

It was Missy's power to win people over, but Curie posed a challenge. By all accounts, the scientist was immune to flattery or to pressures of social convention. Colleagues at scientific meetings had long complained that small talk was not her strong suit. When she wanted conversations to end, she was known to tell people rather tersely that they had disrupted her work long enough. That morning the ailing scientist was pleasant, but by no means solicitous, as Missy would have been had the tables been turned. After introductions, however, she seemed more eager to divulge, or at least to dictate the terms of the interview. She talked about the radium research she knew best, mentioning that her lab had only a single gram of radium with which to run experiments. She rattled off locations where radium was being produced around the world—some in Czechoslovakia, a bit in Austria, some more in Portugal. But the highest radium content existed in the carnotite of the Colorado and Utah mountains, she explained, and no doubt she would love to get her hands on some of it.[7]

On an earlier assignment, Missy had seen the ores Curie was talking about as they were being transferred east to be processed in radium-reduction plants in Pittsburgh. She had been awed by the towering smokestacks of Standard Chemical Company, which alone produced half of the radium in existence. But Curie knew where else in America to find the substance: seven grams of radium were in New York, four more in Baltimore, six in Denver.... "And in France?" Missy asked her. Curie lamented that it was all accounted for, set aside for hospital use, not for research. The war had impoverished France's scientific centers, and her institute was no exception. She was trying to raise money to buy more, but it was prohibitively expensive. In 1920 the going rate for radium was $130,000 a gram, the equivalent of nearly $2,000,000 today. Missy probed deeper into the problem of obtaining radium. "But surely revenues from the patent of radium can pay for more?" she suggested. This was how another of her interviewees, the great Thomas Alva Edison, had been able to perpetuate his research; by the end of his career he had patented nearly eleven hundred of his inventions and processes. Patenting had become the American way. But Curie clarified that there were no patents. "We were working in the interest of science. Radium is an element. It belongs to the people," she told Missy. Her predicament was ironic. Here Curie thought it wrong to profit from a discovery that she thought should be for everyone, and yet American manufacturers had taken advantage, privatized the means of production, cashed in on her science, and essentially priced her out of obtaining more radium.[8]

Missy listened until Curie had nothing left to say. She then asked the scientist what she would want from Americans if she could get it. Curie was mystified by the question. In all her years as a scientist, no journalist had ever asked such a thing. No doubt the radium institute could use a small hospital and radiotherapy service to serve as a school of medicine, she replied after some thought. But more important to her was obtaining another gram of radium and, in the long term, expanding her laboratory, since her research required large quantities of minerals that were nearly impossible to process in her cramped facilities. And there was one other thing: given her ailments of late, she confided that her greatest dream was to build a lab outside Paris, in the countryside, where she would benefit from the fresh air. Her lungs had grown increasingly problematic. As Missy sat there, muffling the coughs that wanted to escape her lungs, she inherently understood what Curie was talking about.[9]

Much to her surprise, Missy left that lab with an altogether different view of Madame Curie than she'd had when she'd arrived. The woman's face was not sad, she decided; it was kind, patient, beautiful, bearing the detachment of a scholar and a willingness to sacrifice for greater good. In later years, Curie's daughter Ève wrote that it was her mother's "scorn for gain, the devotion to an intellectual passion and the desire to serve" that made American women fall in love with her. But in truth, it was Missy. The attributes she chose to see above all others in this intense, socially awkward woman were the ones she was going to reveal to the American public. Most people claimed not to understand Curie's drive, but Missy did. It's why she vowed from that day forward to become the scientist's greatest American champion as well as her devoted friend.[10]

––––––

MISSY HAD PREVIOUSLY ARRANGED passage back to New York with the Transportation Office of the US Navy, figuring that readers might be curious about life on a military transport from a woman's point of view. But now she was distracted, her mind turning over ideas about how to get Curie her radium. She took a faster commercial liner home instead, and by the time she arrived in New York a plan had been hatched. She decided that she would do more than just tell her readers Curie's story; she would galvanize them to make Curie's research, like orphan relief in World War I, a great American cause. Using her well-placed contacts, she would publicize Curie and her work to raise money for a radium fund. The goal would be to purchase a gram of the rare substance, but not for Missy to give to Curie personally. The better headline would read, "Curie's Radium—A Gift of American Women."[11]

A public-relations strategy swirled in Missy's mind that would turn Curie into an American legend in the making: A tragic tale about a woman—a mother—who had sacrificed for the world, yet received nothing in return. She had endured poverty to discover the element that was the leading cure for cancer, but then refused to patent it so that the world could study it readily. She should be heralded a saint, and yet the price of her altruism has been a debilitating lack of funds— not for her own creature comforts but for humanity, who will suffer without her life-saving research.[12]

Curie thought the synopsis extreme when she heard it. French scientists worked under modest conditions all the time, and she was not all that exceptional, she told Missy. But Missy wouldn't listen to her objections. The postwar years were becoming an era of fund-raising in the name of "science as social cause," she explained. Exploiting Curie's image for cancer cures was no different from the recent campaigns exploiting Albert Einstein's for world peace. That said, Missy recognized that the public image put forth of Curie would have to diverge from Einstein's. Despite the growing acceptance of women in higher education and the professions, science and womanhood still seemed incompatible to many. Curie would have to appear to conform to gender expectations in order to make the idea of the "woman scientist" palatable to the American public. Missy understood this from her own experience, for her position of power in the world of journalism would have certainly been contested more loudly had she not proclaimed herself an editor in the name of "nobler womanhood." Her social causes may have been her passion, but they also gave her permission to be in a role of authority, just as they would have to do for Curie. Missy would have to recast Curie as a saint, rather than strictly as a scientist. As the press reported on more deaths linked to radium research, some of which took place at Curie's institute, Curie's dedication to research, couched as work to cure cancer, would seem all the more heroic, because it would look sacrificial. If feminine heroism was embodied in the martyr, the burns on Curie's hands, her jaundice, and her worsening cataracts could make her martyrdom seem unparalleled.[13]

Here is where some of Missy's goodwill toward other editors paid off. Late in 1920 and into 1921, colleagues from magazines and newspapers across the literary spectrum—from the New York Times to Current History Magazine, science reviews, and the Woman's Journal—became mouthpieces for Missy's campaign. No one deviated from her ground rules: publish pieces focused on Curie either as a mother or as Pierre Curie's co-discoverer, or pieces about radium's links to cancer cures. And no one was to mention Curie's alleged love affair or solo career. As a gesture of professional courtesy, Arthur Brisbane, managing editor of the Evening Journal, handed over to Missy his file of press clippings on Curie's sex scandal, promising not to use them. In the American press, Curie was to be reinvented into a humanitarian, which meant sentimentalizing her as a mother, whitewashing the chauvinism and scandal that plagued her in France, and talking about her science as if it weren't really science at all.[14]

The PR campaign worked. In a postwar era in which everyone assured Missy that fund-raising for Curie would be thankless, her fund was oversubscribed within weeks. As a capstone to the campaign, in April 1921 The Delineator ran the headline "The Greatest Woman in the World: Marie Curie." Accompanying it was a cover story titled "That Millions Shall Not Die!" which, consistent with prior articles, linked the radium campaign to a cure for cancer. Next to famed physician William

Mayo's piece "Do You Fear Cancer?" was a portrait of a wistful Curie on a background of white. The following month, Missy printed an article comparing the high-tech extraction of radium from Colorado mines to the cruder methods Curie had employed in her dilapidated shed at the turn of the century; the accompanying photo was of a saintly Curie, her hand gently holding her cheek, an image reinforcing the messaging of the past few months. Casting Curie as the Virgin Mary in black, Missy contended that the scientist had never asked *The Delineator* for help in funding her research, but rather male scientists did after discovering that her research had been halted. In this narrative, Missy and Curie were excised as agents of the radium campaign. It was an art that Missy had mastered: raising money without any show of female assertiveness. The female martyr had to be passive, her success an accident brought forth because of the thoughtfulness of powerful men.[15]

Of course behind the scenes Missy had hardly been passive. Once again, she had turned the Butterick Company offices into a campaign headquarters and formed radium-fund committees divided by sex. The advisory board was a group of scientific and medical men that included the head of the Crocker Memorial Cancer Research Laboratory, the president of the American Medical Association, a Harvard physicist, a Columbia chemist, trustees of the Rockefeller Institute, and the first American surgeon to work with radium. The committee of women was comprised of socially prominent wives—Mrs. John D. Rockefeller, Mrs. Cornelius Vanderbilt, Mrs. John Purroy Mitchel, Mrs. Thomas Alva Edison, Mrs. Herbert Hoover, Mrs. Andrew Carnegie, Mrs. Calvin Coolidge—whose names could attract other potential donors. Other hand-picked members, including Elsie Mead, founder of the American Society for the Control of Cancer, were the workhorses alongside Missy, truly committed to Curie's cause. None of the male committeemen were philanthropists, just as none of the women were scientists. The women looked to be do-gooders and the men looked to be experts, lending prestige once again to Missy's efforts.[16]

Always astute regarding the optics of gender, Missy also understood how appearances around class and patriotism had to be carefully managed in the campaign. Through her descriptions of Curie as coming from nothing, Missy had shaped Curie's quest for truth into a democratic myth, and radium into "a truly American gift." "It represents money from America's richest families and from its poorest. Business girls, clubs, cleaning women, college women, home women, have sent their bits," she reported. She publicly congratulated the working women of the Carroll Club, who collected $1,290 for Curie's cause; and the rose grower who sent Curie bouquets for saving his life; and the old woman who chose to be buried in Potter's Field, so that she could give her meager savings to the Curie fund. Nor did Missy forego the chance to talk up famous men who donated in honor of prominent all-American women. President Harding gave $50 in honor of his mother, Arthur Brisbane $100 in honor of the patriot Julia Ward Howe. "The importance of such human stories as these cannot be stressed too much," Missy told her staff. *They appeal to every class.*[17]

And yet she had supplemented this broad campaign significantly by targeting her wealthier connections. Adding names from her social network to the lists of donors she had already gathered for Liberty Loan and Red Cross campaigns during the war, she also reached out to potential patrons through a letter-writing operation. Part fundraiser, part psychological profiler, Missy individualized each letter to appeal to the human motivations she thought might compel people to give to Curie's cause. It was slow-going work performed for months between the hours of twelve and two, when the men in the office were out to lunch. Like so many women, Missy had mastered the art of being productive in contexts in which work presumably was not performed.[18]

Franklin Lane had put Missy in touch with a chemist at the American Chemical Society who extracted radium for the Interior Department and could obtain a gram of it relatively cheaply. But the bargain hunting wasn't necessary. With tens of thousands of dollars raised over the asking price for Curie's radium, Missy established a trust in the scientist's name, to be managed by a Wall Street company and dispensed with at the radium committee's discretion. Missy had not forgotten Curie's dream to build a lab in the country. She hoped that the trust fund could be used toward that end, as well as to purchase equipment or to hire a chauffeur if doing so would facilitate Curie's comfort and work. She also set aside funds to support future women scientists at the institute. Although this had not been a request of Curie's, it reflected Missy's inclination to try to help not just one scientist but women (plural) for the long term.[19]

———

CURIE WAS BEWILDERED by what Missy had done. What was she to make of this American woman who moved mountains without seeming to want much in return? Pride, patriotism, a reverence for science, a desire to be helpful—these were Missy's motivations. If there was anything self-serving about her campaign, it was in proving that the work of a woman's editor was useful and important. The success of the campaign would lend gravitas to her magazine and to her readers. Consciously aware of it or not, Missy also craved creating connections. She wanted Curie to meet her American admirers much as she wanted Sir Barrie to write for her readers, because she felt gratification in being a sort of matchmaker—identifying the potential love match and then forging the bond. She wanted Curie to see the best of her country as much as she wanted her countrywomen to admire and be inspired by the best in Curie. With these goals in mind, all that Missy really asked for in return was for Curie to provide some autobiographical material for *The Delineator* and for her to come to America to accept the gift of radium in person. She did not envision just one event during this visit, however; Missy wanted a tour across the continental United States, replete with dinners, receptions, ribbon cuttings, and honorary degrees. None of this was to aggrandize herself, but to celebrate Curie and American women and to forge the bond between them.

Curie agreed that it was proper to personally thank the women who had raised funds on her behalf. The problem, however, was that Missy's tour was just the sort of spectacle that she had spent her adult life trying to avoid. The thought of attending public events across the Atlantic horrified her even when she was in good health— and she currently wasn't. Her arms and hands ached. She suffered from kidney disease. She could hardly see, due to her cataracts. And she was too exhausted for an overseas tour that would last for weeks. For Missy, however, there really wasn't any other way for Curie to show her appreciation. Missy offered to travel all the way to Paris to accompany Curie back to New York, in fact, if that was what it was going to take to present the woman scientist to her American admirers.[20]

Missy pictured ceremonies at the White House and at Harvard University as bookend events of the tour, for no American institutions were greater symbols of the prestige she wanted tied to Curie's name. She appealed to Charles Eliot to ask Harvard administrators to grant Curie an honorary degree. Having debated and published his views on coeducation, she knew that she would have to formulate her request carefully. "I feel the coming of this great woman, who is opposed to the movement of Feminism, would be a fine influence in this country," she prefaced.

> When I asked her why she had never been in the United States, she said, "Before I was married, I was too poor to go, and then, after my children came, my obligation, of course, was to stay home and mother them and bring them up properly." Certainly I am not a feminist, but looking upon Mme. Curie as more than a woman— undoubtedly as a great person—I said, "But could you not have made a quick trip, sort of a vacation of six weeks?" She replied that six weeks was too long a time for any mother to be away from her children, except when the War demanded service from her. I only relate this so that you may understand what a simple, conscientious woman she is. Her visit would be a scientific contribution to America; it would also be a spiritual one.[21]

It was true that Curie had put limits on Missy's proposed tour, though her children had little to do with them. "You know how careful I am to avoid all publicity referring to my name. And now I should be very grateful to arrange for my voyage with the minimum of publicity," Curie reminded her host. Her preference was to leave Paris near the end of the French vacation season in October, but Missy insisted on the spring. Missy pressed for a six-week tour, but Curie wanted it shortened. Back and forth they went, Missy requesting permission to add events to the schedule, and Curie whittling them down. Missy won some extra weeks by arranging excursions to the Grand Canyon and Niagara Falls and by slotting quieter days of rest between high-profile events. Curie acquiesced to most arrangements that minimized excessive meeting, greeting, and conversation. This was, she reminded Missy, her earnest attempt to follow her doctor's orders. She was told to engage in as little anxiety-producing social activity as possible, and she had the doctor's note to prove it. Still, Missy talked her into attending a month of social events that she would have declined under any other circumstances, as well as to give speeches, albeit brief ones, at eighteen college ceremonies, while accepting four fellowships, four medals, and nine honorary degrees.[22]

None of which were to come from Harvard. Although Eliot agreed that Curie would "have some good influence while in this country on present discussions of feminism," the Harvard physics department ultimately determined that the woman scientist was undeserving of honors. "Professor Duane says that Mme. Curie 'had a large share in the details of the researches' which related to the discovery of radium, but that 'the credit does not belong entirely to her,'" Eliot conveyed to Missy. "He adds that since her husband died in 1906 Mme. Curie has done nothing of great importance." Apparently her second Nobel Prize was of no consequence in this ultimate assessment of her. Compounding the insult, Eliot himself insinuated that Curie had been the beneficiary of enough American generosity already. His chauvinism reflected an attitude that Missy knew to exist in the exclusive realms of higher learning. All she could do was to remind Eliot of Curie's rare balance of competence and femininity: "She has carried on her scientific work, but the outstanding virtue of these years lies in the fact that having discovered radium and come into prominence, she turned to her home as a normal mother and gave the intimate minute attention to her children which motherhood should impose." Her argument won Curie a modest reception in Cambridge, but not an honorary degree.[23]

None of this snubbing made any difference to Curie, who already thought Missy had planned too much ceremonial pomp. Her anxieties were eased a little by Missy's promises not only to be by her side throughout the tour but to let Curie's daughters accompany her to America. Irène Curie, a tall, sturdier, twenty-three-year-old version of her mother, was polite, obsessed with science, and disinclined toward the social arts. Missy found her gawkiness endearing, her irreverence for appearances, like her mother's, proof that she was occupied by loftier priorities. As for Curie's youngest, sixteen-year-old Ève, Missy predicted that Americans would be utterly charmed by her. Equipped with red lipstick and fashion sense, she effortlessly smoothed over her mother's social edges and made a worthy stand-in when Curie wasn't in the mood to face the public. More important, the presence of both girls would provide the image of doting motherhood that Missy wanted the public to see, even if it belied the mother that Curie was. Unlike Missy, the scientist hadn't taken years off from her career to raise her children; in fact, she had sent them away to be raised by her father-in-law when she didn't want the distraction of parenting. Missy refused to judge. Perhaps it was this acceptance, her earnest attempt not only to appreciate Curie but to understand her on her terms, that made the scientist more responsive to her than to anyone else.[24]

But building that rapport took time. Initially, Curie had her secretary type letters to Missy that felt impersonal, sparse, obligatory. Only gradually did formal missives typed to "Madame" Meloney turn into handwritten notes to "Mon Amie," and eventually "Ma Chère Amie" and "My Dear Friend." Curie stopped apologizing for her clumsy

English and started expressing her mind. She turned conversational, asking after Missy's health. It was a budding show of affection for a woman who seemed, as far as Curie could tell, to want to help her for nobler reasons than getting something in return. Missy made Curie want to be more generous than her reputation suggested.

———————

IN APRIL OF 1921, Missy left New York on the *Olympic* for the single mission of collecting Curie and bringing her back to America. Before departing France, she threw Curie a going-away gala through *The Delineator*'s office in Paris. Famed soprano Sarah Bernhardt serenaded the scientist at the Paris Opera House; it was a taste of what Missy had in store for Curie in the weeks to come, though it was impossible to prepare her fully for the public adoration and paparazzi that would await. Missy tried to make Curie's passage back to New York on the *Olympic* as comfortable as possible by having her daughters on hand as well as Harriet Eager, a young American who went from being Missy's editorial assistant to Curie's personal interpreter and human buffer from American small talk. Passengers on the ship were eager for sightings of the shy scientist during their week at sea, but they were disappointed. Most of the time Curie stayed in her suite below deck, citing seasickness. Figuring she might be reclusive, Missy had booked Curie the most private of accommodations to settle her.[25]

On May 11, the day of their arrival, the atmosphere at the harbor in New York was amped to a level of excitement that made Curie's wooziness worse. Some forty reporters and photographers rushed up the gangplank to get a view of the woman scientist, as Missy warned they would. Curie looked almost miniature in her high-backed chair, as she sat on the ship's deck and took questions from the press. Missy stood by her side, Curie's daughters also nearby as she waited nervously, fingers interlaced in her lap, to get through the snapping of photographs. There was no escaping the raucous welcome at the pier that still awaited her after that. A marching band struck up

Le Marseillaise, while Girl Scouts and Polish women's groups presented the scientist with roses. Curie accepted them awkwardly before being whisked away. Missy had arranged for Louise Carnegie's limousine to take them back to her apartment.[26]

For a year the Meloneys had been living on 12th Street between Fifth and Sixth Avenues, a block in the West Village that felt tucked away compared to the more prominent stretches of Fifth Avenue inhabited by the wealthier women of the radium committee. The crusty facade of the brownstone wasn't fancy; when in need of fresh air, Curie would be able to sit out on one of the iron terraces without courting too much attention. Flowers and cards poured in immediately upon her arrival, but Curie retreated to the guest bed-room, too exhausted to acknowledge them. In the following weeks the apartment became her fortress from the crowds. The Meloneys and their cook were the only people with regular access to Curie and her daughters, though Missy opened her doors to a few potentially helpful friends. There was her personal physician, Harlow Brooks, perhaps the most sought-after medical man in Manhattan, who pre-scribed salves for Curie's fingers and "tonics" (Prohibition sherry) to help her sleep. Edward Bernays stopped by the apartment too; Missy figured it wouldn't hurt Curie to meet the man running publicity for the US Radium Corporation.[27]

There was no facet of Curie's visit that Missy had failed to con-sider. She booked suites, limousines, and train berths and ordered invitations and reply cards, all elegantly embossed at Tiffany's, as well as the ceremonial robes Curie would wear to receive her honorary degrees. She arranged for lawyers and accountants to handle the mon-etary gifts, and visits with eye specialists to manage Curie's cataracts. She responded to the scientist's well-wishers, sending thank-you notes around the country. At the apartment, Missy had notes ready for Curie to sign, staggering the height of the stacks to fit Curie's moods. She corresponded with lab directors, university presidents, and socialites who were planning to host events for Curie, seeing to it that they lim-ited the scientist's speech-giving and interactions with "non-essential" people. She counseled on seating arrangements and ceremonial procedures to allow Curie quick exits, limited hand-shaking, and time to be alone. Missy essentially morphed into hostess, event planner, travel agent, psychologist, motivational speaker, personal assistant, publicist, nurse, and trusted companion whenever the need arose.[28]

It was her calculated decision to make the first social occasion of the tour a luncheon at the home of Mrs. Andrew Carnegie, uptown at 91st and Fifth. This was a private event that Curie couldn't refuse, given the generous scholarship Carnegie's husband had established at her institute during the war. And because Andrew Carnegie had recently passed away, Missy knew that Curie would think it proper to pay his widow her respects. It was a relatively low-key affair that provided an opportunity for Curie to get acclimated to American shows of enthusiasm. Already Curie had admitted that she found Missy's countrywomen a tad more friendly than she was used to.[29]

Curie slept at Missy's that night and was up early the next day to begin her tour of the Seven Sisters schools, where college presidents wanted to honor the scientist who symbolized the potential of women in higher education. Wellesley president Ellen Pendleton wrote Curie to express how pleased she was to break tradition in her case and award an honorary degree, the first at the college for anyone of either gender. Vassar president Henry MacCracken arranged for a car to collect Curie from Smith College to take her to Poughkeepsie, where a welcoming committee arranged pageants and a convocation. Curie found the condition of the grounds, the labs, and the dorms of the women's campuses to be superior to what women enjoyed in France. The students were encouraged to play tennis and to be outdoors, and they had spaces to convene to collaborate and share ideas, all of which contrasted sharply with the cloistered existence of Curie's college years. She wished that she had had access to urban classrooms like the ones she saw at Barnard and Hunter Colleges. The City University of New York's policy of admitting poor yet promising girls left her with a favorable impression, as Missy had hoped it would.[30]

Curie was the honored guest at the annual meeting of the American membership of the International Federation of University Women. Missy had dispensed tickets to the gathering through alumnae associations, and organizers in the Women's University Club forewarned that their venue, the great Carnegie Hall, would be filled to capacity. Curie could barely see past the front rows of college women, thirty-five hundred in all, who came to see her that afternoon. Following Missy's cue, educators who took the podium couched Curie's scientific achievement in maternal terms, her discovery of radium as a gesture of humanitarianism that only a mother could bestow. Bryn Mawr president M. Carey Thomas encouraged the women in the audience to follow in Curie's footsteps and exert their influence on pacifist diplomacy. She hoped that this generation of newly enfranchised women would form a voting bloc to bring about disarmament—"human legislation," as she called it.[31]

At Carnegie Hall, Curie also received the Ellen Richards Memorial Prize—named after an MIT chemist. Oddly, however, Curie was introduced to almost no scientists at these women's college events. Even worse in her mind, she was discouraged from telling her truth: that she loved being a scientist not for humanitarian reasons but simply for doing science for science's sake. It was a strange moment at Vassar College when, against Missy's better judgment, Curie spoke transparently about her discovery of radium. "No one knew that it would prove useful in hospitals," she contended. "The work was of pure science. And this is proof that scientific work must not be considered from the point of view of the direct usefulness of it. It must be done for itself." The humanitarian discovery Missy had projected in the press sounded more like a fortuitous accident, but the optics of a frail Curie spoke louder than her broken English. Needing assistance from the podium, Curie appeared the caricature of feminine sacrifice, just as Missy had cast her.[32]

Missy never revealed her deeper uncertainty about what she wanted Curie—or herself, for that matter—to represent to American women. The modern careerist in her wanted Curie to be an example of competence, proof to male employers that women were worth their investment, because they were men's equals and driven by the same ambitions and capabilities. And yet many middle-class Americans still believed that motherhood and domesticity should be women's sole destiny. Missy, like Curie, sat uncomfortably at the crux of old expectations and new hopes, but the publicist in her sensed that for now, only a traditional portrayal of Curie would do. Most of the women's events she added to Curie's itinerary thereafter were with clubwomen who better enabled her casting of the French scientist as a maternal martyr. The Association of Polish Women in Chicago, cancer philanthropists in New York—throughout the tour these women saw more of Curie than did women scientists.[33]

On May 16, Curie was back at Missy's apartment resting up for a spate of Manhattan events. That week, at a lunch of national chemical societies at the Waldorf Astoria, she nervously held court with the head of the Crocker Center Research Laboratory, the dean of Engineering and Chemistry at Colombia, and the chief chemist at the US Bureau of Mines, followed by receptions at the Museum of Natural History and with the Mineralogical Society. Curie was tired, but there was no time to rest. On May 19 she returned to the Waldorf Astoria to receive a gold medal from the National Institute of Social Sciences, a relatively minor affair compared to the White House festivities to come. Missy had seized the chance to get on the White House calendar while lunching with Vice President Coolidge, and late on the afternoon of May 20, Curie arrived in Washington. The First Lady's personal secretary escorted Curie and party to the White House Red Room, then to the Blue Room, where the French ambassador Jules Jusserand presented Curie to President Harding and his wife. From there, they proceeded to the East Room, where, before ambassadors, congressmen, and Supreme Court justices, Missy emerged from the background to speak on behalf of American women. She presented the president with a silver box to present to Curie, along with a golden key to open it. It was not safe to store actual radium inside the box, but Missy wanted the prop for a photo op of the handing off of Curie's American gift. Everything was being executed as Missy had promised it would.[34]

Dozens of newspapers and magazines covered the event with the solemnity Missy had hoped for. Although Curie's aloofness seemed not to match the grandiosity of the occasion, President Harding's remarks were more befitting:

> We lay at your feet the testimony of that love which all the gener-
> ations of men have been wont to bestow upon the noble woman,
> the unselfish wife, the devoted mother. In testimony of the affection
> of the American people, of their confidence in your scientific work,
> and of their earnest wish that your genius and energy may receive
> all encouragement to carry forward your efforts for the advance of
> science and the conquest of disease, I have been commissioned to
> present to you this little phial of radium.[35]

It had been a long day in a long week, and yet Curie made it to the evening hours in surprisingly good form, charming dignitaries with greetings in English, Polish, or French, as needed. After the White House ceremony, she convened with Robert Milliken and other sci-entists at the National Museum. She dedicated a low-temperature lab at the Bureau of Mines, toured Mount Vernon, and was the honored dinner guest of the French ambassador, followed the next night by dinner with the minister of Poland. She managed mealtime conver-sation with the Speaker of the House and Alexander Graham Bell, helped along by her daughters, Missy, and Bill, who had taken a train from New York to chaperone the women to the evening events; he had grown rather fond of Irène, and Bill Jr. and Ève had become fast friends.[36]

Curie was fatigued, but Missy needed her to soldier on a bit lon-ger. She was expected in Philadelphia on May 23 to receive honorary degrees from the University of Pennsylvania and the Women's Medical College and to attend a meeting of the College of Physicians and Surgeons. On the 24th, Bryn Mawr president M. Carey Thomas threw a garden party for Curie; again, Missy stayed beside her to stave off overly friendly admirers. They moved on to Gloucester, New Jersey, to inspect the labs of the Welsbach Company, which donated fifty milligrams of the radium isotope mesothorium to Curie's institute. She attended a meeting of the American Philosophical Society that night and received the John Scott Medal and an $800 honorarium that Missy added to the others. From there, Curie was supposed to head to Pittsburgh to receive an honorary doctor of laws degree at the city university before touring Standard Chemical Company. But she never made it to Pittsburgh. She reached her limit somewhere in Pennsylvania and was desperate for some time to herself. On May 29 the *New York Herald* reported that Curie had retreated to an undisclosed resort on Long Island. Missy had made arrangements with a wealthy patron of the radium committee to get Curie to her Manhasset home on a moment's notice. Worried that her anemia was getting the best of her, doctors drew blood samples and put her on bed rest.[37]

Two days later, Curie seemed well enough to travel back to Manhattan to tour Memorial Hospital's radium unit. One of her former students escorted her around the facility, which housed four grams of radium, the most in any medical institution in the world. Next on her schedule was a dinner of the Polish Society of America, followed by trips to Dayton and Chicago, en route to her much awaited sightseeing detour at the Grand Canyon.[38]

Back in Paris, Stéphane Lauzanne and his countrymen followed all these events with interest. "Every one realizes that there could be no greater manifestation in honour of French science," he told Missy, assuring her of his entire country's gratitude for everything she had done to host their great scientist. Indeed, the spectacles Parisians read about in the papers had improved Curie's image at home, but Lauzanne hadn't yet heard how his compatriot was deteriorating under the strain of the tour. In the States, Curie was growing more vocal about being tired and anxious, and her daughters were attending more events on her behalf. Journalists soon couldn't help but notice that when she appeared in public she wore a sling to avoid shaking hands. Not knowing what to make of it, some of them presumed that she was irritated with American hospitality, perhaps even bored. She "is 'completely tired out,'" concluded a reporter for the *Times*. "Questions and the 'small talk' of American women and men have fagged her brain."[39]

The plan had been for Curie to go to Los Angeles and Pasadena before returning to Chicago for meetings of the Association of Collegiate Alumnae, the Associated Women's Organizations of Chicago, and the American Chemical Society to receive the Willard Gibbs Medal. She was supposed to attend a luncheon at Northwestern University before inspecting more power plants and taking in Niagara Falls, and there was the final New England leg of the tour, during which Curie was to be honored by the Academy of Arts and Sciences before accepting a degree at Yale. But Missy now confirmed for journalists that Curie was suffering from nervous strain. If she did not improve, she told them, they should expect her to cancel more events.[40]

What Missy didn't tell them was that she, too, was becoming sicker by the day. Perhaps she had grown so much more accustomed than Curie to traveling in less than optimal health that suffering in silence felt normal. Missy never panicked, probably because she was rarely honest with herself about having reached her physical limits. It's hard to know who finally took her aside and gave her permission to confront her decline, but the decision to slow down was undoubtedly prompted by others. As Missy urged Curie and her daughters to continue the trip west to the Grand Canyon, she quietly returned to New York. Rest assured, she told Curie, she was in good hands with Harriet Eager, who would take care of all arrangements in Missy's absence. Even naive Irène sensed Missy's apprehension about leaving them. On the train west she wrote Missy and urged her not to worry—her mother was comfortable. "Our passage through Chicago was allright," she reported. "I hope that you take some rest and do not worry about my dress or any other things of that kind, which I hope Mr. Meloney will forbid you to touch."[41]

Curie was not nearly as sanguine as Irène suggested, however. Without Missy at her side, she became acutely aware of the strange spectacle she had become in America, and she felt anxious to go home. Stepping into the public car of the train was more than she could handle. "I cannot go in and be stared at like a wild animal," she whispered. Ève and Irène made it to the Grand Canyon, but their mother stayed behind. Back in New York, meanwhile, Missy was on the phone, bumping up the Curies' departure and expediting the insurance paperwork on the radium to accommodate an earlier shipment to France. Although it weighed only a gram, the substance proved a challenge to transfer because it was encased in a 250-pound container of steel and lead that took four men to hoist. Missy arranged for government representatives to transfer it the moment the ship arrived in Cherbourg and to deliver it to Curie's lab.[42]

———————

THERE WAS NO AVOIDING the throngs of travelers at the piers the morning the Curies left New York to return to France. In the last week of June, the peak of the summer travel season, the *Herald* reported a record ten thousand passengers boarding seven ships on that day alone. "Perhaps the most tired of the 10,000," a journalist added, "was Mme. Curie, the French scientist, who departed after one of the most exhausting and extensive welcomes ever given in this country to any foreign celebrity." Before hunkering down in her stateroom, Curie managed to pose for photographers and to give a few remarks of gratitude, especially for "Mrs. William Brown Meloney," her protector and caregiver, who had made her trip to America one that she would never forget.[43]

Missy sent Curie home with a gram of radium, lab equipment, $22,000 worth of mesothorium, $7,000 in lecture honoraria, $60,000 of leftover trust money—and a $50,000 book advance. Amidst all the tour accommodations, she had also arranged for Curie to write a biography of her husband for the Macmillan Company. The reserved scientist thought it a daunting task, but once again Missy convinced her that it was for the best. This was a way to share Pierre with the world in her own words, Missy told Curie, and to build a nest egg for her daughters. Curie would have an income for the rest of her life because of Missy's proclivity to play the long game.[44]

It wasn't coincidence that Missy's friends Charlotte and Vernon Kellogg were booked on the same ship the Curies took home from New York. Charlotte was to attend the International Children's Welfare Congress in Belgium, and Vernon traveled as part of his work for the National Research Council, so they made their departure coincide with Curie's, as Missy had hoped they would. From the boat, they confirmed what Missy expected: Ève proved utterly aloof to the flirtations of other passengers, and Irène could not be persuaded to change into the dress Missy had given her for the voyage home, preferring her usual cotton frock, even at supper. As for Curie, Charlotte suspected that she once again feigned illness to avoid other passengers, as well as the task of writing about herself, for the Kelloggs had also been charged with helping her to write her autobiographical piece for *The Delineator.* "I kept away from her and so did Vernon, except when we thought she was bored and might like to talk," Charlotte recounted to Missy. "Her camouflage interests me.... What an easy matter getting the money she wants would be [if] she knew how to make a simple gesture of friendliness and yet protect herself from invasion."[45]

Quiet, media-averse Curie didn't know the lengths to which Missy had gone to ensure good press during her tour. She had suppressed not only details of the Langevin scandal but also slander by anti-French, pro-German members of the New York Catholic community. Missy had turned to Genevieve Brady, a Catholic philanthropist on the radium committee, for help, and Brady in turn threatened to discontinue support of the church if members attacked Curie in print.

It worked—not a shred of bad press could be found in the New York papers. Missy rewarded Brady's good deed by asking Prime Minister Poincaré to decorate Brady, as well as fellow committeewoman Elsie Mead, with crosses as officers of the French Academy. It was yet another instance of Missy bringing women into the limelight, even if it meant their deeds would overshadow her own.[46]

Curie wrote Missy on July 1, 1921:

> My Dear Friend,
>
> Tomorrow we leave the ship and are back to France. We are glad of that but at the same time very sorry that it may be a long time before we see you again. I thank you and your husband for your friendship and your kindness more than I can say. And I will always remember the days we spent together. You made me feel at home in America and I wish that you would come to Paris and be at home with me. You helped me in the most unselfish way in the work I love and I wish that I could be helpful to you in something you want very much to do.[47]

Curie knew she could never repay Missy's kindness in full, but she did request that the French government confer the Légion d'honneur upon her American friend; the president bestowed it personally that December. But for Missy the more gratifying outcome of Curie's tour was the friendship it solidified between her and the scientist, perhaps the deepest Curie would ever have with another woman. For a long time, the relationship remained lopsided, Missy perpetually giving and Curie reluctantly conceding something back. But Missy was patient, understanding that Curie's guardedness was learned, that she was emotionally selfish for her science. During the weeks Curie had spent in America, their sister-like bond had been forged. After her return to France, Curie sent notes to her "Chère Amie" regularly, telling Missy how much she missed her, how much she wished that they could have time together at her country home in Brittany. "Please come soon to Europe and let us talk together again," she wrote Missy from L'Arcouest. It would turn into a regular refrain.[48]

On the surface the women could not have been more different: Curie, more comfortable with empirical facts than with people, and Missy, at ease with a more peopled existence, despite her physical limitations. Curie pushed others away, whereas Missy invariably drew them in. And yet both women had married supportive men who worked in their fields, and both had become mothers whose domestic pangs conflicted with professional ambitions. Their paid work and companionate marriages made them "New Women" who departed from Victorian domesticity, but they still struggled with old expectations. They cleverly allowed others to accept their successful careers by appearing devoted mothers rather than sexual beings. Both shunned organized feminism but lived as independent, powerful public figures. Few women could relate to them as well as they could relate to each other in these respects.

Chapter Seven

HATCHING IDEAS FOR WOMEN READERS, WORKERS, AND VOTERS

1922–1926

THE RADIUM CAMPAIGN WAS PART of a long-time pattern of Missy coming up with grandiose ideas and making them reality. There was the time she approached administrators at Columbia University about developing an "Irish Museum," for which she had already acquired collections. Or when she flew to London from Paris and thought to herself that in the two hours she had spent in the air, she could have been writing out specially made in-flight postcards bought at the airfield. It would be a boon to aviation, she told the British prime minister, and she recommended that a special stamp be printed for publicity purposes. At the outset of World War II, she suggested to the king of England that he broadcast a weekly Sunday prayer over the radio—a gesture that would bring comfort to his people and help His Majesty overcome any self-consciousness he felt as a lifelong stutterer. If the idea was inconceivable to the royal press office at the time, it made perfect sense to Missy, whose instinct to humanize in this instance, as in nearly all instances, didn't fail her, especially when appealing to a female audience.[1]

She would admit to Eleanor Roosevelt that some of her grandest ideas came in her "silent hours," a euphemism for the days, weeks, and months spent lying in bed recovering from illness. Sometimes the only way to cope with her forced convalescence was to dream up something impossible and then brainstorm until an action plan came into view. And although these ideas didn't announce themselves necessarily as female innovations, Missy came up with them bearing women in mind. The radium campaign was a case in point. All she needed was a spark.[2]

A spark like the conversation she had one afternoon at a luncheon of the exclusive Colony Club in Manhattan, which she documented in 1922. She was there to inspire members to give to the radium fund, and when she left the podium one of the club's fashionable hostesses approached her. "Why do you spend your life with a woman's magazine when you could do big work like serving Madame Curie?" the hostess asked Missy. Missy responded that she believed editing a woman's magazine was one of the biggest services that could be rendered to the country, but the woman callously rebuked her, insisting that it was "stupid to print articles about bringing up children and furnishing houses, setting tables and feeding families—or whether it is good form for the host to suggest another service at the dinner table." Missy must have been taken aback, because she grew defensive. She informed her out-of-touch hostess that of the twenty million homes in America, only 8 percent had servants in them. In the other 92 percent, women did their own housework, brought up their own children, and tried to be active in civic life. "They are the people who help make this country the great nation that it is," she added with a tinge of sanctimony. And with that, the conversation came to an abrupt end.[3]

But as Missy was leaving the club another fashionable woman approached who had overheard the conversation and waited to see her out. She offered to have her driver take Missy downtown, and once they were in the car away from the Colony Club the woman felt less inhibited about speaking her mind. She thanked Missy for the attention she bothered to pay average Americans. "You are right," she said, "it is of vital importance to serve the great masses of people. I know. It will probably surprise you to know that when I was fourteen years old I had never seen a table napkin. My family were pioneers in the Northwest and were struggling for mere existence.... People like my family and myself are worth serving and saving."[4]

This woman had been moved by Missy's interest in ordinary people, and Missy was moved by her honesty. Missy begged to know the woman's story, and the woman shared it in sweeping view—from her birth in a Wisconsin log cabin, to her marriage to a Boston diplomat, to her aristocratic life in England. As a Southerner who had acculturated to cosmopolitan New York, Missy identified with this tale more than the other lunching ladies of leisure at the Colony Club ever could.

Missy had an epiphany. What she was hearing, she decided, was a parable for the masses, a sort of enlightened rags-to-riches tale. And thus, much as when she first met Curie, a blurb-like synopsis of this woman's life started writing itself in her head: she is an American woman "who has not sacrificed the strength and honesty of her pioneer girlhood but who added to these qualities that graciousness and charm which have given her distinction on two continents." Missy begged for the chance to present her story to the broader public, and the woman agreed, so long as her identity remain concealed. Honoring her wishes, Missy arranged with Little, Brown to publish *The Log Cabin Lady: An Anonymous Autobiography* in 1922, providing no clue about the woman's identity other than to relate the story of their meeting at the Colony Club in her introductory remarks. To make the little volume more useful yet, she arranged for its proceeds to go toward Curie's research. It was yet another instance of Missy's ideas coming to full bloom—not only for a single woman scientist, but also, with the help of her clever publicity, for a sizable swath of American womanhood who might be inspired by the tale of successful self-making.[5]

———

CAMPAIGNS, CAMPAIGNS, AND MORE CAMPAIGNS—all with women in mind. In the early 1920s Missy arranged with the presidents of the Seven Sisters schools to promote women's college education for the modern age. She asked Smith College president William Neilson for graduation data—specifically, lists of recent graduates and the work sectors they entered in their immediate postcollege years—as research for stories aimed at the economically self-sufficient woman to which *The Delineator* increasingly appealed. Missy believed that the time had come for the female college graduate to have more than just work skills, but also competitive compensation for said skills—and she planned to make the case. She wrote to Marion LeRoy Burton, president of the University of Michigan:

> For twenty-five years and more, women's activities in public life have been subjects for humorous copy in the daily press.... To encourage reporters and city editors to give more consideration to the work of women, and to put proper emphasis on the news of their work, I want the Delineator to offer three thousand dollars to be equally divided between the east, the middle west, and the far west—the prizes to be awarded to the city editor and the reporters responsible for the most constructive interpretation of women's work published in the news column.

Indeed, to a large degree she still saw the legitimation of women's work outside the home as a matter of careful spin and positive press.[6]

Missy wasn't surprised that many of the women on Neilson's lists of recent Smith graduates had gone on to educate the nation's children, both inside and outside the home. Like Catharine Beecher and other nineteenth-century domestic reformers, Missy had no qualms about the cultural presumption that the work of shaping young people, be it paid or unpaid, sat squarely in the hands of the nation's women—her readers—and she used her editorship to call for improved public education and to develop citizenship and literacy in children. Asking her associate editor Harriet Eager to oversee the project, she developed the *Little Delineator,* a magazine for young readers, and ran campaigns that supported children's health initiatives. She commemorated the fiftieth anniversary of the magazine in 1922, for instance, with a campaign dedicated to "The Happy Child" and made it a major mouthpiece for the passage of the Sheppard-Towner Maternity and Infancy Act, legislation first proposed by Congresswoman Jeannette Rankin to combat infant mortality. Under Missy, *The Delineator* took a stance on child labor laws that aligned better with middle-class sensibilities than with working-class realities. But because it was a moralism people had come to expect of a domestic magazine, fewer of them balked when her unexpected nod to women's heightened economic independence was also reflected on the page. In other words, Missy soothed acceptance of her progressive messaging by perpetuating *The Delineator*'s reputation as a "service" publication—that is, a magazine for maternal types rather than for women working for wages. Once again, the key was keeping all the elements in the magazine in careful balance.[7]

As she did in the *Woman's Magazine,* Missy propagated a scientific form of child-rearing in *The Delineator* by staffing its Baby Department with the nation's best medical professionals, including Dr. Luther Emmett Holt, head of the Babies' Hospital of New York. Convincing Holt to join her team had been a coup. Initially he told Missy that medical ethics prohibited his contributing to a woman's magazine, to which Missy rejoined, "There is something awfully wrong with medical ethics when it lets babies die all over the United States because you won't tell what you know to millions of women who read women's magazines." Holt headed west to lecture at the University of California, and Missy sent him telegrams at every train station along the way. "You have now traveled so many miles and wasted so many hours on a ten-day journey to California to talk to 200 medical students, some of whom will flunk out and some of whom will be asleep," she reminded him. "In the meantime, you could have written ten articles which would have reached two million women and have saved the lives of only God knows how many babies." Holt finally succumbed to her requests by the time he reached El Paso.[8]

The more pediatric advice *The Delineator* offered, the more Missy herself turned into an advocate for children's health. The mother who had once contaminated her son's baby bottle now organized child health conferences at the White House and helped to consolidate the American Child Health Association in 1922. At its first annual meeting in Detroit, she delineated what her role in the organization must be as a woman's editor. "You have the information mothers need to give their babies a right start and to keep their children in health," she told medical experts. "We need good physicians—specialists. But to make their knowledge power, we need publicity."[9]

Missy's research suggested that a significant contributing factor in child mortality in the early 1920s was the diminishing health of American women themselves. "Mothers and babies are dying every day—almost every hour—*needlessly* because the simple facts which would save them are not given to the public," she cautioned. "We hold that anything which will help save twenty thousand mothers can be discussed in any national publication and that it is the *duty* of a home publication to carry these messages." Suspecting that the post-war mania to be thin could be contributing to mothers' poor health, she convened specialists to the New York Academy of Medicine for an Adult Weight Conference. And true to her mission to disseminate expert and scientific information, she published the resulting set of weight scales for women based on height in the next issue of *The Delineator*. All of this was part of yet another campaign to improve women's health by demystifying fad diets and fashions.[10]

Other women's magazines reported the latest in domestic-science research, but Missy went one step further, conducting original studies through *The Delineator*'s own domestic institute. Her "Home-makers Editor," Martha Van Rensselaer, was the founder of the preeminent Domestic Service School of Cornell University, and thus the magazine had access to its faculty and collaborated on research. Much the way scientific-management guru Frederick Winslow Taylor called for standardization in American manufacturing, Missy called for American homes to be made more efficient. She kept in regular consultation with English management expert A. P. Young, home economists at the Merrill-Palmer Institute, and Frank and Lillian Gilbreth, whose efficiency studies bore impact in settings from shop-room floors to family kitchens. One project she took as her own was standardizing measurements for better cooking in American kitchens, persuading Vice President Coolidge to help her get a bill through Congress to revise the Standard Container Act as it pertained to fruits and vegetables. She told friends and readers that this wasn't the work of some highfalutin editor, but of a "housekeeper" who wondered why someone hadn't already thought to make food preparation easier this way. It was yet another instance of pulling something from the feminine sphere of influence, turning it scientific, and thus recasting it to legitimate the homemaker, who now looked to be an expert of her own domain.[11]

———

MISSY MADE PRESIDENT HARDING HIMSELF take notice of women's heightened scientific expertise in the home. After visiting a labor-saving kitchen exhibition in Ohio in the spring of 1921, Harding asked for Missy's thoughts on the new domestic technologies on display. She assured him that American women were ready for the newest kitchen gadgets, but she wondered if modernizing just the kitchen was enough. During World War I, residential construction had been halted throughout the country, she reminded him, creating a postwar dearth of new homes. Fewer than 50 percent of American families owned homes, and only an estimated 25 percent of those lived in dwellings that met government standards. Even when Americans could afford to buy, housing experts estimated that a million more houses needed to be built to meet demand. Conservatives grumbled that increased rates of divorce and paid work were causing women to stray from the wholesome tasks of homemaking. But Missy refused to blame women for America's broken home life; she blamed their insufficient homes. The key to perpetuating the American dream was not to demonize bad homemakers, she insisted, but rather to elevate their work and surroundings so they could succeed in their roles. If more women lived and took pride in upgraded, modernized dwellings, American family life would improve, and many of the nation's ills could be solved. Better homes would help make women better citizens, she concluded, thus promoting national security and social tranquility. Perhaps it was the "psychological moment" for a nation-wide movement for better homes.[12]

Harding was intrigued by the idea, but he and Coolidge were too busy negotiating postwar disarmament agreements to play an active role in what Missy had in mind. Worry not, she told him; she had no qualms about starting a nationwide campaign for better homes by herself. Once again, she turned The Delineator offices into a campaign headquarters and her readers into the rank and file of one of her crusades. Persuading the Butterick Company to invest $25,000, she inaugurated Better Homes in America (BHA), a movement to edu-cate Americans on how to build and design living spaces with librar-ies, utility rooms, functional kitchens, yards, labor- and time-saving technologies, instruments, art, and furnishings that encouraged an efficient and cultured home life. "The future history of America will be shaped in large measure by the character of its homes," she told her readers. "Our homes must be attractive, comfortable, convenient, wholesome. They must keep pace with the progress made outside the home." As the organizer of a "domestic" movement, she looked not to be the "public agitator" at which Calvin Coolidge occasion-ally scoffed; rather, she appeared as a republican mother with nobler purpose—and, coincidentally, a platform from which to appeal to women across the country.[13]

Although the BHA was Missy's brainchild from the start, she didn't necessarily want it to look that way. Past experience with the radium fund had proved that the support of prominent men lent legitimacy to women's efforts, so she sought their endorsements whenever she could. Theodore Roosevelt Jr. praised Missy's idea for facilitating the republican values his father had extolled before him, and soon Missy had the full support of Harding's commerce secretary, Herbert Hoover, whose work she had admired during her war-relief cam-paigns in Belgium. Hoover's penchant for solving problems with com-passion and scientific efficiency was just the combination she wanted for the BHA, and having recently founded the Division of Building and Housing within Commerce, Hoover, in turn, liked that the BHA had a grassroots mission in support of increased home ownership, construction, and manufacturing on a national scale. Years later, he continued to laud the BHA as a vehicle of his campaign promise to put "a chicken in every pot." Missy reminded him that it also gave him an in with her readers, the women voters of America. She was a master at creating these mutually beneficial scenarios, in which men with political ambitions were helped along by American women, and both were rewarded in the process.[14]

In selecting the official leadership of the BHA, Missy created optics much like those she had shaped for Curie's radium campaign: the inaugural advisory board included wealthy clubwomen, but the rest were prominent men. Hoover was her figurehead as president, Vice President Calvin Coolidge was the honorary head, and members included Secretary of Agriculture Henry Wallace, Surgeon General Hugh S. Cumming, US Chamber of Commerce President Julius Barnes, and American Institute of Architects fellow Donn Barber. Missy reached out to Will Hays, chairman of the Motion Picture Producers and Distributors of America, to solicit his assistance in producing promotional films for yet another of her ambitious ideas: Better Homes Week. She asked every governor in the United States to establish local committees of women to organize demonstration homes in their communities, built and furnished to BHA specifications for public display during a week in October. Over half the nation's governors supported her efforts, including her former editor Scott Bone, now the territorial governor of Alaska.[15]

Men served as figureheads, but Missy enlisted local committees of women to do the real legwork of Better Homes Week. She provided instructions for forming education and fund-raising subcommittees, and for using slide shows, lectures, window-dressing contests, cooking demonstrations, and block parties to generate buzz around BHA events. Turning local women into publicity agents, she gave them nut-and-bolt directions for erecting miniature playhouses in the public square, holding school essay contests on home ownership, showing BHA films in local movie houses, and collaborating with local newspapers, Rotary and Kiwanis Clubs, real estate boards, business and trade associations, home-building and -furnishing industries, chambers of commerce, women's clubs, and local departments of education, ignoring no grassroots angle of the campaign. Missy was a big-ideas thinker, but she also visualized the follow-through on the granular level.[16]

American women jumped at Missy's call to action for the BHA. Volunteers from the General Federation of Women's Clubs, the Girl Scouts, and women's auxiliaries of the American Red Cross and US Chamber of Commerce organized in some twenty-five hundred American towns to present exhibits or model homes for the inaugural Better Homes Week in 1922. The following year, local committees motivated by design contests, cash awards, and promises of feature spreads in *The Delineator* put some nine hundred homes on display nationwide. Curious to see efforts on the ground in middle America, Missy visited Port Huron, Michigan, to inspect BHA Week activities in person and was overwhelmed by women's local efforts. Club members pronounced the "Best Mother of Port Huron" and gave speeches about how the Better Homes initiative enhanced the town. Next to the local high school stood their prize-wining display house, in which women taught children the basics of running a home. The community invested in a permanent structure, as well as five home-economics labs and teachers. Students had also raised money to erect a clubhouse—the Marie Meloney Club—so named, according to Missy, simply because they liked the alliteration of it.[17]

Missy got her own hands dirty organizing exhibition houses—one in the Bronx, another in Brooklyn, through the Pratt Institute. For a first-place essay prize, she took advantage of her friendship with the sculptor Gutzon Borglum, awarding the original model of his famous sculpture *Lincoln at Washington;* he also designed special medals for the nationwide competition Best Small Home Design. And for clubwomen's essay contests on the ideal home library, Missy awarded copies of books inscribed by her famous friends. With the help of *New York Tribune* marketing executive Helen Rogers Reid, she publicized a model starter home in Larchmont Gardens that featured indoor plumbing, an electric vacuum, sewing machine, basement washing machine, updated kitchen equipment, and washable wall paper. The *Tribune* followed up with praise for Missy herself: "Various magazines have done much to cultivate good taste in furnishings and decorations among women of the country. But the editor of The Delineator, Mrs. William Brown Meloney, has had the vision and the ability to marshal the nation-wide sentiment for better homes into concrete action." It was yet another instance of following through on a grand idea, the scale of which no one thought possible until Missy proved that it was.[18]

Nevertheless, the very bigness of the BHA made it all-consuming, and Missy had a magazine to run. George Wilder gently suggested that she might want to ratchet down the time and Butterick resources spent on a project that looked to have hit its stride, and Missy agreed that the time had come to transfer the BHA headquarters to a government agency. In 1924, she collaborated with Herbert Hoover to reorganize it into a nonprofit service corporation headquartered at the Commerce Department in Washington. She brought a new executive director, Harvard social ethics professor James Ford, up to speed and found a new source of funding, the Laura Spelman Rockefeller Memorial, securing for the BHA $100,000 in annual launching funds for the next three years. The Commerce Department now had the budget to publish annual guidebooks that provided floor plans and photographs of the best model homes from past years, and the BHA had the federal backing that Missy wanted for it, as well as the prestige and staying power that came with government support. Still, despite Missy appearing to have stepped away from the leadership of the BHA, the truth was that she remained integral to its operations for another decade. Again, she was a horticulturist; when she handed off her ideas, she made sure that they continued to be nurtured so they didn't die on the vine.[19]

In hindsight, the larger cultural impact of Missy's BHA campaign is clear. This woman who rented a home in a multioccupant building in Manhattan successfully propagated the private ownership of single-family dwellings as the American ideal, and she might have been more effective than any advertiser or housing expert in selling middle-class domesticity to the masses. Her prescriptions reached millions who toured BHA homes, listened to radio spots, and read her promotional materials in newspapers, *The Delineator,* and government pamphlets. And she exported her version of American domesticity to Australia, the Netherlands, and Belgium, where her contacts formed BHA committees. She told whole communities that achieving a level of cultural respectability she branded "American" required the consumption of modern manufactured goods, establishing soon-to-be suburban norms as few others could in the 1920s.[20]

None of this is to say that her prescriptions for home life, well intentioned though they were, were necessarily within all Americans' financial means. Her version of wholesomeness required indoor plumbing, private bedrooms, and electrical appliances, for instance, that made exhibition homes prohibitively priced for many of the Americans for whom she intended them.

Still, the labor-saving devices she peddled reveal an appreciation for the time constraints of women who worked for a wage, which is remarkable given how few people were promoting efficiency in the 1920s with women in mind. Missy stated flatly in *The Delineator* that "the making of a better home is a mother's duty." And yet, if her focus on home life looked to be a step backward for women, a retrenchment into Victorian domesticity, she preferred to couch her campaign in terms of its modernizing influence. The BHA celebrated traditional homemaking and progressive efficiency at once by exalting women as literal "home makers," consumers, and highly skilled professionals and specialists. She reminded Americans that women's traditional roles were culturally significant, even as she helped women expand them into public realms.[21]

Indeed, if there was irony in Missy's running BHA stories in *The Delineator* alongside pieces like "How I Worked My Way Through College," she claimed not to see it. Covering the Federation of Business and Professional Women's annual convention, she reassured her readers that the women in attendance hadn't become "mannish" by working outside the home:[22]

> Women of leisure, who are in their homes, are always seeking some place to go, but the woman in business needs her home and wants to stay in it when the day's work is done.... These women are chiefly feminine. There was a notable lack of mannish-cut clothing, and practically no evidence of bobbed hair. They were well dressed, well groomed, normal. A large percentage of them were married women—many of them mothers with good-sized families. They were proof that to be successful one must work so hard and with so little self-consciousness that no time is left for fads or affectations.
>
> This generation is the undeniable proof that the woman who makes good outside of home is in most cases just as much a woman as the home-maker who does not have to put her shoulder to the wheel of industry.[23]

No doubt Missy was defending a growing contingent of her readers, but also choices that she had made herself as a professional woman.

———————

THE SUCCESS OF THE BHA was even more proof to President Harding that Missy's instincts rarely failed her. There was something incredibly useful, he thought, in having a woman behind the scenes to whom he could turn for innovative ideas and a distinctive point of view. He was confident that as editor of one of the most successful domestic magazines in the country, Missy had her finger on the feminine pulse of the nation. And thus like Coolidge, he made Missy both his informant and his sounding board on matters pertaining to the domestic life of the nation, but also on matters pertaining to the new female element in politics. Once, in 1921, he called her to the White House to get her thoughts on nominations to head up a woman's council on disarmament. It was obvious to Missy that what Harding wanted more urgently than female nominees was help clearing his conscience, so she gave him that solace too. He had been inundated by requests from women's religious organizations to hold prayer vigils on Capitol grounds, and he denied the requests, citing the separation of church and state. "Mrs. Meloney, have you studied this problem? Have you prayed over it?" he asked her. Missy's response was reassuringly simple: "Yes, Mr. Harding, but I did not pray in the parks."[24]

Missy saw aspects of statesmen that other journalists didn't—their contemplative sides, and occasionally their self-doubt. Most of the time she took her meetings with them as a private advisor, though sometimes she put on her reporter's hat and with pencil and notebook in hand conducted interviews that captured their personalities as no one else did. In 1922, she enlisted a friend, the artist Leonebel Jacobs, to capture the essence of public figures on canvas, taking Jacobs with her to Washington to paint portraits to accompany profiles in *The Delineator*. Scheduling the sittings was a challenge that required coordinating around the appointments of busy officials, but Missy was rarely denied. Harding, Henry Cabot Lodge, Alice Roosevelt Longworth, and the Coolidges were just a few who made the time to sit for portraits. Grace Coolidge loved hers when it was finished. In fact, when Harding died of a heart attack in 1923 and Grace Coolidge's husband became president, her portrait found a prominent place in the White House—and Missy did, too, even more prominent than the one she had assumed under Harding.[25]

Indeed, with the sudden changing of the guard Missy sensed that another PR campaign was in order to endear the new president to the American people—and to American women in particular. Much of the corruption of the Harding administration was only then coming to light, including illegal activity in the Veteran's Bureau and a bribery scandal known in the press as Teapot Dome. In the age of Prohibition, Harding had been a president who drank and had extramarital affairs.

Missy's PR scheme would be helped by the fact that Coolidge was a president who looked honest and earnest in comparison. Unfortunately, he didn't seem especially personable, and likability mattered more and more in American politics. Coolidge didn't much care about his public image, but Missy thought that he should be more concerned now that the women's vote was in play. There was only so much she could do to make over a man so set in his ways, but she knew how to manipulate her impressions of the people and things around him to his advantage. The notes she scribbled after one of her visits to the White House in 1924 reveal a woman astute in very different ways than male journalists might have been, and her observations formed the basis of critiques she reported back, as well as stories she would tell to humanize the Coolidge White House for female voters:

> There is a bronze statue on the mantel of a woman representing Industry and the turning of the wheel of the machinery.
> There is another statuette marked Prosperity. A woman holding a sheaf of wheat, bag of grain.
> Two green pots of ferns and a mahogany clock on the mantel.
> Grey and black carpet—
> Spittoons with yellow roses painted on them
> There are always hot house flowers on Mr. Slemp's desk, also on the President's desk.
> Green plush cushions
> Iron book rests
> The furniture is all of mahogany, or imitation mahogany, very shiny and with black leather upholstery. . . .
> McKenna: Doorkeeper for many years. During Harding's administration was slovenly and unclean. Soiled linen. Frequently—collar open. The Coolidges have made him clean up. Always has a wad of chewing tobacco in his cheek. He knows the names of everybody who calls at the White House.
> The White House offices show the lack of a housekeeper. Floor was cleaned with lye too frequently. This caused removal of varnish

and the floor is badly spotted. Long bench in the hall for reporters. Hundreds of little black spots on the floor and baseboard, where matches and cigarette butts have been dropped. Pots of large ferns in the hall. Formal and cold. McKenna has a way of saying "Goodbye and good luck" which sounds like "Go to Hell."

Most frequent remarks are "practical politician," "Fine fellow," "able," "good Republican," "old line man," "*absolutely* right," "what state are you from," "my job is to get a love feast," "very important meeting," "represents millions of people," "important organization," "one of us," "he was our speaker in 1921," "a coming man," "the people want," "the women demand," "we can't afford to," "I know how busy the President is, but—"[26]

In shaping the Coolidges' public image, Missy was able to draw on a long personal history with the White House. She had recounted for her readers the physical renovations made to the building over the years, as well as its changing aura with each passing administration. As an interesting tidbit, she recounted the days when the executive residence had only two bathrooms, one in the president's quarters and one on the second floor for guests; according to Missy, in the early 1900s visiting world leaders had been startled to see little freshly bathed Roosevelt children dashing past the Oval Room, draped in Turkish towels. She had personalized the Roosevelts by sharing these stories, as well as memories of the cooks, waiters, and chambermaids who had stayed on through administrations and made the White House a home. Like the usher Ike Hoover, who first came to the White House to install push-button electric lights and never left, Missy herself appeared to be a permanent fixture of the Executive Mansion whom readers trusted for honest comparisons from one administration to the next. An inside authority on the private side of the White House, she recalled the china patterns chosen by First Ladies, as well as the origin stories for chandeliers, needlepoints, and portraits that adorned the walls. As she shared these details with women readers, she molded presidential images. And now she was humanizing a president whose personal popularity had political ramifications as never before.[27]

In a media age of newspapers and emerging radio and film, Missy realized that Grace Coolidge was her husband's greatest asset. The attractive and affable First Lady, a former teacher of the deaf and a mother of two, served as a counterbalance to the rough edges and cool temperaments of members of her husband's administration. Missy went to great lengths to cast her role as significant, to shine light on *her* as much as possible. "There is not a mother of ten children, doing her own housework, whose day is longer or more exacting," she asserted to her readers. Having popularized character sketches of political men, now Missy revealed the once private First Lady up close as a charming helpmeet and national hostess, reminding readers of Grace Coolidge's habit of sending flowers from the White House greenhouses to local hospitals to put in the rooms of the sickest patients. "She is as solicitous for her house-guests as would be the simplest home-maker in the country," Missy contended; if American women felt disconnected from her husband, they took solace in a First Lady who was the warmest of neighbors. In later years Eleanor Roosevelt would become famous for responding personally to mail she received from admiring countrywomen, and yet Missy insisted that Grace Coolidge had started the trend.[28]

Missy's impulse to make the First Family seem approachable required a redrawing of old boundaries. She gave readers intimate glimpses of figures once placed on pedestals or outside public view, because the cult of personality reigned supreme in the modern age, especially in the minds of newly politicized women. Indeed, the increase in *Delineator* subscriptions suggests that American women liked how their First Lady had "gone public," even if their glimpses of her and her husband had been carefully curated by a woman editor.

Stories about the First Lady ran in *The Delineator* with other political profiles, romantic fiction, and pieces like "Parking the Baby: Hints for Busy Mothers and Business Mothers." Missy had an expert answer the question "Can Men and Women Be Friends?" and, in a muckraking spirit, announced a piece about what immigrant women suffer at Ellis Island. That photographs of women and children jammed into waiting rooms of Ellis Island accompanied ads for Grape-Nuts and Pepsodent speaks to Missy's appreciation of women as both the moral consciences and the primary consumers of their households. *The Delineator*'s varied content reflected her readers' excitement and ambivalence about the cultural, political, and economic power they were beginning to hold in the modern age; Missy was tuned in to their widening, sometimes conflicting, interests, because she shared them and tried to reconcile them on the page. If anyone questioned the wisdom of her formula, no one could argue with its profitability. Once last in circulation among the Big Six, *The Delineator* stayed either first or second every year Missy remained its editor—a testament to her instincts and follow-through once a lightbulb went off in her head.[29]

Chapter Eight

A WIDOW'S TOUCH AT THE *NEW YORK HERALD TRIBUNE*
1926–1927

I N 1925, BILL'S HEALTH WAS FAILING. Missy made adjustments to his environment, including a move from 12th Street to a rooftop apartment on 9th, hoping that the air on a higher floor would be better for his lungs. But by February he had influenza of a seemingly virulent strain. Missy took him to the Homestead Spa in Hot Springs, Virginia, but he didn't improve. In late spring Bill's condition grew critical; he was struck with double pneumonia and then with an infection in his head. That summer, Missy canceled her annual trip to Europe to stand vigil at his bedside. *The Delineator's* managing editor, Charles Hanson Towne, meanwhile, sailed to London to meet with "Bennett, Galsworthy, Moore, Rebecca West, Willa, Margaret, Maugham—all of 'em," in Missy's stead. When the heat in New York City grew stifling, the Meloneys took themselves upstate to their farmhouse in Pawling. Quaker Hill, as their hamlet was called, was also home to radio broadcaster Lowell Thomas and was located some thirty miles from the Hyde Park estate of Franklin and Eleanor Roosevelt, rising players in the Democratic Party. Despite the visits and well wishes from many prominent New Yorkers, Bill never seemed to improve.[1]

"We have moved him to the hills, but he does not recover," Missy reported to inquiring friends across the country and overseas. Kathleen Norris understood her anguish. "One's heart is an elastic band,

149

and *could* be stretched too far. Missy dear I can only say again that every thought and prayer in these days is for you and your beloved invalid." Curie wrote too, begging for good news, but Missy seemed resigned: "Whatever comes must be faced and after all I have not been hit by the war so cruelly as have many thousands of other women. I try to feel this way about it." Arthur Woods bluntly advised in October that Missy start making arrangements with their priest. If there was any solace in those weeks, it was receiving word from Charlotte Kellogg in Paris that the Curie women were thriving. Ève had performed her first major piano solo inside a packed Paris hall. "It was all that you wished for her, Marie darling," Kellogg reported. Sporting a fashionable "boy-cut" and a straight satin dress, Ève epitomized the New Woman of the Flapper Age. Watching her coyly bow and giggle to the applause, Kellogg found her "deliciously girl-like" and wanted Missy to know. "Your coming into that dear family fructified everything. And how they love you!"[2]

The physician Harlow Brooks had been checking in on Bill throughout his decline and continued his care once Bill had been moved to Pawling. No doubt he knew the inevitable was coming, but for Missy's sake Brooks continued to take sputum samples to monitor any change. Missy sat at Bill's bedside as she tended to her correspondence. One of the people she wrote as her husband lay dying was Dr. Charles Mayo in Minnesota, for she hoped that a friend might benefit from treatment at his clinic. She also finalized lunch plans at the Belgian embassy in Washington, having convinced the Baron de Cartier to bestow the Cross of the Order of the Crown on her colleague Martha Van Rensselaer. Even in her darkest hour, Missy lifted women up and made sure that they were cared for and acknowledged.[3]

Bill died on December 7, 1925. His funeral was days later at the Church of Notre Dame, uptown from where he and Missy had been married twenty-one years earlier. President Coolidge and the First Lady were among the mourners, and pallbearers included Pulitzer Prize–winning journalist Louis Seibold and a tall, stately former Yale man named Ogden Reid, son of Ambassador Whitelaw Reid and heir to both the Mills family's banking fortune in San Francisco and the newly amalgamated *Herald Tribune*. A postmortem exam of forty-seven-year-old Bill revealed a tubercular infection and yet more shrapnel in his lung. Although Bill had managed to complete his biography of John Purroy Mitchel, he had never secured a publisher for it. Missy vowed to have it published posthumously, for the sake of the mayor's reputation as well as to do justice to Bill's legacy.[4] On a scrap of loose-leaf paper, she wrote a poem to her dead husband:

> *Crowds in the street; the sun above*
> *So day*
> *Goes on without you; even I, my Dear,*
> *Go swiftly and am busy there and here;*
> *Yet my soul stays with you and still shall stay.*
> *For, as a sword between me and the rest,*
> *Your memory shines; and still to you addrest*
> *My whole heart's homage; though the show of things*
> *May bring me peace, it is your peace it brings,*
> *And passing by, I know, "He met me here,"*
> *Or, "There he told me such and such a thing,"*
> *So every place spreads shelter like a wing*
> *Above my head, and for your sake is dear*
> *So may I make a shrine of every place*
> *Where I have held your hand and seen your face.*[5]

Every year thereafter the Veterans Administration requested that Missy verify her widow status for her monthly pension, though she would never remarry. Although she had affection for many men, no one replaced the husband she buried. "Time does not cure or ease the heart," she confessed to Charles Norris. "It only accumulates a longer list of confidences of worries and joys to be shared after the doors close on the world.... Work has been the only relief I have known. As much as I adore young Bill, I cannot look at him without seeing his father and being acutely conscious that the close companionship with my old lover cannot be filled by even the best of sons."[6]

According to Missy's friend and former colleague Channing Pollock, after Bill's death Missy "dug herself a mental hole and crawled into it." Harlow Brooks prescribed drugs for the pain mounting in her lungs and suggested that she go back to strapping her chest or wearing a tight corset, if she hadn't forgotten how. He understood that she worked excessively as a distraction, but he also worried that working too hard would kill her if she didn't take a break. "Treat yourself as you would want any of your friends to be treated," he reminded her. "Please remember that there are a great many of us who love you very dearly, and who think that you are an extremely useful person." Kathleen Norris worried too, and begged to know if her "microscopic Highness [was] sleeping and eating respectably?" The honest answer was no. Two months after Bill's death, Missy was suffering too much to take her correspondence in the office anymore. Secretaries sent paperwork to her apartment after she suffered another attack of pleurisy. By March she had landed in a Fifth Avenue hospital.[7]

It was some comfort to Missy to talk about Bill and to remember their life as struggling young reporters. Izola Page reminisced with her about the days when she and Bill had worked together at the *World:* "Arthur, my eldest can remember him . . . because Bill used to let them draw pictures, and kept him happy when I had to go out after something." It pained Missy that her husband, a formidable yet tender presence to children, could not give their own son guidance now, when he needed it most. She would always see Bill Jr. as a boy irrevocably wounded by the death of his father. Already, he suffered lung ailments that prolonged his high school course and delayed his entrance to Williams College. Though he eventually improved enough to study French and English literature, another bout of illness forced him to leave school before getting his degree. Bill Jr. returned to his studies at Columbia, but Missy thought him aimless and searching. "I haven't trusted myself to talk about it because the picture I ought to fit into has to do with a supposedly self-contained, level headed person and things that touch Bill vitally brush aside all other things in my life," she confessed to John Erskine. "He is all I have left from a one-time rich and over-blessed bounty."[8]

Missy was grateful that Erskine, father of the Great Books movement, offered himself up as a paternal figure to Bill in the Columbia English department, for gradually he seemed to set the young man on a path with more direction. "I am sure you haven't any idea of what you have done for that boy," she assured Erskine some months later, in 1926. "He had lost his grip, his interest in life was at very low ebb, he was in rebellion against a system he believed to be a failure and almost criminally wrong. And then—he fell into your hands, and it gave him a new point of view and started him building a philosophy for himself. He got the most priceless of all the gifts of life—a feeling that the game is worth playing. You can't begin without that."[9]

———————

THE GAME IS WORTH PLAYING—that was the philosophy that had always kept Missy focused beyond her ailments. But Bill's death made her confront doubts about the game she was playing at *The Delineator.* Management had changed hands, and she suspected that the new group in charge had ties to the Hearst conglomerate. Concerned almost exclusively with the bottom line, new management was disinclined toward social service and severed ties completely with the BHA and the home economists of Cornell. Missy tried to explain that the Domestic Institute increased ad revenues and that her other innovations had cut costs. As paper got more expensive, for instance, she had called for the reduced size of the magazine, which had saved the Butterick Company over $1,000,000, just on paper alone. But what she said didn't matter. Her vision for *The Delineator* was not in line with the direction her new bosses had in mind.[10]

It turned out to be fortuitous that while Missy sat in mourning she confided much of her dissatisfaction to Helen Rogers Reid, the wife of Bill's pallbearer Ogden Reid of the *Herald Tribune*. Helen was her husband's director of marketing and, as most people knew, the reason why his paper was having a resurgence. Missy and Helen cut similar figures—both were petite, almost fragile, and barely over five feet tall, leading to similar surprised reactions to their grit and professional determination. Both had large, inquiring eyes and were tastefully groomed, Helen often in her signature dress suit with pearls and beret or pill hat. Her look was decidedly feminine, as was her demeanor. She was gracious and soft-spoken, albeit no wilting flower. Not prone to gossip, she, too, was a charming conversationalist who entertained figures of national and world affairs at dinners and weekend parties. Helen and Missy were exceedingly competent, well-reasoned, and direct; they had a work ethic, natural managing abilities, and magnanimity in common.[11]

Once, in a cover profile for *Time,* Helen took issue with the inside story characterizing her as the one in charge of the *Herald Tribune.* She insisted that Ogden was the most independent-minded man she had ever met, to which a reporter replied, "It is Mrs. Reid who often helps that independent mind make itself up." It was not the image she wanted, for like Missy, Helen believed in the "modern trinity"— a job, a husband, and children—though she was ambiguous about their order of priority. She felt most comfortable being all things to all people without fanfare, avoiding publicity that singled her out. And she understood the optics of New Womanhood in transformation, because she, also like Missy, had the broader perspective of coming into New York's elite circles from elsewhere and making her own way. Hailing from Wisconsin, she was the youngest of eleven children and paid her way through Barnard. As a freshly minted graduate she fell into the good graces of Elisabeth Mills Reid, Ogden's aristocratic mother, whose inheritance had kept her husband's flailing *Tribune* afloat. Helen became her social secretary and over the next eight years proved indispensable in tending to Mrs. Reid's affairs, the most concerning of which was Ogden. A law student who drank more than he studied, this eldest heir was too agreeable and laid-back to run the family business, his mother feared, leaving some to speculate that Ogden's blossoming relationship with Helen was, to some degree, a product of his mother's careful engineering.[12]

Indeed, when Ogden and Helen married in 1911, Helen became the stabilizing influence that Elisabeth Reid had hoped for—not just for her son, but also for the family business. Whitelaw Reid died in 1912 and left the paper to a son who liked the editorial side but grew bored with the business of it. Hence why Helen was a crucial addition to the family. When she left her children in the care of her sister to revive the *Tribune*'s advertising department, she had no experience raising revenues for newspapers. But her mother-in-law had witnessed Helen raise $500,000 dollars for the final suffrage campaign in New York and knew she was smart. By the time women won the vote in 1920, the *Tribune* had not only changed its editorial stance on suffrage; it was also in the black, with $4.3 million in gross revenues. Helen went from advertising solicitor to advertising manager to vice president of the marketing department. In five years she nearly tripled the *Tribune*'s ad space, supporting Missy's contention that women's domestic and social roles only heightened their marketing and consumer instincts.[13]

To compete with the *Times* and its modern operations uptown, in 1923 the Reids moved the *Tribune* from the old tower on Nassau Street to a seven-story facility on West 41st. Then, to the shock of the newspaper world, they bought the *Herald*, its second-oldest rival publication, which was steadily in decline. The amalgamated *Herald Tribune* continued representing Rockefeller Republicans with pro-business, internationalist, Protestant points of view. But Helen became a modernizing and moderating influence—not just on the typological conservatism of the paper, but also on the extreme partisanship in editorial. She sought voices that didn't necessarily toe the party line, perhaps because she was a Republican long interested in La Follette progressivism who had even engaged socialists in her college years. The "ism" that guided Helen most was feminism, which she never named though implicitly endorsed as she represented women's perspectives and interests in the *Herald Tribune*. Perhaps this was how she and Missy were most alike as pioneers in New York journalism.[14]

"There are a lot of prejudices against newspaperwomen," Helen acknowledged. "Women have not projected their imaginations toward positions. Ability is still rated as a natural masculine characteristic and is considered an exception among women." Both Missy and Helen had refined their abilities to plan publicity and grassroots campaigns, the former in her magazines and the latter in the suffrage movement, and in the process both also learned to collaborate effectively with and to cultivate able women—and to give them credit when credit was due. "I have been working with women all my life and don't see why sharing honors should be regarded as such a difficult thing," Missy stated flatly to her female secretaries and department editors. She had come a long way since her days of kowtowing to male colleagues as a cub reporter in Washington. Like Helen's, her brand of management was results- rather than ego-driven, and eminently democratic. It was unacceptable to these female leaders to make subordinates do something that they couldn't see doing themselves. Temperamentally and philosophically, Missy and Helen were nearly in perfect alignment.[15]

It was kismet when Helen also discovered that Missy had a mind for the "butter and egg side" of news. She found this out in 1926, when she asked for Missy's thoughts on the newspaper-magazine business, a nut that she and Ogden had yet to successfully crack. Missy told her that she knew from contacts in the Commerce Department that several million dollars annually went into Sunday newspaper supplements that subscribers often thumbed through and threw away before day's end. Readers tended not to consider them keepsakes, as they did stand-alone monthlies, Missy told her, surmising that this was because most newspaper magazines simply hired their regular newspaper staff to generate the content. If Helen wanted to sell Sunday magazines worth keeping, she needed to spare no expense and hire famous writers like those Missy had worked with at *Everybody's*. Continue to include political and financial stories, she urged, but also ones on science and pets and babies, as well as literature that whole families could enjoy.[16]

Missy had a formula for drawing in female and suburban readers—the very ones Helen was trying to win over to her large city paper. The success of *The Delineator* was proof that Missy was a virtual pied piper to this growing readership, and Helen appreciated her innovation. So she offered Missy the opportunity to take over the helm of the *Herald Tribune Sunday Magazine*. Given the autonomy Helen promised her, Missy thought it a proposal too good to refuse. "I have severed my connection with the Butterick Publishing Company," Missy announced to the Norrises in the summer of 1926. "There is no use discussing it, my dear friends, except to say that I was not happy, and if there was ever a time in my life when I need to be happy in my work, it is now. I have had a number of other offers which have sort of buoyed me up and made me feel that I was of some use in the world, and I have finally decided to take over the Sunday Tribune, and with the money they are willing to spend and everything that is in me, make a real Sunday newspaper."[17]

Until now, no woman had ever run a major newspaper's Sunday edition. Still, Mark Goodwin, Missy's former colleague who headed the National Press Club, didn't doubt her ability to return to the "old game" of newspapers and to make her mark in this distinctive way. Curie was shocked that her friend would walk away from a job she had performed so devotedly, but Missy explained that a managing role at a major newspaper, rather than at a woman's magazine, was the challenge and change she had been looking for. She was taking her work for women readers mainstream, and hoping to bring her female readership with her. "The step I am taking is pioneering and not without serious difficulties," she admitted to Curie, "but I need to lose my life in a very exacting task. No one will understand this better than you." She confided to John Erskine that she would need the help of all her friends to succeed in her new undertaking. "Unlike the Delineator, this is not a task which all men agree is a woman's job. But I have worked with men for most of my life and I hope to go on happily in this new field with my brothers under the skin."[18]

It was a rare acknowledgment of the sexism Missy knew would confront her once she left the safe haven of woman's magazines, and yet in some ways she felt well positioned at the *Herald Tribune* to enjoy the best of all worlds. Although she'd be in closer proximity to "hard news," she would also be somewhat shielded from the wrath of men directly. To be sure, the associate editor who worked under her was a man, Richard Lane Field, and Ogden Reid was her boss, but both men remained collegial and respectful of Missy's experience as an editor of successful magazines. She made fast friends with the art critic Royal Cortissoz, with whom she discussed exhibitions, artists, and all things cultural, and she was close personally and politically to the editorialist Walter Lippmann, the celebrity columnist the Reids had poached from the *World*. None of these relationships grew adversarial, probably in part because the men worked in other departments. She never, for instance, suffered direct confrontations with the infamous city editor Stanley Walker, who wrote candidly about his prejudices against women in the newsroom. "They insist that they want to be treated as newspaper 'men,' but when the showdown comes, they instantly become women again," he complained with a less then subtle condescension.[19]

Missy was undoubtedly aware that at the *Herald Tribune*, alcohol aided in dictating the gender dynamics of the newsroom, leveling the playing field for men while helping to relegate women to the peripheries. Despite being in the midst of Prohibition, Walker and his fraternity of reporters drank booze out of paper cups right at their desks, as well as outside the office with male promoters, politicians, and corporate public-relations people at the events they covered. Their favorite drinking hole, Bleeck's, was just downstairs from the office; it was referred to by one reporter as an "old-time barber-shop refuge from feminism." In the new *Herald Tribune* building, Helen's office was on the sixth floor, and Ogden's was on the fifth with the city-room reporters. After six o'clock, when Helen typically went home or to some reception, Ogden often joined his brethren downstairs for a drink, or a couple. Helen's democratic tendencies shone through her style of management, Ogden's through his imbibing with executives and cub reporters indiscriminately. Like Helen, Missy passed on the drinking, but she embraced being a companion, a sounding board, and a reinforcing mirror image of Helen, with her same focus and productivity. She was emboldened by the culture of female competence Helen was cultivating in this male bastion of a major newspaper.[20]

US census figures indicate a doubling of women editors and reporters at American newspapers between 1920 and 1930, suggesting that the increased presence of women at the *Herald Tribune* was consistent with national trends. Nevertheless, these gains were more pronounced at small-town papers, not major New York dailies, making Helen Reid's accumulation of women all the more remarkable. The Floridian Irita Van Doren came over from *The Nation* to assist Stuart Sherman in making over the *Herald Tribune*'s Books Department; when Sherman died in 1926, Van Doren took over the department completely, freshening up the list of titles reviewed for the next forty years. Harriette Underhill was the resident film critic, Margaret Goss and Janet Owen covered women in sports, and Elsa Lang worked in promotions. A female team worked under Helen as advertising solicitors, and her "right-hand man" was in fact a woman named Helen Leavitt, a former suffragist whose daughter wrote features for the Sunday edition. Clementine Paddleford redefined the modern food section, and Dorothy Kiggins was queen of the crossword puzzle. Helen even hired female linotypers in the production department.[21]

The female fiefdoms Helen formed throughout the *Herald Tribune* eventually allowed a few women to alter the sexual geography of Walker's newsroom itself. One was Barnard graduate Emma Bugbee, who started at the *Tribune* on a whim in 1910, when she agreed to take a friend's place over summer vacation, but then stayed for fifty-five years. Her timing had been key, for she had arrived in the all-male city room at the height of the suffrage movement, and thus was able to cover a "woman's" topic that turned into lasting political news. Nevertheless, it took a long time to be granted physical access to the city room; her desk remained awkwardly outside it until Helen arrived. Bugbee was the natural choice in the newsroom to cover Curie's tour in 1921. Similarly, her colleague Ishbel Ross joined the *Tribune* city room in 1919, staying through the merger with the *Herald*. Known respectfully by male colleagues as "Miss Ross," this hard-nosed reporter was logical, dependable, not giddy, a writer of concise prose, never flamboyant or temperamental, and she demanded no special treatment, thus defying all of Stanley Walker's stereotypes, to his own admission. As her reward for blending into the furniture, Walker let her cover murders, kidnappings, riots, fires, and all sorts of catastrophes that made the front page. From the city room Ross observed Helen and Missy working together and felt moved by the "dynamic force between them." "Sometimes they disagree. Both are strong-minded, and passionate in their convictions. But each respects the other," she noted. It gave her some self-assurance that her work as a serious reporter wouldn't be undermined; the female subculture of the paper was understated competence, and it seeped through the city-room walls.[22]

Much as she had at *The Delineator,* Missy seized on the opportunity to expand coverage of traditionally feminine fare by featuring women writers and introducing some controversial content. She published "Woman and Religion" and "Woman and Politics" by the Italian social scientist Gina Lombroso Ferrero, as well as a controversial piece by Marie Belloc Lowndes titled "Why Women Commit Murder." She asked Julia Peterkin, a portraitist of Southern plantation life, to write on former slaves; Dorothy Canfield Fisher about Willa Cather; and Katherine Mayo about her provocative racial theories. Appreciative of Missy's open-mindedness, US Assistant Attorney General Mabel Willebrandt recommended a piece by Republican committeewoman Harriet Taylor Upton, as well as one by her sister on the warlords of China. Missy told Willebrandt that she was happy to read her sister's work so long as Willebrandt considered submitting her own piece on dope and the Justice Department's crackdown on it. She wasn't afraid to push the envelope in a Sunday magazine.[23]

The Reids appreciated that they were getting more than Missy's editorial skills; they were getting her relationships with already-established writers, as well as literary agents at home and abroad. Missy wasn't squeamish about soliciting pieces from the biggest names. Who better to write about the Supreme Court, she figured, than Justice Oliver Wendell Holmes? Or on the "Indian Problem" than the secretary of the interior? She asked Orville Wright to contribute several thousand words on "A Quarter Century of Aviation" and Arctic explorer Vilhjalmur Stefansson to analyze the failings of Umberto Nobile's North Pole expedition. It worked to her advantage that she had relationships with Richard Byrd, Charles Lindbergh, Upton Close, Roy Chapman Andrews, and Amelia Earhart, for American readers loved their adventurists.[24]

Missy's international contacts were the envy of male journalists. She got first dibs on the works of Carlo Sforza, an Italian diplomat forced into exile by Benito Mussolini. He admittedly received bigger checks elsewhere but remained loyal to Missy—"How much more I like the serene and broad atmosphere you create," he assured her. Teddy Roosevelt Jr. buttressed her coverage by sending her reports from his government posts in Puerto Rico and Manila. Anticipating Irish statesman George Russell's visit to New York, Missy asked him if he might submit an article that compared his homeland to America, much like the one she had encouraged Curie to write when she came to New York. She got General Foch to write for her, as well as Edgar Snow, the first Western journalist to cover communism in China. She even asked Wilhelm II, the emperor of Germany, to write a statement on the tenth anniversary of Armistice Day, to which the acting chief of the imperial household responded in disbelief. "You really cannot expect His Majesty the Emperor to make any statement," he chafed. "May I draw your attention to the fact that the Germans consider this date as the day on which they were betrayed by Mr. Wilson and his allies?" Though it didn't pan out, Missy, as always, hadn't seen the harm in asking.[25]

Issues swirled in her mind—education, foreign policy, gender roles, immigration, working-class foment—and she delighted in the challenge of pairing them with the mouthpieces that offered the least-expected insights and the most intriguing points of view. She turned not to a physician or policy man but to University of Michigan football coach Fielding Yost to commentate on "athletic women" amidst debates over physical culture, coeducation, and "race suicide" in white America. She hit up public-relations guru Edward Bernays to contribute articles on "Why Men Fail," figuring that his understanding of consumer psychology could shed special light on the subject. She wanted Connecticut governor Wilbur Cross to write about Prohibition, and Wall Street businessman Dwight Morrow to take up the question "Why Is America Prosperous?" Fannie Hurst was surprised when Missy approached her to write on Jews in New York, as was the film actor Will Rogers when she asked him to write about Alice Roosevelt Longworth from the perspective of a friend outside Washington. "Lord, I don't feel that I'm competent," he told Missy, but she had a way of working with nonwriters, smoothing over their prose without losing their distinctive voice.[26]

Invariably, seeking out big-name contributors meant managing big egos from time to time. Such was the case when physicist Michael Pupin submitted to Missy his latest musings. "I do not know what the custom of the Herald Tribune Sunday Magazine is, but know what my own custom is. It is this: I expect twenty cents a word for my articles which are not more than two thousand words in length." It was a rude awakening when Missy told Pupin that her newspaper budget allowed her to offer only $100 for articles as long as she had room for. Most of the time she accommodated the persnickety, stroked egos, and even endured some mild bullying if she thought it would pay off. Nevertheless, she occasionally put men in their place when she thought a lesson could be learned. Celebrity contributors generally understood that Missy, if her skills were utilized gratefully, could enhance the public presentation of their ideas beyond what other editors could. The Columbia philosopher Irwin Edman initially lacked the confidence to write the articles that Missy proposed, but then he saw how she brought out the best in him. "When I write under your provocation I say things that I really want to say," he marveled. "I do not think there could be any more real compliment to an editor."[27]

Occasionally, when she thought she could do it justice, Missy reserved a story for herself and returned to reporter's mode. The tragic Mississippi flood of 1927 was a story that fell into her lap when Commerce Secretary Herbert Hoover called her and asked her to travel to the flood-damaged area with him. She observed him carefully as he led operations on the ground. Wherever he stopped he was on the phone with an engineer or local official. From the field he wired university agriculturists to learn which crops might grow quickest in soaked lands once the water receded. The consensus was cabbage, so Hoover ordered four million cabbage plants and wired the president to tell him to advise farmers located elsewhere to plant something else and to leave cabbage for the flooded areas. Missy wrote the story, praising Hoover's quick action, and it won her a $500 prize. The piece turned out to be a promotional tool for a commerce secretary with presidential ambitions, as well as a feather in the cap of an editor who generally left most award-winning stories for others to write.[28]

The Reids were impressed with all of it and believed that Missy's innovation in her first two years at the *Sunday Magazine* was a large part of why overall circulation of the *Herald Tribune* began surpassing that of its Hearst competitors and remained only seventy-seven thousand behind the *New York Times*. Now that their paper was operating well in the black, the Reids started construction on a multistory addition to their 41st Street building and designated a whole floor of the new annex for a reinvigorated domestic institute. Yes, Missy's work with home economists, the BHA, White House children's conferences, and the General Federation of Women's Clubs came with her to the *Herald Tribune*. In addition to her editorial duties, she officially replaced Lettie Gay as director of the *Herald Tribune*'s Home Institute in 1930.[29]

Meanwhile, the days of the hollowed-out *Delineator* were numbered. Merging with Butterick's *The Designer*, *Delineator* ("The" had been skimmed off the title) returned to its original domestic focus and targeted a less sophisticated readership than what Missy had cultivated for it. Under editor Oscar Graeve, it went back to being another fashion magazine with homemaking tips. The editorial section shrunk, as did its advertising revenues. The Butterick Company filed for bankruptcy in 1935, forcing *Delineator* to merge a final time with Hearst's *Pictorial Review*. So ended the glory days of the woman's magazine. Missy had moved on and taken her readers with her.[30]

———

MISSY HAD NEVER FOOLED HERSELF about her obsessive habits; working had always been her antidote to despair, her way of tabling pain. If she feared anything, it was an idle mind, and thus she had seized on the challenge of the *Sunday Magazine* as a timely distraction from the loneliness of widowhood. It seemed like Bill Jr., too, had finally begun to find the drive that his mother had wanted for him. He got engaged to a Smith College graduate, Elizabeth Symons of Saginaw, Michigan, and made plans to travel with her to Europe before the start of his senior year. Missy kept tabs on him through the authors she made him visit; novelists W. B. Maxwell and Henry Stacpoole took him in and devotedly reported back to his mother. When Bill suggested that he wanted to interview Benito Mussolini from a "student's point of view," Missy seized on the suggestion and wrote her contacts to request letters of introduction. Bill married in March 1927 in the same rectory of St. Patrick's Cathedral where his parents had exchanged vows, and he graduated from Columbia three months later, his beaming mother boasting that despite the handicap of illness, he had never earned lower than a B+ in his studies. His academic success inspired the newlyweds to move to Paris so that Bill could pursue graduate studies at the Sorbonne. Missy promised to spend Christmas with them and to meet with Curie, whom she hadn't seen since her last time in Paris in 1924.[31]

When the *Berengaria* arrived in Cherbourg with Missy aboard that December of 1927, she was greeted by a son who appeared refreshed and reformed. He traveled with her to Paris by train in a private compartment that provided precious hours of time alone together. "I wanted to look at him—to look through him—to see if in these vital months of his new life, all had gone well with him," Missy remembered. "The clean cut of him, the clear eyes, the steady look, the frank happiness, bridged in those hours some dark chasms in my life. He was older—much older in this half year." Bill and Elizabeth's apartment was spartan, aside from its books, but Missy's first impression was that it "glistened with happiness"; no doubt it reminded her of her simple existence with Bill's father in their cub-reporter days. Her son showed her the necklace he had picked out for his wife's Christmas present; he planned to pay for it with the money he made writing articles for *Century* magazine. His purchases would leave little left to live on for the month, but Missy didn't disapprove. "Elizabeth will have to think about putting away many a dollar—but she will know love and romance and tenderness," she concluded.[32]

More thoroughly than she had during any of her other overseas trips, Missy kept an account of those weeks in Paris, hoping to give it to grandchildren someday. "Now, your grandmother was not a free agent," she prefaced, "and in order to justify leaving my desk for six weeks and spending Christmas with my children in Paris, it was necessary for me to find some important work to do in that part of the world. The record of that work is told in later pages. But the first interest we have, you and I, is the Christmas with your mother and father. The work was the price I paid, and it carried some rewards of its own. You will find this true in your own lives, and you will discover also, that big work, work that succeeds, has to be carefully planned, staged, and much attention given to detail. There is nothing casual about success." Already, she was mentoring children yet to be born.[33]

The important work she referred to included going to the home of former French ambassador Jean Jules Jusserand to arrange for more of his historical writing to be published in the States. When Missy arrived, Jusserand's wife busied herself around a disheveled tea table and propped up her husband in the bed next to it. Since Missy had seen him last, he had been operated on twice for cancer, and the medical bills had set him back. Forced to give up his car and servants, he wondered if he could write something for Missy to supplement his French pension, which, she knew from Curie, hardly supplied enough to live on before medical expenses. He knew American presidents intimately and had stories about the Great War. Missy assured him that he had plenty to tell that Americans wanted to read, leaving him more hopeful than when she had arrived. His *Evolution of the American Sentiment During the War* was published two years later, his American editor undoubtedly crucial in getting it into print.[34]

Though Missy must have seen some of herself in Jusserand, she never let on that she, too, was getting sicker. Given the onset of flu-like symptoms, she agreed to leave for New York sooner than she had planned—but there was no departing Paris without seeing Curie. Missy took Bill and Elizabeth to the scientist's walk-up on the Quai de Béthune. Given Missy's physical struggles, she had to stop several times along the five flights of stairs to sit on windowsills and catch her breath. Curie stood at her door apologizing; she, too, had a hard time with the stairs but wanted Missy to see how much her efforts had made her friend's life more comfortable. Taking her guests from room to room, Curie gushed over the new amenities paid for by American generosity—a small maid's quarters, some appliances in the kitchen, a modernized bathroom. "I shall live here the rest of my life," she luxuriated. Missy thought it sweet. With its old furnishings the apartment didn't look that different from the one she had visited only a few years before.[35]

Missy had never stopped facilitating Curie's science from a distance. She had arranged for an American-made voltmeter, a balance, a millivoltmeter with portable shunt, a galvanometer, and a microampere meter to be donated and shipped to Curie's lab, even enlisting French diplomats to carry items to her in their personal luggage. Dissatisfied with the terms of the trust that contained the leftover monies from the radium fund, Missy had them redrawn so that more money funneled directly to Irène to continue the research of the institute long after her mother was gone. This had been Curie's greatest wish.[36]

Curie had often dropped hints to Missy about another project: fund-raising for more radium, this time for a new institute in her birthplace of Warsaw. "I would not for anything in the world give you more trouble or ask you to start something for the polish radium, I ask you only to express sympathy for the polish undertaking," she wrote Missy, knowing that this was all she had to say for Missy to turn it into a personal mission. As for helping Ève and Irène, Curie didn't have to suggest it; after the tour in America, Missy supported them as if they were her own daughters. As a pupil of the Russian pianist Alexander Brailowsky, Ève had asked if Missy could arrange with New York agents to secure concert dates for him, or possibly even a special recital for First Lady Grace Coolidge, given her love of music. Brailowsky had his American debut at Aeolian Hall in New York City in 1924. Meanwhile, Missy had worked her magazine connections to get Ève a column writing about Paris theater, music, and fashion.[37]

Irène had been harder to cater to, but Missy persistently tried. Preparing to take over her mother's research, Irène had earned her PhD in chemistry and stood second in command at the Curie Institute. Missy offered her lecturing opportunities in American universities, and Irène was grateful. But she was becoming as leery of travel as her mother, partly because she, too, now suffered the effects of radiation exposure. Between intense stints of work at the institute, she followed her mother's regimen of rehabilitation in the mountains. Missy urged her and Marie to consider a trip to America under the auspices of the International Conference on Cancer, but Marie declined for them both since they had already agreed to give lectures in Brazil. Missy proposed that they come straight from Brazil to New York, but again there was a conflict—a happy one: Irène was to be married to a fellow scientist in her mother's laboratory named Frédéric Joliot. Curie initially was skeptical of him, concerned that he would disrupt her partnership with Irène and her inheritance of the radium. But Joliot turned out to be devoted to the Curies' work, as well as to their legacy. He and Irène took the name Joliot-Curie to symbolize the partnership they envisioned—one affectionate, yet also professionally and mutually supportive, much as the marriages of Missy and Marie Curie had been.[38]

Since leaving New York, Curie had undergone four cataract operations, and yet a grayish film still accumulated over her pupils. Ève continued to live with her, devotedly tending to the housework and to her mother's correspondence. Irène now lived with a husband who looked after her, but her mother still worried, for Irène was fragile, even more so than Marie had been at her age. Missy met Irène's baby daughter, Hélène, before heading to Curie's office, "the inner laboratory," where they had first met seven years before. The mood was different this time. They sat by the fire and talked about their children. Curie begged Missy to drive with her to the mountains for New Year's, but sensing that she had reached her physical limits, Missy insisted that she had to go home.[39]

It was likely on the passage back to New York that Missy wrote down what she remembered of those final days in Paris, while every word spoken was still fresh in her mind. She called the piece "Madame Curie" and hoped to publish it for posterity. "I should have enjoyed long quiet uninterrupted hours with you," Curie lamented, and Missy recalled being overwhelmed by the sentiment. "I am so unimportant," she responded. "I have nothing to bring to fill your important quiet hours, except my regard for you, and this can be a useless and cumbersome thing." Curie begged to tell her differently: "You have a great deal to bring me, in mind and in spirit.... Have I not told you that with all we think we know, few things in all the universe are more inaccurate than the human mind—few things truer than kind impulses. I am very fond of you. I like to talk to you, to be with you. It gives me real pleasure."[40]

Missy's last visit with Curie before being driven back to the ship in Cherbourg revealed just how close the two women had become. Curie stroked Missy's hand with her radium-tortured fingers. "She was not the scientist then," Missy observed. "My dear friend," Curie said, "you are not well. You do not take care of yourself. I am afraid you work too hard." Missy gently reminded her that this was coming from a woman who worked eighteen-hour days in the laboratory, but she also supposed that Curie's work was different. "Her labors are worth the cost," she thought to herself. "Mine are only motions." "You should take care for Bill's sake," Curie reminded her. "He will need you a long time and his children will need you, and his wife, and your friends. It would hurt me to have anything happen to you." "I'll die of old age," Missy laughed dismissively. "A human body and brain is a fine instrument," Curie pontificated. "It is the most intricate and delicate equipment in all creation. It is amazing what it can do, despite our abuse of it. We should respect that instrument." Missy ventured to ask Curie just when had she "put the care of [her] 'human instrument' before [her] work?" and Curie chastised her as a mother would: "How you argue!" The scientist's eyes welled up, betraying her real fear of losing her friend. Missy tried to console her, reminding her that she had never been a healthy woman, not even when they first met, and yet here she was—"Tough little old Missy, nothing ever kills."[41]

Although Curie was resigned, she wasn't fooled. She knew that Missy was gravely ill and probably had been for some time. In truth, at no time in those initial years at the *Herald Tribune* or during that trip to Paris had Missy been well or pain free. Curie's admonishments had been repeated by friends in the States before Missy had even left— "You work too much!" "Take better care of yourself!" "I hope you are not working yourself to death, even to save the country!" Harlow Brooks adored Missy, but after Bill's death he believed that he had to become firm with her. "Let me make arrangements to send you to some of the larger sanitariums or health resorts, if you like that name better, where you can be brought back to good health and your normal spirits," he begged Missy. "I am not asking this for your sake, but for the sake of all of us, who are devoted to you."[42]

No one had been surprised back in the summer of 1927 when Missy had suffered another bout of pulmonary tuberculosis. "It is unnecessary to go into the factors which have caused this relapse— you know them as well as I do," Brooks scolded. His prescription had been three to four months of bed rest. "If this is done now, I have every expectation of your recovery," he had told her. "If you try to temporize by less radical measures, you may get out of it but if you do not do something soon, you are going to loose [sic] and we are going to loose [sic] you."[43]

But of course Missy hadn't heeded his warnings. She had continued developing the *Sunday Magazine* at breakneck pace and traveling, spending Thanksgiving with the Coolidges and Christmas with her son and with Curie in Paris. When she finally returned to New York after Curie's tear-filled send-off, her flu worsened into full-blown pneumonia. Brooks beseeched her once again to heed his medical advice, and he stopped in regularly to see that she was off her feet, since there was no other way to make her compliant. If she seemed in denial about how sick she was, perhaps it finally hit her several months later, when she made this stunning admission to James Barrie: "It seems still a little uncertain as to whether I shall be able to go on much further. However, I have followed my old habit of turning to your book 'Courage' in my dark hours."[44]

THREE MONTHS LATER, in the summer of 1928, *Harper's Weekly* editor Norman Hapgood wrote Missy to congratulate her on the fine quality of the *Sunday Magazine,* and she replied with good news: she was over the worst of her illness, she reported, and now "fighting the aftermath." Apparently that summer she had recuperated well enough to stave off death once again. No doubt she minimized her suffering in her letters to friends and authors, but it is remarkable that throughout it all, the *Sunday Magazine* continued to publish apace. As an editor she hadn't missed a beat, and as the dauntless crusader she now returned to her many missions, which soon included the building of a presidential monument, the election of a "woman's candidate" as president, and obtaining for Curie yet another gram of radium.[45]

Chapter Nine

THE WORK OF WEAVING WEBS

1928–1929

I N ADDITION TO BEING AN EDITOR, in 1928 and 1929 Missy became a lobbyist, a campaign director, a fund-raiser, a PR point person—essentially many things to many people. She was making unusual bedfellows behind the scenes, weaving webs among those in her expanding network who she thought could be of service to one another. In so doing, she linked the fate of Mount Rushmore to wealthy friends and presidential campaigns, which she tied to the scientific research of Madame Curie, which she made matter to the expansion of an American university—and on the connections went. It was demanding work, maintenance work, and frankly not often acknowledged as work since so much of it remained unseen, but she forged these connections as if she had no deadlines of her own, and as if illness no longer plagued her. The webs she spun grew so elaborate that it is hard to trace them back to their original impetus. But it was no coincidence that much of this work had the effect of bolstering female efforts as citizens, scientists, and perhaps indirectly as editors of magazines.

BEFORE THERE WAS A MOUNT RUSHMORE, there was Stone Mountain, the Georgia location of the infamously failed project of the erratic yet brilliant American sculptor Gutzon Borglum. In some ways he was the temperamental artist in caricature, but Missy admired him and found ways to make the more stoic, less colorful Calvin Coolidge useful to him. "What a glorious time God had of it when he made you," she once gushed to the artist, and she meant it with all sincerity. Borglum had been a supporter of Teddy Roosevelt's Bull Moose ticket and Leonard Wood's political campaign before the Great War, and by the 1920s he and his wife had become two of Missy's closest friends. He was not merely an artist, just as Missy was not merely an editor. Along with producing sculpture, Borglum painted and sketched, designed roads, reconstructed old buildings, founded a bus company, invented an airplane, wrote scathing political editorials, recruited a Czechoslovakian expeditionary force, and investigated the state of the US air fleet, citing his patriotism as motive. Fashioning himself a Renaissance man, he also submitted articles to Missy on the Cubists. Nevertheless, her favorite works were the sketches and sculptures he made of the great President Lincoln, and he gifted her with a few of them. He shared Missy's penchant for dabbling in a variety of arenas, always purportedly for the good of the country—though quite unlike Missy, his impetuous projects occasionally crashed and burned.[1]

After World War I Missy had traveled to Georgia to observe the remarkable process by which Borglum created templates for his massive sculptures. Onto the eight-hundred-foot-tall granite face of Stone Mountain he had projected images of Confederate soldiers with a contraption of his own invention. She was in awe of the grandiosity of his vision, which would forever alter the natural landscape. But Borglum's tempestuousness and looseness with money concerned members of the memorial association who sponsored the project, and clashes ensued. Borglum felt misunderstood. In a moment of protest and paranoia, he even took to breaking plaster models of his sculptures before fleeing the state of Georgia. His benefactors considered filing charges, and Missy was forced to talk him down. "All of your friends have been outraged at the Stone Mountain atrocity," she assured him. "I understand just exactly how you feel about it, but just as I have had to keep Bill as a precious memory in my life and tried to prevent it being a destroying agony, so must you let your dead child rest and go on with life and the work of today and tomorrow." She adored Borglum and admired his talent, but more and more she placated him until she could help him rechannel his energies, often in the service of others in her network of friends.[2]

While legal disputes continued over Stone Mountain, South Dakota legislators approached Borglum about creating an immense sculpture of presidential busts in the Black Hills, a memorial that came to be known as Mount Rushmore. Senator Peter Norbeck pushed legislation to back the project, and Missy was relieved to get Coolidge's blessing for it and to see Borglum refocused. But the $50,000 in the Mount Rushmore treasury would be exhausted in December of 1927. Work on the project would come to a halt if Congress didn't approve more funds, hence why Borglum was especially invested in the presidential race of 1928. Worried that a changing of the guard in the executive branch could influence legislators and mark the end of his federal funding, he urged Missy to make Coolidge run for a third term. The point was moot, she promised him. The Coolidges were done with the White House, and she was "not the least bit uncertain about Hoover's election." "The best people in the country are behind him," she insisted, the most effective of whom was her.[3]

Indeed, amidst the coverage of the 1928 presidential election, a reporter for *Time* magazine described Missy as a new kind of political operative—the "press handler." "You're dead when they stop writing about you. You are unborn until they begin writing about you," he declared. "Mrs. William Brown Meloney" had become Herbert Hoover's campaign maven, and for his Democratic challenger, Al Smith, it was "Mrs. Belle Israels Moskowitz." It was no coincidence that the reporter mentioned the two women together, for in some ways they were each other's carbon copy. Moskowitz was a Jewish Democrat, Missy a Catholic Republican, and yet both were proving to have substantial influence on political races in New York City, New York State, and nationally. Moskowitz's instincts were born of similar reform circles and women's auxiliaries, through which she, too, demonstrated more innovation in promoting candidates than her male counterparts. Because she and Missy were women, they found it effective—and necessary—to work so far behind the scenes that most of their male counterparts were unaware of them, at least until their discreet machinations made the pages of *Time*. They also differed from male strategists by backing party candidates without becoming overly partisan themselves. Missy had befriended Democrats who shared her progressive agenda, and she eagerly published their perspectives in the *Sunday Magazine*. New York industrial commissioner Frances Perkins was one such friend, as were Democrats Molly Dewson, Ruth Bryan Owen, and the friend they all had in common, the soon-to-be First Lady of New York, Eleanor Roosevelt.[4]

The Republican candidate whom Missy backed in the 1928 election was not the savviest of politicians, which in some ways endeared him to her, for it convinced her that his intentions and methods were pure, not slickened by political gamesmanship. He was an administrator who paid attention to detail, and, as she was, he was results-driven and self-made. Since their cooperative efforts on the Commission for the Relief of Belgium in the First World War, her respect for Hoover had grown, for he had demonstrated not only her same humanitarianism when he was a food administrator, but also her efficiency when he was secretary of the Department of Commerce. They were Republicans of a progressive strain, believing that free enterprise could be a force for social good, and they held up a model of citizenship promoted by the BHA through independent home ownership. As president of the Girl Scouts of America, Hoover's wife, Lou Henry Hoover, also shared Missy's penchant for voluntarism. A geologist with a firm grasp of the issues, she was her husband's intellectual equal, and their marriage, though traditional on the surface, was a companionate partnership, like Missy's had been, making it easy for her to relate to the Hoovers personally as well as politically.[5]

In the summer before the 1928 election, Will Irwin, Hoover's biographer, had urged Missy to work her magic on their candidate's public image, as well as to make the "old goofs" running his campaign more cognizant of women voters. Operatives of both parties recognized that in 1920 and 1924, women remained relatively apathetic about national politics, preferring to back local races when they bothered to vote at all. Harriet Taylor Upton, one of the few women making headway within formal channels of the Republican Party, agreed that since the passing of the Nineteenth Amendment, the woman voter remained an enigma to male operatives. "Men understand their wives, their daughters, their mothers, their cooks, their stenographers and the rest of the woman contingent," she remarked, "but when she appears in the role of voter it's all different." Knowing this was true, Missy cast her candidate anew in a *Sunday Magazine* profile titled "Hoover in Victory," which matched the substance and tone of the following ad, which she assuredly had a hand in placing in the *Woman's Journal* just weeks before the election. Hoover had been remade to appeal to the woman voter:[6]

Thirty-seven leading women tell why they will vote for
Herbert Hoover.

. .

He has the vision to understand great problems, the
courage to undertake them, the ability to conquer them.

. .

No other man knows so deeply the horrors of war and is so
capable of commanding peace.

. .

In 1914 he gave up his mining interests and the certainty of
wealth to feed and clothe ten million war-ravaged people.

. .

He saved the families of thousands of American farmers at
the close of the War by persuading the Allies not to cancel
contracts for American agricultural goods.

. .

He is the great humanitarian of the age and the great
organizer; a man who makes his dreams come true. He

> organized flood relief for 600,000 homeless Americans and
> developed a sound business life for the stricken community.
> Working with 100,000 citizens, he made possible the Better
> Homes Movement to raise our standard of living. He built
> the American Child Health Association, saving each year
> thousands of children.
>
> • •
>
> He exemplifies American opportunity. An orphan at eleven,
> without money or influence, he has made his life one of the
> most useful in history.
>
> • •
>
> Hoover's cause is the cause of the home. Every woman
> should feel the deepest pride that her vote can help make
> this great man the leader of our country.[7]

Missy sensed that women wanted to back a man who was self-made, humanitarian, a champion of Prohibition, and dedicated to maternalist causes, and she didn't seem to mind him taking credit for spearheading projects that had actually originated with her. Borglum was amused at how entrenched her position on Hoover had become and even joked about a campaign button he had designed for Al Smith, to which Missy sniped back that he was betting on a losing horse. She was so adamant that she was right about her candidate that Borglum offered an olive branch—a bas-relief of Hoover with his vice presidential running mate, Charles Curtis, which he could reduce to the size of a button to be struck in bronze, should Missy think it helpful. Still, he teased Missy about her man: "He is not homely. He is just not good looking." "He is homely," Missy conceded, "but so was Lincoln."[8]

She asked Borglum to paint a portrait instead of casting a campaign button, and in return she lobbied to keep Mount Rushmore on the congressional agenda as she solicited rich friends for more funding. John D. Rockefeller was the one most prominent in Borglum's sights. "Now, Missy," he pleaded, "if ever you did anything in your life, or wanted to do anything in your life, other than the great things you have done, and that will rank with the best of them, take this data I am sending you of Rushmore and in your own little hands carry it to John D Jr. and put the case before him. It is up to you—it is up to you!"[9]

Indeed, Missy stood among a nexus of men who needed each other, be it for their money, their talents, or their political power, and she made them aware of that fact. There was consistency in the type of men she connected to each other and to whom she pledged loyalty. Generally, they were hypermasculine in ways idealized at the time, and they carried a record of service from which she could mold their patriotic image in the press. If they did not participate directly in combat, as her husband, Roosevelt, Wood, and Mitchel had, then they resembled a Hoover or Borglum or Charles Evans Hughes as civil servants. "Wild" Bill Donovan fit both molds as the man who had led the 165th Infantry in the Argonne and then became the US attorney known for cracking down on violators of Prohibition. He had arrived in Washington in 1925 and gained political stock in the Republican Party as he took charge of the Justice Department's Antitrust Division. Who better, Missy thought, to be the public face advising Hoover's 1928 presidential campaign? She hoped Hoover could exploit Donovan's personal charisma and in return reward Donovan with a highly coveted administration post; it was no secret that he wanted to be attorney general of the United States, so Missy forged the mutually beneficial bond.[10]

THAT NOVEMBER, HOOVER BEAT the Democrat Al Smith by a landslide, winning the popular vote 21,392,190 to 15,016,443, the electoral vote 444 to 87, and carrying all but eight states. Scientific polling had not yet been invented, but straw polls suggested a gender gap in the electorate that is characteristic of more recent times. A Hearst poll predicted that Hoover would win some 60 percent of the women's vote, versus 56 percent of the men's, and private studies by the Republican National Committee (RNC) suggested a gender differential as wide as 10 percent. Party insiders attributed Smith's failure virtually everywhere but in the South to the female turnout. Surprisingly, he even lost in his home state of New York, where Franklin Delano Roosevelt, also a Democrat, had no trouble winning the governorship. The anomalous results have led political scientists to refer to 1928 as the "year of the woman voter." Although Missy was too ill to celebrate the win with the Hoovers in Palo Alto on election night, the secretary of the RNC reached out to her immediately to thank her for all she had done to shape Hoover into "the woman's candidate." Analyzing the election results with Bill Donovan, Missy admitted that she thought the difference had been Hoover's pull with women, and with "home women" in particular.[11]

She was rewarded for her insights, service, and loyalty with influence beyond even what she had enjoyed with Coolidge when he was in office. Invited regularly to the White House throughout Hoover's presidency, she typically arranged with Lou Henry's secretary to arrive at the Washington train depot, where a presidential car collected her. She lunched at the White House when meetings took her to town, and she accompanied the First Couple to their retreat in the Virginia mountains, Rapidan Camp, on long weekends. Soon she observed enough about Hoover's staff to form opinions and share them with the president, much as she had with Coolidge. Her antennae were always tuned in for this president who lacked an instinct for optics, publicity, and personal motives. At a Polish embassy dinner, she bit her tongue but took copious notes to inform the president of the dubious men around him, one of whom was Hoover's labor secretary. "Looked in on Doak," she scribbled. "So busy playing politics— so grateful to Hoover for making him a cabinet officer—he would say yes, yes to 'The hell with the Pope' or anything else that the President might suggest." She thought Hoover's personal secretary, French Strother, did him no favors with his public comments on the gender and religion wars. The protective publicist in her opined, "Men who are secretaries to presidents should have no passionate convictions and few opinions. They should be machined men who do the harmless and if they reflect any opinion, successfully reflect that of the

President." There were others, too, who she thought lacked discretion and used "their closeness to the White House and their temporary power to preach their own particular sermons." She became a trusted informant to the Hoovers, and they never questioned her intentions, because her sermons never seemed to serve self-interests.[12]

During the trip to Washington when she dined at the Polish embassy, Missy also met with the diplomat Stanley Hornbeck (referring to him in her notes, clearly unbeknownst to him, as "the most pompous man I know"); with Anson Phelps Stokes (who tried to persuade her to donate her correspondence with Curie to Yale); and with the Democratic senator Cordell Hull (about a refugee whose asylum case she had taken up, as well as about an article he had promised her). At the White House, she met with Lou Henry Hoover's former secretary, who wanted a job with the *Herald Tribune,* and she made sure that Arthur and Helen Woods were on the president's dinner list and their children invited to the White House Easter party. She ran into Thomas Costain, a historical novelist and editor for the *Saturday Evening Post,* who, she could tell, was trying to acquire White House usher Ike Hoover's manuscript, "Forty Years in the White House." Allegedly, Ike was not interested in publishing the book unless Missy helped him with it, for he, as did other men in the White House, trusted her judgment about which details to keep to himself. In Washington, as in New York, Missy had earned an impeccable reputation for discretion, which she used in spinning her webs behind the scenes.[13]

Borglum was sure that Missy was his best chance for getting to Hoover and securing more matching funds for Mount Rushmore, and he pressed her hard after Hoover's election. Just before leaving office, Coolidge had officially approved Borglum's Rushmore Memorial Commission. Twelve members were to serve on it, and Borglum wanted Missy to be one of them as his "persona grata" in Washington. He begged her to arrange a first meeting of the commission at the White House, with the new president at the head of the table. She was, Borglum reminded her, his "Warwick behind the throne," referring to the kingmaker of Wars of the Roses fame. "Am counting a lot on you Missy," he reminded her. "Hate to confess it but one must count on somebody sometimes entirely."[14]

This was not necessarily the kind of influence with which Missy was comfortable. She insisted that she was tied to her desk in New York, too busy to join the Rushmore Commission, even though she regularly jaunted off to Washington on short notice if that was Hoover's wish. Nevertheless, she did get Borglum his sitting with Hoover so that he could plead his case himself, and Borglum believed that her intervention was what made the difference. "The big memorial is going fine, largely due to your interference, or, rather, your prodding of the Powers That Be at the White House," Borglum soon reported. By June of 1929, he expected to finish blasting enough Black Mountain rock face to begin sculpting the sixty-foot head of George Washington.[15]

Unfortunately, a particularly disruptive event, one soon known in the annals of history as the Great Depression, would cause long delays in Borglum's work. As a consequence, Mount Rushmore did not get completed until 1941, months after the sculptor's death. But Missy helped to keep the project alive, and Borglum was forever grateful. "Really, Missy, I don't know what I would do without you," he wrote her. "You fill such a big place in so many, many ways, and you must not think that I am counting on you simply for service. You are such a nice soul to just think about and realize that you are alive. . . . I am going to write you some of the things I think Hoover ought to do. You managed to sell him to me, or you made it possible for him to sell himself."[16]

Yes, she had gotten the stubborn Borglum to endorse her man—not through any harsh form of coercion, but merely by whispering in a president's ear and facilitating a meeting of men motivated by enough mutual admiration for her to come to an understanding. From then on, she found plenty of ways to make Borglum as helpful to Hoover as Hoover had been to him.

STILL, MISSY'S ABILITY TO SOFTEN Hoover's edges and soothe his fears had limits. All indications in the summer of 1929 were that economic devastation was coming to many sectors of American society. Since Coolidge's departure, the air of anxiety in the White House had only intensified. The timing was unfortunate. Missy was helping Hoover to acclimate to the presidency at the same time she set out to obtain another gram of radium for Curie's institute in Warsaw. Although it helped that the price of radium had halved since 1921, the predictions of economists meant that speedy fund-raising was now obviously crucial. There was no time to organize a nationwide grassroots campaign that appealed to ordinary Americans like the one she had coordinated in 1921, and Hoover would only be able to help her in a limited capacity. Instead, she turned in 1929 to a wealthy and prominent few, namely Mrs. Andrew Carnegie, Mrs. Thomas Alva Edison, and others who had been generous benefactors eight years before. And there was one other potential donor who had not been involved in the first campaign but who Missy nonetheless decided was in the best position to help the scientist this time around, since he was most in need of what Curie could offer in return.[17]

He was the industrialist Owen Young, a business-savvy patriot who was also president of General Electric and founder of the Radio Corporation of America (RCA). Missy had enlisted him a few years earlier to write a piece for *The Delineator* about electrification and labor-saving devices in rural homes, and the two had remained friends. She had sailed back from Europe with him after receiving an honorary French decoration (one of several) for her work for Better Homes. Young was returning from negotiations of German war reparations when Missy turned his attention to Curie. "It is a fact that Madame Curie has not spent one cent except for a pair of shoes, on personal apparel since they were in the United States," she swore to Young, expanding Curie's already well-established American myth. "Every dollar they can get goes into the work," she continued, filling in the story of scientific success that Young knew with the human details that he didn't. Once again the wheels in Missy's head were turning because she saw a mutually beneficial match to be made: Curie needed resources that a General Electric executive could obtain. But Curie also had something to give: her name and celebrity to an institution of higher education. Young was an alumnus and trustee of St. Lawrence University, and he had told Missy of his desire to bolster the national reputation of his alma mater, especially that of its science departments.[18]

So Missy spun her web and connected her friends. Young arranged for more equipment to be installed in Curie's lab and assisted Missy in getting American funds transferred to a French account that the scientist could access. In return, the grateful Curie allowed her likeness to be placed at the entrance of the new chemistry laboratory at St. Lawrence, an opening gesture of what Missy hoped would become yet another American tour. For years, she had been angling for one, but Curie had always been reluctant when Missy broached the subject openly. "You have been so sick and I don't want to add to your fatigue in any effort like that in 1921," Curie would say. "Also my health has not been good, and my children worry that a trip to America would be too much because they cannot accompany me this time." As sure as Curie sounded about wanting to avoid the journey, Missy remained undeterred. She kept asking for the tour, even through Hoover's election. It was her persistence, coupled with Young's generosity, that finally made the difference.[19]

Curie agreed to travel to America in October of 1929, albeit laying out stricter conditions this time. She whittled the tour down to three weeks, insisting on no major events, speaking engagements, large groups, photographs, autographs, or shaking of hands—and she wanted any visit to the White House to be a more subdued affair than the last one. As for requests to travel to Louisiana, Stanford, Yellowstone, and the Polish embassy, they were nonstarters, she told Missy. Fearing she would catch a cold on a long train ride, she requested to stay along the Eastern seaboard, preferably in the reclusive comfort of Missy's house in Pawling, again citing doctors' orders. The priority, she insisted, was fulfilling her obligation to Young, since he figured most prominently in obtaining her gram of radium. Ceremonies at St. Lawrence were really the only public events that she felt compelled to attend.[20]

Missy didn't meet Curie in Paris this time, but she had friends and French officials check in with her on the ship, and she and Bill (now home from France) met Curie at quarantine the moment she debarked in New York. "I will do my best to take care of you and protect you," she assured her anxious friend. "My happy responsibility [i]s to make sure that America d[oes] not kill you with kindness." She had issued press releases beforehand stipulating that Curie would not be taking interviews or allowing photographs from the ship, and that her itinerary had been reduced to "the least possible number of tiring public appearances." Remarkably, the press fell into line. Curie's party went virtually unnoticed as it made its way down a back stairwell to the lower level of the pier and into limousines Missy had waiting. Curie's luggage was sent for later, this time brought to Missy's new apartment at 1 Fifth Avenue. Curie didn't leave Missy's place until the next day, and only to drive to Owen Young's home on Park Avenue. Harlow Brooks then examined her before she and Missy drove up to Pawling, where the women visited friends of the radium fund and attended a modest tree planting. Curie seemed happy as she relaxed in Missy's garden. It was the quiet before her one great concession: the drive west to attend the Edison Jubilee in Dearborn, Michigan.[21]

The jubilee was exactly the sort of American spectacle that made Curie uncomfortable, but Missy insisted that it couldn't be missed. It was put on by none other than Henry Ford in honor of the fiftieth anniversary of Thomas Alva Edison's invention of the incandescent lamp, and he spared no expense. Whole rooms, trees, and buildings from Edison's New Jersey lab and neighborhood had been transferred to Ford's Greenfield Village, where he had an industrial museum installed and Edison's discovery reenacted in front of the enfeebled eighty-two-year-old inventor himself. President Hoover, John D. Rockefeller, Orville Wright, J. P. Morgan, Albert Einstein, and every major newspaper editor in the country were on the guest list of this celebration of American innovation, and yet when Curie arrived she wasn't awed in the least. The wet weather had made her sick and irritable. When guests approached her asking if she would sign their banquet menus, she flatly refused. Missy read her body language easily: she had made her appearance, and now she just wanted to leave.[22]

Owen Young had his driver take Missy and Curie from Detroit to General Electric in Schenectady, New York, where the labs were closed to reporters and all employees except assistants who ran experiments at Curie's request. The only person who had enjoyed such unfettered access to the labs before was Charles Lindbergh, when he was invited to inspect the company's aeronautical instruments. Curie stayed that night at Young's home in the hamlet of Van Hornesville, insulated from crowds and newspaper coverage of the foreboding market erosion that was becoming apparent on Wall Street. That weekend in Canton, she dedicated the new chemistry building at St. Lawrence and, at Young's urging, received an honorary degree. Young and Missy flanked the scientist at the rear of a grand processional from the campus library to the chapel, where some one thousand students and visitors rose in tribute. George Pegram of Columbia's physics department gave the welcoming address, lauding Curie's "steadfast devotion to science, her patriotic service, her modesty." "We honor her as a wife and mother," he continued. "The nobility of her life is such that our admiration for her character almost turns our attention from her scientific rank." It was much the same saintly rhetoric Curie had heard during the tour eight years before. But on this visit she heard it sparingly, since Missy pushed the maternal narrative with less insistence now. Without more ado, Young escorted Curie to the dais to receive her degree.[23]

At the door of St. Lawrence's gray-stoned Hepburn Hall of Chemistry stood a statue with a saint-like portrayal of Curie. Missy sat to her right as Curie gave the one public address she had agreed to give, again audible only to those directly in front of her. The single activity Curie seemed to relish that day was the tree planting west of the building. Young offered a small shovel, which Curie refused for a bigger one, and with it she vigorously cast aside piles of soil. Young awkwardly handled the miniature implement that had been reserved for his guest, adding some unexpected comic relief.[24]

The next day was Black Tuesday, the date of the infamous stock market crash, but Missy didn't let it impact her plans. Just as she had taken advantage of her ties to Coolidge and Harding to finagle a White House ceremony for Curie in 1921, she managed a more subdued White House event with Hoover in 1929. No one stood more squarely in the eye of the financial storm than this president, and yet he and the First Lady quietly hosted Curie at the White House without uttering a peep about the failing economy. The following evening at the National Academy of Sciences, scientists and members of the diplomatic corps gathered for another ceremonial gift to Curie, this time in the form of a check. Given the financial circumstances surrounding them, nothing was said about the amount written on it, and Missy saw no reason to draw attention to the monetary transaction when Curie's admirers seemed, for the time being, perfectly entranced in the great scientist's presence.[25]

With the big public events of the tour out of the way, Curie returned to New York and took casual dinners in the homes of the Meads and the Reids and even stole an opportunity to go out alone with Missy to a Broadway cinema to see her first talking film. The only formal Manhattan event Missy booked was a dinner of the Society for the Control of Cancer at the Hotel Plaza. And respecting Curie's preference not to speak, Missy gave her own speech and arranged to have it broadcasted over radio so more people could hear it, without Curie having to interact with anyone directly. On November 5, the New York Federation of Women's Clubs honored Curie with a medal, which they presented in Missy's living room. Two days later, on Curie's sixty-second birthday, a handful of Missy's friends celebrated the scientist quietly at the apartment; the Guggenheims, Rockefellers, and Bradys sent gifts and flowers, but didn't burden Curie with an appearance. That afternoon, Curie and Missy motored in Central Park and visited the J. P. Morgan library before dining with the Youngs on Park Avenue; the following day, Missy gave one last luncheon for Curie and the Polish foreign minister before taking her friend to the piers. The presence of paparazzi awaiting Curie was minimal. Personnel on the

Île de France took precautions to shield Curie from the other passengers as she boarded. In planning this tour, Missy had honored Curie's request for restraint, and yet she still had managed to put her in touch with the people who could help her the most. Once again, Missy had woven webs without drawing too much attention to them.[26]

IN 1921, MISSY'S PUBLICITY had generated an image of Curie that overshadowed the reality of her as a working mother or competent scientist. Now, in 1929, American reporters sensed Curie's greater focus on science for science's sake, and although most couldn't get close enough to her to commentate further, a few were unsparing in the details of her reclusive brooding. Yale radiochemist Bertram Boltwood, in fact, decried her single-mindedness in the press, accusing her of making "a good clean up" in America as it fell into economic collapse. Without Missy's tight control over messaging, this time the Curie who emerged in newspapers, when at all, seemed myopic about her science and uncaring about anything else. If it was a bad look, Missy herself had become less apologetic about working with focus and didn't see a need to correct it. Widowhood had hastened the transformation, though such intensity had always been a part of both her and Curie. Perhaps she would have insisted on different optics had she been running another publicity campaign for the masses rather than one for a wealthy few. This tour had become a rare instance of Missy making a big ask to a handful of people without offering more in return. But for Curie, she did it willingly.[27]

If Curie didn't recognize her good fortune in leaving New York moments before the Great Depression with a $50,000 check in hand, Missy most certainly did. Knowing a crash was coming, she had refused any more excuses to postpone the second tour and had gotten Curie out of the country before anyone resented their generosity. Owen Young used his Belgian connections to secure a cheaper price for the radium than what Americans were willing to sell it for. Not only had Missy arranged with Andrew Carnegie's widow to fund another round of Curie Institute fellowships; she had also prevailed upon the Fords to finance another car for Curie in France (hence Curie's mandatory appearance at the Jubilee), and the Moses family a chauffeur to drive it to and from Curie's lab in Paris. The frail scientist could live in the country while continuing to do her research, as she had told Missy she dreamed of doing. Apparently not even an economic crash could deter Missy from fulfilling her plans for Curie's long game. With her uncommon ability to make people useful to each other, she helped Hoover to get his presidential victory, Borglum his funding, and Curie her coveted radium—and just in the nick of time.[28]

Chapter Ten

BEING USEFUL IN A GREAT DEPRESSION
1930–1932

MISSY USHERED IN THE NEW DECADE with a Christmas card that featured a cartoon of a topless Santa:

Lost his shirt but not his heart—coming back next year with a whole new outfit. Blessings on you,

Missy[1]

She was being optimistic: the country's number of unemployed shot up from 1.5 million in 1929 to 4.3 million a year later. Still, during the upcoming years of job loss and economic free fall, Missy would find endless ways to be useful to journalists, artists, writers, and the president himself. She served on the planning committee of Hoover's conference on child health and protection, picking up where she had left off in previous administrations. And having formed a federal committee on unemployment, Hoover asked Missy to recommend members. Arthur Woods naturally came to mind to head it up since he had worked with Bill on veterans' unemployment after World War I. She also suggested Edward Bernays, thinking that the work of the committee would involve propaganda to large degree. Perhaps more surprisingly, she also suggested Lillian Gilbreth, a specialist in scientific management in the home as well as a self-fashioned expert on women's work outside it. Indeed, although Missy was concerned about how all Americans fared during the Great Depression, she was uniquely sensitive to the plight of women, especially the ones who worked.[2]

In reviewing her projects and activities during those years, it's clear that she believed the time was over for glorifying contented domesticity at the expense of addressing women's economic survival. Working women needed strategies for running households on shoestring budgets, without servants, and during the second shift. Missy rebranded the *Herald Tribune* Home Institute as a lifeline for not only full-time homemakers but all women and families surviving the Great Depression. An advisory council that included Martha Van Rensselaer, Children's Bureau director Grace Abbott, home economist Louise Stanley, and Dr. Edna Noble White of the Merrill-Palmer Institute focused less on domestic perfection and more on thrift and efficiency. Long a proponent of standardization in the home, Missy now insisted it was the key to weathering the financial downturn. While designing stripped-down residential demo rooms for the Home Institute, she noticed over fifteen hundred colors of pots and kettles to choose from for the kitchen and over one hundred shades of "buff" for the bathroom alone. Deciding that all that choice was costly, in June 1930 she organized a Color Conference at the *Herald Tribune* that brought industry manufacturers together to consolidate their offerings. That month she also hired Lillian Gilbreth to design a test kitchen to meet the needs of families on budgets, and smaller kitchenettes for dual-income couples. For the BHA, she soon had Gilbreth design a stripped-down "clothery" (combination laundry / sewing room) and nursery for the BHA's "America's Little House," keeping standardization, affordability, and efficiency in mind.[3]

Missy saw the facilitation of domestic thrift as an important strategy for American women, but now she also wanted to ensure their ability to work for a wage outside the home. Her engagement of working women, which had certainly been evident in her *Delineator* days, became more of a priority throughout the 1920s. She became vice president of the Carroll Club, a Catholic organization started by the radium fund's Genevieve Brady; its mission was to sponsor career development and recreation for its working-class members. Many of them were seamstresses, so Missy mobilized them to appear at the Capitol to protest the Vestal Bill, which, with its copyright protections on patterns, had placed undue financial burdens on women who earned money by making garments. At the Carroll Club's anniversary dinner right before the stock market crash, Missy intensified her annual plea for donations to enlarge the summer camp in Pawling that she had established for working women, advancing the logic that she and Curie had come to live by: that long workdays in the city were sustainable so long as one occasionally rehabilitated in nature. She pushed the burgeoning fields of advertising and public relations as gateways into white-collar work for Carroll members, reminding them that they were already intuitive about cultural trends and practiced in mass mobilization through their churches, clubs, and chambers of commerce. And public-relations work could be service work, she told them, the Curie campaign serving as a case in point.[4]

Widowhood had forced Missy to embrace self-sufficiency and no doubt caused her to think more about women's economic dependence on men and also about the self-esteem women gained from having the skills to help themselves. She had always supported women who needed to work, but in the worsening economy she recalibrated her ideal balance between work in and outside the home so that it better matched American women's financial conditions. To an ever greater extent she identified with hard-working women across professions and class lines. Work skills she had once advanced for unmarried women at the *Woman's Magazine* she now thought useful—no, necessary—both in and out of marriage.

If her ideas about women's work seem obvious, at the time they defied the consensus of most male employers and policymakers. Commentators in the 1930s criticized women for taking jobs that "belonged to men" and supposedly unmanning them in the process. A Gallup poll in the mid-1930s revealed that 82 percent of Americans believed that a wife should relinquish her job if her husband already had one. But Missy understood that most ire against working women was misplaced. Indeed, male workers in heavy industrial sectors lost jobs in devastating numbers in the early 1930s, but they didn't lose them to women. And though women who worked in already-feminized service sectors—waitressing, laundressing, and other pink-collar trades—looked to be better off in comparison since fewer of them lost jobs, that was often because they were already underemployed in part-time, seasonal, and underpaid work. The fact was that most women working outside the home in the 1930s occupied positions that men hadn't wanted. And even when people objected to women as primary breadwinners as a matter of old-fashioned principle, women were stepping into that role whether they preferred to or not. Some 1.5 million husbands abandoned their families during the Depression; their wives sometimes had no choice but to make a wage to keep their households afloat. These women struggled with the double burden of housekeeping and wage earning as a matter of survival, so rather than ignore their growing numbers Missy used her platform to champion them and help them succeed in their simultaneous tasks.[5]

Although Missy's job was secure at the *Herald Tribune,* she knew of many female journalists who were being let go at American newspapers in the 1930s. She fought to help them earn a living, imparting her wisdom on occasion at Columbia's school of journalism and growing increasingly active in the New York Newspaper Women's Club. Founded by Martha Coman of the *Herald* in the early 1920s, this organization formalized the gatherings of women journalists who had covered the suffrage movement of the 1910s. A few other female press clubs already existed; Jane Cunningham Croly's Woman's Press Club of New York and the Woman's National Press Association in Washington had been social outlets for women journalists since the 1880s, but Missy had not joined these organizations as an up-and-coming reporter. At the time, she hadn't sought out female camaraderie so much as the acceptance of male colleagues, but her attitude had changed. Now she was well enough established outside the realm of women's magazines to feel as though she could be useful to other women trying to enter the field of hard news. She was elected the first vice president of the New York Newspaper Women's Club in 1929, and she accepted reelection to the position every year until the end of her life.[6]

It proved to be of genuine consequence to women journalists that Missy had influence in the White House, for she may have helped to keep a few of them on the Washington beat. Herbert Hoover had been attending annual Gridiron Club dinners exclusively for male reporters, but the First Lady evidently hadn't considered cultivating relationships with women reporters until Missy suggested that she host them at Rapidan Camp in 1932 and create a feminine White House beat for them to cover. Building these relationships could bring good publicity to her husband's reelection bid, Missy told the First Lady, while boosting up women who were trying to make ends meet as reporters. To maintain the president's popularity with women voters, she also recommended that Hoover allow stories to be run about his female appointments. He had selected women to serve not only in the expected Children's Bureau but also in the Federal Income Tax Bureau, the US Housing Corps, the Employees Compensation Commission, and the Office of Education and Indian Affairs. Not surprisingly, she recommended that these articles be written by female journalists.[7]

Missy's soft spot for female reporters extended to starving artists whose work had dried up with the failing economy. In the 1930s she managed to find or make work for the artists Joseph Cummings Chase, Leonebel Jacobs, and Edward Suydam, best known for his American cityscapes. But she worried, too, about the up-and-coming writers who, due to the dire times, might never be discovered. "An unknown Walter Lippmann, knocking on an editor's door, would not get in," she feared. "The Booth Tarkingtons and Willa Cathers and Edna Millays of this young generation have little chance to survive." She kept writing assignments flowing to the talented Helen

Simpson, a pregnant woman who struggled in the thirties to pay rent and keep up her writing. She lobbied book publishers to buy the poetry of Ada Jackson, and she solicited her prominent writer friends to donate signed first editions of their books to be sold at auction, the proceeds to go toward a relief fund for novice authors. Thinking even more broadly, she convened established literary figures to propose that university faculties and publishers employ young writers to travel to "the backwashes of America" to lecture on cultural topics for six-week stints, with compensation enough to cover their living expenses so they could spend the rest of the calendar year writing.[8]

When most others around her lacked vision beyond their immediate needs, Missy was planning for the future. Witnessing the diminishment of acquisition lists at libraries and museums, she tried earnestly to thwart the trend, raising funds for the Facsimile Text Society to reproduce rare and historic books. Along with proposing stipends for artists, she came up with a project called "Collective Thought on This Crisis in History," which provided cultural custodianship similar to that of the Works Progress Administration to come. Soliciting essays on the current economic crisis from prominent journalists, poets, playwrights, historians, novelists, scientists, educators, industrialists, economists, theologians, and politicians, she proposed creating a time capsule to be housed at the Library of Congress.[9]

At a late-night get-together in Leonebel Jacobs's studio in the Hotel des Artistes, the journalist Louis Seibold mused about Missy's tireless efforts on everyone else's behalf. "Nobody else could stand the amount of work that Missy does—and live," he surmised.

> The only reason she is alive to-day is that she is so taken up with helping other people, that she never has a moment to notice whether she herself is well or ill....One day she's helping President Hoover, the next day she's taking care of Leonebel, and the next she's worrying about my welfare, or more likely, all of us on the same day. And the day after that there are a dozen other people she's planning for and looking after. And,

mind you, all this besides getting out the best Magazine Section there is and spending more time on it than any other editor does. Our tiny little Missy, mothering and business-managing Madame Curie and the Hoovers and the rest of us, is the biggest fine story in the United States.[10]

IN MAKING HIS ASSESSMENT OF MISSY, Seibold hadn't even mentioned the greatest of her Depression-era innovations. In desperate times, she believed that a nation needed its creative souls and brilliant minds more than usual. Artists and intellectuals were struggling and newspapers folding, just when Americans sought inspiration and to be educated out of the doldrums. She had been doing her part to keep ideas in circulation by editing a civic-minded Sunday magazine, but she wanted to do more. And thus, amidst all the other service work and editing duties she had already taken on, she came up with one of the most ambitious of her grand ideas—the *Herald Tribune* Annual Forum on Current Problems—and followed through with a focus at which everyone marveled. It became an esteemed conference of national scope, and it lived on as a paragon of civic engagement well past the Great Depression.

The kernel for the idea had been planted in 1930. Program chairwomen of New York–area women's clubs had been eager to rechannel their efforts to meet the dire times, and they sought Missy's guidance. As a logical extension of the civic campaigns she had already sponsored, she suggested running a local roundtable, but to give it prestige she proposed once again bringing important men into the fold. She offered her connections to the "best informed men in the country," inviting them to discuss the state of the nation and the part women should play in alleviating the social and economic ills of the age. Initially, the registrants for the event were fifty area clubwomen, but of course in Missy's hands that pool grew exponentially. Fifteen hundred women ended up attending the Forum in the first year alone. Even with the expansion of conference space on the eighth floor of the

Herald Tribune building, Missy was forced to relocate the inaugural conference to the Astor Hotel.[11]

Pleas to make the Forum an annual event were immediate. Missy held every Forum thereafter at the Waldorf Astoria to accommodate overflow, and soon people clamored not just to attend but also to get on the speaker lists that Missy carefully compiled to address topics she thought in most need of discussion on a national stage. Each year, tens of thousands of participants from the contiguous forty-eight states, Alaska, and Canada, as well as speakers of national and international reputation, converged in the ballroom of the Waldorf Astoria to discuss a range of topics that included the economy, presidential elections, fascism, incarceration, education, movies, marijuana, sports, national security, medicine, war, marriage, and the very essence of what it means to be American.[12]

Missy called the event simply "The Forum," because that was the operative term. She explained that forums were among the oldest institutions of an open society, occurring as long ago as ancient Athens. They existed for "the discussion of the mighty questions which determine the destiny of free men," and now the destiny of free women too. The relevance of maintaining this format became stark as the 1930s progressed and the economic and cultural problems of the Great Depression bumped up against the dire political consequences of fascist regimes coming into power in Europe. Particularly as Adolf Hitler's intentions for conquest and elimination of "non-Aryans" grew clear in Germany, Missy insisted that there was no more important counteracting force than the free and open discussion facilitated by her Forum. And she made no apologies about drawing women into this public discourse and declaring them crucial to alleviating the nation's problems. This wasn't the time to restrict women to the domestic sphere, or to cordon off the domestic sphere in American minds as a realm having no relevance to the fate of the nation or international affairs. The Forum brought women into public and political conversations, and it made a greater number of these conversations about women.[13]

The point, of course, was wide participation, and yet the broad range of people and perspectives Missy had in mind posed logistical problems. Even as she relocated the Forum to the much larger ballroom of the Waldorf Astoria, she had to turn away thousands who wanted to sit in on the three days of sessions. Looking for a way to make her event more accessible, Missy turned to the burgeoning medium of radio. She had long been urging American homemakers to have a radio in the kitchen to connect them to the outside world and had mastered the use of the airwaves to communicate with homemakers through programs she produced on household tips and the arts. Soon NBC was broadcasting the Forum's keynote speakers and panel speeches throughout the country. Scott Bone reported from Santa Barbara, California, that Missy's voice reached him "as clear as a bell." "It put me into a reverie and sent my thoughts back to good days in Washington, so long gone," he reminisced, unbelieving of how far Missy had expanded her audience and reach since her cub-reporter days in Washington.[14]

FEW PEOPLE WERE BUSIER or more civically engaged than Missy during those early years of the Great Depression. Friends, including Seibold, thought it only a matter of time before she paid the physical toll—and she did. As early as the summer of 1930, she had confided to a few people that she hadn't been well. She was taking long weekends at the farmhouse, hoping that the mountain air would hasten her recuperation. She had obtained the deed to an old schoolhouse near her property with the intention of making it a livable home for Bill and Elizabeth when she could afford to refurbish it. Pregnant, Elizabeth had been renting nearby, while Bill lectured at Columbia, studied law, and worked for Bill Donovan's Manhattan law firm. During the week he slept at the University Club in the city, only coming upstate to see his wife on Sundays. Missy hoped that the renovated schoolhouse would give Bill and Elizabeth their own space, as well as a financial reprieve. It would also bring Bill closer to her when she was in

Pawling, for the truth was that she could use his physical assistance from time to time.[15]

Missy saw Curie in May of 1931, when she traveled to Paris from London. Amidst her usual meetings, she was to dine with the British prime minister and to take Ève Curie to tea before returning to Paris. Curie was so excited to see Missy that she played hooky from the lab to go driving with her for an entire afternoon. In a reversal of roles, she scheduled an appointment for Missy to see a Paris chest specialist and admonished her when she broke the appointment. Missy promised to undergo a thorough examination in New York, but all indications were that she continued to work unabated until the first of August, when she joined the Hoovers for a three-day weekend at Rapidan Camp. The year before, she had had a pleasant time motoring down with President Hoover, but this year's trip with the First Lady was harrowing. In the car she felt woozy; once she arrived at Rapidan, she lost her balance and fell, striking her shoulder and falling unconscious. When she came to, she had a mouth full of blood, and no one was exactly sure why.[16]

With everyone sufficiently concerned about her, Missy was transported back to New York and told to remain off her feet completely. Instead of heeding the advice, however, she spent the next few weeks working through pain. On August 24 she had been in the office for two hours when she spiked a fever, followed by an excruciating headache that finally forced her to go home. She was given drugs for the pain, and when it didn't improve, Mary Day, her good friend and assistant editor, came over with salicylates, which nauseated Missy. At five the next morning, Day called Dr. Morrison, Harlow Brooks's stand-in while he was out of town, and he gave Missy a shot of morphine. By then, she was so sleep deprived that Leonebel Jacobs took her to stay at her studio to escape all distractions and to rest. When Brooks checked in with Missy from out of town, she told him that she was better, but the nurse tending to her reported differently: Missy had pain in her abdomen, her arm, and under her ribs, and her headaches persisted for another five days, unalleviated by ice caps or aspirin. She still was keeping nothing down; medications and painkillers had to be administered rectally. She coughed up some of the mucus clogging her lungs, which was clear at first but then streaked with blood, much to the concern of her caregivers.[17]

Never had she been too indisposed to come to a president's aid, especially Hoover's, but in the fall of 1931 Missy had to decline committees for his Conference on Home Building and Home Partnership. She also had to say no to the journalist Irvin Cobb when he asked her to join the volunteer staff on his Depression-era Speakers' Committee; doctors forbade her from attending the outdoor events he had in mind. It was bad timing when the pilot Lester Maitland wrote her about resuscitating his stunt career by publicizing his flight from Tokyo to New York. Normally she would have asked him to chronicle the flight for the *Sunday Magazine,* but this time she admitted that she was simply too ill to make the calls to find sponsors or to do the public-relations legwork for it. She finally conceded to Harlow Brooks that she felt "like jelly in the bottom of a cup," that her brain was "sluggish," and that her latest trip to Pawling had taken everything out of her. Interior Secretary Ray Lyman Wilbur heard that she was suffering from chills and diarrhea and assumed that it was a relapse of tuberculosis. "We will not expect you to do one single thing for BETTER HOMES for the present," he assured her. "For the sake of every one, do nothing that will bring down your weight, reduce your strength, or interfere with your full and complete recovery." Keeping to his advice, Missy didn't plan a Forum in 1931, despite the success of the inaugural one the year before.[18]

The event that preoccupied her instead that autumn was the birth of a grandson, not so surprisingly named William Brown Meloney VI. She celebrated the birth of this next generation while at the same time making new arrangements to pay the monthly bills for her own invalid mother, who remarkably was still living in a medical facility in Stamford. Her good friend Mina Bruere, founder of the Association of

Bank Women, had been keeping track of Missy's expenditures, sending payments out on her behalf. But now Missy told her lawyer, Henry Moses, that she wanted Bruere to have power of attorney in the case of her own death, which was unavoidably on her mind. With sudden urgency, she revised her will and testament, leaving most of her assets to Bill and earmarking keepsakes for family members and friends. Her father's antique medicine cabinet was to go to Harlow Brooks; a locket containing a picture of her brother to his widow; an ivory Madonna, ten books of his choosing, and letters of Calvin Coolidge to Dr. Menas Gregory. Even as she contemplated death, she was determined to stay useful to her loved ones.[19]

She was far more particular in her directives about Bill Sr.'s writings than any of her own. Drafts of his uncompleted works were to be destroyed, as Missy didn't think he would have wanted them circulated. However, she authorized young Bill to seek counsel regarding his father's unpublished psychological study of Woodrow Wilson and several of his sea poems and finished plays. One copy of Bill's "Life of John Purroy Mitchel" had been stored in the files of Yale University Press, one in her storeroom, and one with her son, and she gave two trunks of papers substantiating the controversial claims in the manuscript to the Library of Congress for safekeeping. Missy kept an itemized list of those contents in a leather hat box that contained the original manuscript, and she requested that her son make final edits before seeking its publication. As for letters that had been written by Bill, she asked that her son hold them for ten years before selectively publishing them—again, not for her sake but for her husband's.[20]

She was a custodian of legacies who never considered her own as particularly remarkable. Writing devotedly to Missy in these months, Curie begged to tell her differently: "My very dear friend, don't think of ending your life while you are young and full of generous thoughts for future work.... Think of how sorry you make those who appreciate and love you as I do." She accepted that Missy wouldn't be able to attend the inauguration of the Warsaw Radium Institute that spring, but insisted on a tree-planting ceremony in her absence. Curie wanted Missy honored in her home country, just as Curie had been honored in Missy's.[21]

———

MISSY STAVED OFF DEATH ONCE AGAIN. By February of 1932 she was writing friends and authors as she always had, assuring them that she was over the worst. Although confined to bed that March, she told the psychologist Havelock Ellis that she was editing the *Sunday Magazine* as usual and that he should continue sending her drafts. "You know better than most people that we can work while the body is halted," she casually added. She was especially eager to start fulfilling the promises she had made to Mary Purroy Mitchel, the mother of the war-hero mayor, who passed away that April. Mary had put family papers and keepsakes in Missy's hands to arrange for deposit at Columbia and the City University. Missy made the annual pilgrimage to John Purroy Mitchel's grave that summer, as she had devotedly done for fourteen years, but this time his mother lay beside him. Now Missy felt as though she was the only one alive who could do justice to their family legacy.[22]

Meanwhile, back in Washington and in upstate New York, there was much political work to be accomplished. Elections were coming up in November, and Missy was committed not only to Hoover's reelection but to Bill Donovan's New York gubernatorial run. In fact, she had been a primary impetus for Donovan's campaign. Hoover had snubbed him for attorney general in 1929, and insiders suspected that his Catholicism had been the reason, a political calculation that crushed both Missy and Donovan's Protestant wife. Hoover asked him instead to be governor-general of the Philippines, but Donovan refused the post. He told Missy that he wasn't bitter, only grateful for what she had tried to make happen for him, and he reiterated how much he valued her friendship. But Missy wouldn't let his political ambitions die. The surest road to the presidency had in the past been by way of the New York governorship, so that was where she focused him for 1932.[23]

Understanding positioning and optics, she had lined up high-visibility events that brought Donovan in contact with key Protestant leaders and New York "drys," as supporters of Prohibition were known. In the meantime, she urged him to write on the judiciary and law enforcement, issues she thought would poll well with female New York voters. She also put her candidate in touch with Edward Bernays, an expert on mass persuasion, whether for hawking products or candidates. He had helped Belle Moskowitz shape Al Smith's gubernatorial platform to appeal to working-class voters, and she hoped that he could do the same for Donovan. Of course, Missy generated her share of publicity too, portraying "Wild Bill" as a self-made lawyer and public servant—a gutsy, high-minded war hero in the vein of Teddy Roosevelt.[24]

As if to make up for the bed rest the year before, Missy planned a full itinerary for the *Herald Tribune* Forum in the fall of 1932. Because it was scheduled to take place weeks before the presidential election, she looked for ways to position Hoover in a favorable light. In the midst of the Great Depression, it wasn't easy. She broke with her own protocol at the *Sunday Magazine* and paid William Allen White double the normal rate for a piece she considered the strongest case in print for Hoover's reelection. Then she published the piece to coincide with Hoover's Forum address on the importance of protecting the welfare of children, which she broadcasted from the White House to the Waldorf Astoria and then over the national airwaves.[25]

Of course, the Forum could not just be about Hoover. Missy made sure that the Democratic presidential candidate, Franklin Delano Roosevelt (FDR), got his time, and other prominent figures made prescient calls for world peace. Virginia Gildersleeve, dean of Barnard College, read aloud a letter written by Curie on this topic; despite her reservations about giving public statements, Curie could never say no to Missy. Owen Young closed his remarks at the Forum by expressing "admiration of the spirit and courage of 'Missy' Meloney, as she is affectionately called by her friends." He described her to the audience as "unconquerable," but only Helen Reid and a handful of others in that ballroom understood all the meaning wrapped up in the term. He was grateful that Missy was to live another day.[26]

His unconquerable friend ended up faring better than her candidates that November. In the throes of the Depression, many voters were desperate to overthrow the party in charge in favor of candidates who appeared to be reformers, and Donovan's service record wasn't enough to blind them to the R next to his name. He lost the gubernatorial race to Democrat Herbert Lehman, and Hoover the presidency to FDR, who captured 472 of 531 electoral votes and won majorities in every state but six.[27]

Hoover knew that his loss was not because of Missy. "I am grateful that I have had such friendship, and I am sure we may all look forward with confidence to the results that will come from the work we have done together," he wrote her after the election. Already he clung to the hope that his legacy would improve with the perspective of time. He needed to feel that he would be vindicated by history, because in the current moment he felt scapegoated, impotent in the face of economic devastation, and ousted by a man with whom he fundamentally disagreed. In the weeks leading up to FDR's inauguration, Missy asked Hoover if he would like an opportunity to defend himself with a parting piece in her magazine, but he told her he wasn't ready. For now, he just wanted her to know what her support had meant to him: "The building up of the Better Homes movement, the Child Health Association and many other activities have been in large degree the result of your able and persistent action. . . . I owe to you many added obligations of purely personal character which are difficult to express in words. I know, however, that you feel in your heart the appreciation which both Mrs. Hoover and I have for your long continued friendship."[28]

Curie had always told Missy that she didn't think it proper for her, a French woman, to comment publicly on American politics, but she knew that, for her friend, Hoover's loss was personal. "I feel sorry for

Mr. Hoover who surely did his best under most difficult conditions," she wrote Missy that November. "I wonder if you have succeeded in deciding whether you [are] to stand by him as previously, or to accept the [election] of Mr. Roosevelt." Curie got right to the heart of the matter, raising an unusual conundrum for a woman who had always been more patriotic than partisan, more pragmatic than fanatical for any single politician. Missy had believed in Hoover the man as well as in his political ideology, for she was leery of dipping too much into public funds to bring relief even to Americans who were suffering greatly. Becoming reliant on paternalistic government was "contrary to the American character," she insisted, and "violently contrary to the spirit of the pioneers." And yet Hoover's measures had been no match for the economic crisis, and his public persona no match for that of his dynamic rival—a Roosevelt not of the Oyster Bay variety but who was a distant Democratic cousin to that side of the family, and whose plan for mitigating the damage of the Depression countered Hoover's in every way. FDR was likable, politically talented, and open to untried ideas. Although his New Deal embodied the Big Government that Missy thought potentially corrupting, it demonstrated the urgency that Americans wanted in 1932.[29]

Missy did not abandon the Hoovers or the Republican Party. When Theodore Roosevelt Jr. called on her marketing savoir faire to sell the National Republican Club to "the younger element," she gladly helped him. But she was too much the facilitator to refuse to work with the new administration, and she almost immediately established herself as its friend rather than adversary. Preceding the inauguration, as speculation abounded over FDR's cabinet picks, she was already showing the soon-to-be president's personal secretary, Louis Howe, her copy on potential labor secretary selection Frances Perkins, allowing him to edit it before it went to print. She would continue to show the administration goodwill every fall, when draft itineraries of the *Herald Tribune* Forums went to the president and First Lady in advance so that they could tweak the speaker lists. In return for her professional courtesy, FDR entrusted Missy with an uncharacteristically candid piece about his polio and rehabilitation at Warm Springs. Soon he was welcoming her to the White House with regularity and engaging her ideas, as Republican presidents had before him.[30]

Under the Democratic New Deal, Missy's municipal work didn't wane. New York Mayor Fiorello La Guardia carved out a PR position for her on the New York State and City "Milk Month" committees, which promoted the buying and drinking of milk to keep dairy prices down and promoted healthier diets among the poor. With all the more urgency, she continued to serve on the planning committee for the annual White House Conference on Children's Health, to run child-welfare conferences under the auspices of the New York State and City Federations of Women's Clubs, and to mobilize consumer drives in the women's auxiliary of FDR's National Recovery Administration (NRA). When Republican men avoided negotiations across the aisle, she talked to them behind the scenes to encourage bipartisan collaboration. Missy was loyal to people and principles, not to parties, and there were still too many ways to be useful during those years of the Great Depression.[31]

Chapter Eleven

FEMALE FRIENDS, FORUMS, FASCISTS, AND FREEDOM OF SPEECH

1933–1934

MISSY KNEW THAT IT WOULD be tricky to fit in all the themes and discussions she wanted addressed at the *Herald Tribune* Forum of 1933. There was no ignoring the rise of fascist regimes in Europe, but there was also the drastic change of tactics for rebuilding the domestic economy brought about by the New Deal. She relied on a vast number of *Herald Tribune* contributors who were experts in international and domestic affairs—men like the Italian writer and political dissident Carlo Sforza and heads of FDR's cabinet and bureaus. But the individual whose perspective she eventually sought out most was someone who was both very much in tune with the administration and increasingly a personal friend—the First Lady, Eleanor Roosevelt.

The six-foot-tall Democrat couldn't have appeared more different from Missy, and yet in ways personal and professional Eleanor was her kindred spirit—a similar combination of "idea person" and "people person" who drew others to her and her causes. She, too, had eschewed the formal suffrage ranks for war relief and had been a stay-at-home mother who wanted to be useful in public life. Neither wealth nor prestige factored into her judgments of people, and thus like Missy's her network was wide, broad, and eclectic. Neither woman was possessive of her friends; in fact, each often brought friends together to forge bonds on their own. Empathetic leaders by nature and magnets for allies, they were women whose personal philosophies and social circles overlapped, despite their affiliations with opposing political parties. Because both prioritized principles and personal relationships over platforms, they represented a different sort of political operative than most of the men around them.[1]

Through New York reform circles, Missy already knew the "Lady's Brain Trust" of the Democratic Party. She had sat on any number of fund-raising, welcoming, memorial, philanthropic, education, and farewell committees with these women, including one that had honored Eleanor Roosevelt as the First Lady of New York. Indeed, in state politics Eleanor had already carved out a life independent of her husband's, following his affair with her social secretary in the 1910s. She had her own car, her own work, and an entire homosocial world separate from the president's. Thus, although Missy became a frequent guest of the First Couple at the White House, more often she saw Eleanor alone, either upstate or in Manhattan, where they each had residences. In these private moments they cultivated a deep friendship and mutual understanding, much like what Missy had with Curie. It was a loyal bond that turned into a formidable political alliance, albeit one virtually undetected within formal party channels. These two women became more helpful to each other personally and politically than anyone would have suspected at the time. In a political world seemingly dominated by men, Missy and Eleanor understood the value of female friendship.[2]

Despite their different titles—editor and First Lady—their accumulated experience in public life was strikingly similar. Missy had edited the *Woman's Magazine* and *The Delineator* and didn't seem at first glance to be a political insider. Eleanor, a political insider, had edited *Babies—Just Babies* and the *Women's Democratic News,* and had written for *Collier's, Redbook,* and other women's magazines, experiences that gave her a heightened acuity with print media and some authority with female readers. Eleanor Roosevelt proved to be the most media-savvy presidential spouse that the country had yet seen, and Missy furthered her education, turning her into a First Lady for modern times. Both were masters of the press conference, the syndicated column, the radio show, the editorial, and the lecture circuit, all of which they utilized to augment their influence. Missy helped Eleanor to fine-tune her messaging behind the scenes and, as she had with Lou Henry Hoover, to turn female reporters into allies.[3]

Although some twelve thousand female journalists now worked throughout the country, they still were largely relegated to writing for women's magazines or women's pages, with limited access to "newsmakers" of power or import. Even the handful of women who covered Washington politics were barred from the National Press Club and excluded from White House press briefings (a practice called "skirting"), and they suffered lower pay and less job security than male reporters. But being the enterprising woman Missy was, she saw in the Depression an opportunity, not just to popularize the human-interest story or to generate revenues by tapping female readerships, but also for women to gain esteem as journalists—and the First Lady would help her do it. Once again, she identified another mutually beneficial match to be made. Eleanor could support women journalists as working women, and women reporters could become mouthpieces for her causes and her husband's administration. Associated Press reporter Lorena Hickok had covered Eleanor as New York's First Lady and confirmed the potential of this relationship, proposing all-female press conferences once Eleanor reached the White House. Now that she was there, Eleanor seized on the idea of women journalists as "interpreters" of the "legislative," "social," and "personal" life of the White House. It was a role that Missy had, in effect, assumed as a woman's editor for decades and now was passing on to the next generation of women.[4]

On the morning of March 6, 1933, male reporters were shocked to see thirty-five of their female colleagues convened in the Green Room of the White House and ushered into the private living area on the second floor. Eleanor walked in with a bowl of candied fruit and passed it around, diffusing all sense of formality. In time the women reporters grew accustomed to sitting on the arms of chairs or on the floor to accommodate the overflow among their ranks. Embracing the informal ambiance, some even took a seat on the couch right next to the First Lady, who seemed not to mind the intimacy. Emma Bugbee told Eleanor that she was curious about the White House living quarters, so Eleanor invited women reporters to a casual lunch and a tour, consenting to their writing about what they saw. "This house belongs to the people and they have a right to know what it looks like," she insisted. No longer were the First Lady and her habitat observed from a distance. Missy's insider access to the White House was now shared by dozens of women reporters.[5]

Eleanor Roosevelt was the first presidential wife to attend an American Newspaper Women's Club tea with her daughter, and the first to invite members of the Women's National Press Club to put on skits at a "Gridiron Widows Party" at the White House. On that occasion she frolicked in peasant attire alongside female journalists who coordinated costumes to portray the Dionne quintuplets. Missy wore a costume made by famed puppeteer Tony Sarg—an elephant with donkey ears, appearing unambiguously bipartisan. The winner of the cleverest-costume contest donned a black dress liberally decorated with acronyms representing a spate of federal agencies: "The Mystery of the New Deal." The more women reporters interacted with the First Lady socially, the more they liked her and grew protective of her. In confidence, they would tell her when they thought she shouldn't broach a topic on the record. When she invited them to picnics on weekends at Hyde Park, they used discretion in writing up what they witnessed of her personal life. This was a First Lady who checked in on them when they were sick, and she knew their families. Not surprisingly, the dynamic was similar to what Missy had cultivated with her contributors over the years, because she and Eleanor lived by the same ethos of personal connection.[6]

Traditionally the exclusive turf of male reporters, the White House was becoming a place where women convened to be briefed ostensibly about "social" rather than "political" news. And yet, by virtue of the venue, much of this reportage moved from the women's section to the front page. Eleanor used the conferences as an opportunity to showcase women within her husband's administration, such as Mint Director Nellie Tayloe Ross, Frances Perkins, and Ellen Woodward, director of women's work in the Federal Emergency Relief Administration. If male reporters were wont to dismiss her Monday-morning briefings as the "docile news" of the "hen house," occasionally Eleanor rolled out announcements that stole the president's thunder. In terms of coverage, her conferences took the trajectory of Missy's magazines, for ever so gradually she, too, encroached on foreign policy, minimum-wage laws, maximum workweeks, impending war— her husband's side of the news—and took a stand on topics that First Ladies of eras past had refrained from weighing in on. Even in a Democratic White House, Missy found a way to exert influence that was discreet yet unmistakable.[7]

MISSY'S GET-TOGETHERS with Eleanor Roosevelt and other women of Washington provided a very different view of power than did her formal meetings with male administration officials. Without holding titles or positions, several women had mastered the art of influence that young Missy had first observed as a teenager at her mother's salons and social functions. Most of Washington agreed that the grand master of them all in those years was Alice Roosevelt Longworth, the eldest daughter of Teddy. A common presence in the Senate press gallery, Longworth knew all the prominent players in the political game and likely knew more about how to grease the gears in government than had her husband, the Ohio congressman turned Speaker of the House Nicholas Longworth, who had died in 1931. She could be a valuable ally but also a formidable foe. After FDR was elected president, Eleanor relied on Missy to be a mediating presence between herself and Longworth, who, despite being the daughter of Eleanor's godfather, seemed to relish being the First Lady's most outspoken critic.[8]

Missy had known Longworth since they were both children and had seen how damning Longworth's judgments of people could be. In Missy's view, her old friend was not so much a gossip as a shrewd manipulator of social information who understood how to wield her feminine power. Although she presented herself to most of Washington society as one of the most put-together hostesses in town, around Missy Alice felt perfectly comfortable sipping tea in an old kimono, her straw-colored hair falling loosely down her back. Missy recalled her once settling into her smoking chair and launching into diatribes—starting with Coolidge, moving on to the effect of Wets and Drys on the Republican Party, touching on issues swaying voters in Pennsylvania, Illinois, and New York, and ending with the differences in the attitudes of Americans in the 1890s versus the present. Alice had been exposed to the issues for so long that her insights seemed more instinctive than anything else. She made time for Missy because Missy was a rare woman who could both challenge and affirm her as a long-time anthropologist of Washington's political habitat.[9]

Missy was also friends with a small yet growing contingent of female bureaucrats who came to Washington from elsewhere and still had a lot to learn. Rather than lord her knowledge of the workings of inner Washington over them, she became their connection and a valuable ally. During the same week when she had met with Alice Longworth to talk old-school politics, she also made dinner plans with Assistant Attorney General Mabel "Maude" Willebrandt and Louise Stanley, chief of the Home Economics Bureau in the Department of Agriculture. Missy had helped to propel both women into national prominence by introducing them to her expansive readership. Stanley and Willebrandt, meanwhile, had adopted a baby together and taken to sharing their parenting philosophy with Missy while she was in town. Willebrandt had divorced her husband two years earlier, and her living situation with Stanley was not public knowledge. But for Missy it was just another fact of the female universe of Washington that male officials didn't know. Male journalists would also never fully comprehend how her relationships with women gave her backdoor access to people and stories, often providing more authentic insights on subjects than a front-door entry could provide.[10]

Missy's relationships with women extended out internationally, as attested by her friendships with various monarchs, wives of diplomats, and the Grand Duchess Romanov. Despite her lineage of note, Romanov was a royal castoff who relied on Missy to help her remake her life, largely by jump-starting her career in America. The granddaughter of Alexander II and an exile of Russia since the Bolshevik Revolution, she came to New York as a two-time divorcée desperate to make an income. Missy helped arrange the American publication of two memoirs and then went one step further, using her connections in the Departments of State and Labor to get Romanov papers to work in the country.[11]

From seamstresses to former royals, women who knew Missy found work during the Great Depression. For Romanov, it was the start toward a new, uneasy sort of independence, and she confessed that back in Europe her family looked down on the compensated work Missy found for her. "The cast I belonged to is horrified of my daring," she told Missy. "In Europe nobody admires success. They are suspicious of it." Clearly, this was where Missy's purported "European point of view" showed its limits. She did everything she could to stimulate the exile's creative juices and earning potential in the States, facilitating her becoming a buyer of Paris fashions for Bergdorf Goodman and promoting her exhibitions of photographs in Manhattan galleries. When the Duchess was short on cash, she counted on Missy for paid writing assignments. "Thanks again and again for all your wonderful friendship and love," she gushed to Missy. "I can not tell you how deeply I feel it. My life here in America has taken another aspect since I have known you."[12]

In return for all the kindness, the Duchess did whatever she could to aid Missy's international activism and reportage, including supplying the following introduction to Alfonso XIII, the king of Spain:

This letter will be handed over to you by one of my dearest American friends—Mrs. William Brown Meloney who not only is a woman of unusual intelligence and insight but also a dynamic personality with a great soul and great ideals.

Mrs. Meloney being what she is commands the confidence and respect of the American government. In the support of her projects both President Hoover and President Coolidge have written for her. Her activities have been astonishingly wide. She had given her disinterested aid and assistance to projects of social and political importance both in America and Europe and with it all has never lent herself to any publicity or cheap journalism. Her journalism is perfect.

Her friendship for England and Belgium during the war made her go in for propaganda work which connected her intimately with the King and Queen of Belgium. As a matter of fact together with General L. Wood she started as far back as 1915 the propaganda movement in America.

She organized for and with Pr. Hoover the American Child Welfare work which utilized the war funds of America remaining after the Armistice.

Two or three years ago Mrs. Meloney organized herself and lead [sic] a vast campaign all through America in honour of Mme. Curie which made it possible for the scientist to go on with her work in Europe.

And this is just a few of her activities.

She has been the intimate and trusted friend of many European statesmen—I wish you would see her and talk to her. Mrs. Meloney is one of the few Americans who has got an absolutely European point of view on political problems and your acquaintance with her might be of great and general importance under present circumstances.[13]

Missy had always carried letters of introduction with her to Europe, and increasingly these admiring correspondents were women, some well-established through inheritance, others by professional reputation, or both. Men may have failed to see the value in gaining such endorsements, but Missy understood that her female network, which extended across continents and the political spectrum, provided access to people and stories on altogether different tracks than the obvious ones available to men. Women were her access, her alternative vantage point, and her loyal brigade of friends who wanted her to succeed. Hence why the painfully shy Madame Curie pushed herself to speak and write publicly to Americans, and why the British novelist Marie Belloc Lowndes threw parties introducing Missy to her country's literary lights. "Of the many kind friends I have here, not a single one has done as much as you in the many years that I have been in touch with America," Lowndes told her when she visited New York in 1933. Her outpourings could just as easily have been uttered by any number of women grateful for what Missy did to promote their interests and propel their careers in years when they were discouraged from competing with men.[14]

———

WOMEN TURNED OUT to be Missy's solace in that frustrating summer of 1933. She had sailed to Europe at the end of June to visit authors, the pope, and several rising dictators of Western Europe for interviews. Thankfully, she also managed to slip in precious time with Curie, which counterbalanced the craziness that ensued.[15]

While in Rome, Missy planned to sit down with Mussolini, and not for the first time. Back in 1928 she had met him at his summer palace to interview him for the *Herald Tribune,* becoming one of the first American journalists to gain access to him. She had been introduced to the premier as he posed for a portrait in his throne room, and afterward she recorded her mental snapshot of him: "above medium height, stocky," she wrote, but not overweight. His forehead was broad, Augustan; she decided that his nose would have been large on any other face. He had strong hands and mesmerizing eyes, but she was struck most by his massive jaw—"so powerful and set," she later wrote, "that one knows only death could move it." He spoke about Christianity and American authors and was curious about what made people tick. His magnetism and love of horses reminded Missy of Teddy Roosevelt, and she wondered if, in the Italian head of state,

Americans had an ally in the making. She wrote of him favorably in 1928, concluding that in the five years since he had taken power, he had done much to educate his people. Underneath his intimidating facade she saw a lover of science, an admirer of intellect, a unifier of a country—not yet an instigator of war.[16]

Her impression of the Italian dictator hadn't changed two years later, when she interviewed him a second time. Now, in 1933, she wanted to check in with him again in preparation for the third *Herald Tribune* Forum. That year she devoted many of the panels to discussions of America's international commitments, and sounded alarms about Adolf Hitler's growing power in Germany. Along with speeches from prominent clubwomen, Walter Lippmann, the president and First Lady, Frances Perkins, and Ruth Bryan Owen, now the minister to Denmark, Missy hoped to record a message from Mussolini to be broadcasted on Columbus Day, just before the Forum was scheduled to close. "There will be two million school and college students, many of whom are of Italian extraction, in all parts of the United States and Canada listening in on the radio to a conference which will be held in New York," she told officials in a bid to see their head of government. "The depression in this crisis in history directs a hard blow to these young people.... He could inspire a multitude of people. That he could do this in English would endear him to many."[17]

Working through "front-door" channels—the Italian embassy in Washington and the American embassy in Rome, which was headed by Ambassador Breckinridge Long—Missy got word that Mussolini was willing to see her and to be recorded for the broadcast. Nevertheless, cables she received also suggested that details were far from nailed down. She sailed to Europe with the understanding that she would meet with Mussolini in Rome sometime between July 24 and August 1, only to discover that her audience had been delayed. Not one to fret, she stayed at the Carlton Hotel in London and with Curie in Paris until Long recommended that she come to Rome to wait it out at the Excelsior Hotel. Missy arrived—and stayed for twelve days. To help her pass the time, Alexander Kirk, counsellor at the American embassy, hosted her and tried to find out what was blocking Missy's interview. When Kirk heard nothing, he took Missy to the Foreign Office, where she inquired with more Italian officials. Go back to the hotel, they told her. They promised her that she'd get a call.[18]

Kirk was happy for this extended time with Missy; even from a distance she had been a sort of guardian angel to him and a voice of reason over the years. A man best known for his lavish entertaining, in middle age Kirk was having doubts about whether his career "as a society whore" was useful to diplomacy. Missy reminded him of his worth more convincingly than anyone else, and in return he was unconditionally devoted to her. She had the same effect on Nicholas Roosevelt, first cousin once removed to Teddy, who was the minister to Hungary in the years Kirk was assigned in Rome. Roosevelt seemed to think that his selection for the post had been Missy's doing entirely. "I have shuddered to think of the terrible responsibility you undertook when you had me sent here," he told her, fearing that he was "a dud as a diplomat." He hinted that he wouldn't object to being transferred to Holland or Switzerland, or even back to Washington in an assistant-secretary role, but Missy always reminded him of his usefulness in that corner of the world.[19]

Jusserand, de Cartier, Roosevelt, Kirk—all diplomats who wondered at one point or another whether Missy was better attuned to the cultural nuances of their work than they were. Kirk admired her ability to maintain sight of grander goals, even as she received the runaround from Italian bureaucrats in that summer of 1933. Her interactions with officials were polite yet firm; she was patient, but clear that she wasn't leaving until she got her interview. "The more I watch you, Missy, the more I marvel at your restraint," Kirk told her. "You are simply built for achievement no matter what value the object may have in your scheme of things or what fuel you must burn in getting that object." He knew she was physically struggling and refusing to let it show. "If I could only give you my health, you'd do so much with it," he supposed.[20]

But through the grapevine there were whispers that Mussolini had left town and had no intention of seeing Missy. Confusion mounted one day when Missy was told confidentially that the real holdup was Mussolini's exclusive contract with the Hearst Company. She reiterated to officials that her request for the Columbus Day address shouldn't pose any conflicts; she was not asking for rights to his writing, just for his voice to be recorded. The Italian secretary of state and the head of the press bureau apologized for the runaround, but they, too, were unable to nail down a date for the interview. By now, Missy figured out that it had been over a year since a member of the foreign press had been granted permission to meet with Mussolini one on one, and that he had only been taking questions at public functions. Yet another rumor circulating at the American embassy was that Mussolini had been angered by an earlier interview with the journalist Fredericka Blankner, but Missy knew that was preposterous since he had earlier praised Blankner for her journalism.[21]

No, what was happening, she was pretty sure, was that she was being intentionally blackballed. Rather than relent and go home, however, she asked Breckinridge Long "to insist upon a showdown." His persistence got her an appointment at the Palazzo Chigi with the Italian secretary of state, who told her that Mussolini would finally see her, "but no questions . . . sometime in early September." Allegedly, Missy's philanthropic war record, not her journalism, had won her this access, which made her furious. She shot off a note that she asked the secretary to give to his head of government:

I do not know whether the insult is intended for me personally—which is unlikely since I am not here in a private capacity—or an insult to the great paper I represent, or to its owner, Mr. Ogden Reid—or whether the intent is merely to be offensive to Americans. The suggestion has been twice offered that I see the head of the government as something other than a journalist. I offer no apology for my profession. I am proud of my connection with the New York Herald Tribune, one of the greatest newspapers in the world today—and owned and edited by a man of intelligence and integrity. I do deplore however that sensational and destructive school of journalist which is owned and directed by a man without conscience [she was talking about Hearst]. I especially regret that such a man may be so trusted and honored in foreign countries, to the detriment of better international relations and the fair treatment of fair minded journalists. . . . I shall not be in Rome in September.

I do however hope that in the future, journalists who come to Rome on your invitation will be more fairly dealt with.[22]

Missy hated feeling as though she had wasted her time, but she didn't stew over the failed interview. She caught up with other European contacts until she received a letter from one of her German connections, Richard von Kühlmann, formerly the secretary of state for foreign affairs, who asked her to come to his country. Only one thing would entice her to come, she told him—an interview, if not with Paul von Hindenburg then with Hitler himself. Von Kühlmann explained that the former no longer gave interviews but that perhaps the latter could be compelled to break his silence with American journalists. Now Missy was interested. She waited for word from the Foreign Office and meanwhile wired a request to the *Herald Tribune* office in New York to have funds available to her in London should she go to Germany. She stopped in at Rapallo to see one of her writers, Max Beerbohm, before heading to the French Riviera for visits with Carlo Sforza, Thomas Mann, Lion Feuchtwanger, and Arnold Zweig, more of her authors in exile. Feuchtwanger was in the middle of writing "The Fascinating Nonentity," an article for Missy about how Hitler, a man of "no personality," managed to speak to the masses. It was to replace the piece that had gone up in flames when the Nazis torched his library.[23]

Missy couldn't stay with her exiles for long. She had promised to meet up with Curie in Chamonix, and it was the portion of her trip she looked forward to most. Curie eagerly awaited the visit too, but she also had some somber business to discuss. There were details she wanted to finalize in her will, and Missy was disturbed by her urgency. Nevertheless, on one of their days together the women stole a moment to make their way to a clearing in the mountains, where they sat together in silence, as if time were briefly standing still. Missy had no words to describe the beauty of the French Alps at sundown; to have Curie in her presence was to keep some perspective and to forget the frustrations of the last few weeks for a while. They collected cups of the blue stones that lay abundant among the peaks; Curie promised to send them to America—a memento of their brief but precious time together. She could offer Missy no better access to interviews that summer, but she recorded some remarks for the Forum to promote science and international peace. Missy assured her that coming from the most heralded woman scientist in the world, these words would be more meaningful to Americans than Curie could imagine.[24]

On August 8, a dispatch was waiting for Missy at the *Herald Tribune* office in Paris, announcing that her interview with Hitler had been granted for any day that week at three p.m. She verified the dispatch with the embassy, wired for more instructions, and phoned von Kühlmann to schedule a date for the interview. He told Missy to meet him in Munich, and he would drive her from there. She flew to England first to tie up loose ends and coordinate her passage home from Cherbourg on August 16. Von Kühlmann confirmed that the interview had been arranged for the next Saturday at Hitler's summer palace and told Missy to be in Munich by eight a.m. She flew as far as Frankfurt, saw that she could make the rest of the trip by train, and phoned von Kühlmann to tell him not to meet her at the flying field. But he had bad news: the interview with Hitler had been canceled. "If you will stay on in Germany, by the middle of next week he will tell you when he will see you," von Kühlmann directed. Missy couldn't hide her annoyance. "If I had been a journalist at large I might have called his bluff," she remembered thinking, but she had a Forum to organize, and time was running short. She bought a ticket on the night train to Paris, spent her few remaining hours people-watching in Frankfurt, and, after chatting with locals about the Nazi emblems everywhere, decided that she would settle for submitting a story titled "Conversations in Frankfurt" before returning to New York.[25]

The trip back to Cherbourg was harrowing, but enlightening. A conductor on the train from Frankfurt to Paris declared that Missy was leaving Germany with too much money in her purse; he forced her off the train and even threatened her with jail. Although she bought a first-class ticket on the Paris train the next morning, she was taken to the third-class car. Space had been made in first class for military officers en route to Brussels. "I saw many old time officers and boys who seemed not more than fourteen or fifteen in uniforms and with side arms—their eyes shining," she recalled, and then wrote a note to self: "There is a disturbing excitement in Germany."[26]

In Paris, another dispatch had caught up to her from Italian officials: apparently Mussolini had had a change of heart since she had left Italy. While he still wouldn't do Missy's radio broadcast, he decided that he would see her immediately if she returned to Rome. This time, however, she didn't take the bait. She was two weeks late on her plans and missing out on precious time with a new grandson, her second, who had been born just before she left New York. "I hope you will approve of my decision not to return to Rome," she wrote to the Reids. "I'd like to have had the interview with Mussolini, but it is one story—and I think something bigger is at stake. I feel sure the time has come for ethical journalists to demand respect." Breckinridge Long investigated what had happened in Rome, but Missy told him that it didn't matter. She was pretty sure that the increased discretion and militancy of Mussolini's people reflected changes in the man himself. She suspected that he didn't want to appear critical of Hitler's aggressions, making an anti-war message more consistent with his cultural work in 1928 than now. Missy documented for the Reids her failed attempts to get audiences with autocrats that summer: "I want to preface this memorandum with this statement: Germany and Italy are getting ready for war."[27]

––––––––––

ENTER MARGHERITA SARFATTI, another European woman whom Missy brought into her orbit. She was an Italian Jewess and a talented journalist, who, as an expert art critic, had ties to artists around the world and wanted to break into the American lecture circuit. She and Missy shared interests and acquaintances, but where Missy served as an advisor to US presidents, Sarfatti had the ear of Mussolini. In 1911 the married Sarfatti had had a love affair with the future autocrat and had remained one of his most trusted cultural advisors ever since. She enjoyed a mysterious pull with the dictator; it was influence comparable to what Missy held with presidents, though sexualized and more sinister than Missy might have initially realized. Sarfatti had introduced Mussolini to theories not only of fascism but also of racial hierarchy, making him all the more complicit with Hitler's racial policies when Italy allied with Germany later in the 1930s. Sarfatti had long espoused the need to grow the ranks of the white race against the "Yellow Peril"; she held clear prejudices against Asians, though for obvious reasons her rhetoric never turned anti-Semitic. She had little reason to worry about becoming a political dissident in 1933, and yet she ironically fueled the ideas that eventually forced her to flee Italy. Seeing Missy as her ticket out, she positioned herself as Missy's inside contact to Mussolini as well as her intimate protégée, much the way Curie had been.[28]

Missy had been corresponding with Sarfatti before and during the summer debacle in Rome. As her attempts to meet with Mussolini through "front-door" channels failed her, she had turned to Sarfatti as her "backdoor" female connection. As for Sarfatti, apparently her job, from Mussolini's perspective, was to smooth things over with Missy so that his ties to the American media were not permanently severed. Apologetic for the miscommunications in Rome, Sarfatti told Missy that Mussolini regretted having missed the chance to see her. What could she do personally, she asked, to make up for the wasted trip? Sarfatti sent Missy home with consolation prizes: signed photographs of Il Duce and a copy of the biography of him that she had written in 1924, inscribed, "To 'Missy' Meloney with the expression of my best thanks for her kind, hearty and ready sympathy, which gave me the unexpected pleasure of a sudden 'old' friendship." Sarfatti's intimate language made it clear that she wanted to be in Missy's inner circle.[29]

And it seems that she left a favorable impression. Missy reported to the Reids that Sarfatti was one of the most remarkable women she had come across in years. "She is the woman back of the Fascist Movement—a journalist, owner of several papers, official biographer of Mussolini. She is a titled woman, the author of a number of meaty books. She worked with Mussolini on his first newspaper, and is very powerful in Italy." In letters, Sarfatti met Missy's admiration with words of affection: "I embrace you with all my heart" ... "I am willing to do anything you like me to do, darling!" ... "How heartily I wish all good + happy things to be piled on your dear darling beautiful clever sweet head! I am quite homesick for you, Darling girl...I hug you affectionately." Perhaps this was the conventional effusiveness of an Italian woman, but it was also strategically expressed. Although Mussolini never recorded a radio address that summer, Sarfatti proved eager to record one herself and to have it played in the ballroom of the Waldorf Astoria at the Forum of 1933. In it, she called for the solidarity of "White Civilization" and Italian fascism as the way forward in uncertain economic times. In the name of Mussolini's regime, she was laying down groundwork, whetting the appetites of white Americans for more to come. "Do you think there is any chance of effectually realizing your beautiful kind plan for my visit to America?" she asked Missy. Her scheme was becoming clear. In return for access to her head of government, she wanted the benefit of Missy's positive press and personal connections, the former for Mussolini and the latter for herself.[30]

Her persistence worked. Missy started preparing for an American tour for Sarfatti, dispatching a reporter to Rome to interview her for a piece later titled "Italy's Heroine of Fascism." Along with making inquiries to speaker agencies and getting Sarfatti on the social calendars of her well-positioned friends, Missy circulated translations of her biography, *Dux*, to academicians and published her editorials, several of which rolled out pronatalist programs. Although Sarfatti's tour was no match for Curie's in 1921 in terms of publicity, Missy scheduled as many activities for her Italian guest, if not more, since she was amenable to a frenetic pace. Missy jammed opportunities into the schedule for Sarfatti to publicize herself and to add people to her network. A virtual Who's Who of New York was in attendance at a party Missy threw for Sarfatti at Leonebel Jacobs's studio in the Hotel des Artistes, including Fiorello La Guardia, Sinclair Lewis, his wife Dorothy Thompson, Norman Bel Geddes, Condé Nast, the Reids, and Fannie Hurst. Knowing that Sarfatti wanted to meet big people in publishing, academia, and film, Missy spared nothing in making introductions. She even won Sarfatti access to the White House, where the First Couple welcomed her as Mussolini's official consort. Sarfatti found the president charming and attentive, though she couldn't rid Eleanor of her skepticism of fascist regimes, of both the German and the Italian variety.[31]

If Missy seemed swept up by the charms and troubling dogma of Margherita Sarfatti, one must remember how much her perceptiveness, patriotism, and international informants served as counteracting forces against the woman's seductions. For all the opportunities Missy afforded Sarfatti to extol the virtues of Italian fascism, Missy herself never publicly endorsed them. And although Sarfatti played down the increasing terror of Mussolini's regime, Carlo Sforza reminded Missy of what life was like for an Italian intellectual in exile, and she published his views regularly. Missy believed in the power of free speech and the free dissemination of information so that Americans could evaluate multiple viewpoints themselves. She fostered this independent thinking because she thought it the lifeblood of democracy. Missy likely sensed Sarfatti's precarious position as Mussolini's political mouthpiece who also feared becoming his political casualty. But there was an implicit understanding between the two women. Each provided the other with access to people and resources that men, for all their outward power, couldn't or wouldn't offer them.[32]

On June 9, 1934, Sarfatti left New York to return to Italy; Missy was already en route, having left on the *Olympic* the day before. This time she traveled with Leonebel Jacobs, who doubled as Missy's personal nurse and the portraitist of her European authors. Sarfatti was anxious to return the hospitality lavished on her in New York, but Missy had much to do before meeting up with her in Rome. She planned to see the novelist Cosmo Hamilton and his brother Sir Philip Gibbs, as well as Frank Swinnerton and Virginia Woolf, whose portrait Jacobs was scheduled to paint for the *Sunday Magazine.* Most important, she was to join the four hundred delegates of the Twelfth International Congress of PEN in Edinburgh, presided over by Missy's longtime friend H. G. Wells.[33]

Missy had no doubt that the air would be charged at the congress. At the one in Dubrovnik the year before, the American delegate Henry Seidel Canby had submitted a resolution of the New York executive committee that denounced the German PEN chapter for expelling pacifist, Jewish, and communist writers from its ranks. Still, the censorship continued. Missy was in Edinburgh to defend Germans whose writings had been banned in their homeland and who had been forced to flee. One of them, the Jewish playwright Ernst Toller, confided to her that he suspected he had been in danger of being kidnapped and thrown into prison before going into hiding. Deaths of German writers that the SS called suicides were really murders by strangling, he told her, and he feared for the lives of several of his imprisoned friends.[34]

Literary freedom was the preeminent concern of PEN members in 1934, but Missy had been fixated on the issue since the 1910s, when she had asked Charles Eliot to write about the press as a bedrock of the American Republic. "Everything Americans hold dear depends on the freedom of the press," she told students in a speech at Bates College, qualifying that an independent press also had to be a responsible one. In 1929 she had helped American PEN president Will Irwin draft a position paper on irresponsible journalism—"that kind of literature deliberately calculated to create international distrust." Americans had to be discerning of the information they consumed and to defend honest outlets when threatened, she asserted. In a radio broadcast, she reminded listeners of Peter Zenger, the German printer who over two hundred years earlier had published his *New York Weekly Journal* as protest against censorship and had gone to jail for his convictions.[35] In Edinburgh, she sounded the same alarms. "We are living in one of the most critical hours in history," she exclaimed. "It calls for great living, clear thinking, and courageous acting." She continued:

> There can be no growth in any nation where there is no intellectual freedom.... The ban upon the intellectual work of the Jewish people in Germany is not confined to the political leaders[,] not to the economists[,] not the philosophers. It seeps through and poisons the entire intellectual structure of one of the great and learned nations of the world.... It is an old atavistic recurrence in the cycle of time, but it is not to be tolerated....
>
> What comes out of this depression from the loss of money, of power, of personal prestige, may quickly be healed by the turn of fortune, but what happens to damage a character, either in an individual or in a nation, requires generations to wash out.... In the name of nationalism, persecution becomes fanaticism, the child of cowardice and ignorance. There is only one weapon with which to fight this reversion—the courage to establish before the civilized world a standard of right thinking and right living, and then persistently to support that standard. To this end the members of the P.E.N. have dedicated themselves.[36]

———

AFTER SPEAKING IN EDINBURGH, Missy visited briefly with Curie in Paris before returning to London for author meetings; although Curie had been struggling that spring with pneumonia, Missy didn't suspect that her friend had been sicker than usual. Marie Belloc Lowndes planned a cocktail party so that her American editor could meet up with Countess Margot Asquith, P. G. Wodehouse, and some rising talents she hoped to bring to the American market. But her plans came to a halt when Missy received a distressing cable from Ève Curie. It appeared that since Missy had seen her just a week before, Ève's mother had taken a drastic turn. Worrying now for Marie's life, Ève begged Missy to return to Paris to be with her. While Missy was making arrangements, another relapse in Curie's condition forced a further change in plans. Doctors advised Ève to transfer her mother to the mountains, and on July 2 she wrote Missy from Sancellemoz, a hospital in the Haute-Savoie. Doctors had reached the conclusion that they had wrongly treated Curie for tuberculosis, rather than whatever ailment was affecting her bones and causing her pain. "The journey was awful," Ève reported.

> Since our arrival, mother is extremely ill and weak: enormous fever, suffering in all the body, extreme weakness. It is not anymore in the chest—and maybe it never was. It is something else that we don't know...perhaps pernicious anem[ia]....It's terrible. I had the greatest doctor of Geneva here, Professor Roch—he has no hope anymore—but we don't know if it is going to last a few days, or a few weeks. The poor creature is suffering so much that I cannot look at her and have to go out of her room to cry out of her sight.

When Irène arrived at the hospital the next day, her mother's suffering was too much for her to bear.[37]

Missy didn't arrive in time to see her friend alive. Curie died the following morning, July 4, 1934. Ève sent a cable informing Missy of her mother's burial that coming Friday, and Missy canceled the rest of her appointments in London to stay in France.[38] Before day's end, Missy had written a statement to supplement the cover obituary in the European edition of the *Herald Tribune:*

> In the death of Mme. Curie the world has lost one of its immortal characters. Her life and her work have inspired millions of people. She has been a challenge and an inspiration to her generation, and especially to the women of her time. In America she will always be revered as she was loved in her lifetime. Scientists, educators, public

leaders and plain people shared a profound respect for her. Her death will come as a personal loss to many of my countrymen.

I saw Mme. Curie last week and though she was ill and suffering, as always, she was courageous and cheerful. Her thoughts then, as through her entire life, concerned her work and the well being of other people.

In her lifetime she was a champion of peace. The finest tribute which we may pay to her memory will be in that cause. . . . I salute her memory and grieve for the loss of a precious friend.[39]

James Barrie and Carlo Sforza were among those who immediately sent Missy cables of sympathy, having heard so many of her stories about the reclusive scientist over the years. Sarfatti, too, seized on the moment to send condolences. "I know how sad + lost you must have been for the great Marie Curie's loss," she wrote Missy. "She has run her race, fought her battle, won her prize. . . . I kiss you with love + tenderness as well as admiration + gratitude." She expressed the sentiments one would to a friend in pain, but the stream of letters that followed suggests that Sarfatti also saw Curie's death as an opening— an opportunity to fill a void in Missy's inner sanctum and to take advantage of her goodwill and network of friends to get established in America. And thus although Missy's interview with Mussolini was thwarted again that summer, Sarfatti continued to hold herself out to Missy as her best chance for another bite at the apple.[40]

Chapter Twelve

PUBLICLY TURNING A PAGE
1934–1936

FOR ALL HER GOOD INTENTIONS, Missy wondered over the years if she hadn't pushed Curie to her physical limits and hastened her decline. Ève had always allayed her worries. "I ha[d] never seen Mother in better health and humor than when she came back from the United States," she once assured Missy from Paris. "You have taken such care of her, and have been so kind for her, that I felt that, in spite of all the tiresome dinners and ceremonys [*sic*], she had a happier time in America than she ha[d] here." Curie's daughters were grateful to the American editor who had been the one person in their mother's life who wanted nothing more than to help the scientist succeed. Recognizing Missy's service to Curie's institute in Warsaw, the Polish government awarded her the Order of Polonia Restituta in 1935, and Missy accepted it graciously. But perhaps more meaningfully to Missy, Ève had set aside her mother's watch for her, the very one that Pierre Curie had given his wife to time their famous experiments and that Marie continued to use in widowhood. Ève took great pains to see it transported to America from the table next to her mother's deathbed and placed directly into Missy's hands. It reminded Missy that despite her great loss, there was still precious work to be done.[1]

Missy understood the Curies' anguish in losing their mother, for she had also lost hers in 1934. After decades of invalidism, Sarah Irwin Mattingly had made it to the ripe age of eighty-two before finally succumbing to her ailments. The year before, Missy had recovered editions of her mother's magazine and proudly displayed them at the Century of Progress World's Fair in Chicago. Although few people had recognized it at the time, Sarah had been one of the first female editors in the country, and Missy had finally come around to seeing her mother, not her father, as the one who had ordained her professional path. Alexander Kirk consoled her from Rome: "I don't suppose it is any satisfaction to you now to realize that you yourself have added to her stature." One North Carolina obituary lauded Sarah as "an 'Independent Woman' by nature, by ability, and by interest." "She started no movement, sponsored no cause, waged no fight on behalf of any particular interest but she proved to the world of her day that after all being a woman is no hopeless handicap." This description, a tribute to a woman who was largely unsung and yet who lived by discreet example, was one Missy took pride in emulating.[2]

On the heels of her mother's death, Missy learned that King Albert of Belgium, whom she considered an exceptionally compassionate sovereign, had died in a freak mountaineering accident. She grieved him, as well as the more stoic Calvin Coolidge, who had died of a heart attack in Massachusetts the year before. That October, Missy dedicated a library to the former president in the National Women's Republican Club, personally escorting Grace Coolidge around the refurbished space. She tried to be a comfort to the former First Lady, as well as a guide to productive widowhood, much as Curie and her own mother had been for her. Despite their very real losses, those women had turned widowhood into an opportunity to live the intellectual life they had wanted for themselves. Missy had taken their cues when she lost her husband, pouring her grief into tackling new challenges, hence why she had plunged into uncharted waters at the *Herald Tribune Sunday Magazine*. But now, faced with so much more loss, where would she navigate next?[3]

First, she wanted to shore up Curie's legacy in the United States. Missy lobbied the Board of Aldermen and Mayor La Guardia to rename a stretch on Manhattan's Upper East Side "Marie Curie Avenue." At a ceremony at 77th and the East River, officials representing the Polish and French consulates joined Missy in eulogizing the fallen scientist. Polish Americans danced to the music of their homeland, and schoolchildren unveiled a portrait of their heroine. It was a scene Missy had long fantasized about: establishing New York as Curie's honorary home.[4]

There were rumors of unauthorized biographies being written about Curie, both in Europe and in the States, so Ève begged Missy for advice. The savvy publicist told Ève to write her mother's story, a full-length biography, before others swooped in. Despite Irène lobbying to have their mother's papers destroyed, Ève thought about it and ultimately agreed with Missy: "I think it ought to be a book mainly about Mother's person and Mother's life—which are beautiful, I think, like a sort of legend." Irène meanwhile thought her mother's science more important to pass down to posterity than her personal story. Just in time, Missy had successfully had the legal rights to the American radium transferred to the Sorbonne so that Irène could have unrestricted use of it. Finally, that December, the monies from her mother's fund were turned over to Irène completely. "It will help us in the new field of work opened by the 'Artificial Radioactivity,'" Irène assured Missy. Despite the devastations of that year, she worked doggedly in the lab with Frédéric, as her mother would have wanted, and won a Nobel Prize the following year. Less than enthusiastic about attending the award ceremony in Stockholm, Irène, as her mother had done, tried to get away with refusing to accept the award in person and staying put in the lab. "My mother would have been glad to see all that," she told Missy, "but not so glad as of the work itself."[5]

The work. Though its nature had differed for Curie and Missy, their belief in the sanctity of work had bonded them. Both women had taken on too much of it as a way to stave off grief, to prove their worth, and to make meaning in their lives. And yet because they inherently understood how work was each other's comfort, each voiced concern, but never judgment, when it led to the other's physical decline. Missy's way of dealing with the loss of Curie, her mother, and her friends in 1934 was the same as it had been after Bill's death—simply to stay busy with work while she could. The country remained in the throes of a Depression, after all, making it hard for Missy to justify slowing down to catch her breath. She worked undaunted on Home Institute projects and reinvigorated efforts for the BHA under FDR with the passing of the Housing Act of 1934, which encouraged improvement in housing standards and created the Federal Housing Administration (FHA). Late in September, Missy joined Eleanor Roosevelt and the poet Joseph Auslander to dedicate "America's Little House" at Park Avenue and 39th. Although she could barely be seen speaking through the unfinished window frames of the house, Missy was heard clearly over the Columbia radio network urging lenders to lower interest rates and builders to erect affordable homes with up-to-date conveniences for wage earners who needed time freed up to punch the clock.[6]

Indeed, the words and actions of this wisp of a woman reverberated widely, especially now that her Forum attracted international figures to New York and reached countless more over the radio. A mere four months after Curie's death, a reporter for *Time* described the frantic scene as the Forum of 1934 commenced: "Trailing a thousand different perfumes, an endless procession of women surged through the lobbies of Manhattan's swank Waldorf-Astoria.... This year no less than 38,000 women applied to the Herald Tribune for tickets, and 25,000 actually registered for the five sessions. The ballroom had seats for only 2,500. A thousand others packed the adjoining halls to hear the program from loudspeakers." The sheer scale of the event was astounding, and yet no detail was too small for Missy—from choosing the discussion themes, to editing remarks, to selecting publicity photographs. When panels were in session, she even pushed cards that read, "You have one more minute," into the speakers' view. If it seemed like busy work that might best be relegated to others, it was also a much-needed distraction from the personal loss she had endured. Edward Elliott, president of Purdue University, was in such awe of her generalship at the Forum that he asked her to give a keynote address on campus as one of the most influential public servants of her generation. "Whenever I think of lionhearted crusaders," he later wrote her, "I think of you."[7]

It hadn't been lost on reporters covering the Forum that year that more women were speakers, not just attendees. Soon-to-be Nobel Prize–winning author Pearl Buck and the aviator Amelia Earhart joined more established figures such as Queen Mary, Eleanor Roosevelt, and Fannie Hurst in giving remarks that went over the airwaves. One reporter described Missy's female participants as women "holding down men's jobs in a man's world," adding, too, that they spoke to an American female workforce that had doubled to over ten million since the turn of the century. Missy also provided Labor Secretary Frances Perkins a platform from which to set the record straight about working women, and the secretary informed her audience that 95 percent of married women in jobs were the sole supporters of their families, refuting the common assumption that women wage earners worked for "pin money" or had taken their husbands' jobs.[8]

It was no accident that in this year of the woman Missy booked fellow journalist Dorothy Thompson to deliver a major keynote. As the former chief of the Berlin office of the *New York Post,* Thompson had been the first American woman journalist to head a major foreign bureau, and she seized on the opportunity to propel herself to national fame. Having interviewed Adolf Hitler as the National Socialist Party was on the rise, she recorded her underwhelming impressions in *I Saw Hitler* and was kicked out of Germany for her views. Missy was convinced that this moment, when the Germans were trying to suppress Thompson, was exactly the time to invite her to speak at the Forum, and she assured the audience that they could "accept her word and her guidance" as a "disinterested observer" of international events. With her physical stature, strong opinions, and booming voice, Thompson appeared at the podium as an unexpected feminine force. This was a woman who drank, smoked, dominated conversations, and wore her ambitions on her sleeve. She was a new kind of heroine, one who felt comfortable sporting a masculine self-assuredness.

Though their styles differed, Missy greatly admired Thompson's work and happily put in a good word to help her land a radio show of her own. No doubt Missy was also a factor in Helen Reid hiring Thompson two years later to write the syndicated column On the Record, adding a bold new voice to the female influence already present at the *Herald Tribune*. Once the champion of a famous woman scientist, now Missy championed many women wanting to be seen, heard, and paid in professional careers. Perhaps it was her way of honoring a mother who had also pioneered a path to self-realization in the public sphere, albeit more quietly than Thompson did it.[9]

———

DESPITE ALL HER PROJECTS, Missy remained restless for a fresh editorial challenge, even if the timing was dreadful for launching new publishing ventures. In the 1930s some four hundred newspapers nationwide had either been absorbed into other papers or folded altogether, unable to generate sufficient advertising funds amidst the depressed economy and the burgeoning era of radio. A few reader-friendly newcomers proved successful with innovative formats—compartmentalized news rags like *Time* and *Newsweek,* for instance, and the more eye-catching *Look* and *Life*. Nevertheless, a cost-saving measure that made increasing sense for publishers was subscribing to syndicated columns, rather than hiring reporters to create original content for a premium. The *Herald Tribune* was syndicating nationally recognized Walter Lippmann and soon did the same with Dorothy Thompson. Even Eleanor Roosevelt took advantage of the trend, disseminating her messages across the country through her syndicated column My Day, which appeared in sixty-two newspapers by 1938.[10]

Missy considered ways to combine syndication with a popular-magazine format that would inspire and inform in the current times. She discussed with the Reids starting "a clearinghouse for Sunday copy," a weekly supplement filled not just with news, but with fiction too, as she had done in her Butterick publications. In the Depression it was a risky proposition, given the cost of big-name authors, and yet her success with them in the past convinced her that they must remain the centerpiece of any new concept she pitched. Having purchased some $4,000,000 in fiction over the years, she had established relationships with some of the most revered literary figures alive and had a few favors to call in.[11]

She jotted down what she envisioned: a magazine "popular and entertaining," but also "original, sufficiently sensational to be talked about, and completely without smut." As she had with *The Delineator*, Missy looked to tap into a middlebrow readership that may or may not have been college educated but that nonetheless had grown increasingly more sophisticated through its expanding access to public education, university extension courses, radio, moving pictures, and Chautauqua lectures. Many of them were middle-class suburbanites and women who, as she put it, remained alien to editors who never wandered beyond Fifth Avenue, Broadway, and Seventh. She had already convinced the Reids that her background in women's magazines made her an expert in this modern reader and in generating popular appeal. All she needed were investors who would entrust her with the editorial side of such a project.[12]

Missy's proposal was made more feasible by the fact that the Reids and a few others had started to think along similar lines. Both because and in spite of the Depression, a group of businessmen broached the idea of a nationally syndicated Sunday magazine with Joseph P. Knapp, the principal owner of the Crowell-Collier Publishing Company. Knapp had built a printing empire at American Lithographic and had revolutionized high-speed four-color printing at his company Alco-Gravure. Now, he was principal investor in the United Newspaper Magazine Corporation, which pitched a syndicated Sunday supplement to city papers. With Missy's blessing, the Reids enlisted in the venture, and their *Herald Tribune* joined the Baltimore *Sun*, Boston *Herald*, Chicago *Daily News*, Washington *Star*, and over a dozen other city papers in launching a new magazine called *This Week*. In February of 1935, its first issue was distributed in major cities and surrounding areas throughout the country. With all her ideas for appealing to women, suburbanites, and middlebrow readers at the forefront, Missy was the obvious choice to be its editor, and her *Herald Tribune* staff became the nucleus of the new editorial group.[13]

And so Missy paved an unprecedented path in magazines—advancing from the editorship of a fringe woman's publication, to a more successful one, to the Sunday magazine of a major New York newspaper, and now to a Sunday magazine with a national distribution that she would, once again, build from scratch. No other woman in the business had so much reach or so much content to choose from, for in addition to her broad range of news and editorial, she was also given the green light to print fiction. She had come full circle, back to when she first acquired content for *Everybody's* in the 1910s. For the debut edition of *This Week* she reached out to her old friend P. G. Wodehouse, paying for his piece herself, before acquiring the initial installment of a serial from Sinclair Lewis. Rupert Hughes and Fannie Hurst also provided fiction for the first issue, and Missy called in favors from Lord Strabolgi, scientist Roy Chapman Andrews, and artist Neysa McMein. In subsequent issues, more A-listers helped her out on the relative cheap. Somerset Maugham submitted stories as Missy peddled his manuscripts to fund his scholarships for novice British authors, and Joe Auslander submitted poems, telling her, "Maybe I'm making a mistake. But my love for you is no mistake, and an awful lot of it goes to you with this." Sherwood Anderson and Robert Frost submitted pieces on request, and Zona Gale had previously given her the short story "Papa LeFleur" for the day she could go back to printing fiction.[14]

This Week started with a combined circulation of four million. Missy's task was to keep this sprawling readership hooked and then to grow it, albeit with more cooks in the kitchen than she was used to. The corporation's editorial committee was supposed to meet regularly, but Missy's health rendered most in-person meetings impossible. She told Knapp that her time would be more productively spent if the committee met only as crises arose, which, if history proved anything, would be almost never. Still, she planned to work closely with her assistant editors, advertisers, illustrators, and designers. She had strong opinions regarding the magazine's look and feel, all of them informed by studies and data she collected about the reader experience. The feedback supported her priorities of fresh editorial and first-run fiction, namely stories with backdrops, themes, and plots coinciding with what was happening in the news. To add female interest, she brought in more "dos and don'ts" by etiquette guru Emily Post and tweaked the ratios of serials to articles, and celebrity profiles and romances to current events and adventure. She featured glamorous personalities from movies and radio, and moderns such as Ève Curie and Amelia Earhart, and she brought in pieces from sports legends Babe Ruth, Jack Dempsey, and the swimmer Gertrude Ederle to appeal to men and women across the generations.[15]

Given its wider audience, *This Week* couldn't be as heavy as the often somber *Herald Tribune Sunday Magazine*. And yet Missy fought pressure to make her publication resemble Hearst's glossier, more whimsical *American Weekly*. It pained her to run consecutive features on the sensationalized Dionne quintuplets and to pose Hollywood starlets on the cover. Missy preferred "thinking" stories and "storytelling covers"; if Greta Garbo had to feature, then she preferred her visage to be interpreted and set in context by someone like the artist Neysa McMein, rather than photographed in a vacuum. "Some feel that the way to meet Hearst competition is to be like Hearst; others feel that the way to fight fire is with water," she explained to Knapp, showing clear preference for the latter. It was affirmation when a *Time* reporter praised *This Week* for less "gaudiness" than *American Weekly* and determined its "genteel white-haired editor" the reason.[16]

Indeed, Missy seemed to have struck a winning balance in terms of the *type* of editorial she printed. It was the shrinking *amount* of it that displeased her. Having to kowtow to the business minds of the magazine, she managed a drastic reapportioning of editorial to ad space, which left a mere nine and a half pages to work with, compared to thirty-four in *Collier's* and forty-seven in the *Saturday Evening Post*. Where, she asked Knapp, was she supposed to fit serious pieces on domestic and world affairs? Her goal was to produce a "family" magazine, "an instrument in the making of a better America," she reminded him. Upon an executive's uninformed suggestion that she hire a male assistant to "get important articles," she snapped back that she could get them just fine on her own. The problem was having the space to print them.[17]

Perhaps for the first time in her entire career, Missy was starting to wonder if she, as a woman editor, might have been put in a position to fail. She had always prided herself on exceeding expectations with the budget and hand she had been dealt. But eventually she was feeling constrained to the point of handicap. At the Butterick Company, she had been sheltered from critics outside the realm of women's magazines, and at the *Herald Tribune* the Reids had shielded her from male critics by putting her in charge of the Home Institute and a brigade of female personnel who valued her vision. But at *This Week,* number crunchers unfamiliar with editorial were weighing in and being critical. Rather than relent to their criticism, Missy sent a memo to Knapp laying out, in no uncertain terms, her take and her expectations:

I do not think it does THIS WEEK any good for people other than the editor to ask advertising agencies, newspapers and former editors to point out what is the matter with the magazine....I have had a good many years of experience in this game and I know that editorial job. I undertook to make a national magazine in this small space against the advice of every friend I have in the editorial world because I believed in the future of THIS WEEK. I welcome, and have on many occasions sought constructive criticism, but criticism which does not take into account all the factors and limitations involved is of very little value—like suggesting that what the nations of Europe should do is just to forget their enmities and love one another. Such criticism is the easiest in the world to make. I could take any one of the most popular and successful mags on the stands today and tell you how it could be improved.

She didn't hold back, listing the obstacles imposed on her as she saw them:

a. 21 papers with violently opposing ideas to be satisfied.

b. At least two editors violently opposed to my appointment as editor of THIS WEEK, either because I was a woman or because they had personal friends to offer as candidates.

c. The largest mass audience in the world to please and the smallest space of any mag in the world in which to do it.[18]

The list went on. It was a rare moment when Missy felt the need to actively defend her turf, rather than simply letting her results speak for themselves. She told Knapp that it made no sense to stop letting her run serials, which, although the biggest drain on her budget, also proved to be the bread and butter of Knapp's other successful, more generously subsidized publications. "You pay Kathleen Norris more for one serial than the entire manuscript and art budget of THIS WEEK for four months," she reminded him, and added that even with the limited budget and space afforded her, she had already found a way to increase the circulation of *This Week*'s partnering papers. She begged Knapp to remind critics of the scanty page count she had to work with, and she closed with an ultimatum: "I suggest that you either recommend that I be given, at this point, complete authority and responsibility for the result, or that you select another editor."[19]

It had never been Missy's style to issue demands, but now she made it plain that she would not be sabotaged by uninformed men. Her strategy worked—it was the last time Knapp came to her with criticism that wasn't his. In fact, it might have been the last time he came to her with criticism at all, even when she asked for it, because he saw with subsequent issues that her editorial instincts were on point. As she proved that quality control didn't preclude profit, Knapp deferred to her more frequently and then entirely on all editorial matters, and he defended her to the rest of the corporation. Like so many of the men who collaborated with her, Knapp went from being her boss, to her admirer, and then her affectionate friend. In the early years, editing *This Week* was a drawn-out dance of steps forward and steps back, sometimes more steps back than seemed recoverable. Still, Missy held fast to her vision, as she tweaked and pleaded and skimped and willed success. As she always told people, there was no luck to it. She simply worked harder than everyone else.[20]

———

WITH BILL MELONEY having been gone nearly a decade, and her mother and Curie having been laid to rest, Missy was turning a page in her personal life. She was not interested in another husband, but she was most definitely in want of a roommate. For a woman used to being so independent, it was hard to admit that living in an apartment by herself was lonely and physically challenging. She had come to rely on the assistance of Leonebel Jacobs when she traveled, and steadily this relationship bloomed. In 1935 Missy left her apartment at 1 Fifth Avenue to keep house with Leonebel at 1 West 67th, in the Hotel des Artistes. Centrally located near artists and writers, Jacobs's studio was a convenient base of operations. Leonebel was like a sister, a nurse, and a personal assistant in one; when Missy could not be reached by phone or was slippery in answering inquiries about her health, friends turned to Leonebel for the rundown. Whether they were introducing European friends to New York society or promoting art or philanthropies, Missy and Leonebel soon became an inseparable pair, hosting dinner parties together, often even midweek and late into the night. The guest list at any one of their soirées in 1935 included an eclectic mix of personages—from Charles and Anne Lindbergh, to RCA's David Sarnoff, the *New Yorker's* Harold Ross, and celebrity dog breeder Albert Payson Terhune. Not coincidentally, there was occasional overlap between the names on their dinner cards and the bylines in the pages of *This Week*.[21]

The time had also come for Bill Jr. to turn a page, so his mother believed. For years, he had appeared to find his way only to lose it again, perhaps because his well-intentioned mother still did much of the navigating in his life. No doubt at Missy's strong suggestion, he had agreed to study for his law degree and to join the New York firm of Bill Donovan. Bill Jr. landed there after his mother had helped Donovan run for New York governor, and he later took over the running of the *Pawling Chronicle* as he served as an upstate correspondent for the *Herald Tribune* and the *Times*. What good were a mother's connections if they couldn't help her only son get back on his feet? Nevertheless, there were signs that Missy's machinations were not necessarily what Bill needed to feel fulfilled. He claimed to be frustrated by the fact that he could not follow in his father's footsteps by serving in the military; his lungs had allegedly remained too impaired to allow him to register for active duty. The closest he would get to the military, in fact, was when he scoured the papers of the War Department to find George Washington's original directive creating the Order of the Purple Heart. Somehow the command had been forgotten until Bill Jr.'s find. When his discovery was brought to the attention of army officials, they considered awarding Bill Sr. a Purple Heart posthumously, but Missy believed that her husband would have refused the honor when other worthy men had not been considered for it over the years. Instead, she asked military officials to recognize her son as the Purple Heart's official historian—her way, perhaps, of making him a hero, as his father had been.[22]

Bill had written his mother late at night from the offices of the *Chronicle* after one of his employees leaned into the meshing gears of the press and mangled his arm. After filling out workers' compensation papers, it occurred to Bill that he was overwhelmed. "It was good to hear your voice the other evening and to have the benefit of your greater wisdom and advice," he told Missy. "I have a lot to learn about my trade and one of the things that I lack is a good mental sounding board—a sharp, keen and vivid mind against which to try my thoughts. Sometimes I feel myself thinking in a vacuum and then I know that it is time to sing out for help." Indeed, Missy already sensed that he could use her guidance. His relationship with Elizabeth had grown visibly strained. He had had an affair with a woman named Priscilla Fansler Hobson in New York City, and rumors abounded that she had aborted Bill's child before marrying the notorious Alger Hiss. Bill went back to Elizabeth, but more and more they lived apart. Now his boys were at Elizabeth's parents' home in Michigan; Missy suppressed her disappointment at seeing her grandsons only in pictures. Her advice to her son was to regroup out West, where he could start fresh. His father's Hollywood friends took Bill in as a script-writing apprentice, and Missy, too, arranged for him to meet up with her West Coast contacts. The Armenian-American director Rouben Mamoulian assured Missy that Bill dutifully came to his Beverly Hills home for lunch, as she had arranged.[23]

Missy had been unable to reach Bill on the phone to wish him a happy thirtieth birthday that May of 1935. When he called her back, he reported that he had been working on a film "full tilt," putting in fifteen-hour days at the studio. He was also trying to develop a script for Lionel Barrymore but confessed to not knowing if he had "the gift" to make it as a screenwriter. It helped to have the mother he did. "You know more about fiction than anyone I know.... Roy Cohen praised you as the best—and to the author the most useful—fiction editor in the game today," he told her. Missy brushed off the compliment and, as a mother would, assured Bill that he indeed had the gift; but as an editor would, she also warned him that struggle would be inevitable. Many of the best writers knew rejection many times over, she reminded him, adding that Roy Cohen had been turned down all over the place and was flat broke when she took a chance on him. "Here he is twenty years later, a successful writer who has made money and a reputation, and some of his work will certainly last in American letters as a distinct contribution to Americana. And, yet, even now he has to turn to occasionally rewrite a story. He has re-written two for me since he has been in California.... Writing is just like everything else, only more so—it has to be struggled with, fought and bled over, and it has to be loved."[24]

It pleased her to coach her son the way she had coached so many authors over the years, but a mother's advice had its limits. With Bill now divorced and working long hours across the country, Missy worried that he was lonely. Sometimes he was, Bill admitted, though he was trying to ameliorate the situation. That weekend he drove with friends to see some desert flowers, and one of the women who joined him was a writer a few years his senior—a New York transplant and mother of three named Rose Franken. Missy was thrilled—and also partially responsible. Months before, she had been visiting her longtime friend Menas Gregory, the recently retired head of psychiatry at Bellevue. Since Bill's death, Gregory had invited her regularly to his bachelor apartment atop the Buckingham Hotel, and on one occasion he introduced Missy to Franken, whose late husband had been his medical colleague. Something told him that the two women would get on famously, for Franken was a self-taught writer who had published her first novel in 1925, followed by a critically acclaimed play in 1932. Now, as a widow, she was making a surprisingly good go of it writing for the Hollywood screen.[25]

"Mrs. Meloney was already ensconced in a great Charles II needle-point wing chair when I arrived," Franken recalled of that first meeting at Gregory's apartment. "My first impression of her was that her feet didn't quite reach the floor. She was extremely tiny, and I wondered, vaguely, as her hand so firmly pressed mine, how such vitality and strength could be packaged in so small a body." By now, Missy's hair was stunningly white; Franken found the contrast to her brown eyes "intensely arresting." Watching Gregory watching Missy, Franken decided that he was deeply in love with her, and probably had always been. But as sweetly as Missy talked to him, Franken could tell that his feelings would never be returned, for she referred to "Big Bill" over and over, as if he were still alive. "I wish you'd look up Little Bill when you get back to Hollywood," Missy suggested to Franken as they rose from Gregory's dinner table. Over the meal she had explained that Bill was learning the ropes at Twentieth Century Fox. Out of politeness—and because Missy charmed her—Franken agreed to check in on Bill when she returned to California. Missy gratefully drew her in to kiss her. "God love you," she professed.[26]

When Franken met "Little Bill," his cultured voice belied his mother's nickname. He was tall, extremely thin, and dressed impeccably in Harris tweed and polished oxfords. She was struck by his immaculate hairline and tidy moustache. "He had an outstanding nose, almost beaked," she noticed, and yet it contributed to, rather than detracted from, his distinguished bearing. "My mother's friends who look me up bring out the worst in me," Franken remembered Bill confessing, "especially professional women." There was no immediate chemistry, but in time Franken bonded with Bill over their love of animals and, unexpectedly, their fluid collaboration on writing projects. They would sit opposite each other, Bill typing out plots as Franken conjured up dialog. One would leave the typewriter and the other continue intuitively where the first had left off. In 1935 they wrote the script *Thirsty Soil*, followed by *Beloved Enemy*, establishing themselves as the writing duo "Franken Meloney." In a matter of months, Bill looked to have found renewed health, purpose, and companionship, much to his mother's relief.[27]

———

IT FINALLY APPEARED as though Missy would get her interview with Mussolini. A few foreign journalists were being granted access to him in the summer of 1935, including Anne O'Hare McCormick, foreign correspondent for the *New York Times*. As the Germans departed from the League of Nations, Mussolini told McCormick that he still intended to reduce armaments in Europe, as most Americans hoped to hear. Missy doubted his sincerity; her contacts in Rome confirmed her sense that the leader she had met in 1928 had been seized by a megalomania similar to what had emerged in Hitler. It made her keen to meet with Mussolini once again in person to discern his intentions for herself, and she had asked Sarfatti to make it happen.[28]

And Sarfatti did. Having bypassed official channels, she allegedly used her personal sway with Mussolini to determine a specific time and place for Missy's long-awaited interview. Better yet, she reported that the Italian government had installed radio equipment that would allow Missy to broadcast Mussolini's words for the Forum that fall. Cautiously optimistic, Missy booked another summer trip to Europe, scheduling plenty of other meetings in case she was once more given the run around. An interview in Germany was again a possibility. Meanwhile, she attended a play with Phillips Oppenheim in London; had tea with Strabolgi at the House of Lords; lunched with the feminist magnate Lady Rhondda; and arranged to see Honoré Willsie Morrow, who now lived in Devon. Missy's assistant editor Mary Day worried about her stamina, but Morrow wrote to assure her that Missy had been holding up beautifully when she saw her in London. "She managed between strawberries, callers and telephones to find out what my present novel covers and to express a real interest in it," Morrow marveled. It was Missy in her usual form.[29]

Having arranged the Mussolini interview for July 19, Sarfatti met Missy in Rome and accompanied her in a limousine to the palace. Sarfatti gently reminded her American guest of what she, as a friend of the Italian government, would probably be expected to write following the meeting. Indeed, before Missy had even arrived and asked her first question, Sarfatti was encouraging her to emphasize all the investment opportunities Mussolini would open up to Americans if Ethiopia fell into Italian hands. At that moment, Missy's excitement turned into a more subdued sense of clarity. Now she properly understood why she had been granted the interview, if she hadn't somewhat suspected it already. Sarfatti had essentially summoned her to Italy as part of a spin campaign, and that knowledge made Missy feel cheapened and played.[30] The next day, her write-up appeared in the *Herald Tribune*:

ITALY'S DUTY IS TO CIVILIZE ETHIOPIA, MUSSOLINI HOLDS
Il Duce Explains and Defends His "Mission" to
Mrs. Meloney, Editor of This Week: His People,
Asked If They'll Go, Reply "Certainly"

ROME, July 19—Just twenty-four hours before Haile Selassie I, Emperor of Ethiopia, appealed to his people to resist Italian invasion, Premier Benito Mussolini, in an interview with me at the Palazzo Venezia, said this: "After fifty years of well-meant but futile attempts, we are now determined to settle once and for all the problem of our relations with Ethiopia. Italy fully realized the mission of civilization that she has to accomplish in Ethiopia, not only on her own behalf but also on that of the whole Western World." [. . .]

This statement comes from a Mussolini who is strikingly in contrast to the Mussolini I interviewed seven years ago.[31]

Missy went on to disclose the shocking news that the premier planned to invade Ethiopia on the first dry Monday in September. She used discretion about injecting too many of her own opinions into the piece, largely quoting Mussolini verbatim, without commentary. Nevertheless, the story was a scoop, and it reverberated throughout Europe and back home. It signaled the unraveling of the League of Nations and the beginning of a wave of bellicose nationalism throughout Europe. Although Missy had once seen potential for good in Mussolini's rise to power, now she felt disillusioned. She had hoped that Americans would listen to the premier over the airwaves in 1935 and come to the same positive conclusions she had during her face-to-face meeting with him in 1928. But after the debacle of 1933 and facing him now, she realized that there was no point in recording him. Her hopes of any alliance with the leader had been vanquished. He was an altogether different man, with altogether different intentions.

In the interwar years she had grown introspective about the costs of war, joining prominent women such as Emily Newell Blair, Jane Addams, Carrie Chapman Catt, Dorothy Canfield Fisher, Mary Woolley, and Eleanor Roosevelt in contributing to the volume *Why Wars Must Cease*. Whereas the other contributors generally told of the demoralizing effects of war, Missy focused concretely on its monetary costs—from veterans' relief to insurance, lost production, war settlement claims, community restoration, interest on war debts, and postwar military operations. Of course her personal experience as a pensioner of the Veteran's Bureau spoke equally to the emotional costs of war, but her essay sounded less like a sentimental plea of moral suasionists past than a pragmatic call against waste. Maintaining peace did not mean remaining passive about the rising tensions in Europe, however, she believed that Americans had propagated a terrible "self-deception" in staying neutral for so long during the First World War. Now, with fascists signaling their intentions, she urged her countrywomen not to be complicit in another deception.[32]

It was Sarfatti's grave misfortune that after the Ethiopian invasion, Mussolini aligned with Hitler and changed his stance on anti-Semitism. Suddenly, Jews in Italy were barred from mixed marriages, professional jobs, and government service. As the Jewish Sarfatti became a second-class citizen in the country she had spent decades building up to the world, her influence on Mussolini waned. She stopped being subtle in expressing her desire to come to America, but her support of the Ethiopian invasion had changed the country's perception of her and closed many of the doors that Missy had opened in 1933. As her situation grew dire, so did her pleas. Could Missy get her money through the embassy? Paid lectures? A visa? New York accommodation? A book deal? Introductions to Hollywood filmmakers? In melodramatic fashion, she called on Missy's humanity, her friendship, her compulsion to do right. "Darling, I long to come over to America, do all you can for me," she begged. "You will save my life by doing so." "Help me out of this hell for Heaven's sake!"[33]

Columbia University president Nicholas Murray Butler asked Missy if she had found any opportunities for Sarfatti in the States, though by then Missy had stopped trying. She was undyingly loyal to the most flawed of her friends, so long as they were honest with her, and Sarfatti hadn't appeared to be. How long had she known of Mussolini's plans, and what was her role in shaping them before they spiraled out of control? Sarfatti had wanted to replace Curie in Missy's affections, only to find in Missy something that Curie never could: the limits of her good graces.[34]

———

MISSY HAD WRITTEN PROFILES and articles on any number of world leaders throughout her career, but somehow the magnitude of her war-announcing scoop propelled her into the public consciousness as nothing else had. Newsmen had long respected her journalism, but to the general public she seemed to suddenly explode onto the scene after her interview with Mussolini. And although she had been the mind behind the scenes of the *Herald Tribune* Forum for five years, the amazing success of that event also boosted her exposure in the press. In previous years, Hermann Hagedorn, director of the Theodore Roosevelt Memorial Association, had asked Missy to recommend men for the memorial's Distinguished Service Medal, thinking that no one was in more "constant touch with the main streams of activity in the country." But now, he considered Missy as one of his esteemed honorees. "I have been watching your march up the ladder with affection and a bunch of personal pride (I knew her when...)," he gushed, like a proud father. Missy was finally receiving acclaim for work she had always done.[35]

She continued to speak at expositions on women's "better buying" and on radio programs like WJZ's "Let's Talk It Over," still in the voice of the domestic expert. But it was no longer some insider secret that her expertise extended beyond the woman's sphere into politics, media, and marketing. Missy sat on panels alongside the president of NBC Radio and officials of the Federal Housing Administration. Nelson Rockefeller called on her to stimulate the housing market in New York City as he stood on the precipice of completing Rockefeller Center. She chose the winner of the Irwin D. Wolf Award for the best idea in packaging, alongside retail executives and professionals of the Pratt Institute and the Metropolitan Museum of Art. Who better to judge, organizers figured, than this unsurpassed packager of American ideas and ideals?[36]

Although Helen Reid ran the marketing department of the *Herald Tribune*, Missy's campaigns for Curie, the BHA, children's health, Milk Month, the Junior Red Cross, efficient kitchens, and American presidents now solidified her reputation as a marketing maven. As the keynote speaker at the annual meeting of the American Association of Advertising Agencies, she elicited a response so positive that *Advertising and Selling* and the *Washington Post* reprinted her remarks for wider circulation. The president of Beech-Nut Packing Company concurred that she stole the show, outperforming speakers like Arthur Brisbane and the head of General Motors. Missy was flattered but torn; although she liked being heeded as a marketing expert, she had never intended to market herself.[37]

The shift from *making* the news to *being* the news gratified yet unnerved her at once. Despite her sheepishly passing off the credit to the Reids, the press proclaimed the frail organizer of the Forum an expert on current events and the American woman's point of view. Even the *New York Times* acknowledged her "tireless labor in bringing together the best minds of the world to discuss the problems before the women of the United States," quoting her Forum keynotes as if they were the words of statesmen. In 1936 the woman who had once organized the awarding of Curie's honorary degrees was honored with a doctorate of human letters at Russell Sage College. Missy sat humbly as her host spoke from the podium: "By thus helping thousands of American women citizens interpret the great national problems of the present and the future in terms of sound economic laws and the controlling social ideals of our times, you have plowed well and deep that a finer social order may grow."[38]

The result of her gaining attention in male realms of influence was more praise by groups such as the League of Business and Professional Women, which honored Missy as a "Woman of Achievement" in 1936, defining "achievement" in the virile, careerist sense. Meanwhile, the First Lady thought no one better to make a case for melding the traditionally feminine sphere of social service with masculine public policy than the founder of the Forums, and she asked Missy to give a White House address calling for the establishment of a National Academy of Public Affairs. That year Missy also presided over the Forum's Round Table Conference on Crime and Youth, at which Mayor La Guardia and FBI Director J. Edgar Hoover hashed out ideas she had proposed for improved courts and recreational outlets for the nation's children.[39]

By putting social reformers in conversation with federal officials and policy wonks of all sorts, Missy had transcended the boundaries both of political party and of gendered sphere. Because she remained so visibly useful through the remaining years of the Depression, her efficacy was no longer something she could disguise or attribute to men. Still, she continued to try. Though Missy had grown and changed in many ways, her reluctance to step into the spotlight was one thing that remained constant. Fame was not her aspiration; *mastery* was— over national crises, political scenarios, the distribution of national magazines, and, at the core, her physical shortcomings. Perhaps only a woman of her generation and constitution could truly understand.

Chapter Thirteen

ILLNESS AND IMPENDING WAR

1937–1940

ALL THE ACCOLADES AND PUBLIC PRAISE didn't distract Missy from making *This Week* the best that it could be. In the summer of 1936 she met with advertisers in Cleveland, Chicago, St. Louis, and Dallas, trying to live up to her claim to know middle America better than the magazine executives on Seventh Avenue did. Knapp admired her work ethic, but he worried about her too—as Charles Eliot, Harlow Brooks, and any number of men had before him. It was no secret that despite his editor wanting to be everywhere at once, her health had relapsed again, though she obscured to what extent. He implored her to take some time off in Pawling, and she did at the end of July, albeit with to-do lists in hand. "I am working here from the neck up," she promised him. "This note goes to you via Dictaphone by the side of my bed. Don't worry about me. I am going to get well quickly....Dr. Morrison told me that I had my best work ahead of me—if I take time to overhaul the engine now."[1]

Knapp knew that was a big "if," but true to her word Missy canceled her trip to Europe; her managing editor Mary Day took over her meetings in London. Missy reported to an inquiring Eleanor Roosevelt that she was improving in Pawling, but shortly after that she was admitted to Doctor's Hospital, a favored rehabilitation spot of the New York elite, located opposite Gracie Mansion on the Upper East Side. Once again, she refused to make physical incapacitation an

excuse to avoid helping her friends. Owen Young came by the infirmary with paperwork for Missy to sign as trustee of Mary Mitchel's
estate, and from her bed she also tied up financial ends for the socialite
Emilie Grigsby, who had resorted to pawning jewelry to pay her lawyers. While in the hospital, Missy planned tributes for the Memorial
Committee of Harlow Brooks, her beloved physician, who had died
of an infection from the very bacillus he had discovered in the 1890s,
no doubt contracted while he was tending to patients without taking adequate precautions. The fact that Brooks had treated patients
until the very end of his life was emblematic of the heroism Missy
had known in her physician father and of the selflessness that had
made Brooks her kindred spirit. Likewise, Missy had no intention of
relinquishing her work while she lived, especially now, as tensions in
Europe convinced her that war was impending.[2]

With ambitions to return to Germany in 1937, Missy reached out
to her contacts again, requesting a sit-down with Hitler once she
was well enough to travel. She was careful with her tone. "I don't
want to risk the kind of disappointing experience I had the last time
I went," she reminded the German consul general, and yet she didn't
admonish too harshly in light of the recent explosion of the German
airship *Hindenburg,* which had tragically killed thirty-six in New Jersey.
Although tensions had risen between the Germans and Americans,
she thought it essential to keep channels of communication open,
so she continued to solicit German contributors to *This Week* to get
scoops that other American journalists increasingly couldn't under
Hitler's regime.[3]

But the trip to Germany was never to be. The truth was that after
two decades of regular overseas travel, Missy's body could no longer withstand the physical strain of it. The last time she had gone
to Europe she had been accompanied by a medical entourage, and it
had made her self-conscious. "A few people think that I am high hat
'traveling with a maid,'" she told Channing Pollock. "*You* know why
I can't make it alone." She had always prided herself on being able
to travel on planes, trains, and boats on a moment's notice to get to

people and stories before other journalists swooped in. But now she coordinated too many moving parts to be spontaneous. For the first time, she consciously refocused on projects that required little travel and were longer term. Notre Dame president John Francis O'Hara offered her a standing invitation to lecture on campus once her health was restored, but in the meantime, he scolded her: "If you don't take time enough to rest, you are going to see Notre Dame from above." The following summer he wondered half jokingly if he should extend his invitation, if only to force Missy into the campus infirmary.[4]

Indeed, as 1937 wore on, Missy didn't appear to be getting better. She found herself back in the hospital, this time at St. Luke's in Manhattan, her convalescence shrouded in more secrecy since she was no longer allowed to have visitors. A concerned Eleanor Roosevelt sent her notes, as did friends from around the world. Cecil Roberts corresponded like a regular pen pal, keeping her abreast of his recovery from his own nervous breakdown; he had been grateful to Missy for helping him get through his writer's funk, even as she lay in a bed of her own. Alexander Kirk checked in regularly too, wanting advice as he moved between diplomatic posts. "I would give anything to be able to talk to you about what I have seen . . . it frightens me," he reported from Moscow. Berlin, of course, was no better; he likened it to "impending Hell." "You are the one who always can do something and my membranes are tearing with the necessity of doing something or of seeing that something one has done, brought results," he wrote her despairingly. Hitler's reign of terror was no longer just rumor and speculation.[5]

It pained Missy not to be in Europe facilitating diplomacy in her quiet, effective way. For now, all she could do was encourage, advise, console from a distance, and perhaps carry out small favors where she saw they were needed. During that summer she reached out to European contacts through her secretaries, requesting that they assist friends and reporters traveling overseas. Lord Strabolgi obliged her requests to entertain FDR's naval secretary, Frank Knox, during King George's coronation weekend. *New York Times* correspondent Anne

O'Hare McCormick was another American whom Missy asked Strabolgi to take around the House of Lords; the access she provided no
doubt contributed to McCormick's reportage that summer, which
won her a Pulitzer Prize, the first for a woman journalist. She also
helped Helen Reid's son "Whitie" follow in his father's footsteps and
become a journalist at the family's newspaper. To facilitate his work as
an overseas correspondent, Missy called upon her contacts in the British government to provide the young Reid access to stories. "I shutter
[sic] at the thought of the work you have done on my behalf in writing
all of London," Whitie wrote her, but Missy did it gladly. It was the
least she could do to reciprocate for his mother's support over the
years, and all it required was sending out dispatches from bed.[6]

Missy didn't leave the hospital for good until after New Year's Day
of 1938. Rather than return to the Hotel des Artistes, however, she
took up temporary residence in the Biltmore, which was virtually
next door to the United Newspaper Magazine Company offices in
the Graybar Building. Despite doctors' orders for continued bed rest,
hers was a revolving door; she conducted as much business in her
hotel suite as in the office. Recalling the occasion with bewilderment,
Edward Bernays entered Missy's suite at the Biltmore just as the president of the General Federation of Women's Clubs was departing. Gift
packages and baskets of unopened fruit sat on the chiffonier, while
secretaries and typewriter desks heaped with paper stood next to the
bed. Dressed in a coffee-colored negligee, Missy was propped up on
cushions on a sofa in the corner, holding court as if working from
an executive's desk. When Bernays entered the room Missy turned
away from the couch and greeted him ebulliently. Despite having a
collapsed lung, she insisted that she felt fine, joking that she didn't
see the need for more than one lung anyway. Bernays told her that he
worried, but Missy implored him not to. She had plans to save enough
money to retire with a nursing staff and to take on all those books
she had threatened to write, she told him. Bernays marveled at her
optimism.[7]

Before long Missy shifted her base of operations again, from the Biltmore to the Waldorf Astoria, which was more central to her abundant New York projects. Mayor La Guardia was a regular caller, as Missy continued to run many of his local relief committees, and the executive board of PEN conducted meetings right there in her residence. Although she continued to travel to Pawling, she admitted to Eleanor Roosevelt that the trips to and from the city were getting onerous. One mere excursion from the farmhouse to the dentist in Manhattan had set her recovery back weeks. Her saving grace was an Irish nursemaid named Geraldine, who tended to her devotedly on either end of the commute.[8]

By the summer of 1938, it grew clear to those who wanted to talk to Missy in person that they were less likely to find her in the city and that they'd have to make the pilgrimage upstate. She welcomed visitors and put them up in museum-like accommodations. The works of Borglum, Jacobs, and Jo Davidson were on display throughout Missy's main house and the adjoining guest house and cottage, along with trinkets, portraits, masks, textiles, lithographs, books, and figurines that had been gifted to her over the years. Early American and Victorian pieces were mixed in with Louis XVI and Queen Anne–style footrests and writing desks, Italian credenzas, carved Madonnas, and Chinese vases in jade. Some pieces had once been in the White House; others had belonged to emperors. Even the walls of the nurse's room and secretarial office were adorned with Civil War needleworks and original landscapes. In the attic, Missy kept a collection of autographs and the glass slides that Borglum had used to project his images onto the mountainsides he blasted into sculptures.[9]

Bill and Rose Franken had become fixtures at Quaker Hill since getting married in April of 1937. Missy accepted Rose and her boys unconditionally as family. "Barriers did not exist for her," Rose appreciated. She wondered if Bill knew the rarity in having two strongminded women cultivate such affection between them, but he had seen it before. Missy conveyed to Eleanor Roosevelt that her new daughter was "a rarely gifted and lovable person," and from then on Rose became a regular and favored guest at the White House. With newfound confidence and contentment, Bill published his first major novel, *Rush to the Sun*. A reviewer for the *New York Times* called Bill "outspoken," like "a Faulkner or a Caldwell"; John Erskine thought the novel the best thing Bill had written, until he published *In High Places* two years later. Bill had become the full-time author his mother had mentored but could never be herself. Although her marriage had been a happy union of writers, she and Bill Sr. had never ventured into a literary collaboration like Franken Meloney, which produced the plays *Strange Victory* in 1939, *When Doctors Disagree* in 1940, and *American Bred* in 1941. It pleased Missy equally to see her son so supportive of his wife's solo efforts, for the greatest successes between them were Rose's alone, based on her character Claudia, the heroine of stories that appeared in *Redbook* and *Good Housekeeping*, in eight novels, on the Broadway stage, and eventually on radio, film, and television.[10]

On the night of the Washington stage premier of *Claudia*, Rose dressed early to allow time to stop off at the Waldorf Astoria to see her mother-in-law, who was too feverish to accompany her. Missy looked unwell, and yet the moment Rose came in her face brightened, as if she were on a stage. "How I wish I could be there tonight," she said, lifting Rose's hand to her lips. "I'm so proud of my beautiful daughter." Rose remembered thinking it one of Missy's sweet conceits, since she had never considered herself particularly pretty. Skeptical by nature, Rose believed Missy to be the one person who hadn't a disingenuous bone in her body. After that Washington premier, Missy wrote Rose to tell her that Eleanor Roosevelt had taken friends to the play and that they had enjoyed it thoroughly. She attached a clipping from the First Lady's column My Day, just to prove that what she was telling her was true.[11]

ON AUGUST 18, 1938, Missy dictated a letter to Joseph Knapp that reported a cleaner bill of health. "Dear Boss. . . . My temperature has been normal for two months. My sputum test has been negative for three months. I am five pounds overweight for my normal health. The last X-ray showed all the lung expanded except a small area in the upper lobe." Knapp was happy to hear the update and sent a cheery note back, signing off, "Your boss. Ha, ha!"[12]

Several times while returning home from salmon fishing, Knapp had stopped in at Quaker Hill to see Missy in person; it was becoming the only way to truly know how she was faring, since she tended to oversell her health in her written reports. Although sometimes still in bed, she was always brimming with ideas for *This Week*, and most of the time she had already begun reaching out to potential authors. She had collected reactions to the new marriage-license law and enlisted J. Edgar Hoover to address high school students as soon-to-be voters. Deciding to profile the inventor of white lines on highways, she had sent an assistant off to inquire at the US Patent Office. That August she also proposed a "success story" contest, for which young male and female readers shared accounts of how they "made good" during the Depression. She wanted to devote that same issue to the twentieth anniversary of the signing of the Armistice at Versailles, soliciting Pershing in America, Foch in France, von Hindenburg in Germany, and Fisher in England to write about which battle each man believed to be decisive in that terrible war. Their perspectives were to go alongside remarks from Mussolini, Hitler, Chamberlain, Daladier, FDR, and Hoover in reaction to a premonition Georges Clemenceau had shared with her a decade earlier: that the Versailles Treaty would sow the seeds of the next world war. The story needed to run soon, she told Knapp, since Clemenceau had predicted tensions to erupt before the year's end.[13]

Eleanor Roosevelt had come to Missy's farmhouse that summer as well and was relieved to see in her friend "no signs of being an invalid." In fact, Missy had been anxiously awaiting Eleanor's arrival with a puppy for her son, which Eleanor kept for herself. Missy looked well but was admittedly still too frail to organize that year's Forum by herself. Reluctantly, she asked Helen Reid to take over many of her tasks and Eleanor to assist in any way she could. "No one who has never organized a Forum has any conception of the work, the strain, and the disappointments involved," she confessed. She tried to stay useful, even from Pawling, by drawing up the Forum program to include panel discussions on charged issues. During another of Eleanor's visits, Missy elaborated on why it was crucial to have a Forum panel that hashed out pending immigration legislation, including a bill granting citizenship to illegal aliens with no criminal record. "So many of them have come believing that they were entering the country properly and have been victims of graft and blackmail ever since," she explained of many recent immigrants. "The Bill, as I understand it, sounds like a very humane and just one." Given the rising panic about unchecked immigration, much of it with nationalist undertones, she believed that some sensible, fact-based discussion was overdue in a national venue.[14]

Missy got a chance in the weeks leading up to the 1938 Forum to discuss issues with the president himself at Quaker Hill. "I have been eager to have a quiet talk with you for some time," she told him, admitting that she had not been well enough to come to him. One of the ideas on her mind was a biography of the president's former right-hand man Louis Howe, who had passed away in 1936. As a Democratic operative during the 1932 election, Howe had been a formidable adversary, but that didn't diminish Missy's appreciation of him: "Although a semi-invalid, he was a tower of strength." She admired his public-relations acumen and identified with his battle against chronic ailments, as well as his continuing to direct operations from hospital beds near the end. "I think a study of his life could be made a most appealing human story. And his faith in F.D.R. and his reasons for believing in him could bear telling to the country," she contended. She, of course, would never have considered telling the similar tale of her relationship with Herbert Hoover; there was no benefit to recounting her story, whereas Howe's life could help in making a public case for FDR's third term. Only after much pressing of the point did she convince the First Couple to address the idea head-on at the Forum that year. They feared that a third term was a political third rail, but Missy insisted that "the question [wa]s in the minds of people" already. "The news coming from the eastern and western parts of the world would seem to indicate that by 1940 we shall be involved in a war[,] if not as participants at least as peacefully on the defensive," she reminded them. Given the prediction, she was sure that Americans would want continuity in the presidency, despite the opposing opinion of the *Herald Tribune*.[15]

That October, thousands gathered at the Waldorf Astoria in anticipation of intensified political theater at the Forum. In a coup, Missy had convinced Herbert Hoover to be on the agenda, speaking on "America and the World Crisis" and directly preceding FDR's closing remarks. There was also the unanticipated drama of her carrying her weakened body across the Forum stage to deliver her speech, "A New World Power—Mass Opinion." Her remarks were as prescient then as they would be now:

> To believe in democracy is not enough. To keep it alive we shall have to fight for it with every weapon we have; ultimately, God forbid, we may have to go to war for it. . . .
>
> Science has now made it possible to mobilize, in a few hours, the emotion if not the opinion of the whole world when great events are in the making. . . .
>
> We must remember that in a dictatorship, opinion is dictated. Only one side of a story is ever told.
>
> In a democracy, we have an opportunity to learn all sides of debatable questions so that in democracies *only* it is possible to crystallize an informed public opinion. The greatest danger America faces in this situation is the possibility of mass emotion riding over sentiment for one side or the other. . . .
>
> The whipping up of mass emotion is one of the favorite devices of dictatorships, but though mass emotion is powerful, I believe that informed mass opinion is even more powerful. . . .
>
> I have believed that one of the chief aims in the life of a civilized human being should be the pursuit of truth and yet I repeat to you

today that the history which has been made in the past ten years convinces me that in a crisis the truth is not as important as what people believe.

But remember also, that truth is without use until it is given to the people. It is without power until the people accept it. You must be a vital part of this new power of mass opinion.[16]

Owen Young was not present to hear Missy speak in person, but he heard her over the radio. "I could not help admiring your loyalty in undertaking such a task, and at the same time I could not help regretting that you felt it necessary to submit to that added strain," he wrote her. The radio audience could detect the physical exertion of the undertaking, but Young praised Missy's performance as a necessary one, no less.[17]

———————

WHILE THE FORUM WENT ON in New York, Irène Curie was writing Missy disquieting dispatches from Paris: "We are more than ever depressed by the International events. It is a sad comedy to see papers celebrating as saviors of the peace the madmen Hitler and Mussolini." She was disgusted by the racist, anti-Semitic, sexist policies of fascist leaders, but frankly also by the noninterventionism of Americans, which made her receptive to Russian communism as a form of resistance. When France and England finally declared war in September of 1939, Irène wrote Missy more despondent than before. Her husband, Frédéric, had been put in charge of a group of laboratories for war purposes, and she felt compelled to work with him, even if Hitler's regime set the research agenda. "It seems to be impossible to live on the same continent with the Germans," she lamented. "Let us hope that some bomb will not change that state of things.... I am not sorry that my mother died before she could see all of this again."[18]

Irène imagined life in the States as blissfully removed from war, but that wasn't entirely true. Americans had yet to suffer attacks on their home soil or to declare war, but tensions were palpable. Americans feared that violence could come to their shores, and the Depression, which was not yet over, continued to reduce their confidence in established institutions. Politically radical movements and "anti-American" groups were on the rise. The FBI monitored the subversive activities of communists, fascists, and organizations who supported the overthrow of the government, only adding to the paranoia and mistrust. Missy tried to help the FBI by selling their amped-up surveillance tactics in her magazine, albeit adjusting the tone of the rhetoric to avoid leaving readers panicked or dubious of her good intentions. She recommended that rather than sounding impersonal alarms, FBI director J. Edgar Hoover share his personal thoughts on "what the man on the street should know" about foreign sabotage and how citizens could do their part to thwart it. Meanwhile, she amassed her own intelligence files in unmarked, sealed envelopes and handed them off to unnamed agents to give to Hoover. The information was sufficiently concerning to dispatch field agents to Quaker Hill for follow-up questions. Grateful for Missy's vigilance, Hoover promised her access to inside stories he wasn't offering other news outlets. Once she was well enough, he vowed to escort her personally to Quantico for one, so that she could see firsthand how FBI agents trained to combat methods of modern espionage.[19]

As she had before World War I, Missy thought it her civic duty to aid in matters of national security, but it was also her mission as an editor to keep up her readers' morale. The dual obligations posed a challenge for an editor trying to strike a balance between content that was both practical and escapist, patriotic and philosophical, that informed but also inspired. She solicited winsome pieces from Walt Disney, as well as from the deaf, blind philosopher-pacifist Helen Keller. Despite being ill, she made her pleas to Keller in person, knowing full well that the human connection would be crucial. Keller, too, had been a Southern transplant to New York (Forest Hills, Queens) whose overcoming of physical limitations had inspired those around her; Missy thought there was no one better to encourage her readers. Her visit with Keller led to the publication of "The Beauty I Have Seen," a rumination about being grateful. Keller signed, and her secretary dictated, a letter afterward: "'Missy'—a tender intimate name to love you by. It is so like the pressure of your hand." In the same vein, Missy convinced baseball great Lou Gehrig to write for her as his battle with ALS was ending his illustrious career. She proposed the piece carefully, arguing that sharing his story with readers would give his suffering a larger purpose; it was not unlike the case she had made to James Barrie years earlier, for, as Barrie had been, Gehrig was initially reluctant to write for her. What changed his mind was Missy's own physical perseverance at the Forum. "I marveled at your vitality and admired your courage to overcome this obstacle," he wrote her. "If, in a small measure, I am able to match your fortitude, I shall be very proud."[20]

Missy's patriotism was multifaceted in those tense months of 1939. It showed in her acquisitions for *This Week* and was evident, though less visible, in the advice she passed on to the First Lady during their visits alone together. Missy floated the idea of the president making Herbert Hoover his chief relief administrator, a move that could be uniting as a bipartisan gesture, she argued. Who better to bring relief to Americans than the man who had provided food for millions in the Great World War? Because Hoover was a patriot, she believed he would accept the call to service. It was an opportunity to remind the public of the gallantry of his earlier career and to reestablish his legacy as a civil servant. Eleanor took the idea to FDR, and he approved. But to Missy's disappointment Hoover wasn't interested in the scheme that she had proposed. Still bitter about the election of 1932 and fundamentally opposed to the New Deal, he wanted nothing to do with the present administration. Missy thought it sad. She had forgiven many slights over the course of her career, but apparently the bruised egos of men took longer to heal. Eleanor agreed that in situations like these, men could be "slower than women"; male egos had a tendency to complicate matters in ways that compromising, selfless women like Missy could not entirely understand.[21]

This political tribalism of men was inconvenient, but Missy didn't let it thwart her final preparations for the Forum that fall. She secured some fifty A-list speakers, including governors, mayors, the Polish ambassador, King Leopold of Belgium, Harvard president James Bryant Conant, the scientist George Washington Carver, and Madame Chiang Kai-shek. The panel discussions "Nazi Propaganda in the United States" and "Communism in American Labor" were prominent on the docket, as Missy saw no need to talk around them. FDR planned to speak on the war in Europe, and the First Lady to give the speech "Humanistic Democracy: The American Ideal." It took some persuading, but Eleanor finally mustered the courage to speak on the ideas she had been fine-tuning with Missy in Pawling. "You, who have championed Marian Anderson and the poor people at Reidsville, are anointed to say something about humanistic democracy," Missy assured her. "To this enormous audience you must give a thought that will send them back to do something about it."[22]

When the day of the Forum finally arrived, doctors decided that Missy was too ill to preside over the sessions, and Helen Reid took her place. Given the political climate, it pained Missy to sit this one out, so she pulled herself out of bed to record some remarks in Lowell Thomas's broadcast booth in Pawling. She was self-conscious as she spoke into the microphone, worried that her Forum audience would detect how weak she had become. But she felt compelled to make a call to action—or to faith, at least—in a speech she titled "What Man Cannot Destroy." "Hitler came to power through faith," she began. "We, the American people, must not lose strength through lack of faith.... How dare we have less faith in freedom than the Nazis of Germany have in regimentation?"[23]

The winter that followed the Forum was one of the worst that Missy could remember, and her failing lungs forced her to stay at Quaker Hill for the duration. All she could do to feel effective was to continue inquiring remotely regarding the whereabouts of her European friends. She was desperate to hear word of the Belgian queen mother, Elizabeth, who had been facilitating the escape of Jewish children from the Nazis and now could not be reached. As she waited to hear news from officials in Washington, Missy felt helpless and isolated. Blizzard conditions prevented her secretaries from getting to her, and by the time they arrived Missy had to be transported to the city for an operation. Eleanor fished for details, though all she got were assurances that the procedure had gone well—and more requests for favors: Could she use her sway to help the British poet Ada Jackson and her family get out of Europe? Could she put a good word in My Day about Rose and her latest stage production? Might the president consider hiring Lillian Gilbreth to make ergonometric adjustments to his desk chair? Even in the most desperate of times, Missy tried to position her friends to their advantage. She also happily reported to Eleanor that Dorothy Thompson had had a change of heart and was going to "come out for the President" in 1940. With FDR's third term so hotly contested, she figured that the news would come as some relief. It was something to talk about in lieu of the bigger elephant in the room: Missy's deterioration, and the reality that it was seriously impairing her work.[24]

Joseph Knapp had long been content with letting Missy dictate her work arrangements as she saw fit, but for the first time in her career Missy doubted her own ability to overcome her physical limitations well enough to maintain the production schedule of her magazine. With mixed emotions, she decided to look for a second in command, an editor who did more than take dictation and carry out orders, and who in time could make important editorial decisions in her absence. Her ideal candidate would be someone experienced, though not yet stuck in his or her ways; someone already capable, yet still able to be groomed in her philosophical mold. That person turned out to be William I. Nichols, a Harvard graduate and Rhodes Scholar, whom Missy poached from Sunset magazine. It appeared that their admiration was mutual. Nichols called Missy "a powerhouse of energy... with radar-like sensitivity and intuition." He marveled at her ability to "wheedle an article over the telephone from an overworked Cabinet officer, and former President, or the latest winner of the Nobel Prize." He could name no other editor he would prefer to emulate. For her part, Missy was convinced that Nichols had abundant potential. Early on she wanted him to meet Eleanor Roosevelt, prefacing to her that he was "a charming young man...sympathetic to the New Deal."[25]

Before long Missy reported to Knapp that she had "worked out a program and a technique for work with Nichols' help." He stood in for her at editorial meetings, at first just reading Missy's prepared statements, but developing his own voice over time. In April of 1940 he conveyed good news to the board of *This Week:* advertising revenues were up a whopping 73 percent that quarter. Through Nichols, Missy reminded the board of what a "challenge to editorial ingenuity" the increases had been, given that she had only 2 percent more space with which to make them. It helped, of course, that four more newspapers had been brought into the corporation, thus increasing circulation of *This Week* by another two million readers. With full faith in Nichols, Missy welcomed the growth. She was learning to admit her limitations, to make adjustments to her workload, and to share the burden of work, not just the rewards it eventually reaped.[26]

During the following summer, Eleanor Roosevelt motored to Pawling several times, for Missy had a lot on her mind. To begin with, Alexander Kirk was pleading for reassignment, and Missy had strong thoughts on where his skills should be utilized next. She also wanted to share the latest dispatches she had received from Irène about the Curie Institute in Warsaw. The radium for which Missy had raised funds had gone missing, likely stolen by the Germans, though possibly hidden by the institute's director; Irène said that she couldn't be sure, since he, too, had gone missing. American reports confirmed similar atrocities in France, where the American gift of radium had been looted by the Nazis and then shipped to Berlin. Although Irène wanted to retreat to the mountains, she told Missy that she couldn't stray from her lab, given the circumstances. Her children had been sent to the country, but she had no way to confirm their well-being, nor did she know the whereabouts of her sister since she had fled to England and joined the Resistance. The Fighting French kept a low profile for obvious reasons.[27]

Irène was still bitter about America's lack of involvement in the war. "The great rich democracy of the United States has given nothing for the defence of democraties [*sic*]," she railed. Missy sympathized with her frustrations. She considered herself a citizen of the world, opposed to Charles Lindbergh, Alice Longworth, and others of her friends who had publicly aligned themselves with the isolationists of "America First." Eleanor had launched a "No Foreign War" crusade in 1937, only to abandon it as her husband's third term loomed. Now she came out for putting bullies in their place—with force, if necessary, explaining to My Day readers that she and Missy were of like mind in this regard. In the meantime, the two women recommitted themselves to the kind of war relief they had provided during the First World War. Missy sat on the Women's Division of the Commission for Relief in Belgium and became a director of the Commission of Polish Relief, an organization that coordinated food and shelter for Polish refugees. With the death toll rising in Europe, Missy's physical decline was no excuse not to act. Anticipating American war on the horizon, she was determined to stay as useful to the country as she had ever been.[28]

Chapter Fourteen

A WOMAN'S WORK IS NEVER DONE
1940–1943

MISSY HAD LONG ENTRUSTED herself with preserving the legacy of her friends, but now this work took on urgency, as if she were running out of time. When she heard that La Guardia wanted to name a city high school after John Purroy Mitchel, she proposed as a more fitting honor the publication of Bill's biography of the former mayor. Mitchel's still-unorganized personal papers had been a casualty of Missy's editorial deadlines, but now she finished sorting the fourteen trunks of documents in her care, delivering some to Columbia University and transferring others to the Library of Congress to remain unopened until she could tease out the items that she thought unsuitable for public viewing. Such were the wishes of Mary Mitchel, who had always trusted Missy's judgment.[1]

Missy was in regular contact with Librarian of Congress Archibald MacLeish about other documents in her possession. "I would just like to know that they are safe," she told him, especially the ones historians would need to tell the stories of great men to future generations. There was the written record of her interview with Mussolini on his fiftieth birthday and a Confederate order book from the Battle of Bull Run, signed by the officers who had led the charge. She deposited various manuscripts and letters of Calvin Coolidge, Theodore Roosevelt, and Charles Eliot, and convinced Alexander Morgan Hamilton to deposit family letters he had collected with his grandfather J. P.

Morgan so that historians would give Alexander Hamilton his proper due as a Founding Father. She possessed some of Leonard Wood's handwritten notes from discussions with President Wilson, and a resignation letter written by former War Secretary Lindley Garrison that Wilson had refused to accept. "Secretary Garrison was an old friend of mine, and I happened to be in his office when he returned from the White House," she explained to MacLeish. "He laughingly said, 'I'll resign to you, anyway. Here is a little souvenir you can keep secret until after the war.'" Missy wanted to transfer custody of these relics—and their stories—while she was still around to give them context.[2]

Aside from her Curie memorabilia, most of the items Missy had collected by and about women over the years represented women in the collective, rather than as individual standouts. There were the textiles that she gave to the Metropolitan Museum of Art, and a collection of three thousand books by and about women "from Sappho to Eleanor Roosevelt" that she proposed donating to a worthy institution, perhaps a woman's college or a home-economics department like the one at Cornell. Eleanor seconded the idea, so long as Missy was sufficiently honored for the giving. But therein lay the problem. Missy didn't think that her role as a custodian was particularly noteworthy. She likened herself to a historian more than to an agent of history; a journalist who reported the news, rather than being the news; a facilitator of greatness, but not a great individual, like her beloved Curie. As much as she had accomplished in her role as a reporter or editor, this one was best performed inconspicuously.[3]

It had been Missy's plan to write a biography of Curie, not to profit financially but because she thought she could convey the scientist's greatness in ways that would endure. Loyalty prevented her from writing something for publication until Ève Curie's book, published in the States in 1937, had had its run. Nevertheless, she told Ted Roosevelt Jr., vice president of Doubleday, that the story of Curie's American tour was begging to be told. "I have about one hundred letters from Madame Curie, some of which are too personal to be quoted from, and all of which I took to her at Cherbourg in the summer of

'24 or '25," she told him. "I did not want to preserve anything to which she might object. She let me keep the most important letters although I had to argue very strenuously about some of them."[4]

Curie's daughters remained protective of their mother, too, objecting to third parties telling her story, but Missy warned that in America it was nearly impossible to stop them. She had recommended letting Bill register Ève's *Madame Curie* with the Motion Picture Association, but Warner Brothers had registered a version of her story already. Sam Goldwyn of MGM had also reminded the Curies that he didn't need their blessing to produce a biopic of his own. Fine, Missy conceded, let the filmmakers do what they're going to do. But she urged Ève to take back control by getting them at least to agree to use her book as the basis of any depiction of her mother's life.[5]

Through PEN, Missy already had a hand in drafting legislation that protected authors' rights in similar cases, which was a tad ironic. Here she wanted women to tell their own stories their own way, and yet in the case of her story, she preferred not to tell it at all. She shaped legacies, but what was worth remembering about hers? She was an invalid, an editor, a connector, a creator of optics—in the service of good, she liked to think. Still, she couldn't imagine anyone wanting to know about a woman whose best contributions to public life had been performed behind a curtain. On occasion, however, the most famous American woman alive would lift that curtain enough to give a brief glimpse. On the eve of the *Herald Tribune* Forum of 1940, Eleanor Roosevelt announced some good news in My Day: "Mrs. William Brown Meloney, who has always been the real inspiration of this forum, is well enough to be on the platform."[6]

In the ballroom of the Waldorf Astoria, Missy made her way to the dais to rousing ovations. As she had grown sicker over the years, she had also grown more ambivalent about being so visible. Her modus operandi had always been to conceal her illness, to suffer away from the public, but there was no hiding it in that venue. Her impulse was to diffuse and redirect the shows of gratitude. "When I was ill in 1938 Mrs. Reid put her shoulder to the wheel, interviewed speakers and introduced them from this platform," she told the audience. "She had to carry the heaviest part of this work in 1939, and this year, despite her added work and her natural concern about that gallant young son of hers who is a war correspondent in the most dangerous spots in England, she ha[s] done more than her share."[7]

Despite the good fortune of Missy's presence, the air at the Forum was palpably tense. Assuming that the country was on the precipice of war, participants sounded grave and alarmist. And a presidential election was only two weeks away. FDR was running for his third term against Wendell Willkie, the Republican challenger endorsed by the *Herald Tribune,* and also the not-so-secret lover of Missy's colleague Irita Van Doren. In the interest of fairness, Missy allowed an equal amount of time for all the candidates to make impressions. In her own broadcasted speech, she professed that there was no other time in the nation's history when liberty was in greater need of ardent defending: "A year ago we could not have believed that the people of Paris would lift their eyes to Notre Dame and see the flag with the crooked cross waving in the spring sunlight.... If this should happen in our own community, or if any other visible evidence of treachery should come to your attention, I beg you to remember our Forums and to demand an assembly of the people in order to avenge so serious an attack and a challenge."[8]

––––––––

FDR WON HIS THIRD TERM handily that November. Willkie secured 82 electoral votes to the president's 449, and though Missy had let them air their views at the Forum, Socialist and Prohibition candidates didn't eke out a single electoral vote. Again, her sense had been right: on the brink of war, Americans wanted continuity in leadership, a president who had already proven himself and helped them to weather a depression. Gearing herself up for another four years in the White House, Eleanor took a personal day just before Thanksgiving to run errands in Manhattan and to see Missy at the Waldorf Astoria. In the next installment of My Day, she remarked about those precious moments with her "ever courageous and inspiring friend": "Here is a woman who, in spite of months of illness, has managed to keep her guiding hand on the production of a weekly magazine, [and] has given her thought to the arrangements of one of the best known forums in the country.... Her spirit has remained an outgoing spirit in spite of all the limitations of pain and weakness. There is something very stimulating in talking with this gallant woman."[9]

Ruth Gruber was another woman who went out of her way to see Missy at the Waldorf Astoria before returning to Washington. She was a much younger reporter who, with Missy's encouragement, had been writing for the *Herald Tribune* about women under totalitarian regimes and had just returned from a stint in the Soviet Arctic. When Gruber arrived at her suite, Missy wasn't dressed, but Geraldine let Gruber in to see her anyway. There Missy was, propped up in bed in a pink flannel nightgown, her alabaster hands protruding slightly from its sleeves. She said that she was embarrassed, but then she fell right into her usual mentoring, asking the young journalist to hand over the copy of *This Week* that was sitting on the table. "This is the kind of thing I would like you to think about writing for us," she showed Gruber, turning over the cover to her special editorial section, Page 2, where Missy featured the opinions of a wide range of journalists, authors, and public figures. It was one of the most popular features of *This Week*, but Missy had needed to sell it hard to management. "When I first broached the idea, men at the office snickered. I said, 'well, *This Week* is my responsibility. If it fails, I fail. I'm going to try it.'"[10]

Decades later, Gruber recalled that visit with awe. The woman lying before her looked so fragile and feminine, and yet she was such a force. Missy "balanced her life as wife, mother, journalist, editor, and lecturer, and did it all with grace," Gruber marveled. And she hadn't been selfish with her success but instead had shared her collected wisdom with journalists of the next generation. "Remember the men around you may know a lot about life. But you do too," Missy reminded Gruber, for she had been no stranger to the impostor complex that came with covering topics and regions of the world that women were considered too sentimental to tackle. But Missy had long overcome any feelings of inadequacy, and she helped women on similar journeys. Gruber pulled out a pair of fur moccasins from her travels in Alaska, and as she did with all gifts, Missy delighted in them. "I brought you these as a tribute because all these years I have sat at your feet," Gruber said, and Missy politely protested. It was the kind of adulation she had always taken pains to avoid, and yet Gruber was insistent; she thought Missy the rarest of people, both humble and great at once.[11]

Channing Pollock was another journalist who thought Missy emanated greatness, and he wanted the world to know it. As the most prolific contributor to Page Two, he amassed his pieces for Missy into *Guide Posts in Chaos* (1942), dedicating the book to "A Great Editor and a Good Friend." He thought Missy's editorial instincts second to none and proposed publishing a tribute to her in *Reader's Digest*, with the blessing of its editor, DeWitt Wallace. Missy was flattered but uncomfortable with the in-depth profile Pollock had in mind. She recommended angling the piece to feature what she called "the real success story"—*This Week*—and proposed edits that focused on the magazine and the men on its business side. Pollock said that he would make some slight adjustments, but *she* was the success story he wanted to reveal. "Some embarrassing friendly praise has sometimes bowled me over," she confessed. "I have been a hard worker for a great number of years and that is the answer to most of what is called my success." Reading over the litany of accomplishments Pollock included in his piece, Missy decided that they were "drab and unimportant." "Measured by events of our time it seems terribly piffling and I honestly think that I have done only two things to justify my rich and happy life. I gave William Brown Meloney to the world and helped Madame Curie get back to work."[12]

An exasperated Pollock pushed back, insisting, among other things, that all her accomplishment amidst illness made her exceptional. But Missy wondered why he needed to mention illness at all: "I suppose you have to say that my health cracked up again and again but I wish it weren't necessary. Everyone who knows me, knows I am lame.... Few knew I had a bad lung until this last pneumonia and the empyema that followed it. But even so, I have gone on working my regular hours.... Do you think you might cure the legend of invalidism by saying that I have flown 25,000 miles covering my job?"[13]

Even now, she didn't want to be seen as special, or as suffering. Eventually, she decided that she didn't want to be seen at all, for when the piece was finished and Wallace asked for Missy's go-ahead, she hedged. Perhaps her boss should also give it a read, she suggested. "If credit for making THIS WEEK successful were given to me and then I should slip out of life, it would do the magazine a lot of harm," she warned. At this, Pollock was mystified. "If I write that George Washington was a great man, who had much to do with the creation and greatness of his country, will that persuade anyone that the country became worthless with the death of George Washington?"[14]

His reasoning made no difference in the end. The most Pollock was able to reveal about Missy in print came in his memoir, *Harvest of My Years,* two years later: "Mrs. Meloney and I had been cub reporters together on the Washington Post—though she was an even younger cub than I. She is one of the ablest and most amazing women I have ever met, but her story cannot be written while she lives." "When I am gone, say anything you wish," Missy told a disappointed Pollock as consolation, "and if some star in the heavens blinks a little more brightly for you, know that Missy is sending her love."[15]

The sad irony of the words Pollock wrote in his memoir was that Missy was alive when he wrote them, but not once they were published for anyone else to read.

———

THE LAST TWO YEARS of Missy's life were much like the ones that came before them, if measured by her influence on people and her ability to get things done. She continued to work hard, mostly from bed, and right up until the end. A war raged in the distance, and she made herself of consequence to it, even before Americans were formally combatants. As 1941 approached, Naval Secretary Frank Knox was already conferring with her about which national security details to disclose in *This Week*. Even more so than in World War I, Missy became central to the propagandizing of the military to generate morale and to prepare for war.[16]

In January of 1941, she felt strong enough to attend a tea Eleanor Roosevelt was hosting in the city, but she also finally listened to friends who urged her to sojourn west for rehabilitation, as she had done as a younger woman. She rationalized the trip by scheduling business- and story-related meetings during her travels, finalizing advertising agreements with Louis B. Mayer in Hollywood and interviewing local FBI agents in Phoenix for more national-security articles. J. Edgar Hoover's admonitions to her to avoid returning to New York until she had completely recovered went unheeded—Missy likely wasn't even sure what a full recovery felt like after so many years of living with her ailments. By March she went home to New York to continue working full-time. Anticipating a formal declaration of war by the president, she voiced strong opinions about how his cabinet should proceed. She took to task her longtime friend William Castle in the State Department for boycotts and sanctions of the Japanese, fearing that the measures were too hostile, too soon. More urgently, she presented to Secretary of State Cordell Hull a plan for providing food relief to European allies. "I have considered the humanitarian question of saving millions of lives as the transcendent purpose," she prefaced, and argued that wise food control was key to winning the war, as well as the peace.[17]

Missy shuttled between beds at Quaker Hill and the Waldorf Astoria that spring, spending less and less time in Washington. It gave her comfort knowing that her editor and proxy Bill Nichols was in the capital doing her bidding. "Here are the appointments I have made for you," she wrote atop an hour-by-hour itinerary of meetings at the Navy Department Building, at the White House executive offices, and with various cabinet secretaries and bureau directors. Of course when Nichols couldn't be her stand-in in Washington, she still relied on the ever loyal Eleanor Roosevelt, who seemed happy to be the same eyes, ears, and legs for Missy that Eleanor had been for her husband. Feeling "not quite up to snuff" in late May, Missy asked Eleanor to call on her soon to help her with a list of items that needed attention. Some were personnel suggestions to Henry Morgenthau in the Treasury Department, others she directed to the president about the Department of Labor. She also asked Eleanor to look over a manuscript that had come in about Edwin "Pa" Watson, FDR's appointments secretary, for she still refused to publish any references to the president without his or his wife's approval.[18]

Meanwhile, harrowing news continued to come from Irène Curie in France. A lack of heat and food rations had led to another break in her health, and she was back in the hospital. Missy feared that Hitler's regime would wear down Irène's resistance and force her to use her atomic science in its service, if the harsh conditions didn't kill her first. Worried for the safety of Irène's husband and children as well, Missy urged Eleanor to help her evacuate the whole Joliot-Curie family to America. The president was willing to go to great lengths to get them Stateside, Eleanor assured her; exchanging the family for German prisoners was not out of the question. Eleanor conducted talks with the State Department and personally delivered Missy's messages to Irène through department officials to bypass the censors. Among other news, Missy wanted Irène to know that she had secured commitments from Columbia University and the California Institute of Technology to take Irène into their labs, if she could get herself out of France.[19]

Europeans were astonished at how Missy was able to lend them aid from her sickbed. She continued to organize relief for children of the Allied nations, and intent on raising funds for the British, she came up with a new public-relations vehicle: a celebrity cookbook—written not just by any celebrity, but by Wallis Simpson, the American turned British duchess. After the king abdicated his throne to marry her in 1937, the elegant Simpson became famous and infamous at once, for in the eyes of many Brits she was the divorcée who seduced a beloved monarch away from his people and his royal duties. Missy thought that the cookbook could domesticate her in the British mind, making her likable, much as Curie had become in Missy's hands. To assure the success of the venture, she promised not only to have domestic economists of the Home Institute assist in compiling the recipes but also to get the First Lady to write the cookbook's introduction and Charles Scribner's Sons to donate a fourth of the book's proceeds to British aid. The *Herald Tribune* agreed to put up several thousand dollars to publish parts of the cookbook in the January 1942 edition of *This Week,* proceeds to go to the British War Relief Society. Missy still had a way of conjuring up ideas that were a win for everyone involved.[20]

That autumn, Eleanor saw Missy to shore up details of the cookbook, only to marvel at her "looking so well and surrounded with work." This work did not include Forum planning, however. Missy suspected that the administration would be better served by focusing on the impending war, which, as she predicted, came quickly. The Japanese attacked Pearl Harbor on December 7, and FDR declared war on Japan the following day. Three days later, Congress declared war on Germany, an ally of Japan, which had declared war on the United States. Having resigned himself to the inevitable, FDR had instituted a peacetime draft in 1940, which meant that 2.2 million American troops were ready to be deployed. Irène Curie and the Baron de Cartier were a few of Missy's friends who wrote from Europe to tell her that they were relieved that the Americans had finally entered the fray.[21]

With America officially at war, Missy turned to the public-relations work she knew best. She gave the First Lady a slogan, which she claimed to have borrowed from Calvin Coolidge, to inspire the home-front readers of My Day to do their part as a resurging "second line of defense": "Eat it up. Wear it out. Make it do. Do without." Meanwhile, *This Week* underwent wartime adjustments similar to the ones Missy had made to *The Delineator* during the First World War. The physical size of the magazine's pages shrunk to make it look more like the competing *Collier's,* which cut costs (and line counts) amidst wartime rationing. Missy focused on making her limited editorial space meet the psychological times. Once 80 percent fiction, 20 percent non, *This Week* dropped its serials and shifted the ratio of content closer to half and half. Managing editor Mary Day worried that the move would put off women, who took over as the magazine's base readership as more men enlisted for war. Missy assured Day that she knew from the last war that female readers wanted more than escapism. Although issues included pictorial essays by the photojournalist Margaret Bourke-White and military cartoons, women were not ignored in Missy's war coverage, which included pieces on nurses, WACs, WAVEs, women civilian defense workers, and tips for how housewives could make do with wartime rations. Her editorial decisions proved to be good ones, and in 1942 *This Week* moved from tenth place in revenues among American magazines to seventh, passing *Good Housekeeping* and *McCall's*. A *Time* reporter was astonished by *This Week's* success, given the health of its "tiny, fragile" editor, to which Missy allegedly told him, "I have been lame since 15, and had a bad lung since 17 and have done the work of three men ever since."[22]

It was uncharacteristic bravado from a woman who once again was out of commission for a "slight operation," and who begrudgingly headed south to recuperate. Grace Coolidge gave Missy a list of her favorite North Carolina inns, but Missy didn't stay away long. Her illness worsened, forcing her to return to New York for intensified medical care. "In a little while I shall feel more like myself," she assured the Duchess of Windsor to alleviate any worries about the cookbook. Ada Jackson sent Missy an Easter verse, and Herbert Hoover sent proofs of his recent book with a note attached: "It was a great pleasure to see you again, and to see the most imperishable of human souls." Alexander Kirk typed Missy a long letter from Cairo, where he served as ambassador to Egypt: "So many times in the past I have rebelled against the impacts you have been dealt and marveled at the courage and endurance you have shown in countering them that I now feel that the only way for those who care for you to show their affection is to meet your inspired stoicism in kind."[23]

That winter, in a letter to Bill Donovan, Missy admitted that the time had finally come to consider downsizing, specifically selling the farmhouse in Pawling to move into an adjacent cottage on the grounds.

The truth was that her physical world had already been shrinking; she was entertaining less often, and it was hard to stay on top of the maintenance of her sprawling grounds. Although she consolidated her space, her search for timely pieces for *This Week* continued vigorously. She asked Sumner Welles of the State Department to ruminate on Hitler as the tenth anniversary of his "attempt to dominate the world" approached, offering $1,000 for the piece. Intelligence official and *This Week* contributor Stanley Hornbeck scolded her for not resting enough, but she couldn't resist the urge to pitch more policy measures from bed. That December she even contacted the vice president and the secretary of agriculture about a scheme to raise Danish Landrace pigs on the nation's farms to augment the wartime food supply. She also shared her thoughts on military strategy, industrial efficiency, women's productivity, and lowering crime, as if preparing for an annual Forum.[24]

Indeed, it was at her moments of greatest physical incapacitation when her mind raced the most. As she pitched policy, she also continued writing friends on behalf of other friends, making requests and arranging quid pro quos. When she reached out to Herbert Hoover at the start of 1943, this time it wasn't to interest him in a role in the administration, but rather to tell him a bit about the Serbian-born scientist Nikola Tesla. He was down and out, even more so than Curie had been when Missy first met her in Paris. "His contribution to the sum-total of American civilization is almost beyond calculation," she told Hoover. "Hundreds of billions of dollars of American wealth are ascribable to his inventions. They are at the very center of our war effort. No man living has added more substantially to the potentialities of human life than Tesla. Yet today, when he is past 90, he is worse than penniless. He is extremely frail, weighing less than 90 pounds. His health is poor, and he has grown somewhat bitter against the U.S.A. No doubt his current poverty is his own fault. However, I think that ordinary standards do not apply to Tesla. He was always the pure scientist, never interested in money, always impractical about material existence."[25]

Missy was not asking Hoover for money; she wondered, rather, if the former president, who had once been a fellow scientist, knew someone who could take care of Tesla without seeming to, all while assisting with his notes and experiments to preserve what might be of value in them. It was the sort of support she had given Curie, in addition to securing her radium. But Tesla died in his room at the New Yorker Hotel three days after Missy inquired on his behalf. Although he was alone, apparently he was not forgotten. A champion of scientists, Missy vowed that since she couldn't rescue Tesla, she would redouble her efforts to save Irène Curie from Hitler, and she wired her more funds in Switzerland. Irène's mother would have wanted her to do everything possible, after all, to save her daughter and her science.[26]

In the coming weeks, Missy kept her secretaries busy. Sumner Welles received more of her letters to forward to Alexander Kirk and the French general Henri Giraud, commander in chief of Allied forces in North Africa, from whom she wanted a statement for *This Week*. She asked J. Edgar Hoover to write a piece about "the rising tide of crime among youth," and he sent her working drafts. Still, Rose Franken wrote Eleanor in April to tell her that despite the mountains of work emanating from Missy's bedroom, her mother-in-law was sicker than usual, so sick that Rose decided to stay with her for a while. It's hard to know if the women of the New York Newspaper Women's Club were aware of how poorly Missy was faring, but it probably didn't matter, for that May they once again reelected her to another consecutive term as first vice president. No doubt it was a show of affection and appreciation for all Missy had achieved as a woman in the field of journalism.[27]

JUNE 4, 1943: Missy sent a note to Frank Knox of the navy. She gave him her editorial remarks on his latest *This Week* submission and then, nearly buried at the end of the letter, announced some slight adjustments at the magazine—nothing that should worry him. Although she was not giving up her duties at *This Week* entirely, she was stepping down as editor to become "Editorial Director." Just what that role entailed, she didn't say. "I am not surprised," Knox responded. "I have long wondered how you could keep up the pace." Days later, Missy's news to Knox went public in the pages of *Time:* "Out goes fragile, ailing Mrs. William Brown Meloney, 60, a dominating organizer who has been described as 'fine lace made of cable wire.' In comes her hand-picked successor, genteel William Ichabod Nichols."[28]

Missy said nothing about the shake-up at *This Week* in a letter she sent to Rose the next day. She was much more concerned with Rose's latest Broadway production, a psychological drama called *Outrageous Fortune,* and she had to say her piece while she could:

> Dearest Rose, I haven't read your play and I don't even know the name of it, but after reading this week's article in the June 5th issue of the New Yorker about Gilbert Miller, I am worried about it. Remembering "Claudia" and its wholesome influence I am worried about what Miller will do with the three characters you have mentioned to me— a prostitute, a Jew, and a homosexual. I can't believe the play will last, or that it will be a credit to you, produced by this man who was not the least bit flustered when the police closed "The Captive." You were headed for the fine, tender plays which help the world along. I hope I will love to see you do another such play as "Claudia," and not something that has to do with decadence.
>
> I know what the critics will be apt to say about you, and the frame of mind in which they will report your next play. No matter how beautifully done, a prurient play neither succeeds nor is a credit to its author. Remember Oscar Wilde. He never lived down the reputation he made in England. If this play has to be produced, I wish it would come out under another author's name.
>
> I love you with all my heart, or I would not say this to you. This is something the war has done to you, as it has to many others, but we need a balance and you know how to give it.
>
> God love you, Mother[29]

Rose was not the first author Missy had scolded, but it was strange that she worried that Rose had pushed the envelope too far. Missy had long encouraged explorations of the grittier facets of life, as well as of mar-

ginalized people, and yet now her input seemed to border on the prig-
gish. Rose scrawled across the bottom of the letter, "one of Missy's few
errors in judgment!" but she had the good sense to put Missy's comments in perspective. Missy had never been naive about who people
were. This was a woman who had mentored Jewish and homosexual
writers for years; her fear was not in exposing them to an unaccepting
public, but in exposing them to the public in ways that did them no justice. Rose knew that underlying Missy's words was less judgment than
protectiveness. As she lay dying, Missy's instincts as a mother and a publicist were to shield Rose from the critics, for she knew that bold ideas
had to be presented carefully, that the public had to be steadily primed
for them, or they wouldn't be well received. No doubt she would have
trusted her own rendering of Rose's characters over that of Gilbert
Miller. Had there been more time to steer a PR campaign, Missy likely
wouldn't have told Rose, "Don't do it," but rather, "Don't do it yet."

Missy's mantra had always been to uplift, and her modus operandi
was to change minds discreetly, without anyone detecting that she
was doing it. For a woman of her generation, working in stealth had
become an effective way to shift the cultural winds. She didn't see wartime as an appropriate moment to deliver unconventional statements,
in art or in life. But Missy's own experience during and after World
War I suggests that the opportunity to make controversial gestures
would have come, and people could have been prepared for them. In
Missy's plea, Rose heard a woman who had more work to do, but who
knew that she was running out of time.

That Missy had given up the reins of *This Week* without immediately
replacing it with a different venture was yet another sign that she knew
she was nearing the end. After a lifetime of incessant work, she looked
to be finally slowing down, without fear of the void that she had always
filled with work. A tiny brook babbled in her garden in Pawling, snak-
ing between banks of roses, irises, and early annuals. The long deck
chair she normally sat in as she hosted houseguests sat empty on the
terrace, the blanket at its foot folded and undisturbed. The doctor had
left painkillers for her chest, and she took them so that she could sit

up and talk to her children without their suspecting her decline. They of course weren't fooled. Rose and Bill had made a pact not to say it out loud, but they knew that the malady she had held at bay since age seventeen was taking its final toll. Geraldine hoped that Rose might coax her patient into taking a bit of broth at supper, but she refused to press the issue. Missy gazed on Rose gratefully as she carried her untouched dinner tray back to the kitchen. Rose and Bill stayed the night in Pawling, and then the next, and the next... until there was no longer a reason to stay. Missy died peacefully on June 23, 1943.[30]

Days later, some five hundred mourners gathered to find her casket draped in daisies and smilax at the entrance of St. Patrick's Cathedral. Even in death, she inspired people across industries and parties to come together. Herbert Hoover and Owen Young joined David Sarnoff and James Farley, chairman of the New York State Democratic Party, as honorary pallbearers. In attendance were many male associates from her professional life who had become friends, including Ogden Reid, Joseph Knapp, Louis Seibold, John Erskine, Bill Nichols, and Missy's editorial staff. But there, too, sitting in the pews, were Leonebel Jacobs, Fannie Hurst, Helen Reid, Lou Henry Hoover, and many other of her female intimates who mourned her deeply. Ève Curie made her way to New York to drive with Bill and Rose to Woodlawn Cemetery, where Missy's plot, together with the Purroys' and the Mitchels', had been consecrated by a Catholic priest.[31] Her obituary in the *Times* seemed unusually heartfelt, perhaps an indication that, as did most journalists in New York, its author knew and appreciated her:

> It needs no long memory to recall that time when hardly one woman was employed by a daily newspaper. There have been woman writers, correspondents, but the news room was strictly a masculine reservation. In the days before typewriters even a secretary was masculine. Mrs. William Brown Meloney, whose deeply regretted death was announced yesterday, was one of the pioneers of the triumph of women in the newspaper field....

She was a leader as well as a precursor.... To common sense and judgment she added imagination. Some instinct in her reached out and told her what people wanted. The Herald Tribune's Forum on Current Problems, now a national institution, was her child. Her place in the community was a large one. Her useful and humane activities were many and varied. She knew and worked with many of the most generous spirits of our time, [no one] any more generous than she.[32]

Eleanor Roosevelt waited a few days before paying her "small tribute" to Missy in My Day. "I felt that many others had known her longer than I have and had a right to speak first," she explained. "I have known her well only since she had begun her extraordinary fight against pain and illness, so always to me she will be the flame of a spirit which nothing, not even death, can extinguish." She continued:

One never came away depressed from seeing "Missy" Meloney. One always felt that the world was so full of interesting things that there was something important for everyone to do and she was urging you on to do your share. I know that even in the future, if I am sometimes weary and think that perhaps there is not use in fighting for things in which I believe against overwhelming opposition, the thought of what she would say, will keep me from being a slacker. She believed that women had an important part to play in the future. She not only helped such women as Madame Curie, who were great women, but she helped many little people like myself feel that we had a contribution and an obligation to try to grow. I do not want to think of Mrs. Meloney as dead. I want to think of her vivid spirit living on in those who loved her, giving them strength to conquer bodily ills and courage to achieve more than they believed themselves capable of achieving. Most of her messages and letters finished with the same sentence. She used it to me and I am sure she did to all her other friends. And so I say "God love you," Missy dear.[33]

EPILOGUE

N*EW YORK TIMES*, AUGUST 29, 1943:

To Honor Woman Editor

Washington, DC: The Maritime Commission announced today that a Liberty ship named for Mrs. William Brown Meloney would be launched Thursday at the Bethlehem-Fairfield Shipyard in Baltimore.[1]

Writers, artists, editors, and Washington elite convened in September 1943 for the launch of the SS *Marie M. Meloney*. Rose was tasked with breaking the ceremonial bottle of champagne across the hull of the ship before it glided out to sea. Suddenly overwhelmed by emotion, she couldn't stop the flow of tears. Eleanor touched her gently from behind and kissed her cheek. The First Lady's solemnity was then replaced by her signature toothy grin. "I was so pleased to read in the newspapers that *Claudia* will be coming back to Washington," she said in an attempt to change the mood. "Franklin and I would so enjoy having you and your husband stay with us again." Rose had written of Eleanor's kindnesses in *Redbook* that spring and donated the proceeds from the piece to the Red Cross and the March of Dimes to aid war relief and the president's pet cause, the treatment of infantile paralysis. The two women had become part of each other's inner circle, just as Missy had wanted.[2]

Missy would have also been heartened to know that by the time she died, women made up 50 percent of newspaper staffs in smaller American cities, a significant number of World War II correspondents (127 of them cleared by the State Department and accredited by the War Department), and 25 percent of American journalists as a whole. Nearly 100 women reported from the Capitol press galleries, and the tradition of female excellence at the *Herald Tribune* continued with women such as Ruth Gruber, war correspondent Marguerite Higgins, and Woman's Page editor Dorothy Dunbar Bromley. When Ogden Reid died in 1947, Helen formally took over the reins of the paper, though she had long been in charge already. Thanks to Eleanor Roosevelt, more than 100 women continued to cover her White House press conferences until FDR died in 1945. In the words of historian Kathleen Cairns, "If World War I cracked the newsroom door and the Depression opened it wider, World War II finally demonstrated that women belonged in front page journalism." It was a trajectory that Missy had a heavy hand in helping along.[3]

She also would have been gratified to know that her efforts to aid Curie's daughters were not in vain: both Ève and Irène survived the war. Irène continued her science. Ève won the National Book Award for *Madame Curie,* published a compilation of her writings as an international war correspondent, and earned a nomination for the Pulitzer Prize. Missy's earlier introduction of Ève to Eleanor Roosevelt led to her giving lectures in the United States on French women in the war, and she published extensively on the subject before becoming a philanthropist and an American citizen in 1958. Coincidentally, she, too, married a Nobel Prize winner—but for peace, rather than for science. Ève lived to be 102, but her sister suffered symptoms similar to her mother's until she died of leukemia in 1956, no doubt the result of radiation poisoning.

Six months after Missy's death, MGM released *Madame Curie,* directed by Mervyn LeRoy and starring Greer Garson as Marie. Focused on Curie's collaboration with her husband, the film showed nearly nothing of her longer solo career, which was, Missy knew, how

Curie would have wanted her story told. To this day the Curie fixed in the American imagination is largely the one conjured by Missy in 1921.[4]

Missy won accolades that have been measures of greatness for men in public life, but they meant little to our humble heroine. Any references to the eight foreign decorations she received in her lifetime have existed in the writings or utterances of others. She played down her honors and publicized the feats of her friends. Today, we might scold her for being sacrificial—yet another woman who allowed herself to be overshadowed by those around her. But in so doing, she propelled other women into prominence and women's issues into public discourse. And although it is generally true that she preferred being heard to being seen, she did make public appearances when she wanted the convictions of her words known. Syndicated columnist Elsa Maxwell pronounced her one of the most effective speakers in the country, an assessment seconded by George Palmer Putnam, who put Missy on his list of "best conversationalists" the way others put women on the "best dressed" list. In a rare acknowledgment of her subtle but effective mode of operating, one reporter said of her late in life that she demonstrated two aptitudes: "a sympathetic understanding of the needs and desires of people in every walk of life, and an X-ray ability to see through to the heart of public problems and frequently to predict the outcome or suggest the solution." Indeed, his observation supports those of her intimate friends who admired her ability to communicate, but also to listen. She absorbed nuggets of wisdom from the experiences of others and synthesized them into a more nuanced understanding of the world that she willingly shared to make life better for women, Americans, and their allies.[5]

Missy often said that she regretted little in life, though she did lament never having time to write the books she often talked about. Had she gotten around to it, she told Ted Roosevelt, she would have written one called *Great Days and Little Men*, highlighting moments in which she witnessed "smart Men dawdle with time or blindly play with great stakes." She had over thirty years of anecdotes to draw on, starting with "the disillusionment and manhandling of Admiral Dewey," moving on to her frustrations with War Secretaries Daniels and Baker in World War I, to her fundamental disagreements with President Wilson, and concluding with Mussolini, "who, in a reckless moment, sat down and wrote the answer to eight important questions beginning with, 'Will you invade Abyssinia?'" Roosevelt would have been happy to publish *Great Days and Little Men* or anything from Missy's pen, and in 1938 he implored her to get writing before it was too late. Rather than heed his advice, however, she kept up her manic work schedule and passed along the names of friends she thought more deserving of book deals. Roosevelt was frustrated. Missy had so many stories to tell. Acknowledging her role as "the confidential adviser of the great men of these times," one reporter supposed "that if ever she were to 'tell all'—which she never will—a good many books would need to be rewritten."[6]

But Missy took almost all those confidences to the grave. Although she had a hand in shaping actions of prominent men and in directing political winds, she avoided situations that would have outed her as someone who knew the inside story or was an actor of any consequence. Her molding of the images of Mitchel, Curie, Hoover, Coolidge, and so many other famous personages is proof of how adept she was at historical mythmaking, which causes us to wonder if the historical obscurity that befell her was of her conscious design.

An admission Missy made to Eleanor Roosevelt in 1939 might partly explain why she stopped short of writing anything in which she featured, even as a bit player: "I had been told that women had always been held down and were the inferior sex. My mother, who was a progressive, had some bitter battles to fight. I didn't fight them; I just stepped aside and worked and worked, and I am still working."[7] For all her efforts to legitimize women as authors, journalists, scientists, artists, and professionals, Missy didn't view them as "fights," or as "feminism," or as accomplishments worthy of including in a record to be passed down to posterity. It helped to think of herself as a worker bee, not as the queen, because projecting that role made her less conspicuous as she manipulated cultural and political levers. And work was her comfort. The more she worked, the more she proved to herself that she was not the invalid of her own sob story. Her ailments helped to shape her definitions of success. Rather than setting out in search of fame, she sought efficacy, because that was better proof that she had conquered her limitations and become the master of her own domain.

Historians have observed similar sensibilities in other women of her generation and reform circles. Coming of age when men and women still deeply internalized the gender ideology of separate spheres, they lived a paradox, allowing their unprecedented achievements in the male public realm to be couched as feminine sacrifice. Missy wanted others to see her paving of paths of female professional expertise as service, and the strategy ultimately demanded a price. Although she achieved some public acclaim in the 1930s, ultimately her connecting, and organizing, and listening, and publicizing, and advice giving, and trendsetting went unrecognized as acts of leadership or of historical consequence. She was heralded more often as a remarkable mother, not a mentor; as a survivor, not a success story in the heroic tradition of great men. Like most of us, she may very well have craved acknowledgment for her efforts, but she also feared it, because such scrutiny may have reminded people that what she was doing, conventionally speaking, was inappropriate and not so "womanly" after all.[8]

ALMOST TWENTY YEARS after Missy's death, in 1962, Bill Jr. gave his mother's papers to Columbia University; to no one's surprise, almost all of them told more about the accomplishments of the people Missy had helped than about herself. Helen Reid nonetheless wrote a tribute to Missy to commemorate the gift. Trying to sum up the life of a woman who had made inroads into so many spheres of activity wasn't easy, and she knew that Missy would have been embarrassed by the attention. She turned to journalists from across the country to start, relying on their memories of Missy in her prime. Dorothy Thompson described her narrowly as "one of the most civilized people in New York City." An editor of a newspaper put out by a federal corrections facility called Missy "an Editor Extraordinary"—"She kn[e]w how to do her job so well that she ha[d] no contemporaries." A Southern journalist gave up altogether on attempting to capture Missy: "Writing about her is like trying to put *Gone with the Wind* on a post card." Reid tried anyway, forming her tribute of Missy around professional benchmarks and "firsts," but then including accomplishments that the public at large might not have understood as innovations. "A keystone of her editorial formula was linking both fiction and articles close to the world news and signing up as contributing writers a vast number of men and women—cabinet members, public officials, educators, labor leaders, scientists—who were in the forefront of new developments," she explained. "In whatever she did she kept the image of journalism at its highest and best and those who worked closely with her emerged with the knowledge that they had touched someone unique."[9]

Surprisingly, in a milieu in which a woman's worth was still determined largely by her prowess in the domestic sphere, Reid didn't refer to "Mrs. William Brown Meloney" as wife and mother. She simply called her "Missy" and focused on character traits rarely acknowledged in public tributes of men, ones she nevertheless believed had made Missy highly effective in her personal and professional life. There was, for one thing, her undaunted vivacity, despite her obvious physical frailties. "Hers was energy of the atom before the atom had been discovered," was how Reid put it. And there was Missy's "radarlike sensitivity and intuition," a phrase borrowed from William Nichols, which allowed her to "anticipate history while it was still in the making." Reid marveled at how Missy "seemed literally to manufacture time for worth-while activities, and give them the necessary drive for going ahead." "Perhaps her top capacity," Reid concluded, "lay in being able to give ideas to others as well as to receive them." Indeed, she emphasized Missy's knack for cultivating relationships of affection and reciprocity. Whereas such proclivities are rarely mentioned in the biographies of great men, Reid was sure they had made Missy one of the best team players and useful people she had ever known.[10]

Reid's impression of Missy as the extraordinary woman, yet everywoman, was hardly hers alone. Go back to Missy's days as editor of *The Delineator,* when she participated in BHA festivities in the town of Port Huron, Michigan. She was greeted at the local train station by the mayor, town officials, a band, and some one thousand children who had been let out of school early for her arrival. The local teachers had decided to make Missy the day's civics lesson, assigning students essays about their guest visitor. "She is a woman of national and international fame but she is so unaffected and simple," one student wrote. Candidly, another student, an immigrant girl, confessed:

> My first impression of Mrs. Meloney was that she was a very ordinary looking person and it seemed almost impossible for me to believe that she was as important as I had heard people tell. She didn't seem as pretty as she looks in the picture. *THEN I NOTICED HER EYES.* They were like two dark *coals and they snapped.* When I saw them I changed my mind quickly. They told that she was great *WITHIN.* Then when she got up and began to talk to us, I was so ashamed of myself for the false opinion I had formed too soon of her, and later when I had a personal talk with her I felt still more ashamed of myself, for I saw where her nobility was, in her great mind and soul.[11]

The woman who Helen Reid, monarchs, First Ladies, children, colleagues, and yet-to-be-discovered authors cherished was one who didn't lord over people; she collaborated. Whereas virtually every man in charge whom she knew adhered to top-down models of management, Missy positioned herself in the middle of networks that radiated outward and drew people in, making her accessible to Pulitzer Prize winners and presidents, as well as to their spouses and young upstarts hoping for a break. In 1939, when she was too sick to leave her bed, she sent encouraging missives to Donald Jeffrey Hayes, an African American poet who she hoped would soon be published. She gave him advice and placed two of his poems in *This Week*, but she wanted to do more. Thinking his other poems more appropriate for the editorial page of the *Times*, she had Hayes send them there, instructing him to mention her name. In the meantime, she asked for his forty best poems so that she could work on getting him a book deal. Illness didn't stifle her enthusiasm for undiscovered talent. She was never too established to help the unknown become known.[12]

People gave Missy their best work not because she intimidated, but because she commanded their respect. They appreciated her faith in them, and she knew just what to say to draw out their best. She made the most of her instincts about human nature and social and cultural trends to incite change in the world, and she converted lofty ideas into tangible deliverables. She never self-aggrandized; her decisions carried purpose beyond her immediate needs. She brought gravity to female perspectives in American politics and culture and had a way of elevating everyone through her understated accomplishments, making her more than a female martyr or trailblazer, but rather a leader who has yet to be acknowledged as such. Many would describe her style as feminine, which shouldn't diminish her in the least. And yet regrettably, the silence about her in the annals of history suggests that it already has.

We have found ways to damn women in nearly any style of leadership they choose, because in the popular imagination a powerful woman remains an oxymoron. The roots of this image run deep, as Missy's life attests, and have lasted, as recent presidential elections attest. But Missy has also given us ways to reimagine the powerful woman, if we care to see them. Unbeknownst to her, *this* might be her most important campaign.

Despite the fact that she would have protested, we unveil her shrouded methods and place them under the light. With a need like never before for her type of advocacy and efficacy, the time has come to give Missy and her undervalued set of skills their due. She had a better read on what women wanted and needed and how to advance their stature in the public sphere than men in public office ever could. Although she could have used her access to powerful people to enrich herself, she decided to bring other women into the fold, facilitating national conversations in which women had bearing as chroniclers, artists, experts, mothers, and political beings. In this way and in so many others, she was a uniquely powerful woman, an unsung maker of American queens.

ACKNOWLEDGMENTS

THANK YOU to everyone who has taken interest in Missy and who understands why now is the time to tell her story. I have been blessed with a wonderful editor, Leah Stecher, who understood from the get-go what I wanted to say about Missy and through Missy, and she has helped me to convey it better. Thank you Claire Potter for your enthusiasm for women's history, and to Melissa Veronesi for your expertise in book production. And thank you Kelley Blewster for being a master copy editor. Like Missy, you women know the work of being meticulous behind the scenes; your gratification is in the work itself. But once in a while I think it's important to pull back the curtain and acknowledge women being masterful—and helpful to other women.

Anyone who writes knows that it is often a lonely labor of love. I'm lucky to have family and friends who take interest in my solitary work and who ask me about it when I come up for air. Thanks to my kids, Joy and Bastian, for inspiring my writing in ways you don't realize. Thank you for granting me the time to think and to get to know Missy better over the past few years.

I researched Missy's life on one end of the country and embarked on the writing after a move to the other. It has been an introspective time, made much better by the fact that my twin, Jory, now lives across the San Mateo Bridge from me, and also by the crazy coincidence of my college roommate moving across the country at the very same time to live only three blocks away. Neha, we've been lucky to come together again at this time in our lives. So much of what we talk about is reflected in Missy's life, which reminds me of how timeless she truly is.

In the last three years, I've met some women in Silicon Valley whom I would call "girls' girls" in the best sense of the term. Cristina Spencer, Lisa Wong, Kristen Guggeis, Libby Moulton, Lamya Alaoui, Diane Kratz, Chiara Portner, Mona Sabet, Deirdre Lum, and Maureen Mahoney have made me feel more at home and wonderfully aware of the power of Missy's relationships with women, though I had a pretty good idea already. In World War I, the Great Depression, and World War II, Missy turned to women and women turned to her to contribute to American life in valuable ways. I channel her in this perilous time in our nation's history to remind women of their ability to shift the tides.

NOTES

People referred to Marie Mattingly Meloney as "Missy Meloney," "Missy," "Marie Meloney," and "Mrs. William Brown Meloney." She is referred to in the notes simply as "MMM."

Unless otherwise specified, all archival material cited below comes from the Marie Mattingly Meloney papers (MMM), Rare Book and Manuscript Library, Columbia University Libraries, New York, New York. Material from Marie Mattingly Meloney (MMM) has been organized into correspondence (boxes 1–28), catalogued manuscripts (boxes 29–30), miscellaneous material (MMM misc. material, boxes 32–34), and Marie Mattingly Meloney manuscripts (MMM manuscripts, boxes 35–37). If no designation is specified, it belongs to the correspondence boxes, which are organized alphabetically.

PREFACE

1. Julie Des Jardins, *The Madame Curie Complex: The Hidden History of Women in Science* (New York: The Feminist Press, 2010), pp. 23–52.

2. Handwritten note on loose sheet, n.d., MMM manuscripts; MMM to Mary Day, n.d., note attached to undated autobiographical piece, MMM manuscripts (referred to hereafter as "MMM autobiography"); Shirley Temple to MMM, April 27, 1936.

3. See Des Jardins, *The Madame Curie Complex,* and *Lillian Gilbreth: Redefining Domesticity* (Boulder, CO: Westview Press, 2012).

4. See Carroll Smith-Rosenberg's classic essay, "The Female World of Love and Ritual: Relations Between Women in Nineteenth Century America," *Signs,* vol. 1, no. 1 (Autumn 1975), pp. 1–29; Julie Des Jardins, *Walter Camp: Football and the Modern Man* (New York: Oxford University Press, 2015).

5. Kahlil Gibran to MMM, n.d.; Stanley Hornbeck to MMM, December 12, 1938.

6. Harriet Eager Davis, *World on My Doorstep: A Venture in International Living* (New York: Simon and Schuster, 1949), p. 6; Ruth Pratt to MMM, September 15, 1932.

7. Examples of such gift giving are too numerous to cite here. See, for example, Grace Coolidge to MMM, January 6, 1938; John Erskine to MMM, March 30, 1937; Rouben Mamoulian to MMM, February 5,1936; Edna Ferber to MMM, February 2, 1936.

8. MMM to Bruce Barton, October 30, 1934.

9. Harlow Brooks folder, MMM misc. material.

10. See, for instance, her talk to the NCCWW, "The Immigrant: A Defender or an Enemy of the Republic?" December 1, 1925, and draft of New Year's speech, n.d., MMM manuscripts; draft on American values and opportunity for all, n.d., MMM manuscripts.

CHAPTER 1: THE MAKINGS OF A SOB STORY

1. The women journalists covering the Thaw trial were Dorothy Dix, Winifred Black Bonfils, Ada Patterson, and Nixola Greeley-Smith. See Jean Marie Lutes, *Front-Page Girls: Women Journalists in American Culture and Fiction, 1880–1930* (Ithaca, NY: Cornell University Press, 2006), p. 65; typed description of cub reporter years, MMM autobiography, p. 25.

2. Jan Whitt, *Women in American Journalism: A New History* (Urbana: University of Illinois Press, 2008), pp. 4–5.

3. Fairfax's real name was Marie Manning, and Dix's was Elizabeth Meriwether Gilmer. Maurine Beasley and Sheila Gibbons, *Taking Their Place: A Documentary History of Women and Journalism* (Washington, DC: The American University Press, 1993), p. 10; Marion Marzolf, *Up from the Footnote: A History of Women Journalists* (New York: Hastings House, 1977), p. 35; Lutes, *Front-Page Girls*, p. 8.

4. Ishbel Ross, *Ladies of the Press: The Story of Women in Journalism by an Insider* (New York: Harper and Brothers, 1936), pp. 16–17; Lutes, *Front-Page Girls*, p. 2; Marzolf, *Up from the Footnote*, pp. 32–33; Elizabeth L. Banks, *The Autobiography of a Newspaper Girl* (London: Methuen and Company, 1902), pp. 199, 197–214.

5. Ross, *Ladies of the Press*, p. 17; MMM autobiography, p. 13.

6. On several occasions, MMM's sojourns to the South were announced in the local papers, albeit with no mention of her medical diagnosis. See, for instance, the *Washington Evening Star*, February 22, 1894, p. 24.

7. Birth records corroborate that MMM was born December 8, 1878, but passports, census records, obituaries, and self-reports place her birth later. For a photograph of her grave site, see www.findagrave.com/memorial/47423197. See the US Federal Census data for MMM in 1880 and 1900, which list her birthdate as "about 1879" and "February 1879," respectively. (Year: 1880; Census Place: Bardstown, Nelson, Kentucky; Roll: 435; Family History Film: 1254435; Page: 188C; Enumeration

District: 205. And Year: 1900; Census Place: Washington, Washington, District of Columbia; Roll: 158; Page: 32B; Enumeration District: 0012; FHL microfilm: 1240158.)

8. "Shadows in the Morning," handwritten manuscript, n.d., MMM manuscripts.

9. Although Louis Philippe spent some twenty-one years in exile, some of the time in Philadelphia, Boston, and New York, I have found no evidence that he spent time in Bardstown. Mattingly Spalding, a town historian and a nephew of MMM's, treats the stories of Louis Philippe's associations with Bardstown as lore, but he states, too, that the royal's initial meeting with Father Joseph Flaget, the town's first bishop, "probably took place in 1799," and that he consequently gifted art to the Bardstown Catholic Diocese. See Mattingly Spalding, *Biography of a Kentucky Town* (Baltimore, MD: printed by author, 1942), pp. 8, 10 (typed book inscribed to "Aunt Missy," Rare Book and Manuscript Library, Columbia University, New York, NY); John S. C. Abbott, *History of Louis Philippe: King of the French*, 2nd ed. (Sandycroft Publishing, 2017 [1871]), pp. 32–47; "'Once the Athens of the West,' Bardstown, KY, Was in the New York Class in 1808," New York *Sun*, April 26, 1908; "Shadows in the Morning."

10. "Biographical Sketch of Cyprian Peter Mattingly, MD," Bardstown, KY, n.d., MMM catalogued manuscripts; enclosed Mattingly family history in MMM to Joe Mattingly, January 14, 1938; "Medical Societies," Twelfth Annual Meeting of the American Medical Association, *Medical and Surgical Reporter*, June 2, 1859, p. 205; "University of Louisville," *The Western Journal of Medicine and Surgery*, April 1847, p. 364; C. P. Mattingly and R. S. Strother, "A Medico-Legal Case," *The Western Journal of Medicine and Surgery*, vol. V (May 1847), p. 404; Spalding, *Biography of a Kentucky Town*, pp. 50–51.

11. "Shadows in the Morning."

12. Some sources suggest that Cyprian Mattingly may have had nineteen children from three different wives. See Ishbel Ross, "Marie Mattingly Meloney," in *Notable American Women*, ed. Edward James (Cambridge, MA: Harvard University Press, 1971), p. 525; Samuel J. Rogal, *A William Somerset Maugham Encyclopedia* (Westport, CT: Greenwood Press, 1997), p. 177.

13. Kentucky Marriage Records, 1852–1914 (online database), Provo, Utah, Ancestry.com, 2007, http://search.ancestry.com/cgi-bin/sse.dll?indiv=1&db=KY marriages1...e&_phsrc=Xoi11&_phstart=successSource&usePUBJs=true&rh Source=8054; "Biographical Sketch of Cyprian Peter Mattingly"; MMM to Joe Mattingly, January 14, 1938; MMM to George Mattingly, April 3, 1937; Spalding, *Biography of a Kentucky Town*, p. 21.

14. "Mrs. Mattingly, 82, Educator, Is Dead," *New York Times*, January 7, 1934, p. 31; draft of writing on "Sallie Irwin," December 9, 1940, MMM manuscripts.

15. Handwritten genealogy, Sarah Irwin Mattingly file, n.d., MMM misc. material; Ross, "Marie Mattingly Meloney"; announcement of the *Kentucky Literary*

Magazine in *South Kentuckian,* May 4, 1880, p. 2; *Eclectic Teacher and Southwestern Journal of Education,* vol. 4, no. 10 (June 1880), pp. 361–362; "Mrs. Mattingly, 82, Educator, Is Dead"; Spalding, *Biography of a Kentucky Town,* 79; "The Kentucky Literary Magazine," Hartford, KY, *Herald,* May 5, 1880, p. 3.

16. "Recollections of Father," n.d., MMM manuscripts.

17. "Recollections of Father"; "Shadows in the Morning."

18. "The Patriot," handwritten draft, n.d., MMM manuscripts.

19. "Recollections of Father"; "Shadows in the Morning"; handwritten recollections of Nellie Cotton incident and learning not to fear, n.d., MMM manuscripts.

20. Draft of speech MMM gave at St. Lawrence University, March 18, 193[0], p. 18, MMM manuscripts; George Mattingly to Aunt Missy, March 1937; MMM to George Mattingly, April 3, 1937. For an analysis of the crisis in elite masculinity in America at the turn of the century, see Michael Kimmel, *Manhood in America: A Cultural History* (New York: Oxford University Press, 2006).

21. "Social Matters," Washington *Evening Star,* December 25, 1891, p. 1.

22. Mary Roberts Rinehart, *My Story* (New York: Farrar and Rinehart, 1931), pp. 340–344.

23. MMM autobiography, pp. 1–2.

24. Donald Ritchie, *Press Gallery: Congress and the Washington Correspondents* (Cambridge, MA: Harvard University Press, 1991), pp. 148–151.

25. MMM autobiography, p. 18; draft on Mrs. Coolidge at the White House, June 12, 1924, MMM manuscripts.

26. 1900 United States Federal Census, Washington, DC; Roll: 158, Page: 32B; "Local News of All Sorts," *Washington Times,* September 9, 1894, p. 3; *A Handbook of American Private Schools,* 3rd ed. (Boston: Porter E. Sargent, 1917), p. 204; ad for Sarah Irwin Mattingly's school in *Confederate Veteran,* vol. 22, no. 9 (September 1914), p. 429; "Prizes for Girl Students," Washington *Evening Star,* June 6, 1894, p. 8; "For Damages," Washington *Evening Star,* July 21, 1897, p. 3.

27. MMM autobiography, pp. 43–45.

28. Channing Pollock, "Missy," n.d. (and included drafts), Pollock file, MMM misc. material.

29. MMM autobiography, pp. 2–3.

30. MMM autobiography, pp. 2–4.

CHAPTER 2: A CUB REPORTER IN 1900

1. For a discussion of how the ideology of separate spheres supported anti-suffragist arguments at the turn of the century, see Anne Myra Benjamin, *Women Against Equality: A History of the Anti-Suffrage Movement in the United States from 1895–1920* (Lulu Publishing Services, 2014); Susan Goodier, *No Votes for Women: The New York Anti Suffrage Movement* (Urbana: University of Illinois Press, 2013);

Brian Harrison, *Separate Spheres: The Opposition to Suffrage in Britain* (New York: Routledge, 2012).

2. Lutes, *Front-Page Girls*, p. 1; Ross, *Ladies of the Press*, pp. 10, 21–22; Kathleen Cairns, *Front-Page Women Journalists, 1920–1950* (Lincoln: University of Nebraska Press, 2003), p. xii; Patricia Bradley, *Women and the Press: The Struggle for Equality* (Evanston, IL: Medill School of Journalism, 2005), p. 127; Banks, *Autobiography of a Newspaper Girl*, p. 239.

3. It is unclear how old Missy was when she got her first reporter job. Many sources say she was in her teens, but if she was born in 1878, as census records indicate, she would have been in her early twenties when she first met Scott Bone—if that encounter was in 1899 or 1900, for that also is unclear. In her own account, she collapses the time between her first meeting with Bone and her covering of the political conventions of 1900 to an unknown extent. Beasley and Gibbons, *Taking Their Place*, p. 8; Pollock, "Missy," n.d.; "Noted Woman Editor Won Job as Reporter by Getting First Story of Dewey Marriage," clipping from unknown publication, n.d., MMM manuscripts; MMM autobiography, pp. 28, 13.

4. Ross, *Ladies of the Press*, p. 380; "Noted Woman Editor."

5. MMM autobiography, pp. 5–6.

6. "On Getting a Job," n.d., typed draft, MMM manuscripts; MMM autobiography, p. 7.

7. Banks, *Autobiography of a Newspaper Girl*, pp. 16–17; MMM autobiography, pp. 8–10.

8. "Dewey Married—Brings Bride Here," New York *World*, November 10, 1899, pp. 1–2; "On Getting a Job."

9. William S. Solomon, "The Site of Newsroom Labor: The Division of Editorial Practices," in *Newsworkers: Toward a History of the Rank and File*, eds. Hanno Hardt and Bonnie Brennen (Minneapolis: University of Minnesota Press), pp. 120–126; MMM autobiography, pp. 11–12.

10. "Noted Woman Editor"; MMM autobiography, pp. 14–16.

11. George W. Wilder, "The Delineator's Editor," *The Delineator*, March 1921, p. 1; MMM autobiography, pp. 16–18.

12. MMM autobiography, pp. 19–21.

13. Mrs. William Henry Jones of Salt Lake City, Utah, and Mrs. J. P. West of Lewiston, Idaho, served as alternate delegates to the convention that year. See Jo Freeman, *A Room at a Time: How Women Entered Party Politics* (New York: Rowman and Littlefield, 2002), p. 65; Stan M. Haynes, *President-Making in the Gilded Age: The Nominating Conventions of 1876–1900* (Jefferson, NC: McFarland, 2016), p. 248.

14. MMM autobiography, p. 22.

15. MMM autobiography, p. 23.

16. MMM autobiography, pp. 24–25, 45–46.

17. MMM autobiography, pp. 25–28.

18. MMM autobiography, pp. 30–31; Pollock, "Missy."

19. MMM autobiography, pp. 30–31.

20. MMM autobiography, p. 32.

21. MMM autobiography, p. 34.

22. MMM autobiography, pp. 34–37.

23. MMM autobiography, p. 37.

24. Untitled social news, Washington *Evening Star*, July 21, 1900, p. 7; MMM autobiography, pp. 37–39.

25. Marzolf, *Up from the Footnote*, p. 34; Ross, *Ladies of the Press*, p. 64.

26. MMM autobiography, p. 41.

27. MMM autobiography, p. 40.

28. Agnes Wright Spring, "Theodore Roosevelt in Colorado," *Colorado Magazine*, vol. XXXV, no. 4 (October 1958), pp. 242–251.

29. MMM autobiography, pp. 42–43.

30. MMM autobiography, pp. 46–47.

31. MMM autobiography, pp. 47–48.

32. MMM autobiography, p. 49.

33. MMM autobiography, pp. 50–53.

34. MMM autobiography, p. 53.

35. MMM autobiography, pp. 55–56.

36. MMM autobiography, p. 57.

37. MMM autobiography, pp. 58–62.

38. MMM autobiography, pp. 62–65.

39. Untitled piece on MMM in *The Intermountain Catholic*, September 1, 1900, p. 2; MMM autobiography, pp. 66–67.

40. MMM autobiography, pp. 66–67.

41. Marie Mattingly, "'Convict No. 1924' Visit to Capt. Carter in the Prison at Fort Leavenworth, Kansas," *Washington Post*, November 7, 1900, p. 5.

42. MMM autobiography, pp. 68–69; MMM, "'Convict No. 1924.'"

43. MMM autobiography, p. 25.

44. President Fillmore had discouraged Swisshelm from requesting a gallery seat, insisting that the experience of being a woman in a bastion of men would be unpleasant, but she arranged to write letters in Horace Greeley's *Tribune* and couldn't be persuaded to leave. Initially, Greeley liked the novelty of a woman political correspondent, but Swisshelm's time in the gallery was short-lived. She wrote a scathing piece on Daniel Webster, revealing him as a drunkard who sired mulatto children, and men in the newspaper establishment thought she had crossed a line. One didn't reveal the private indiscretions of public men. See Sylvia D. Hoffert, *Jane Grey Swisshelm: An Unconventional Life, 1815–1884* (Chapel Hill: University of North Carolina Press, 2011); Ritchie, *Press Gallery*, pp. 4–5, 43–46, 85, 121, 145–146; Ross, *Ladies of the Press*, pp. 16, 323–326; Beasley and Gibbons, *Tak-*

ing Their Place, p. 9; Irvin Molotsky, "You've Come a Long Way, Scribe," Special to the *New York Times,* October 18, 1985, p. 20; "The World Her School," *Los Angeles Herald,* September 3, 1896, p. 5.

45. MMM autobiography, pp. 70–71.

46. MMM autobiography, p. 74.

47. Ibid.

CHAPTER 3: MANHATTAN, MARRIAGE, MOTHERHOOD, MAGAZINES—AND MODERNITY, 1901–1914

1. "Miss Marie Mattingly," *Arizona Republican,* August 8, 1901, p. 4; August 1, 1908; local news of the *Arizona Weekly Journal-Miner,* January 8, 1902, p. 3.

2. MMM to Channing Pollock, February 6, 1941; Kevin C. Fitzpatrick, *The Algonquin Round Table: A Historical Guide* (Guilford, CT: National Book Network, 2015), pp. 127–129.

3. Ross, *Ladies of the Press,* p. 22; Cairns, *Front-Page Women Journalists,* pp. 14–16; Bradley, *Women and the Press,* pp. 138–139.

4. Ross, *Ladies of the Press,* p. 143; "On Getting a Job"; "Her Field Widening: Miss Marie Mattingly Now a Contributor to N.Y. Herald," *Arizona Republican,* November 28, 1902, p. 8; "Memoranda for order of jobs in writing book," n.d., MMM manuscripts; Nanette Lincoln, "Southern Women Journalists in New York," *Bob Taylor's Magazine,* May 1906, pp. 166–167.

5. Robert V. Hudson, *The Writing Game: A Biography of Will Irwin* (Ames: Iowa State University Press, 1982), pp. 37, 40–41, 47.

6. "Nation's Safety Lies in Freedom of the Press," Lewiston *Evening Journal,* December 7, 1934, p. 20; Elting Alexander Fowler to MMM, August 10, 1915; Ross, *Ladies of the Press,* p. 143; Wilder, "The Delineator's Editor," pp. 1, 72; "Noted Woman Editor."

7. Ida M. Tarbell, *The History of the Standard Oil Company* (New York: McClure, Phillips and Company, 1904); Brooke Bailey, *The Remarkable Lives of 100 Women Writers and Journalists* (Holbrook, MA: Bob Adams, 1994), pp. 182–183; Bradley, *Women and the Press,* pp. 144–145; Marzolf, *Up from the Footnote,* p. 41.

8. Freeman, *A Room at a Time,* pp. 64–65.

9. Ross, *Ladies of the Press,* pp. 21–22, 87–89, 94; Banks, *Autobiography of a Newspaper Girl,* pp. 287, 289.

10. John William Leonard and Albert Nelson Marquis, *Who's Who in America, 1920–21,* vol. 11 (Chicago: A. N. Marquis Company, 1920), p. 1947; William Brown Meloney, "Our Police Disease," *Outlook,* October 5, 1912, pp. 260–268; William Brown Meloney, "Slumming in New York's Chinatown," *Munsey's,* vol. 41 (September 1909), pp. 818–830; William Brown Meloney, "Strikebreaking as a Profession," *Public Opinion,* vol. 25 (March 1905), pp. 440–441; William Brown Meloney, "Joseph Pulitzer," *American Magazine,* vol. XXI (November 1909); 1880 US Federal

Census, San Francisco, CA, Roll: 74, Family History Film: 1254074, Page: 747C, Enumeration district: 059; "Births-Marriages-Deaths," *San Francisco Call,* May 1, 1898, p. 14; "Esola Charges Before Police Commissioners," *San Francisco Call,* January 19, 1900, p. 12; "Trial of Morrisey and Flynn Is Ended," *San Francisco Call,* March 6, 1902, p. 12; "Witnesses Assaulted," *San Francisco Chronicle,* January 22, 1900; "Short and Sharp," San Francisco *Record-Union,* January 25, 1898, p. 4.

11. "One Killed and Thirty Injured in Wreck of Train," New York *Evening World,* June 11, 1906, Final Results Edition, p. 3; MMM, "The Last Magic," for the American Association of Advertising Agencies 18th Annual Meeting at the Greenbrier, White Sulphur Springs, WV, April 12, 1935, MMM manuscripts.

12. "In Society's Circle," *Washington Times,* Evening Edition, June 7, 1904, p. 6; "Meloney-Mattingly," *New York Tribune,* June 7, 1904, p. 5; wedding announcement in Washington *Evening Star,* June 7, 1904; "Mary Irwin Expires at Garfield Hospital," *Washington Times,* December 29, 1903, p. 3; MMM to Joe Mattingly, January 14, 1938; Ross, *Ladies of the Press,* p. 332.

13. "In Society's Circle"; "New Haven Commuters Kick," New York *Sun,* August 12, 1904, p. 5.

14. Izola Page to MMM, March 9, 1933.

15. William B. Meloney, "What Women Have Accomplished Without the Ballot," *Munsey's,* vol. XVIV (November 1910), pp. 197–203.

16. Beasley and Gibbons, *Taking Their Place,* p. 131.

17. Edited manuscript, n.d. (paginated a, b, c, etc.), MMM manuscripts; 1910 US Federal Census, Manhattan Ward 12, New York, NY, Roll: T624-1025, Page: 4A.

18. "Gaynor Finds Idle Police," New York *Sun,* April 6, 1910, p. 1; "After Alderman Markert," New York *Sun,* March 26, 1910, p. 2; "Steadily Gaining, Say the Mayor's Doctors," *New York Tribune,* August 15, 1910, pp. 1, 2; "City Hall Routine Resumed," New York *Sun,* August 11, 1910, p. 2; secretary of MMM to Schuyler N. Warren, June 6, 1939, box 7, William B. Meloney–John Purroy Mitchel Collection, Rare Book and Manuscript Library, Columbia University, New York, New York.

19. "Meloney Leaves Mayor," *New York Tribune,* June 2, 1911, p. 14; "News of Plays and Players," New York *Sun,* October 2, 1911; "$1,132,000 for New Schools," *New York Times,* February 11, 1910, p. 10; Joseph Cummings Chase, *My Friends Look Good to Me* (New York: Sears Publishing Company, 1933), pp. 183–186.

20. "Newspaper Folk in New York," *The Wasp (The Pacific Coast Weekly),* January 3, 1920; William Brown Meloney, *The Girl of the Golden Gate* (New York: Grosset and Dunlap, 1913); Arrival: New York, New York, Microfilm Serial: T715, 1897–1957, Microfilm Roll: 2235, Line 16, Page Number: 179 (Ancestry .com New York, Passenger Lists, 1820–1957), Provo, Utah, Ancestry.com, 2010, http://search.ancestry.com/cgi-bin/sse.dll?indiv=1&db=nypl&h=4014575822 &tid=&pid=&usePUB=true&rhSource=3030.

21. Rinehart, *My Story*, pp. 81–84, 86, 111, 134–135; Jan Cohn, *Improbable Fiction: The Life of Mary Roberts Rinehart* (Pittsburgh, PA: University of Pittsburgh Press, 1980), pp. 28–30; Kathleen Norris, *Noon: An Autobiographical Sketch* (Garden City, NY: Doubleday, Page, and Company, 1925), pp. 53–58.

22. Mary Ellen Waller-Zuckerman, "'Old Homes, in a City of Perpetual Change': Women's Magazines, 1890–1916," *Business History Review*, vol. 63, no. 4 (Winter 1989), pp. 719, 727; Sidney R. Bland, "Shaping the Life of the New Woman: The Crusading Years of the *Delineator*," *American Periodicals: A Journal of History, Criticism, and Bibliography*, vol. 19, no. 2 (2009), pp. 166–167, 170.

23. MMM, "The Last Magic"; MMM to Bill Nichols, August 6, 1940, MMM manuscripts.

24. Bland, "Shaping the Life of the New Woman," pp. 168, 174–181; Frank L. Mott, *A History of American Magazines, 1865–85*, vol. 3, 4th ed. (London: Oxford University Press, 1970), p. 487; Waller-Zuckerman, "'Old Homes, in a City of Perpetual Change,'" p. 732; Mary Kosut, ed., *Encyclopedia of Gender in Media* (Purchase College, State University of New York: Sage Reference, 2012), pp. 436–437.

25. Mott, *History of American Magazines*, pp. 482–483; Kosut, *Encyclopedia of Gender in Media*, p. 436; Waller-Zuckerman, "'Old Homes, in a City of Perpetual Change,'" pp. 747, 750, 753–754; Carolyn M. Goldstein, *Creating Consumers: Home Economists in Twentieth-Century America* (Chapel Hill: University of North Carolina Press, 2012), pp. 39, 45.

26. MMM's speech on the *Woman's Magazine*, typed draft, n.d., MMM manuscripts, pp. 3–5; David S. Shields, *The Culinarians: Lives and Careers from the First Age of American Fine Dining* (Chicago: University of Chicago Press, 2017), p. 536.

27. *Woman's Magazine*, January 1914, vol. 29, no. 1, cover; *Woman's Magazine*, March 1914, vol. 29, no. 3, cover; MMM's speech on the *Woman's Magazine*, p. 2.

28. "Memorandum of Educational Matters to Mr. Ridgway," [1914], p. 7, MMM manuscripts.

29. MMM to Charles Eliot, March 9, 1914, Charles Eliot folder, MMM misc. material.

30. Pollock, "Missy."

31. Charles Eliot to MMM, July 28, 1914, August 24, 1914, September 8, 1914, March 19, 1915, July 27, 1915; MMM to Charles Eliot, March 15, 1915, April 1, 1915, July 22, 1915, August 3, 1915.

32. Charles Eliot to MMM, April 22, 1915, September 20, 1915.

33. MMM to Charles Eliot, April 30, 1915, September 18, 1915, September 23, 1915.

34. William Howard Taft to MMM, February 15, 1916; Gifford Pinchot to Harriet Ide Eager, March 12, 1917, MMM correspondence; Eliot Wadsworth to Harriet Eager, October 16, 1917, MMM correspondence; Franklin K. Lane to MMM, January 29, 1915, April 15, 1915, April 12, 1916, March 21, 1919.

35. For a discussion of strategies for this generation of women journalists, see Bradley, *Women and the Press,* pp. 134–136.

36. Charles Eliot to MMM, March 19, 1915; MMM to Eliot, March 15, 1915.

37. Charles Eliot to MMM, December 6, 1920; MMM to Eliot, December 11, 1920.

CHAPTER 4: WHAT IT MEANS TO BE A PATRIOT (THE SUFFRAGIST WHO WASN'T), 1915–1920

1. "Francis C. Mattingly Dead," *Washington Herald,* March 6, 1908, p. 2; "Francis C. Mattingly Dead," Washington *Evening Star,* March 5, 1908, p. 2; "Francis C. Mattingly Dead: Newspaper Man and Lawyer Succumbs to Rheumatic Fever," *Washington Post,* March 6, 1908, p. 2; "Gonzaga Cadets," Washington *Evening Star,* October 9, 1897, p. 16; wedding announcement in Washington *Evening Star,* September 26, 1906; "Final Services Today," Washington *Evening Star,* March 7, 1908, p. 18.

2. MMM to Colonel Roosevelt, December 26, 1916, Theodore Roosevelt file, MMM misc. material; Wilder, "The Delineator's Editor," p. 72; Theodore Roosevelt to MMM, Christmas 1909, MMM manuscripts (reprinted, August 5, 1916). To understand American women's role as the "second line of defense," see Lynn Dumenil, *The Second Line of Defense: American Women and World War I* (Chapel Hill: University of North Carolina Press, 2017), pp. 1–2.

3. Dumenil, *Second Line of Defense,* p. 34; Andrew Carnegie to MMM, November 2, 1914 (Missy's letter of October 23, 1914, is quoted in Carnegie's letter).

4. "Rich Young New Yorkers Drill in Rain to Learn How to Be Real Soldiers," New York *Evening World,* August 10, 1915, p. 2; "Strenuous Life at Plattsburg Business Men's Camp," Special to *New York Times,* August 15, 1915, p. xi; "Private Mitchel Juggles Trunks; in Bed at 8 P.M.," *New York Tribune,* August 11, 1915, p. 14; "Tenting on Busy Camp Ground, Where Business Men of New York Are Conquering Mysteries of Military Lore from Reveille to Taps," *New York Tribune,* August 12, 1915, p. 9; "City Men Drive at Army Work," Special to *New York Times,* August 11, 1915, p. 5.

5. Dumenil, *Second Line of Defense,* pp. 19–20; MMM to Dr. J. G. Schurman, November 24, 1914; Schurman to MMM, December 3, 1914; Wilder, "The Delineator's Editor," p. 1; MMM to Colonel Roosevelt, November 13, 1914, November 14, 1915, Theodore Roosevelt file, MMM misc. material; Mott, *History of American Magazines,* p. 487.

6. Dumenil, *Second Line of Defense,* p. 34.

7. Charles Chaplin to Harriet Eager, March 30, 1918, MMM correspondence; Bland, "Shaping the Life of the New Woman," p. 181; schedule of features in *Woman's Magazine* and *The Delineator,* August 1915 to December 1922, MMM manuscripts.

8. P. van den Ven, Belgian Information Service, Washington, DC, to MMM, June 19, 1918, in "Notes—including Hollywood," MMM misc. material; Wilder, "The Delineator's Editor," p. 72; Baron de Cartier to MMM, July 27, 1918. For a discussion of women's relief efforts in the nineteenth century, see Lori Ginzberg, *Women and the Work of Benevolence: Morality, Politics, and Class in the Nineteenth-Century United States* (New Haven, CT: Yale University Press, 1990).

9. MMM wrote in a letter to Channing Pollock, "I developed the plan for the Junior Red Cross and have some letters from H.P. Davison and President Wilson." See MMM to Channing Pollock, n.d., Pollock file, MMM misc. material; Julia Irwin, "Teaching 'Americanism with a World Perspective': The Junior Red Cross in the U.S. Schools from 1917 to the 1920s," *History of Education Quarterly*, vol. 53 (August 2013), pp. 255–279.

10. Dumenil, *Second Line of Defense*, pp. 105–106, 162; Ross, *Ladies of the Press*, p. 120; Annalena McAfee, "Women on the Front Line," *The Guardian*, April 15, 2011, www.theguardian.com/books/2011/apr/16/women-war-reporting-annalena -mcafee; "War to Open Newspaper Field to Many Women," *Editor and Publisher*, August 25, 1917, vol. 50, part 1, p. 15; Beasley and Gibbons, *Taking Their Place*, pp. 139–140; Ross, *Ladies of the Press*, pp. 376–377.

11. Franklin Lane to Robert Lansing, December 5, 1917, MMM correspondence.

12. "Notes on trip to Brussels to see Queen," n.d., MMM manuscripts.

13. "Notes on trip to Brussels"; contract for Queen Elizabeth biography, New York City, February 11, 1926, MMM manuscripts; "Queen Elizabeth," typed draft, n.d., MMM manuscripts.

14. MMM to My Friend, n.d., MMM manuscripts; Helen Rogers Reid, "'Missy' Meloney," *Columbia Library Columns*, vol. XI, no. 2 (February 1962), p. 32.

15. "Society," Washington *Evening Star*, November 29, 1917, p. 12; "600 Made Officers at Ft. Oglethorpe," New York *Sun*, August 15, 1917, p. 6; MMM to General Wood, April 4, 1917.

16. Leonard Wood to MMM, November 11, 1918; MMM to General Wood, November 8, 1918; MMM to Theodore Roosevelt, November 9, 1918.

17. MMM to General Wood, January 6, 1919, General Wood file, MMM misc. material; MMM to General Wood, March 13, 1919.

18. MMM to General Wood, April 3, 1919, May 9, 1919; letter of Theodore Roosevelt, February 6, 1917.

19. MMM to General Wood, October 11, 1918, September 25, 1919.

20. General Wood to MMM, June 30, 1919.

21. MMM to General Wood, April 9, 1919, September 25, 1919; General Wood to MMM, April 11, 1919, June 30, 1919, July 8, 1919.

22. Elaine Weiss, *The Woman's Hour: The Great Fight to Win the Vote* (New York: Viking, 2018), pp. 84–85, 92, 122, 132.

23. MMM to Major H. L. Reese, April 28, 1937; Edward V. Riis, "Ex-Mayor Mitchel's Death Described in Detail by His Flying Instructor; Struggled to Right Self in 500 Foot Fall," clipping, n.d., box 7, William B. Meloney–John-Purroy Mitchel Collection, Rare Book and Manuscript Library, Columbia University Libraries, New York, New York.

24. "Thousands Pay Tribute to Mitchel," *New York Tribune,* July 11, 1918, pp. 1, 4; "Mitchel's Body Arrives at Home of His Mother," New York *Evening World,* July 9, 1918, pp. 1, 3; "Funeral of Mitchel to Be Open to All," New York *Tribune,* July 10, 1918, p. 5; "21 Flyers to Soar over Mitchel Bier," New York *Sun,* July 9, 1918, p. 9.

25. Mrs. Purroy Mitchel to William Brown Meloney, January 1920, box 7, Meloney-Mitchel Collection.

26. Franklin Lane to MMM, May 31, 1918, August 26, 1918. See bound volume *Jobs for Soldiers,* C. B. Hammond to William Brown Meloney, October 7, 1919, MMM correspondence; "Major W. B. Meloney Dies; Victim of War," *New York Times,* December 8, 1925, p. 25.

27. Helen Woods to MMM, March 16 [1919]; Arthur Woods to MMM, February 22, 1919, July 2, 1919; Belgian Consul to MMM, October 23, 1919, Belgian correspondence file, MMM misc. material.

28. "Mrs. Meloney Decorated," New York *Sun,* December 26, 1919, p. 9.

29. Wilder, "The Delineator's Editor," pp. 1, 72.

30. Peyton Conway March to Col. T. B. Mott, March 30, 1920, MMM correspondence; March to MMM, November 16, 1920; MMM to General P. C. March November 13, 1920.

31. Robert Poole, *On Hallowed Ground: The Story of Arlington National Cemetery* (New York: Bloomsbury Publishing, 2009), p. 146.

CHAPTER 5: CULTIVATING RELATIONSHIPS AND BEST SELLERS FOR AND BY WOMEN, 1920S

1. Wilder, "The Delineator's Editor," p. 1.

2. Talk by MMM to *The Delineator* staff, Thursday 2:50 p.m., n.d. [1925], MMM misc. material.

3. William Brown Meloney, "Calvin Coolidge, America," *Everybody's,* December 1919, p. 28; typed draft on MMM's first visit to Calvin Coolidge at the Massachusetts State House, October 1919, pp. 1–3, MMM manuscripts; typed draft on Calvin Coolidge writing for MMM, n.d., p. 2, MMM manuscripts.

4. Typed draft on MMM's first visit to Calvin Coolidge, pp. 3–4; typed draft on Calvin Coolidge writing for MMM, p. 3.

5. Typed draft on MMM's first visit to Calvin Coolidge, pp. 4–5; typed draft on Coolidge writing for MMM, pp. 3–4.

6. Typed draft on MMM's first visit to Calvin Coolidge, p. 5.

7. Typed draft on Calvin Coolidge writing for MMM, p. 1; typed draft on MMM's first visit to Calvin Coolidge, pp. 9–11.

8. Calvin Coolidge to MMM, March 7, 1921, Calvin Coolidge folder, MMM misc. material.

9. Typed draft on Calvin Coolidge writing for MMM, pp. 5–7, 9.

10. Typed draft on MMM's first visit to Calvin Coolidge, p. 12.

11. MMM to Georges Lecomte, June 19, 1920; Berta Oliver to MMM, June 26, 1920; William John Locke to MMM, June 25, 1920; talk by MMM to *The Delineator* staff [1925].

12. MMM to William Brown Meloney, April 18, 1920, MMM misc. material.

13. Ibid.

14. Franklin K. Lane to MMM, November 18, [1920]; MMM to May Sinclair, June 22, 1920; Alfred Charles Harmsworth to MMM, May 3, 1920; J. S. Fletcher to MMM, June 15, 1920; Neil A. Lyons to MMM, June 15, 1920; Jerome Klapka Jerome to MMM, June 24, 1920; MMM to H. de Vere Stacpoole, June 17, 1920; MMM to Mrs. Stacpoole, June 30, 1920, English correspondence 1920, MMM misc. material; Joseph Conrad to MMM, June 25, 1920; Arthur Conan Doyle to MMM, June 26, 1920; MMM to John Galsworthy, June 17, 1920; MMM to Lady Warwick, June 29, 1920, English correspondence 1920; secretary of MMM to Sir Anthony Hope Hawkins, June 21, 1920; MMM to John Collis Snaith, June 19, 1920; MMM to F. Brett Young, June 18, 1920, English correspondence 1920; A. M. Spinks to MMM, June 21, 1920; Ella King-Hall of Mr. Fitzgerald Arbuthnot Literary and Dramatic Agents to MMM, June 22, 1920; H. Matheson, political secretary of Lady Astor, to MMM, June 29, 1920.

15. Hughes Massie to MMM, June 28, 1920; MMM to Mrs. Massie, June 30, 1920; John Sherlock to MMM, June 21, 1920; MMM to John Sherlock, June 17, 1920, June 22, 1920; Jessie Conrad to MMM, March 22, 1926.

16. Arthur Stuart-Menteth Hutchinson to MMM, June 5, 1920; talk by MMM to *The Delineator* staff [1925].

17. Arthur Bliss Lane to MMM, June 26, 1920; MMM to Sir Eric Drummond, June 30, 1920; Drummond to MMM, July 3, 1920; MMM to E. H. Jones, June 22, 1920; MMM to J. S. Fletcher, June 17, 1920.

18. MMM to Professor P. van den Ven, May 28, 1920; Emile Cammaerts to MMM, May 3, 1920; Marie Kefer-Mali to MMM, May 31, 1920; MMM to Kefer-Mali, June 23, 1920; Comtesse van den Steen to MMM, January 2, 1920; Therese Hymans to MMM, May 23, 1920; MMM to Madame Paul Hymans, June 13, 1920, July 1, 1920; MMM to Viscomte Henri Davignon, May 26, 1920, June 30, 1920.

19. MMM to Abbe Felix Klein, June 16, 1920, MMM misc. material; MMM to Mme. Henri Carton de Wiart, June 9, 1920, June 30, 1920, Belgian correspondence file, MMM misc. material; MMM to P. van den Ven, May 27, 1920, MMM misc. material; MMM to George Robey, June 17, 1920, June 24, 1920; Sir Gilbert Parker to MMM, June 23, 1920.

20. "Some Memories of Sir James M. Barrie," typed manuscript, n.d., J. A. Barrie folder, MMM misc. material.

21. Talk by MMM to *The Delineator* staff [1925].

22. "Some Memories of Sir James M. Barrie."

23. State Department Certificate [1919/1920], MMM manuscripts.

24. MMM's account of her visit with Barrie is part of her talk to staff at *The Delineator* offices [1925]. See also the draft of the speech she gave at St. Lawrence University [1930]; "Barrie," typed draft, January 21, 1926, MMM manuscripts.

25. Ibid.

26. "Barrie."

27. "Some Memories of Sir James M. Barrie"; "Barrie."

28. MMM to Maynard Greville, June 28, 1920.

29. MMM to Channing Pollock, February 6, 1941; MMM, memorandum on the Norrises, March 25, 1924, CG and Kathleen Norris file, MMM misc. material.

30. Lynn Dumenil, *The Modern Temper: American Culture and Society in the 1920s* (New York: Hill and Wang, 1995), p. 154; "The Gossip Shop," *Bookman*, June 1925, p. 501; "Sequelae," *Time*, April 20, 1925, p. 22; Zona Gale to MMM, August 22, 1923; Isabel Paterson to MMM, July 12, 1921; MMM to Gutzon Borglum, March 3, 1930.

31. Joan Shelley Rubin, *The Making of Middlebrow Culture* (Chapel Hill: University of North Carolina Press, 1992), pp. xi–xii.

32. Fannie Hurst, *Anatomy of Me: A Wonderer in Search of Herself* (Garden City, NY: Doubleday, 1958), pp. 241–242; Julie Goldsmith Gilbert, *Ferber: A Biography of Edna Ferber and Her Circle* (Garden City, NY: Doubleday and Company, 1978), p. 404; Edna Ferber to MMM, February 6, 1928, April 30, 1935; J. M. Barrie to MMM, December 19, 1934; Willa Cather to MMM, August 26, 1934, May 29, 1935. Mary Roberts Rinehart was another of Missy's authors who struggled with critics who thought her writing was more commercial than elevated. See Cohn, *Improbable Fiction*, p. 65.

33. Kathleen Norris, *Family Gathering* (Garden City, NY: Doubleday, 1959), p. 106; Charles G. Norris to MMM, July 25, 1921, August 23, 1922, March 23, 1923; MMM, memorandum on the Norrises, March 25, 1924, MMM correspondence; memo from "MM" to Mr. Gannon, March 23, 1923; MMM to Charles Norris, August 28, 1922; MMM to Kathleen Norris, March 13, 1922; MMM to Ceegee, May 3, 1926, CG and Kathleen Norris folder, MMM misc. material.

34. Will Irwin to MMM, December 4, 1931, n.d.; Hudson, *The Writing Game*, p. 143; "Galsworthy in New York," *New York Times*, April 10, 1926, p. 17; "Book Notes," *New York Times*, April 14, 1933, p. 23; John Erskine to MMM, May 8, 1930.

35. MMM to E. V. Lucas, December 17, 1924, January 24, 1925; Lucas to MMM, January 13, 1925.

36. MMM to Mr. Moore, in-house memorandum, April 30, 1926, Rinehart file, MMM misc. material.

37. Theodosia Faulks to MMM, April 1, n.y.; Eugen Boissevain to MMM, February 28, 1931, May 1931, November 18, 1931.

CHAPTER 6: THE PUBLICIST OF MADAME CURIE, 1921

1. MMM to M. Stéphane Lauzanne, April 7, 1921, Stéphane Lauzanne file, MMM misc. material; Lauzanne to MMM, May 19, 1920, June 5, 1920, July 2, 1920.

2. Julius Mendes Price, chromolithograph of the Curies, *Vanity Fair,* December 22, 1904; Emily Crawford, "The Curies at Home," *World To-Day,* vol. 6 (1904), p. 490.

3. Edward L. Bernays, *Biography of an Idea: The Founding Principles of Public Relations* (New York: Open Road Media, 2015), unpaginated e-book; Adam Wishart, *One in Three: A Son's Journey into the History and Science of Cancer* (New York: Grove Press, 2008), p. 47; William J. Mayo to MMM, March 16, 1921; Rachel A. Koestler-Grack, *Marie Curie: Scientist* (New York: Chelsea House, 2009), p. 115.

4. MMM, introduction to *Pierre Curie,* by Marie Curie (New York: Macmillan, 1923), pp. 12–16.

5. For an account of Marie Curie's struggles as a married woman in science, see Julie Des Jardins, *Madame Curie Complex,* pp. 33–35.

6. MMM, introduction to *Pierre Curie,* pp. 12–16.

7. For an account of MMM's interview with Curie, see Des Jardins, *Madame Curie Complex,* p. 25.

8. Des Jardins, *Madame Curie Complex;* Susan Quinn, *Marie Curie: A Life* (New York: Simon and Schuster, 1995), p. 383.

9. Marie Curie to MMM, March 9, 1921; "Helping Madame Curie to Help the World," *Woman's Journal,* March 12, 1921, p. 1062.

10. Wishart, *One in Three,* pp. 52–53; "Nazis Find Mme. Curie's Radium," *Fort Dodge Iowa Messenger Chronicle,* December 5, 1940, Correspondence, box 40, Rose Franken Papers, Rare Book and Manuscript Library, Columbia University, New York, New York.

11. MMM to Lt. Colonel W. C. Koenig, June 17, 1920, July 26, 1920.

12. Des Jardins, *Madame Curie Complex,* p. 26.

13. Marie Curie to MMM, November 7, 1920, box 1, William B. Meloney–Marie Curie Special Manuscript Collection, Rare Book and Manuscript Library, Columbia University, New York, New York (hereafter MCC); MMM, introduction to *Pierre Curie,* pp. 15–16; Don Arnald, "Einstein on Irrelevancies," *New York Times,* May 1, 1921, p. 50; Daniel Kevles, *The Physicists: The History of a Scientific Community in Modern America* (Cambridge, MA: Harvard University Press, 1987), p. 212; Des Jardins, *Madame Curie Complex,* pp. 26–27.

14. "News Notes of the Fortnight," *Woman's Journal,* May 21, 1921, p. 1234; Des Jardins, *Madame Curie Complex,* p. 37; Robert Reid, *Madame Curie* (London:

Collins, 1974), p. 256; Colbey Emmerson Reid, "Glamour and the 'Fashionable Mind,'" *Soundings: An Interdisciplinary Journal,* vol. 89, no. 3/4 (Fall/Winter 2006), pp. 303, 315n7.

15. "The Greatest Woman in the World," cover, "That Millions Shall Not Die!" p. 1, William Mayo, "Do You Fear Cancer?" p. 35, all in *The Delineator,* April 1921; Waldemar Kaempffert, "How Radium Is Extracted," *The Delineator,* May 1921, p. 7. See also, Mayo, "If This Malady Is Attacked Early," p. 29, and "A $100,000 Thimbleful," p. 1, both in *The Delineator,* June 1921.

16. Charlotte Kellogg to Mrs. C. N. Chipman, April 4, 1921, box 2, MCC.

17. MMM, "The $100,000 Thimbleful" (draft), MMM manuscripts; notes on MMM's publicity course for the Carroll Club, March 23, 1925, MMM manuscripts; "Hardings Help Curie Fund," *New York Times,* April 20, 1921, p. 2; A. Brisbane to MMM, March 14, 1921, box 1, MCC.

18. Notes on MMM's publicity course, MMM manuscripts.

19. Franklin K. Lane to MMM, Los Angeles, n.d.; Franklin K. Lane to Col. William Brown Meloney, January 31, 1921. Accounts differ about the amount of money left over from the radium campaign from which Missy started the fund. She claimed that $84,000 remained, but according to the "Declaration of Trust by the Equitable Trust Company of New York," signed May 31, 1921, the fund was created with $56,413.54. See box 4, MCC.

20. For an account of MMM's planning and Curie's hesitation, see Des Jardins, *Madame Curie Complex,* pp. 39–43.

21. MMM to Charles Eliot, December 11, 1920, box 2, MCC.

22. Marie Curie to MMM, January 31, 1921, March 4, 1921, box 1, MCC; March 5, 1921, March 19, 1921; Dr. Roche to MMM, January 28, 1921, box 2, MCC. The honorary degrees were from Smith College, the Women's Medical College, the University of Pennsylvania, the University of Pittsburgh, Columbia University, the University of Chicago, Northwestern University, Wellesley College, and Yale University. Curie was made a fellow of the Mineralogical Society of New York, the Museum of Natural History, the Radiological Society of the American Medical Association of Boston, and the Academy of Science in Buffalo, New York; and she was awarded the Naples Table Award, the Gold Medal of the National Institute of Social Sciences, the Gold Medal of the American Philosophical Society, and the Willard Gibbs Scientific Medal.

23. Charles Eliot to MMM, December 18, 1920, box 2, MCC; MMM to Eliot, December 24, 1920, box 2, MCC.

24. Des Jardins, *Madame Curie Complex,* p. 36; Koestler-Grack, *Marie Curie,* pp. 117–118; Diana Preston, *Before the Fallout: From Marie Curie to Hiroshima* (New York: Walker and Company, 2005), pp. 57–58.

25. "Olympic to Sail Crowded," *New York Times,* April 19, 1921, p. 16; "Notables on the Olympic," New York *Evening World,* Wall Street Edition, April 20, 1921,

p. 12; Preston, *Before the Fallout,* pp. 57–58; Mrs. Robert G. Mead to Dr. H. Mac-Cracken, May 4, 1921; Quinn, *Marie Curie,* p. 391.

26. "Mme. Curie Here Today," *New York Times,* May 11, 1921, p. 8; "Mme. Curie Lands, Cheered by Crowd," *New York Times,* May 12, 1921, p. 1; Wishart, *One in Three,* pp. 54–55.

27. Tom Miller, "The 1895 Ardea Apartments," June 7, 2012, Daytonian in Man-hattan, http://daytoninmanhattan.blogspot.com/2012/06/1895-ardea-apartments-nos-31-33-west.html; Dr. Harlow Brooks to MMM, n.d.; John J. Moorhead, *Harlow Brooks: Man and Doctor* (New York: Harper and Brothers, 1937), pp. 6–7; Bernays, *Biography of an Idea*; 1920 US Federal Census, Manhattan Assembly District 10, Roll: T625-1202, Page: 11B.

28. White Star Line to Elsie Mead, June 30, 1921, MMM correspondence; receipt from Tiffany and Company to Marie Curie Fund Committee for items, May 1921, box 4, MCC; invoice for velvet gown and Oxford cap, c/o Dr. Mary Carey Thomas, Bryn Mawr College, n.d., MMM correspondence; MMM to Mrs. C. N. Chipman, May 22, 1921, box 2, MCC.

29. Marie Curie, "Impressions of America," typed draft, n.d., p. 3, box 3, MCC.

30. Wellesley College Bulletin, *Annual Reports, President and Treasurer, 1919–1921,* series 10, no. 11 (Wellesley, MA: December 1921), p. 18; Ellen Pendleton to Marie Curie, May 13, 1921, MMM correspondence; Ellen Pendleton to MMM, June 1, 1921; William Allen Neilson to MMM, May 9, 1921; H. N. MacCracken to Mrs. R. G. Mead, February 24, 1921, May 8, 1921, MMM correspondence; MMM to Dr. MacCracken, March 3, 1921; "Memo to Madame Curie for the Press," n.d., box 3, MCC; Curie, "Impressions of America."

31. "Welcome to Madame Curie from the American Association of University Women," announcement of ceremony, April 1921, program of meeting, May 18, 1921, box 3, MCC; "Says Women Can and Must Stop War," *New York Times,* May 19, 1921, p. 11; "College Women Hail Mme. Curie as Their Own," *New York Tri-bune,* May 19, 1921, p. 13; Des Jardins, *Madame Curie Complex,* p. 40.

32. Marie Curie, "The Discovery of Radium," address at Vassar College, May 14, 1921, boxes 3, 5, MCC. The myths MMM created around Curie are also dis-cussed by Susan Quinn in *Marie Curie,* pp. 386–388.

33. Des Jardins, *Madame Curie Complex,* pp. 39–40.

34. "Science Medal Bestowed upon Madame Curie," *New York Tribune,* May 20, 1921, p. 6; memorandum (on White House ceremony), May 20, 1921, box 4, MCC.

35. "Remarks of the President in Presenting to Madame Curie a Gift of Radium from the American People," May 20, 1921, box 5, MCC.

36. Invitation to the dinner honoring Curie by Ambassador and Madame Jus-serand for May 21, 1921, box 4, MCC; Elise Jusserand to MMM, May 14, 1921; Prince Casimir Lubomirski to MMM, May 26, 1921; "Dinner for Madame Curie,"

New York *Herald,* May 22, 1921, p. 14; "Dinners and Luncheons for District's Society," Washington *Evening Star,* May 22, 1921, p. 5.

37. Invitation of M. Carey Thomas and the Philadelphia Marie Curie Radium Fund Committee for garden party, May 24, 1921, box 4, MCC; "Madame Curie Receives Gram of Radium and Many Honors," *Journal of Industrial and Engineering Chemistry,* June 1921, p. 573; program of University of Pittsburgh Convocation, May 26, 1921; "Mme. Curie Must Begin Rest at Once," New York *Herald,* May 29, 1921, p. 9; "Mme. Curie's Blood Is Under Analysis," New York *Evening World,* May 30, 1921, p. 5.

38. Edith H. Quimby, "The Marie Curie Correspondence with Marie Mattingly Meloney," *Columbia Library Columns,* vol. XI, no. 2 (February 1962), p. 18.

39. Stéphane Lauzanne to MMM, May 24, 1921; "Mme. Curie's Brain Fagged by 'Small Talk' of Americans," *New York Times,* May 28, 1921, p. 1; "Memorial Hospital Greets Mme. Curie," *New York Times,* May 29, 1921, p. 16; Des Jardins, *Madame Curie Complex,* p. 42.

40. "Trip Benefits Mme. Curie," *New York Tribune,* June 24, 1921, p. 3; Wishart, *One in Three,* pp. 56–57.

41. MMM to Prince Lubomirski, June 9, 1921; Irène Curie to MMM, Friday, n.d. [June 1921], box 2, MCC.

42. Reid, *Madame Curie,* pp. 262, 266; Des Jardins, *Madame Curie Complex,* p. 42; Asst. to Passenger Traffic Managers, International Mercantile Marine Co. to Elsie Mead, June 8, 1921, box 4, MCC; Rolling Burdick Hunter Co., Marine Department, Insurance, June 21, 1921, MMM correspondence; Harland Miner, Chief Chemist, Welsbach Company, to MMM, June 8, 1921, June 29, 1921; "Madame Curie Sails for Home Bearing Gifts," *New York Tribune,* June 26, 1921.

43. "10,000 Sail in Day on Seven Big Liners," New York *Herald,* June 26, 1921, p. 7. See also draft of Curie's "Impressions of America."

44. Jean Jules Jusserand to MMM, June 10, 1921; "Plan Life Income Now for Mme. Curie," *New York Times,* July 30, 1921, p. 7.

45. Charlotte Kellogg to MMM, [June] 1921, July 30, 1921.

46. MMM to Stéphane Lauzanne, March 11, 1922; Lauzanne to MMM, May 19, 1922, July 22, 1922.

47. Marie Curie to MMM, July 1, 1921, box 1, MCC.

48. Jean Jusserand to MMM, December 6, 1921; Marie Curie to MMM, April 14, 1922, August 8, 1921, box 7, MCC.

CHAPTER 7: HATCHING IDEAS FOR WOMEN READERS, WORKERS, AND VOTERS, 1922–1926

1. MMM to Philip M. Hayden, Asst. Secretary, Columbia University, September 16, 1929, Nicholas Butler file, MMM misc. material; John Erskine to MMM,

September 27, 1929; MMM to J. Ramsay MacDonald, May 14, 1931, MacDonald file, MMM misc. material; MMM to Lord Tweedsmuir, November 15, 1939, November 24, 1939.

2. MMM to Eleanor Roosevelt, July 28, 1938.

3. MMM, preface to *The Log Cabin Lady* (UK: Dormouse Press, 2011 [1922]), pp. 1–4.

4. Preface to *Log Cabin Lady*.

5. Alfred McIntyre to MMM, January 7, 1922; James Calvert, "Worldly Bardstonian Had a Way with Words," *Kentucky Standard*, September 24, 2011; Marie Curie to MMM, April 8, 19[30], October 10, 1933, box 7, MCC.

6. William A. Neilson to MMM, March 16, 1922, April 14, 1922; MMM to Neilson, March 21, 1922; "Occupations of the Class of 1919, 1920," Ada Comstock folder, MMM misc. material; MMM to Marion LeRoy Burton, October 30, 1923, MMM manuscripts.

7. "For the Children" and "Child Labor," in From the Editor's Point of View, *The Delineator*, April 1923, p. 1; "The Hope of the World," and "For the Children of To-morrow," in From the Editor's Point of View, *The Delineator*, June 1922, p. 1; "The Happy Child," in From the Editor's Point of View, *The Delineator*, August 1922, p. 1; Steven L. Schlossman, "Philanthropy and the Gospel of Child Development," *History of Education Quarterly*, vol. 21, no. 3 (Autumn 1981), p. 292; Molly Ladd-Taylor, "Hull House Goes to Washington: Women and the Children's Bureau," in *Gender, Class, Race and Reform in the Progressive Era*, eds. Noralee Frankel and Nancy S. Dye (Lexington: University Press of Kentucky, 1991), pp. 110, 122.

8. MMM, "The Last Magic."

9. "Detroit Health Conference," *Lansing State Journal*, July 26, 1923, p. 7; *Detroit Free Press*, October 17, 1923, p. 10; MMM, "Broadcasting the News of Child Health," in *Public Health, Michigan Health Almanac*, vol. 11 (Lansing, MI: Department of Health, 1923), p. 402; MMM, "Child Health," in From the Editor's Point of View, *The Delineator*, May 1923, p. 1.

10. Draft on Child Welfare Movement, n.d., MMM manuscripts; "Child Health," in From the Editor's Point of View, *The Delineator*, May 1923, p. 1; "Neither Too Fat Nor Too Thin, Doctors Warn 20,000 Women After Adult Weight Conference," Longmont, Colorado, *Daily Times*, March 20, 1926, p. 2; "'Boyish Figure' Aim Brings Health Test," *New York Times*, February 22, 1926, p. 3; "World News About Women," *Woman's Journal*, June 1926, p. 34.

11. Martha Van Rensselaer to MMM, October 22, 1920; MMM to R. M. Adams, October 23, 1920; Mary Ellen Zuckerman, "Martha Van Rensselaer and the *Delineator's* Homemaking Department," *Journal of Historical Research in Marketing*, vol. 5, no. 3 (2013), pp. 373–374, 377; A. P. Young to MMM, April 27, 1923, April 21, 1924, April 15, 1925; MMM to Young, May 6, 1924, March 25, 1925; typed

draft of Butterick Cookbook, n.d., MMM manuscripts; Henry A. Wallace, Dept. of Agriculture, to MMM, February 21, 1922; MMM to Channing Pollock, n.d., Pollock file, MMM misc. material. For the rise of home institutes, see Goldstein, *Creating Consumers,* pp. 200–207.

12. Draft on Better Homes Campaign, August 7, 1922, MMM manuscripts; Kendrick Clements, *The Life of Herbert Hoover: Imperfect Visionary, 1918–1928* (New York: Palgrave Macmillan, 2010), pp. 222–224; Regina Lee Blaszczyk, "No Place Like Home: Herbert Hoover and the American Standard of Living," in *Uncommon Americans: The Lives and Legacies of Herbert and Lou Henry Hoover,* ed. Timothy Walch (Westport, CT: Praeger, 2003), pp. 113, 119; Jeffrey Hornstein, *A Nation of Realtors®: A Cultural History of the Twentieth-Century American Middle Class* (Durham, NC: Duke University Press, 2005), p. 128; Janet Hutchinson, "The Cure for Domestic Neglect: Better Homes in America, 1922–1935," *Perspectives in Vernacular Architecture,* vol. 2 (1986), p. 168.

13. MMM quoted in Mary Drake McFeely, *Can She Bake a Cherry Pie? American Women and the Kitchen in the Twentieth Century* (Amherst: University of Massachusetts Press, 2001), p. 43; Janet Hutchinson, "Shaping Housing and Enhancing Consumption: Hoover's Interwar Housing Policy," in *From Tenements to the Taylor Homes: In Search of an Urban Housing Policy in Twentieth-Century America,* eds. John F. Bauman, Roger Biles, and Kristin Szylvian (University Park, PA: Penn State Press, 2000), p. 88; talk by MMM to *The Delineator* staff [1925].

14. Bland, "Shaping the Life of the New Woman," p. 182; Theodore Roosevelt Jr. to MMM, July 7, 1922, August 21, 1922; talk by MMM to *The Delineator* staff [1925]; MMM to Charlotte Kellogg, June 1, 1922, Kellogg file, MMM misc. material; Hornstein, *A Nation of Realtors®,* p. 128; Clements, *Life of Herbert Hoover,* pp. 222–224.

15. Draft on Better Homes Campaign; Will Hays to MMM, July 19, 1922, MMM, "Better Homes in America Plan Book for Demonstration Week, October 9 to 14, 1922," e-book #7992, Project Gutenberg, 2012, http://www.gutenberg .org/cache/epub/7992/pg7992-images.html; "Better Homes for America," and "National and State Officials Who Are Supporting *The Delineator's* Better Homes for America Campaign," in From the Editor's Point of View, *The Delineator,* September 1922, p. 1; Blaszczyk, "No Place Like Home," pp. 128–129; talk by MMM to *The Delineator* staff [1925].

16. MMM, "Better Homes in America Plan Book for Demonstration Week, October 9 to 14, 1922."

17. "World News About Women," *Woman's Journal,* September 23, 1922, pp. 22–23; Clements, *Life of Herbert Hoover,* p. 224; talk by MMM to *The Delineator* staff [1925].

18. "Better Homes Week in City Oct. 9–14," *New York Times,* October 1, 1922, p. 143; "Small House Plans Receive Awards," *New York Times,* October 5, 1930,

p. RE14; "Broad Campaign for Better Homes: Demonstration Houses Will Open Today in More Than 1,000 American Cities," *New York Times,* June 4, 1923, p. 14; memorandum of MMM to Colonel Woods, n.d., Colonel Woods file, MMM misc. material; MMM to Gutzon Borglum, October 3, 1930, November 3, 1930; "Tribune's Ideal House Is Ready for Inspection," *New York Tribune,* October 8, 1922, p. 5; "Better Homes," *New York Tribune,* October 9, 1922, p. 8.

19. Hornstein, *Nation of Realtors®,* 128; Ellis W. Hawley, "Herbert Hoover, the Commerce Secretariat, and the Vision of an 'Associative State,' 1921–1928," *Journal of American History,* vol. 61, no. 1 (June 1974), p. 134; Blaszczyk, "No Place Like Home," p. 130; Hutchinson, "Shaping Housing and Enhancing Consumption," p. 89; MMM to Charles Eliot, January 22, 1924; Clements, *Life of Herbert Hoover,* p. 256; ad in *New York Times* announcing incorporation of Better Homes, "Better Homes in America," February 16, 1924, p. 28.

20. There are differing claims about the number of local BHA committees formed by 1930, though there is agreement that the BHA's reach was widespread. Barbara Burlison Mooney claims 5,960 committees, and Janet Hutchinson notes that the BHA administration claimed 7,279 committees. See Barbara Burlison Mooney, "The Comfortable Tasty Framed Cottage: An African American Architectural Iconography," *Journal of the Society of Architectural Historians,* vol. 61, no. 1 (March 2002), p. 61; Hutchinson, "The Cure for Domestic Neglect," p. 173; Janet Hutchinson, "Better Homes and Gullah," *Agricultural History,* vol. 67, no. 2, *American Rural and Farm Women in Historical Perspective* (Spring 1993), p. 103; Hutchinson, "Shaping Housing and Enhancing Consumption," p. 89; MMM to Channing Pollock, n.d., Pollock file, MMM misc. material; talk by MMM to *The Delineator* staff [1925].

21. Fred Bjornstad, "Herbert Hoover, Housing, and Socioeconomic Planning in the 1920s," in *Uncommon Americans,* Walch, ed., p. 109; US Treasury Department's Internal Revenue Service, *Statistics of Income from Returns of Net Income for 1922* (Washington, DC: Government Printing Office, 1925); Department of Commerce, Bureau of the Census, *Mortgages on Homes in the United States* (Washington, DC: Government Printing Office, 1923), p. 172; "Better Homes Week in City"; McFeely, *Can She Bake a Cherry Pie?,* pp. 43–44; Martha Swain, *Ellen S. Woodward: New Deal Advocate for Women* (Jackson: University of Mississippi Press, 1995), p. 22; notes on MMM's publicity course, MMM manuscripts.

22. "How I Worked My Way Through College," *The Delineator,* September 1922, p. 15.

23. From the Editor's Point of View, *The Delineator,* November 1922, p. 1.

24. Draft of recollection of conversation with Warren G. Harding, n.d., MMM manuscripts.

25. Leonebel Jacobs, "Seeing Things with a Pencil," *The Delineator,* June 1922, pp. 16–17; Lucia Moore, Nina McCornack, and Gladys McCready, *The Story of Eugene* (Eugene, OR: Lane County Historical Society, 1995), p. 204.

26. In-house memorandum on the White House, January 10, 1924, MMM misc. material.

27. Draft on Mrs. Coolidge at the White House, June 12, 1924, pp. 1, 4, 8–9, MMM manuscripts.

28. "The President's Wife," in From the Editor's Point of View, *The Delineator*, March 1923, p. 1; draft on Mrs. Coolidge at the White House, pp. 2, 5–6, 7, 10, MMM manuscripts.

29. "Parking the Baby: Hints for Busy Mothers and Business Mothers," *The Delineator*, February 1921, p. 2. See W. L. George's "Can We Be Comrades," p. 2, Genevieve Parkhurst, "Does This Mean 'Sex-War'?" pp. 7, 62–64, and "Where Bad Citizens Are Made," pp. 8–9, 54, all in March 1921 edition of *The Delineator*; Zuckerman, "Martha Van Rensselaer," p. 372; Bland, "Shaping the Life of the New Woman," p. 165.

CHAPTER 8: A WIDOW'S TOUCH AT THE *NEW YORK HERALD TRIBUNE*, 1926–1927

1. MMM to Charlotte Kellogg, July 29, 1924; MMM's secretary to Charlotte Kellogg, June 17, 1925; Charles Hanson Towne to MMM, May 12, 1925; "William B. Meloney Critically Ill," *New York Times*, December 5, 1925, p. 3.

2. MMM to Elsie Barber, August 19, 1925; MMM to Charlotte Kellogg, August 12, 1925; Kathleen Norris to MMM, September 14, 1925; MMM to Marie Curie, July 27, 1925, box 2, MCC; Arthur Woods to MMM, October 2, 1925; MMM's secretary to Marie Curie, September 23, 1925, box 2, MCC; Charlotte Kellogg to MMM, November 10, 1925, November 12, 1925.

3. Harlow Brooks to MMM, July 23, 1925, box 7, MCC, November 17, 1925; Charles Mayo to MMM, December 2, 1925; Baron de Cartier to MMM, November 26, 1925, December 5, 1925.

4. MMM to Major H. L. Reese, April 28, 1937; "Major W. B. Meloney Dies, Victim of War," Obituary for Lieutenant Colonel William B. Meloney, *New York Times*, December 9, 1925.

5. "At Midday," n.d., MMM manuscripts.

6. Marie Curie to MMM, December 28, 1925; MMM to E. L. Bailey, Director of Dependents Claims Service, February 2, 1935; Bailey to MMM, February 6, 1940; R. J. Hinton to MMM, August 1, 1942, MMM manuscripts; MMM to Ceegee Norris, January 20, 1926.

7. Channing Pollock, "Missy," n.d. (and included drafts), Pollock file, MMM misc. material; Harlow Brooks to MMM, March 24, 1926; Kathleen Norris to MMM, n.d.; MMM to Charlotte Kellogg, March 11, 1926.

8. Izola Page to MMM, March 9, 1933; MMM to John Erskine, August 21, 1926.

9. MMM to John Erskine, August 21, 1926.

10. The claim of $1,000,000 in savings was MMM's and has not been substantiated elsewhere. MMM to John Erskine, July 21, 1926; Zuckerman, "Martha Van

Rensselaer," pp. 381–382; MMM to Channing Pollock, n.d., Pollock file, MMM misc. material.

11. "Mrs. Ogden Reid Dies Here at 87," Special to the *New York Times*, July 28, 1970.

12. Richard Kluger, *The Paper: The Life and Death of the New York* Herald Tribune (New York: Vintage, 1986), pp. 171–177, 180–181, 285; Marzolf, *Up from the Footnote*, pp. 63–64; "Mrs. Ogden Reid Dies Here at 87"; Bradley, *Women and the Press*, pp. 216–217; Ross, *Ladies of the Press*, pp. 135–140.

13. Bradley, *Women and the Press*, p. 217; Ross, *Ladies of the Press*, pp. 135–137; Kluger, *The Paper*, pp. 182, 201–204.

14. Kluger, *The Paper*, pp. 212–214; Ross, *Ladies of the Press*, p. 137.

15. Marzolf, *Up from the Footnote*, p. 64; talk by MMM to *The Delineator* staff [1925]; Ross, *Ladies of the Press*, p. 138.

16. Pollock, "Missy"; MMM to Pollock, n.d., Pollock folder, MMM misc. material.

17. MMM to Channing Pollock, February 6, 1941; Mark L. Goodwin to MMM, July 24, 1926; MMM to Charles Norris, July 20, 1926, CG and Kathleen Norris file, MMM misc. material.

18. MMM to Marie Curie, July 23, 1926, box 2, MCC; MMM to John Erskine, July 21, 1926.

19. Royal Cortissoz to MMM, January 27, 1928, March 2, 1928, August 2, 1928; Ronald Steel, *Walter Lippmann and the American Century* (Boston: Little, Brown and Company, 1980), pp. 274–279; Stanley Walker, *City Editor* (Baltimore, MD: Johns Hopkins University Press, 1999 [1934]), pp. 248–249.

20. "Herald Tribune's Lady," *Time*, October 8, 1934, p. 67; Kluger, *The Paper*, pp. 263–267.

21. With the doubling of women in the newsroom in this decade, they numbered nearly twelve thousand, about a quarter of the total nationally. See Cairns, *Front-Page Women Journalists*, p. 20; Ross, *Ladies of the Press*, pp. 138–139; 403–404, 412–413, 469; Walker, *City Editor*, pp. 260–261; Kluger, *The Paper*, pp. 286–288; Kelly Alexander and Cynthia Harris, *Hometown Appetites: The Story of Clementine Paddleford, the Forgotten Food Writer Who Chronicled How America Ate* (New York: Gotham Books, 2008); Bradley, *Women and the Press*, pp. 216–217; "Herald Tribune's Lady."

22. "Reminiscences of Emma Bugbee, 1974," Women Journalists Project, Oral History Research Office, Columbia University Rare Book and Manuscript Library, New York, New York; Catherine Gourley, *War, Women, and the News: How Female Journalists Won the Battle to Cover World War II* (New York: Atheneum, 2007), pp. 25–26, 29; Marzolf, *Up from the Footnote*, pp. 39, 44–45; Ross, *Ladies of the Press*, pp. 12–13, 122–123, 126, 141; Stanley Walker, "Foreword," in Ross, *Ladies of the Press*, pp. xi–xii; Walker, *City Editor*, pp. 260–261, 288; Kluger, *The Paper*, p. 221.

23. MMM to Gina Lombroso Ferrero, July 16, 1928, September 24, 1928, Lombroso file, MMM misc. material; Marie Adelaide Lowndes to MMM, February 7,

1933; Julia Peterkin to MMM, March 24, 1931; Dorothy Canfield Fisher to MMM, February 18, 1933; Katherine Mayo to MMM, n.d., September 30, 1927; Mabel Walker Willebrandt to MMM, March 26, 1927, April 29, 1928, April 8, 1929, September 4, 1929, November 29, 1929.

24. MMM to E. V. Lucas, August 12, 1926; Oliver Wendell Holmes to MMM, November 18, 1927; MMM to Andrew Mellon, November 30, 1928; Ogden L. Mills to MMM, September 6, 1928; Hubert Work, Secretary of the Interior, to MMM, August 6, 1926, September 8, 1927; MMM to Orville Wright, October 27, 1928; Vilhjalmur Stefansson to MMM, June 18, 1928, July 10, 1928, July 15, 1928; MMM to Upton Close, February 28, 1933.

25. Carlo Sforza to MMM, April 14, 1930; Theodore Roosevelt Jr. to MMM, September 2, 1930, March 8, 1932; MMM to George Russell, December 19, 1927, Russell file, MMM misc. material; MMM to J. J. Jusserand, July 22, 1927; S. Bernard Thomas, *Season of High Adventure: Edgar Snow in China* (Berkeley: University of California Press, 1996), pp. 31–32; Robert M. Farnsworth, *From Vagabond to Journalist: Edgar Snow in Asia, 1928–1941* (Columbia: University of Missouri Press, 1996), p. 158; MMM to His Imperial Majesty, Kaiser Wilhelm, The Second, September 11, 1928; Wilhelm II, Emperor of Germany (signed by Count Schmettow) to MMM, October 1, 1928.

26. Fielding Yost to MMM, September 8, 1928; Karl Menninger, "Reading as Therapy," *ALA Bulletin*, vol. 55, no. 4 (April 1961), p. 317; MMM to Wilbur Cross, November 22, 1932; MMM to Dwight Morrow, August 31, 1927; MMM to Fannie Hurst, April 22, 1927; Brooke Kroeger, *Fannie: The Talent for Success of Writer Fannie Hurst* (New York: Times Books, 1999), pp. 128–129; Will Rogers to MMM, October 3, 1927.

27. Michael Pupin to MMM, June 25, 1928; Irwin Edman to MMM, October 20, 1932.

28. Typed notes on Mississippi flood, May 20, 1942, MMM manuscripts.

29. Kruger, *The Paper*, p. 232; MMM to Dr. Edna N. White, April 11, 1930, box 64, folder 8; February 1, 1928, box 1, folder 62, Merrill-Palmer Institute: Edna Noble White Records, Walter P. Reuther Library, Wayne State University, Detroit, Michigan.

30. "Butterick Magazines to Merge," *New York Times*, June 17, 1926, p. 12; Bland, "Shaping the Life of the New Woman," p. 183; Kosut, *Encyclopedia of Gender in Media*, p. 437.

31. MMM to John Erskine, July 21, 1926, August 21, 1926; MMM to Vernon Kellogg, May 18, 1926; W. B. Maxwell to MMM, June 17, 1926; Henry Stacpoole to MMM, September 28, 1926; MMM to Charlotte Kellogg, June 9, 1927, June 15, 1927; Frank Swinnerton to MMM, May 12, 1926; "Meloney-Symons," *New York Times*, March 6, 1927, p. E8; "18,000 Guests to See Graduation of 5007," *New York Times*, June 1, 1927, p. 20.

32. Draft of MMM's account of her time with Bill and Elizabeth in Paris, [1927], MMM manuscripts, pp. 2–3.

33. Draft of MMM's account of her time with Bill and Elizabeth in Paris, p. 1.

34. "A Few Memories of January 1928, also Christmas 1927," MMM manuscripts.

35. MMM, "Madame Curie," January 22, 1928, typed draft, MMM manuscripts, pp. 1–2.

36. Marie Curie to MMM, December 15, 1921; March 17, 1922, box 1, MCC; April 14, 1922, box 1, MCC; May 20, 1922, box 1, MCC; March 31, 1922, October 6, 1922, box 2, MCC; Elsie Jusserand to MMM, November 5, 1922; Jean Jules Jusserand to MMM, January 16, 1923, May 15, 1922, June 5, 1922, box 2, MCC; MMM, "Madame Curie," p. 4.

37. Marie Curie to MMM, December 10, 1921, box 1, MCC; Ève Curie to MMM, November 21, 192[2], January 8, 1923, November 18, 1927.

38. H. E. Hawkes to MMM, December 2, 1924; Irène Curie to MMM, May 8, 1925, box 2, MCC; Marie Curie to MMM, March 21, 1925, April 21, 1925, April 30, 1926, May 10, 1926, May 29, 1926, June 23, 1926, July 23, 1926, box 7, MCC; Preston, *Before the Fallout*, pp. 57–58; Koestler-Grack, *Marie Curie*, pp. 117–118.

39. Marclene F. Rayner-Canham, *Women in Chemistry: Their Changing Roles from Alchemical Times to the Mid-Twentieth Century* (Philadelphia: Chemical Heritage Foundation, 2005), p. 105.

40. MMM, "Madame Curie," pp. 4–5.

41. MMM, "Madame Curie," p. 7.

42. A. N. Arcibol to MMM, July 5, 1929; Henry Breckinridge to MMM, December 3, 1928; Harlow Brooks to MMM, July 30, 1927.

43. Harlow Brooks to MMM, August 9, 1927.

44. Chase, *My Friends Look Good to Me*, pp. 82–83; John Galsworthy to MMM, January 10, 1928; MMM to Galsworthy, February 10, 1928; MMM to St. John Ervine, February 2, 1928; Harlow Brooks to MMM, August 27, 1928; MMM to Sir James M. Barrie, May 4, 1928, J. A. Barrie folder, MMM misc. material.

45. MMM to Norman Hapgood, August 6, 1928.

CHAPTER 9: THE WORK OF WEAVING WEBS, 1928–1929

1. MMM to Gutzon Borglum, August 24, 1922, November 5, 1925, June 8, 1926; Borglum to MMM, August 23, 1922, October 12, 1927, in Gutzon Borglum folder, MMM misc. material; Robert Casey and Mary Borglum, *Give the Man Room* (Indianapolis: Bobbs-Merrill Company, 1952), pp. 19–20, 107, 137.

2. MMM to Gutzon Borglum, March 28, 1928, August 25, 1930, September 29, 1930; Borglum to MMM, July 27, 1923; Casey and Borglum, *Give the Man Room*, pp. 206–220; John Taliaferro, *Great White Fathers: The Story of the Obsessive Quest to Create Mt. Rushmore* (New York: Public Affairs, 2002), pp. 74, 98.

3. Casey and Borglum, *Give the Man Room,* pp. 16–17, 288; telegram, MMM to Gutzon Borglum, n.d., in Gutzon Borglum folder, MMM misc. material; MMM to Borglum, August 2, 1923, November 5, 1925, June 16, 1928, June 19, 1928; Borglum to MMM, July 27, 1923, October 12, 1927, February 29, 1928; Howard Shaff and Audrey Karl Shaff, *Six Wars at a Time: The Life and Times of Gutzon Borglum, Sculptor of Mount Rushmore* (Sioux Falls, SD: Center for Western Studies, 1985), pp. 255–256.

4. "How It's Done," *Time,* November 24, 1930, p. 17; Elisabeth Israels Perry, *Belle Moskowitz: Feminine Politics and the Exercise of Power in the Age of Alfred E. Smith* (Boston: Northeastern University Press, 1992).

5. Walch, ed., *Uncommon Americans,* pp. 1–17; Dumenil, *Modern Temper,* pp. 7–8; Nancy Beck Young, "Searching for Lou Henry Hoover," in *Uncommon Americans,* Walch, ed., pp. 21–23.

6. Will Irwin to MMM, July 6, 1928; Jo Freeman, "Gender Gaps in Presidential Elections," letter to the editor, *P.S.: Political Science and Politics,* vol. 32, no. 2 (June 1999), pp. 191–192; Upton quoted in Melanie S. Gustafson, *Women and the Republican Party, 1854–1924* (Urbana: University of Illinois Press, 2001), pp. 3–4; MMM, "Hoover in Victory," *New York Herald Tribune Sunday Magazine,* June 24, 1928, pp. 1–3. For a discussion of Republican women's indirect strategies to have influence on the Republican Party leadership in the 1920s, see Catherine E. Rymph's *Republican Women: Feminism and Conservatism from Suffrage Through the Rise of the New Right* (Chapel Hill: University of North Carolina Press, 2006), pp. 2–5, chapters 1 and 2.

7. Advertisement for Herbert Hoover, *Woman's Journal,* September 1928, p. 51.

8. MMM to Gutzon Borglum, February 11, 1928, June 27, 1928, September 27, 1928, telegram n.d.; Borglum to MMM, October 1, 1928, November 2, 1928; Shaff and Shaff, *Six Wars at a Time,* pp. 255–256.

9. Borglum to MMM, May 5, 1928.

10. Anthony Cave Brown, *The Last Hero: Wild Bill Donovan* (New York: Times Books, 1982), pp. 73, 79, 87, 89, 103–104.

11. Freeman, "Gender Gaps in Presidential Elections"; Franklin W. Fort to MMM, November 4, 1928; MMM to Colonel William Donovan, November 13, 1928.

12. Polish embassy dinner notes, March 28, 1931, in 1931 file, MMM misc. material; Mildred Hall to MMM, n.d., April 8, 1929; MMM to Mary Day, October 17, 1930, MMM manuscripts.

13. Polish embassy dinner notes, March 28, 1931.

14. Gutzon Borglum to MMM, February 26, 1929, March 11, 1929, March 16, 1929, March 27, 1929, telegram from San Antonio, Texas, n.d.

15. MMM to Gutzon Borglum, March 27, 1929, January 27, 1930; Borglum to Herbert Hoover, December 2, 1929, January 24, 1930, MMM correspondence.

16. Borglum to MMM, August 20, 1929.

17. MMM to Ted Roosevelt Jr., August 5, 1938; Des Jardins, *Madame Curie Complex,* pp. 44–45.

18. "Dawes Plan Works, Young Declares," *New York Times,* November 21, 1924, p. 3; Josephine Young Case and Everett Needham Case, *Owen D. Young and American Enterprise: A Biography* (Boston: David Godine, 1982), pp. 389–390; MMM to Owen D. Young, July 17, 1925, December 6, 1924.

19. Owen D. Young to MMM, January 30, 1925; Marie Curie to MMM, December 3, 1924, March 21, 1925, April 21, 1925, December 28, 1925, October 4, 1927, November 9, 1927, July 27, 1928, box 7, MCC.

20. Marie Curie to MMM, July 28, 1929, August 19, 1929, August 30, 1929, box 1, MCC; Owen D. Young to Madame Curie, June 23, 1926; MMM to Vernon Kellogg, October 3, 1929.

21. Marie Curie to MMM, July 27, 1928, August 19, 1929, September 16, 1929, box 7, MCC; Marie Curie to Mrs. Robert G. Mead, August 30, 1929, September 16, 1929, MMM correspondence; MMM to Curie, October 12, 1921, September 25, 1929, box 2, MCC; "Mme. Curie Arrives 'Happy to Be Back,'" *New York Times,* October 16, 1929, p. 30; "Mme. Curie Is Guest of Friends in Country," *New York Times,* October 17, 1929, p. 9; "Mme. Curie Plants Tree," *New York Times,* October 19, 1929, p. 19.

22. Edward Bernays, *Biography of an Idea;* "Mme. Curie Has a Cold," *New York Times,* October 28, 1929, p. 22; "Mme. Curie's Aversion to Giving Autograph Extends to Endorsing Charity Checks," *New York Times,* February 15, 1931, p. 54.

23. "Mme. Curie Examines Schenectady Plant," *New York Times,* October 24, 1929, p. 3; Program, "Madame Curie at St. Lawrence University," October 25–26, 1929, box 5, MCC; "Mme. Curie Serenaded," *New York Times,* October 26, 1929, p. 21; "Mme. Curie Speaks at St. Lawrence," *New York Times,* October 27, 1929, p. 24.

24. Case and Case, *Owen D. Young,* pp. 390–391, 468–469; program, "Madame Curie at St. Lawrence University."

25. "Mme. Curie Has a Cold"; "Mme. Curie at White House," Special to *New York Times,* October 30, 1929, p. 21; Ruth Fesler to MMM, October 21, 1929; "Remarks of the President on the Occasion of the Presentation to Madame Curie of a Gram of Radium in the Building of the National Academy of Sciences and National Research Council," October 30, 1929, box 4, MCC; "Mme. Curie Receives $50,000 Radium Gift; Hoover Presents It," *New York Times,* October 31, 1929, p. 1.

26. "Mme. Curie Observes 62d Birthday Today," *New York Times,* November 7, 1929, p. 15; "The Microphone Will Present," *New York Times,* October 27, 1929, p. 20; "Hail Mme. Curie at 62," *New York Times,* November 8, 1929, p. 25; "Mme. Curie to Be Guest at Dinner," *New York Times,* September 23, 1929, p. 35; "Mme. Curie to Get Medal," *New York Times,* October 21, 1929, p. 16; "Clubwomen Give

Mme. Curie a Medal," *New York Times,* November 6, 1929, p. 27; Marie Curie to MMM, December 14, 1929; "Mme. Curie to Sail on Île de France," *New York Times,* November 8, 1929, p. 25; "Mme. Curie Sails Thanking America," *New York Times,* November 9, 1929, p. 9.

27. Des Jardins, *Madame Curie Complex,* 46.

28. Owen Young to Nelson Dean Jay, Morgan Company, September 20, 1933, MMM correspondence; Louise W. Carnegie to MMM, January 23, 1930, February 6, 1930, box 1, MCC; Marie Curie to MMM, November 23, 1929, December 4, 1929, box 4, MCC; Curie to MMM, January 25, 19[30], February 11, 1930, box 7, MCC; Curie to MMM, January 27, 1930, February 15, 1930, February 18, 1930, July 12, 1930, box 1, MCC; Des Jardins, *Madame Curie Complex,* p. 44; Edna Noble White to MMM, January 1, 1930; MMM to White, December 17, 1929, January 14, 1930, February 18, 1930; White to Mrs. Edsel Ford, January 16, 1930, box 64, folder 8, Merrill-Palmer Institute: Edna Noble White Records; MMM to Curie, January 15, 1930, February 7, 1930, February 27, 1930, box 2, MCC.

CHAPTER 10: BEING USEFUL IN A GREAT DEPRESSION, 1930–1932

1. Christmas card, n.d., MMM's Christmas cards file, MMM manuscripts.

2. For annual unemployment numbers during the Great Depression, see "Unemployment Statistics During the Great Depression," United States History website, accessed March 2019, www.u-s-history.com/pages/h1528.html; "Educational News and Editorial Comment," *Elementary School Journal,* vol. 30, no. 1 (September 1929), p. 3; MMM to Mary Day, October 20, 1930, MMM manuscripts; Bernays, *Biography of an Idea;* Martha H. Swain, "Prelude to the New Deal: Lou Henry Hoover and Women's Relief Work," in *Uncommon Americans,* Walch, ed., pp. 153–154.

3. MMM to Dr. Edna N. White, n.d. (letter about Color Conference), box 64, folder 8, Merrill-Palmer Institute: Edna Noble White Records; "Home Making Centre Will Open Tonight," *New York Times,* March 15, 1929, p. 34; "As the Business World Wages: Where Business Can Help," *Nation's Business,* October 1930, p. 11; MMM to Dr. Edna White, n.d. [1930]; Joseph Cummings Chase to MMM, n.d.; draft of preface of institute cookbook, n.d., MMM manuscripts; Laurel D. Graham, "Domesticating Efficiency: Lillian Gilbreth's Scientific Management of Homemakers, 1924–1930," *Signs,* vol. 24, no. 3 (Spring 1999), pp. 661, 666fn.42; Des Jardins, *Lillian Gilbreth,* pp. 135–136.

4. "Carroll Club Circus," *New York Times,* April 23, 1927, p. 9; MMM to Robert Bacon, May 21, 1926; "Dinner Pays Tribute to the Working Girl," *New York Times,* February 18, 1929, p. 19; "Benefit on Ship for Vacation House," *New York Times,* March 9, 1928, p. 23; MMM to Kathleen Norris, January 23, 1929, CG and Kathleen Norris file, MMM misc. material; notes on MMM's publicity course, MMM manuscripts.

5. Susan Ware, *Beyond Suffrage: Women in the New Deal* (Cambridge, MA: Harvard University Press, 1981), p. 2; Des Jardins, *Lillian Gilbreth*, p. 129.

6. "1,100 Young Editors Meet at Columbia," *New York Times*, March 12, 1927, p. 6; "Student Editors Meet Thursday," *New York Times*, March 4, 1934, p. N3; "Heads Newspaper Women's Club," *New York Times*, May 7, 1931, p. 34; Marzolf, *Up from the Footnote*, p. 49; Bradley, *Women and the Press*, pp. 213–215; Ross, *Ladies of the Press*, p. 126.

7. Nancy Beck Young, *Lou Henry Hoover: Activist First Lady* (Lawrence: University of Kansas Press, 2005), pp. 151–152; Lenna Lowe Yost, "President and People Govern Together," *Woman's Journal*, November 1930, p. 23.

8. Edward Howard Suydam to MMM, August 4, 1931, February 6, 1932, April 7, 1932, n.d. [post 1933]; MMM to Dr. Stephen Wise, November 17, 1932; George Shively to MMM, January 11, 1934; Jim Putnam to MMM, March 6, 1934; "Proposed Project: Collective Thought on This Crisis in History," n.d., MMM manuscripts.

9. MMM to Ann Morgan, December 10, 1930; "Proposed Project: Collective Thought on This Crisis in History."

10. Seibold quoted in Chase, *My Friends Look Good to Me*, pp. 142–144.

11. "The New York Herald Tribune Forum, 1930–1940," in *1940 Forum Report*, box 40, MMM; draft of speech for the Tenth Annual Forum, September 24, 1940, MMM manuscripts; MMM to Mary Day, October 20, 1930.

12. "Events Today," *New York Times*, October 25, 1938, p. 23; *Report of the 8th Annual New York Herald Tribune Forum on Current Problems: "America Facing Tomorrow's World,"* Waldorf Astoria, October 25–26, 1938, New York World's Fair, October 27, 1938, box 40, MMM; *Report of the 9th Annual New York Herald Tribune Forum on Current Problems, "The Challenge of Civilization,"* Waldorf Astoria, October 24–26, 1939, box 40, MMM.

13. Draft of speech for the Tenth Annual Forum.

14. "The New York Herald Tribune Forum, 1930–1940"; draft of speech for the Tenth Annual Forum; McFeely, *Can She Bake a Cherry Pie?*, p. 46; "Today on the Radio," *New York Times*, October 3, 1927, p. 27; Scott Bone to MMM, October 13, 1932; Bone to Louis Seibold, October 22, 1933, MMM correspondence.

15. MMM to Lucy Moses, July 24, 1930; MMM to Marie Curie, July 21, 1931, box 2, MCC.

16. Invitation for lunch with the Prime Minister and Miss MacDonald, May 6, 1931, Europe letters, 1931 folder, MMM misc. material; Ishbel MacDonald to MMM, May 13, 1931; Marie Curie to MMM, May 8, 1931, May 12, 1931, May 16, 1931, May 19, 1931, box 7, MCC; "Hoovers Go to Camp Today," *New York Times*, August 1, 1930, p. 3; "Hoover Goes to Camp for a Few Days' Rest," Special to *New York Times*, August 1, 1931, p. 6.

17. MMM's memorandum to Dr. Brooks, October 1, 1931; memorandum by Nora Scannell to Dr. Brooks, n.d. [August–September 1931], MMM manuscripts.

18. Secretary Robert Lamont to MMM, September 9, 1931; MMM to Lamont, September 18, 1931; Irvin Cobb to MMM, October 22, 1932, November 3, 1932; MMM to Cobb, October 24, 1932; Lester Maitland to MMM, September 17, 1931; MMM to Maitland, September 28, 1931; MMM's memorandum to Dr. Brooks, October 1, 1931; Ray Lyman Wilbur to MMM, September 29, 1931, February 18, 1932.

19. MMM to Henry Moses, October 16, 1931; Moses to MMM, November 12, 1930; "Memorandum for Changes to Be Made in Mrs. Meloney's Will," October 16, 1931, MMM misc. material.

20. "Memorandum for Changes to Be Made in Mrs. Meloney's Will"; memorandum to Henry L. Moses, October 16, 1931.

21. Marie Curie to MMM, October 23, 1931, MMM correspondence; B. Dluska to MMM, May 4, 1932, box 1, MCC; MMM to Dluska, May 17, 1932, box 2, MCC.

22. MMM to Havelock Ellis, February 13, 1932; E. V. Lucas to MMM, September 22, 1932; "Estates Appraised," *New York Times,* March 15, 1933, p. C34; "Meet Again to Pay Homage to Mitchel," *New York Times,* July 20, 1932, p. 18.

23. MMM to Bill Donovan, March 8, 1929, MMM misc. material; Donovan to MMM, February 14, 1929, February 14, 1929 (two different letters); Brown, *Last Hero,* 107, 112.

24. MMM to Bill Donovan, February 7, 1929, March 8, 1929; Bernays, *Biography of an Idea;* Perry, *Belle Moskowitz,* pp. 140–141.

25. MMM to William Allen White, October 27, 1932; "Hoover to Speak Today," *New York Times,* September 29, 1932, p. 23.

26. "End of Child Labor Is Urged by Hoover," *New York Times,* September 30, 1932, p. 1.

27. Steel, *Walter Lippmann and the American Century,* p. 297.

28. Herbert Hoover to MMM, December 6, 1932, January 5, 1933.

29. Marie Curie to MMM, August 8, 1928, November 12, 1932, box 7, MCC; draft of New Year's speech, n.d., MMM manuscripts; Timothy Walch and Dwight M. Miller, eds., *Herbert Hoover and Franklin D. Roosevelt: A Documentary History* (Westport, CT: Greenwood Press, 1998), pp. xvii–xviii.

30. Theodore Roosevelt Jr. to MMM, June 11, 1934; typed manuscript of a conversation between MMM and FDR dated December 11, 1938, Franklin Delano Roosevelt file, MMM misc. material; Eleanor Roosevelt to MMM, December 8, 1933; Louis Howe to MMM, December 23, 1932; Missy LeHand to MMM, October 20, 1933; Eleanor Roosevelt to MMM, August 21, 1935; MMM to Eleanor Roosevelt, July 28, 1938.

31. "Milk Committee Named by Mayor," *New York Times,* September 24, 1934, p. 20; "Child Health Put Above Economics," *New York Times,* October 15, 1932,

p. 17; "Political Parties Asked by Whalen to Aid NRA Drive," *New York Times*, August 27, 1933, p. 1.

CHAPTER 11: FEMALE FRIENDS, FORUMS, FASCISTS, AND FREEDOM OF SPEECH, 1933–1934

1. Robin Gerber, *Leadership the Eleanor Roosevelt Way: Timeless Strategies from the First Lady of Courage* (New York: Portfolio, 2002), pp. xxvi–xxix, 11, 13, 208–212, 217, 221–222.

2. Lou Henry Hoover to Mrs. Mead, February 19, 1929, MMM correspondence; Ware, *Beyond Suffrage*, pp. 6–7, 15–17, 32–33; Fannie Hurst to MMM, May 1, 1933; Eleanor Roosevelt to MMM, August 2, 1935, August 9, 1935.

3. Maurine H. Beasley, *Eleanor Roosevelt and the Media: A Public Quest for Self-Fulfillment* (Urbana: University of Illinois Press, 1987), pp. 16–17; Blanche Wiesen Cook, "Introduction," in *My Day: The Best of Eleanor Roosevelt's Acclaimed Newspaper Columns, 1936–1962*, David Emblidge, ed. (New York: DaCapo Press, 2001), p. xiii.

4. Beasley, *Eleanor Roosevelt and the Media*, pp. 25, 36; Gourley, *War, Women, and the News*, p. 30; Rodger Streitmatter, ed., *Empty Without You: The Intimate Letters of Eleanor Roosevelt and Lorena Hickok* (New York: Free Press, 1998), p. xxiv; Michael Golay, *America 1933: The Great Depression, Lorena Hickok, Eleanor Roosevelt, and the Shaping of the New Deal* (New York: Free Press, 2013).

5. "Reminiscences of Emma Bugbee, 1974"; Beasley, *Eleanor Roosevelt and the Media*, p. 47; Gourley, *War, Women, and the News*, pp. 30, 33; Ross, *Ladies of the Press*, pp. 309, 315–317; Gerber, *Leadership the Eleanor Roosevelt Way*, pp. 133–135.

6. "Costumes Novel at White House," Special to the *New York Times*, December 9, 1934, p. 40; "Reminiscences of Emma Bugbee, 1974"; Beasley, *Eleanor Roosevelt and the Media*, p. 49; Gerber, *Leadership the Eleanor Roosevelt Way*, p. 120.

7. Beasley, *Eleanor Roosevelt and the Media*, pp. 58–59, 119–120; Streitmatter, *Empty Without You*, p. xxiv; Gerber, *Leadership the Eleanor Roosevelt Way*, pp. 136–137.

8. Stacy Cordery, *Alice: Alice Roosevelt Longworth, from White House Princess to Washington Power Broker* (New York: Penguin, 2008).

9. Handwritten note dated October 28, n.y., MMM manuscripts; notes dated April 12, 1926, "on a rough train from Washington," MMM manuscripts.

10. Notes dated April 12, 1926, MMM manuscripts.

11. Romanov's memoirs were titled *The Education of a Princess* (1930) and *A Princess in Exile* (1932). MMM to William N. Castle, April 14, 1931, June 12, 1931; secretary of MMM to Castle, April 20, 1931, October 28, 1931, MMM misc. material; Polish embassy dinner notes, March 28, 1931; William W. Husband to MMM, April 9, 1931, April 18, 1931, June 5, 1931, February 26, 1932.

12. Invitation for May 24 [193?], Marie Romanov folder, MMM misc. material; Marie Romanov to MMM, July 1, 1931, July 1931, July 10, 1936.

13. Grand Duchess Marie Romanov to Alfonso XIII, King of Spain, Troy, New York, 1931, MMM correspondence.

14. Marie Belloc Lowndes to MMM, November 4, 1933.

15. "M'Reynolds Sails for Europe Today," *New York Times*, June 30, 1933, p. 15; Isabella Howard to MMM, August 19, 1933; MMM to Howard, August 24, 1933.

16. Draft of interview with Mussolini dated January 16, 1928, MMM manuscripts, pp. 5–11.

17. "President to Talk to Women Here," *New York Times*, October 8, 1933, p. N2; "Ban on War Urged by Mrs. Roosevelt," *New York Times*, October 13, 1933, p. 21; memorandum on proposed interview with Mussolini, August 31, 1933 (retyped with note, September 12, 1933) and attached memo dated August 23, 1933, MMM catalogued manuscripts; Ruth Bryan Owen to MMM, October 16, 1933; MMM to Breckinridge Long, July 18, 1933, Breckenridge Long file, MMM misc. material.

18. Telegrams from Foreign Office to MMM, July 22, 1933, July 23, 1933, [to Paris, 1933], MMM catalogued manuscripts.

19. Alexander Kirk to MMM, n.d.; Nicholas Roosevelt to MMM, Budapest, September 12, n.y., March 21, 1931, April 21, 1931, January 5, 1932, February 10, 1932.

20. Alexander Kirk to MMM, March 6, n.y., n.d. (two different letters); MMM to Kirk, [July 1933].

21. Memorandum on proposed interview with Mussolini; Fredericka Blankner to MMM, August 29, 1933; MMM to ? Sourdi, n.d., MMM catalogued manuscripts.

22. Memorandum on proposed interview with Mussolini.

23. Richard von Kühlmann to MMM, August 3, 1933; telegram, MMM to Wilbur Forrest, n.d. [July 1933], in typed notes of German experience, summer 1933, MMM catalogued manuscripts; Carlo Sforza to MMM, July 22, 1933; Lion Feuchtwanger to MMM, June 18, 1933, July 11, 1933, December 27, 1933.

24. Marie Curie to MMM, August 2, 1933, September ?, 1933, October 10, 1933, box 7, MCC; MMM to Alexander Kirk, [July 1933].

25. Hubert Roemer to MMM, August 19, 1933 (enclosure: Report by Renee Brasier on Hitler interview); MMM to Baron von Kühlmann, August 10, 1933; MMM's memorandum to Mr. Reid, August 28, 1933, in typed notes of German experience.

26. MMM to Honorable W. L. Lowrie, American Consul General, Frankfort, August 14, 1933, in typed notes of German experience; memorandum to Mr. Reid, August 28, 1933.

27. "Son Born to Mrs. W. B. Meloney," *New York Times*, April 9, 1933, p. N4; memorandum on proposed interview with Mussolini; MMM to Herr Leitner, German Embassy, Washington, DC, September 10, 1933; Leitner to MMM,

September 11, 1933, in typed notes of German experience; Breckinridge Long to MMM, October 12, 1933; attached memo to memorandum on proposed interview with Mussolini, August 23, 1933.

28. Philip V. Cannistraro and Brian R. Sullivan, eds., *Il Duce's Other Woman* (New York: William Morrow and Company, 1993), pp. 419, 448.

29. Margherita Sarfatti to Missy Meloney, n.d. [July 1933]; memorandum on proposed interview with Mussolini.

30. Margherita Sarfatti to MMM, n.d., n.d., January 17, ? [Rome]; Cannistraro and Sullivan, *Il Duce's Other Woman,* p. 413.

31. Cannistraro and Sullivan, *Il Duce's Other Woman,* pp. 410, 419, 422–434; Robert M. Hutchins, University of Chicago, to J. E. Samuelson, September 25, 1933, MMM correspondence; Frank Knox to MMM, May 14, 1937; Margherita Sarfatti to MMM, March 4, 1934; "Italian Writer Greeted," *New York Times,* April 9, 1934; Fannie Hurst to MMM, June 3, 1934; Margherita Sarfatti to MMM, January 17, n.y.

32. Carlo Sforza to MMM, May 24, 1934; Cannistraro and Sullivan, *Il Duce's Other Woman,* pp. 446–447.

33. "Ocean Travelers," *New York Times,* June 8, 1934, p. 24; MMM to Cosmo Hamilton, June 27, 1934; Frank Swinnerton to MMM, June 23, 1934; Virginia Woolf to MMM, June 22, 1934.

34. Henry Seidel Canby, "Report of the PEN Congress, American Delegation, and Speech Made at the Congress by Ernst Toller Representing Exiled Authors, 1933," Ernst Toller file, MMM misc. material; "Nazis Face Attacks at Writers' Meeting," *New York Times,* June 18, 1934, p. 7; "Wells Denounces Curb on Free PEN: He Tells World Writers They Dare," Special Cable to the *New York Times,* June 19, 1934, p. 17; James J. Barnes and Patience P. Barnes, *Nazi Refugee Turned Gestapo Spy: The Life of Hans Wesemann, 1895–1971* (Westport, CT: Praeger Publishers, 2001), p. 110; MMM to Baroness Marie Budberg, June 29, 1934; Ernst Toller to MMM, July 28, 1934, March 28, 1935, April 27, 1935, May 27, 1936.

35. MMM recalled her conversation with Eliot in a letter to John Galsworthy, September 27, 1928; Will Irwin to MMM, October 16, 1929; "Nation's Safety Lies in Freedom of the Press," *Lewiston Evening Journal,* December 7, 1934, p. 20.

36. Draft of speech on a free press, n.d., MMM manuscripts.

37. A. P. Young to MMM, July 3, 1934; Ralph Hale Mottram to MMM, July 3, 1934; Marie Belloc Lowndes to MMM, June 15, 1934, June 26, 1934, June 29, 1934; Ève Curie to MMM, June 1934, June 11, 1934, July 2, 1934.

38. Ève Curie to MMM, July 4, 1934.

39. "Mme. Curie, Co-Discoverer of Radium, Dies in Savoy," cover, special to the *New York Herald,* European Edition of the *New York Herald Tribune,* July 5, 1934, clippings in box 4, MCC; "Mme. Curie's Life and Work Lauded by Mrs. Meloney," special to the *New York Herald.*

40. James Barrie to MMM, July 5, 1934; Carlo Sforza to MMM, July 6, 1934; Margherita Sarfatti to MMM, n.d. [July 1934], July 3, 1934.

CHAPTER 12: PUBLICLY TURNING A PAGE, 1934–1936

1. Ève Curie to MMM, December 27, 1933, July 27, 1934, box 1, MCC; "Mrs. W. B. Meloney Honored in Capital," Special to the *New York Times*, November 7, 1935, p. 28; Emil Lengyel to MMM, June 8, 1935; Ève Curie to Gerard Swope, August 25, 1934, box 4, MCC.

2. Death notice for Sarah Irwin Mattingly, *Statesville Record and Landmark*, January 26, 1934, p. 4; "Mrs. Mattingly, 82, Educator, Is Dead," *New York Times*, January 7, 1934, p. 30; Spalding, *Biography of a Kentucky Town*, p. 79.

3. Alexander Kirk to MMM, March 2, 1934; Paul May to MMM, March 9, 1934; "Library Dedicated by Mrs. Coolidge," *New York Times*, October 31, 1934, p. 21.

4. "Mayor Dedicates Marie Curie Ave.," *New York Times*, June 10, 1935, p. 19; program of the Dedication of Marie Curie Avenue, June 9, 1935, in John Jay Park, 77th Street and East River, Manhattan, box 4, MCC; documents relating to the naming of "Curie Street," 1935, box 4, MCC; Joseph W. Wieczerzak, "Marie Curie Avenue, New York: A Street That Was," *Polish Review*, vol. 44, no. 2 (1999), pp. 143–150.

5. Ève Curie to MMM, July 27, 1934, box 1, MCC; "Daughter Will Use Mme. Curie's Radium," *New York Times*, July 20, 1934, p. 6; Irène Curie to MMM, December 30, 1934, December 5, 1935, box 2, MCC.

6. "President's Cares Described by Wife," *New York Times*, September 26, 1934, p. 23; "Mayor Urges Aid for Better Homes," *New York Times*, July 31, 1934, p. 19; Hutchinson, "Shaping Housing and Enhancing Consumption," p. 93; "New Ideals Urged by Mrs. Roosevelt," *New York Times*, September 27, 1934, p. 9.

7. "Herald Tribune's Lady"; "Crime Study Opens Conference Today," *New York Times*, September 26, 1934, p. 3; Lawrence Tibbett to Mary Day Winn, September 15, 1934; MMM to Tibbett, August 9, 1934, September 11, 1934, September 18, 1934; Edward Elliott to MMM, October 3, 1934, June 11, 1938.

8. "Ridgewood Will Send Delegates," Hackensack *Record*, September 25, 1934, Correspondence, box 40, Rose Franken Papers; "Group to Hear Talk by Mrs. Roosevelt," *New York Times*, August 27, 1934, p. 17; "Launching and Conference Radio Sweetmeats Today," *Springfield Republic*, September 26, 1934; "Herald Tribune's Lady."

9. Sinclair Lewis joked that he'd write a "girl's" book titled *Helen, Missy, Irita and Dotty, Or: The Herald Tribune Girls in Harlem*. It's worth noting that Helen Reid knew Thompson before Missy's intervention, as both women were active in the New York suffrage movement. See Peter Kurth, *American Cassandra: The Life of Dorothy Thompson* (Boston: Little, Brown, 1990), pp. 218–219, 232; Dorothy

Thompson to MMM, May 26, 1934, November 9, 1934; "Mrs. William B. Meloney Presents Dorothy Thompson," in Guy R. Lyle and Kevin Guinagh, compilers, *I Am Happy to Present: A Book of Introductions,* 2nd ed. (New York: H. W. Wilson Company, 1968), p. 112; Gourley, *War, Women, and the News,* pp. 36–38, 44–47; Cairns, *Front-Page Women Journalists,* p. 27. Missy recalled extending her first invitation to Thompson to speak at the Forum in her speech "A New World Power: Mass Opinion," at the 8th Annual Forum in 1938, Mass Opinion folder, MMM manuscripts.

10. Barbie Zelizer, "Words Against Images: Positioning Newswork in the Age of Photography," in *Newsworkers,* p. 138; Steel, *Walter Lippmann and the American Century,* pp. 279–280; Emblidge, ed., *My Day;* Beasley, *Eleanor Roosevelt and the Media,* pp. 90–91.

11. Channing Pollock, "Missy."

12. MMM memo, October 31, 1933, MMM manuscripts.

13. William I. Nichols, *New Patterns in Publishing: The Story of* This Week *Magazine* (New York: Newcomen Society of North America, 1960), box 40, MMM; "Sunday Battle," *Time,* October 15, 1934, p. 60.

14. Richard Lingeman, *Sinclair Lewis: Rebel from Main Street* (St. Paul, MN: Borealis Books, 2002), p. 443; "Knapp's Week," *Time,* February 25, 1935, p. 54; Somerset Maugham to MMM, July 24, 1935; MMM to Maugham, August 2, 1935; Ted Morgan, *Maugham: A Biography* (New York: Simon and Schuster, 1980), pp. 389, 463; Joseph Auslander to MMM, July 31, 1940; Sherwood Anderson to MMM, November 7, 1940; Robert Frost to MMM, March 14, 1933; February 12, 1934; Zona Gale to MMM, February 17, 1931; MMM to Gale, February 19, 1931.

15. Memorandum to Mr. Knapp, September 8, 1933, Joseph Knapp to MMM, October 22, 1936, MMM to Knapp, October 25, 1936, all in MMM manuscripts.

16. "Comments from Country's Most Noted Field Investigator," in "Survey of April 7th, 1935 Issue of *This Week,* 10 Cities," MMM manuscripts; MMM, "Memorandum," 1936, MMM manuscripts; MMM to "Boss" [Joseph Knapp], June 8, 1936, MMM manuscripts; "Memo on the Dionne Quintuplets," n.d., MMM manuscripts; MMM memo to Knapp, n.d., MMM manuscripts; "Knapp's Week," *Time,* February 25, 1935, p. 54.

17. MMM memoranda to Mr. Knapp, September 1, 1936, September 12, 1936, MMM manuscripts.

18. MMM memorandum to Knapp, September 1, 1936, MMM manuscripts.

19. Ibid.

20. MMM to Channing Pollock, February 4, 1941.

21. Margaret Widdemer, *Golden Friends I Had* (Garden City, NY: Doubleday, 1964), p. 339; Anne Morrow Lindbergh to MMM, November 11, 1935; Harold Ross to MMM, April 8, 1935; David Sarnoff to MMM, November 1, 1935, March 7, 1937; Albert Payson Terhune to MMM, April 1, 1935.

22. "Fortescue Fun," *Time,* September 10, 1934, p. 51; MMM to Major Reese, April 28, 1937, June 9, 1937.

23. William Brown Meloney to MMM, October 26, 1933; G. Edward White, *Alger Hiss's Looking-Glass Wars* (New York: Oxford University Press, 2004), p. 14, 257n; MMM to Bill Meloney, May 7, 1935; Rouben Mamoulian to MMM, November 22, 1935, December 15, 1935, February 5, 1936.

24. Bill Meloney Jr. to MMM, May 3, 1935, MMM misc. material; MMM to Bill Meloney, May 7, 1935, MMM misc. material.

25. "Rose Franken, 92, Author of the 'Claudia' Stories: Magazines, Books and Broadway Used the Series," *New York Times,* June 24, 1988, p. B6.

26. Rose Franken, *When All Is Said and Done: An Autobiography* (Garden City, NY: Doubleday, 1963), pp. 161–163.

27. Bill Meloney's 1940 draft card lists him as six feet, one inch and 165 pounds. See "Draft Registration Cards for Connecticut, 1940–1947," Record Group: Records of the Selective Service System, 147, box 277, accessed September 28, 2017, http://search.ancestry.com/cgi-bin/sse.dll?indiv=1&db=YMDraftCard...e&_phsrc=Xoi10&_phstart=successSource&usePUBJs=true&rhSource=7488 (no longer available); Franken, *When All Is Said and Done,* pp. 170–175, 190, 200; Charlotte Hughes, "Woman Playmakers," *New York Times,* May 4, 1941, p. SM10.

28. Cannistraro and Sullivan, *Il Duce's Other Woman,* p. 468.

29. Cannistraro and Sullivan, *Il Duce's Other Woman,* p. 468; MMM to Baron Richard von Kühlmann, June 21, 1935; MMM to Phillips Oppenheim, June 22, 1935, Oppenheim file, MMM misc. material; Lt. Commander Joseph Montague Kenworthy Strabolgi to MMM, June 15, 1935; Margaret Haig Rhondda, 2nd Viscountess, to MMM, June 19, 1935, June 24, 1935; F. Britten Austin to MMM, May 30, 1935; Gladys Bronwyn Stern to MMM, July 1, 1935; Honoré Morrow to Miss Winn, July 10, 1935, MMM correspondence.

30. Cannistraro and Sullivan, *Il Duce's Other Woman,* p. 468.

31. "Italy's Duty Is to Civilize Ethiopia, Mussolini Holds," *New York Herald Tribune,* July 20, 1935, newspaper clipping in MMM catalogued manuscripts.

32. Rose Emmet Young, ed., *Why Wars Must Cease* (New York: Macmillan Company, 1935), pp. x, 46, 56–62. Friends praised Missy for her efforts to promote international peace in the interwar years. See James T. Shotwell to MMM, October 22, 1935, February 13, 1936; Henriette, Princess of Belgium, to MMM, February 13, 1936; Eleanor Roosevelt to MMM, September 20, 1935.

33. Margherita Sarfatti to MMM, August 8, 1934, August 13, 1935, October 31, 1937, 1938 [Paris], July 30, 1938; Cannistraro and Sullivan, *Il Duce's Other Woman,* pp. 474, 496–497, 512–513, 518, 523.

34. Nicholas Murray Butler to MMM, January 27, 1939.

35. Hermann Hagedorn to MMM, June 10, 1939, January 22, 1940.

36. "President Presses Neutrality Stand," *New York Times*, October 18, 1935, p. 1; "Women Get Advice on Better Buying," *New York Times*, October 1, 1935, p. 25; David Sarnoff to MMM, October 19, 1935; "Behind the Scenes," *New York Times*, November 24, 1935, p. X15; "Home Economics Held Vital Study," *New York Times*, March 22, 1935, p. 25; Nelson A. Rockefeller to MMM, June 4, 1936; "Packaging Jury Named," *New York Times*, December 15, 1936, p. 47.

37. MMM, "The Last Magic"; Felix Bruner to MMM, n.d., F. C. Kendall to MMM, April 25, 1935, Bartlett Arkell to MMM, April 24, 1935, Guy Smith to MMM, April 23, 1935, all in MMM manuscripts.

38. "Women Organize to Aid World's Fair," *New York Times*, January 24, 1937, p. 39; "Kudos," *Time*, July 29, 1935, p. 16; "Doctorates Given to Three Women Leaders," *New York Times*, June 2, 1936, p. 25; diploma, Doctor of Human Letters, Russell Sage College, June 1, 1936, MMM manuscripts; "Marie Mattingly Meloney," remarks given with honorary degree, Russell Sage College, 1936, Russell Sage Libraries, Troy, New York.

39. "Colleagues Honor 24 'Career Women,'" *New York Times*, March 19, 1936, p. 22; Winifred Mallon, "General Federation Board Session to Study Project for Academy of Public Affairs," *New York Times*, January 12, 1936; "Women Join Fight on Juvenile Crime," *New York Times*, March 13, 1936, p. 25; "Crime Rise Is Laid to Child Neglect," *New York Times*, March 12, 1936, p. 23.

CHAPTER 13: ILLNESS AND IMPENDING WAR, 1937–1940

1. MMM to "Boss" [Joseph Knapp], n.d. [1936], MMM manuscripts; MMM to Knapp, July 31, 1936.

2. Eleanor Roosevelt to MMM, October 28, 1936, December 14, 1936; Owen Young to MMM, December 9, 1936; Young to Emily J. Sheppard, October 27, 1937, MMM correspondence; "Tabulation of Securities Held by City Bank Farmers Trust Company as Custodian Emilie Busbey Grigsby," n.d., Owen Young file, MMM misc. material; Shane Leslie to MMM, December 10, 1934, December 31, 1934, February 15, 1935; "Dr. Harlow Brooks Dies," *Montreal Gazette*, April 14, 1936, p. 18; Harlow Brooks Memorial program (1936), Dr. Harlow Brooks folder, MMM misc. material; Moorhead, *Harlow Brooks*, pp. 267–274.

3. MMM to Dr. H. Borchers, March 10, 1937; Borchers to MMM, May 13, 1937.

4. MMM to Channing Pollock, n.d., Pollock file, MMM misc. material; John Francis O'Hara to MMM, October 3, 1936, June 14, 1937, June 28, 1937.

5. Cecil Roberts to MMM, September 30, 1937; Alexander Kirk to MMM, October 20, 1937, Alexander Kirk folder, MMM misc. material; Alexander Kirk to MMM, June 8 [1938], August 28 [1939].

6. Lord Strabolgi to MMM, March 10, 1937, May 18, 1937, July 1, 1937; Gourley, *War, Women, and the News*, pp. 48–49; Whitelaw Reid to MMM, August 6, 1940; Kluger, *The Paper*, p. 335.

7. MMM to Joe Mattingly, January 14, 1938; Walter Lippmann to MMM, February 24, 1938; Edward Bernays, *Biography of an Idea*.

8. Mayor La Guardia to MMM, November 28, 1938, January 10, 1939, July 24, 1940; Robert Nathan to MMM, n.d. [1939]; MMM to Eleanor Roosevelt, September 13, 1939.

9. Frederick Britten Austin to MMM, July 20, 1938; ledger, Consolidated Appraisal Company, New York, "Catalog and Appraisal of Property Belonging to Mrs. William Brown Meloney," made for her property located at South Quaker Hill, Pawling, New York, February 6, 1940, MMM manuscripts.

10. Franken, *When All Is Said and Done*, pp. 246–251, 284; MMM to Eleanor Roosevelt, October 11, 1939; Eleanor Roosevelt to MMM, August 11, 1937; John Erskine to MMM, August 23, 1937; Edith Walton, "A First Novel Which Has Power and Beauty: William Brown Meloney's 'Rush to the Sun' Successfully Blends Poetry and Realism," *New York Times*, August 29, 1937; Stanley Young, "'In High Places,' by William Brown Meloney, and Other New Fiction," *New York Times* [1939], p. BR4; "Rose Franken, 92, Author of the 'Claudia' Stories"; Charlotte Hughes, "Woman Playmakers," *New York Times*, May 4, 1941, p. SM19.

11. Franken, *When All Is Said and Done*, pp. 254–255; MMM to Rose Franken, February 20, 1942, Correspondence, box 1, Rose Franken Papers.

12. MMM to "Boss" [Joseph Knapp], August 18, 1938, MMM manuscripts.

13. Joseph Knapp to MMM, n.d.; MMM to Knapp, August 19, 1938, October 19, 1939, June 27, 1940; MMM's memo, "Success Story Contest," and MMM's notes on Armistice Day feature for *This Week*, August 19, 1938, MMM manuscripts.

14. Eleanor Roosevelt to MMM, July 8, 1938, July 13, 1938; *Report of the 8th Annual New York Herald Tribune Forum on Current Problems;* MMM to Eleanor Roosevelt, July 28, 1938, August 5, 1938.

15. MMM to Franklin Delano Roosevelt, August 23, 1938, MMM to Eleanor Roosevelt, August 18, 1938, both in Franklin Delano Roosevelt file, MMM misc. material; MMM to Eleanor Roosevelt, July 28, 1938, August 5, 1938; Joseph P. Lash, *Eleanor and Franklin: The Story of Their Relationship Based on Eleanor Roosevelt's Private Papers* (New York: Konecky and Konecky, 1971), pp. 614–615.

16. MMM, "A New World Power: Mass Opinion," speech for the 8th *Herald Tribune* Forum.

17. Owen Young to MMM, November 2, 1938.

18. Irène Curie to MMM, October 4, 1938, March 3, 1939, September 11, 1939, box 2, MCC.

19. Athan G. Theoharis, *The FBI and American Democracy: A Brief Critical History* (Lawrence: University Press of Kansas, 2004), pp. 42, 44; MMM to Joseph Knapp, February 26, 1940, MMM manuscripts; J. Edgar Hoover to MMM, October 24, 1939, December 4, 1939, January 4, 1940, January 19, 1940, July 2, 1940, July 30, 1940, October 23, 1940, November 6, 1940.

20. Helen Keller to MMM, February 10, 1938, June 26, 1942; Lou Gehrig to MMM, August 14, 1939.

21. Walch and Miller, eds., *Herbert Hoover and Franklin D. Roosevelt,* pp. 169–170; 176–177; Eleanor Roosevelt to MMM, September 10, 1939, September 17, 1939, October 8, 1939.

22. MMM's letter to Eleanor Roosevelt was attached to a memo Roosevelt's secretary wrote dated October 23, 1939, Franklin Delano Roosevelt folder, MMM misc. material.

23. *Report of the 9th Annual New York Herald Tribune Forum on Current Problems,* "*The Challenge of Civilization,*" Waldorf Astoria, October 24, 25, 26, 1939, box 40, MMM; Eleanor Roosevelt to MMM, October 15, 1939; MMM, *What Man Cannot Destroy* (New York: New York Herald Tribune, 1939), pp. 13, 17.

24. MMM to Prince de Ligne, November 14, 1939, Prince de Ligne file, MMM misc. material; MMM to Oliver St. John Gogarty, February 29, 1940; Eleanor Roosevelt to MMM, April 16, 1940, May 6, 1940, May 27, 1940; MMM to Roosevelt, May 21, 1940.

25. MMM to Joseph Knapp, October 19, 1939, January 8, 1940, February 26, 1940, MMM manuscripts; William I. Nichols, "New Patterns in Publishing," pp. 15–16; MMM to Eleanor Roosevelt, January 29, 1940.

26. "Statement by Mrs. Meloney," April 20, 1940, MMM manuscripts.

27. Eleanor Roosevelt to MMM, June 5, 1940, July 3, 1940, July 12, 1940; MMM to Roosevelt, July 15, 1940; Irène Curie to MMM, May 14, 1940, box 2, MCC; "Nazis Find Mme. Curie's Radium."

28. Irène Curie to MMM, May 14, 1940, July 25, 1940; Gerber, *Leadership the Eleanor Roosevelt Way,* pp. 180–181; clipping of Eleanor Roosevelt's My Day, July 13, 1940, Franklin Delano Roosevelt file, MMM misc. material; Beasley, *Eleanor Roosevelt and the Media,* p. 124; "Groups Meet Today for Belgian Relief," *New York Times,* June 11, 1940, p. 34; "National Group Formed Here for Polish Relief," *New York Times,* September 28, 1939, p. 27; Martin Harris, "Discuss Plans for Polish Relief Concert," *New York Times,* November 5, 1939, p. 38.

CHAPTER 14: A WOMAN'S WORK IS NEVER DONE, 1940–1943

1. MMM to George Bell, January 6, 1939; MMM to Philip M. Hayden, January 10, 1939; MMM to Raymond Fosdick, January 5, 1939; MMM to Philip Arnow, March 5, 1937; MMM to Dr. C. K. Jones, Hispanic Foundation of the Library of Congress, July 25, 1941, box 7, Mitchel folder, Meloney-Mitchel Collection.

2. MMM to Archibald MacLeish, September 9, 1940; February 25, 1942, box 7, Mitchel folder, Meloney-Mitchel Collection.

3. MMM to Archibald MacLeish, July 12, 1940, September 9, 1940, February 25, 1942, Mitchel folder, box 7, Meloney-Mitchel Collection; "Bequests, Donors, and Lenders," *Annual Report of the Trustees of the Metropolitan Museum of Art,* no.

72 (1941), p. 41; "Notes," *The Metropolitan Museum of Art Bulletin,* vol. 37, no. 2 (February 1942), p. 46; MMM to Eleanor Roosevelt, October 11, 1939; Roosevelt to MMM, October 15, 1939.

4. MMM to Theodore Roosevelt Jr., August 5, 1938, August 12, 1938.

5. Ève Curie to MMM, November 20, 1937, February 12, 1938, box 1, MCC; MMM to Ève Curie, October 17, 1934, box 4, MCC; MMM to Ève Curie, January 21, 1937; Irène Curie to MMM, October 25, 1936, box 2, MCC.

6. Eleanor Roosevelt, My Day, Richmond, California, *News Leader,* October 24, 1940, Correspondence, box 40, Rose Franken Papers.

7. Draft of speech for 10th Annual Forum, September 24, 1940, MMM manuscripts.

8. Kluger, *The Paper,* pp. 322–326; Kurth, *American Cassandra,* p. 321; "Forum to Present Campaign Rivals: Roosevelt and Willkie to Make Addresses," New York *Sun,* October 4, 1940, Correspondence, box 40, Rose Franken Papers; "Herald Tribune Forum Oct. 22–24 Will Hear Roosevelt and Willkie," *New York Herald Tribune,* October 4, 1940; "President, Willkie to Address Forum," *New York Times,* October 4, 1940, p. 21; draft of speech for 10th Annual Forum.

9. Eleanor Roosevelt, My Day, *Toledo Blade,* November 27, 1940, Correspondence, box 40, Rose Franken Papers; Eleanor Roosevelt quote from My Day, November 18, 1938, Eleanor Roosevelt Papers, Digital Edition, www2.gwu.edu/~erpapers/myday/displaydoc.cfm?_y=1938&_f=md055114.

10. Ruth Gruber, *Inside of Time: My Journey from Alaska to Israel* (New York: Carroll and Graf, 2003), pp. 129–130; Bradley, *Women and the Press,* 219.

11. Gruber, *Inside of Time,* pp. 131–132.

12. Channing Pollock, *Guide Posts in Chaos* (New York: Thomas Y. Crowell, 1942); Pollock to DeWitt Wallace, January 24, 1941, MMM correspondence; MMM to Pollock, February 19, 1942, January 26, 1941, February 4, 1941, n.d., Pollock file, MMM misc. material; Pollock, "Missy."

13. MMM to Channing Pollock, February 6, 1941, n.d., Pollock file, MMM misc. material.

14. MMM to Channing Pollock, July 18, 1941, August 7, 1941; Pollock to MMM, July 12, 1941, July 19, 1941.

15. Channing Pollock, *Harvest of My Years* (Indianapolis: Bobbs-Merrill Company, 1943), p. 330; MMM to Pollock, November 17, 1941.

16. Frank Knox to MMM, December 31, 1940.

17. Eleanor Roosevelt, My Day, Bridgeport *Star,* January 28, 1941, Correspondence, box 40, Rose Franken Papers; Kluger, *The Paper,* p. 350; J. Edgar Hoover to MMM, February 24, 1941, March 21, 1941; MMM to William Castle, February 29, 1940; MMM to Cordell Hull, March 27, 1941, MMM misc. material.

18. MMM to William Nichols, May 16, 1941, MMM manuscripts; MMM to Eleanor Roosevelt, May 28, 1941, Franklin Delano Roosevelt file, MMM misc.

material; MMM to Eleanor Roosevelt, June 24, 1941; Eleanor Roosevelt to MMM, June 17, 1941.

19. MMM to Eleanor Roosevelt, June 24, 1941; Eleanor Roosevelt to MMM, July 2, 1941; Malvina Thompson to MMM, July 23, 1941.

20. MMM to Eleanor Roosevelt, October 10, 1941, October 27, 1941, Windsor file, MMM misc. material; MMM to Eleanor Roosevelt, November 19, 1941; MMM to Lady Halifax, November 18, 1941; Whitney Darrow to MMM, January 5, 1942; MMM to Darrow, January 5, 1942; MMM to Winthrop Aldrich, December 12, 1941; Wallis Windsor to MMM, October 27, 1941, May 6, 1942; MMM to the Duchess of Windsor, October 10, 1941, October 22, 1941, October 25, 1941.

21. Eleanor Roosevelt, My Day, Clarksburg, West Virginia *Exponent-Telegram,* October 12, 1941, Correspondence, box 40, Rose Franken Papers; Baron de Cartier to MMM, December 18, 1941.

22. Eleanor Roosevelt, My Day, Wheeling West Virginia *News-Register,* February 24, 1942, clipping in Correspondence, box 40, Rose Franken Papers; memo by Mary Day enclosed in MMM to Mr. Gilleaudeau, July 25, 1942, MMM manuscripts; MMM's notes, August 19, 1942, MMM manuscripts; letter sent from MMM to editors and publishers, May 14, 1942; Tom Cathcart, "Confidentially," July 24, 1942, MMM manuscripts; "Different *This Week,*" *Time,* January 5, 1942, p. 34.

23. Grace Coolidge to MMM, March 11, 1942; MMM to the Duchess of Windsor, April 22, 1942; Windsor to MMM, May 6, 1942; Ada Jackson to MMM, March 8, 1942; Herbert Hoover to MMM, June 1, 1942; Alexander Kirk to MMM, June 18, 1942.

24. MMM to Bill Donovan, September 4, 1942, box 7, Mitchel folder, Meloney-Mitchel Collection; MMM to Secretary Welles, November 30, 1942; Stanley Hornbeck to MMM, December 16, 1942; Henry Wallace to MMM, December 8, 1942.

25. MMM to Herbert Hoover, January 4, 1943, Herbert Hoover folder, MMM misc. material.

26. Sumner Welles to MMM, February 16, 1943.

27. Rose Franken to Eleanor Roosevelt, April 4, 1943, Correspondence, box 1, Rose Franken Papers; J. Edgar Hoover to MMM, April 26, 1943, June 4, 1943; Sumner Welles to MMM, April 26, 1943, May 4, 1943; MMM to Welles, June 9, 1943; "Newspaper Women Elect," *New York Times,* May 20, 1943, p. 24.

28. Frank Knox to MMM, June 3, 1943; "This Week's Spirit," *Time,* June 14, 1943, p. 90.

29. MMM to Rose Franken, June 15, 1943, Correspondence, box 1, Rose Franken Papers.

30. Franken, *When All Is Said and Done,* pp. 283–285; "Mrs. W. B. Meloney, Noted Editor, Dies," Special to the *New York Times,* June 24, 1943.

31. "Leading Woman Journalist Dies," Schenectady *Union Star,* June 24, 1943, clipping in Correspondence, box 40, Rose Franken Papers; "Notables Attend

Meloney Service," *New York Times,* June 26, 1943, p. 13; MMM to Shuler N. Warren, April 20, 1939, box 7, Meloney-Mitchel Collection.

32. "Mrs. William Brown Meloney," *New York Times,* June 25, 1943, p. 16.

33. Eleanor Roosevelt, My Day, clipping from the Hollywood, California, *Citizen News,* June 29, 1943, Correspondence, box 40, Rose Franken Papers.

EPILOGUE

1. "To Honor Woman Editor," *New York Times,* August 29, 1943, p. 29.

2. "Ship Gets Editor's Name," *New York Times,* September 5, 1943, p. 19; Franken, *When All Is Said and Done,* p. 294; Rose Franken to Eleanor Roosevelt, April 4, 1943, Correspondence, box 1, Rose Franken papers; Rose Franken, "Second Thoughts on the First Lady," *Redbook,* June 1943, Correspondence, box 41, Rose Franken Papers; Basil O'Connor, President of National Foundation for Infantile Paralysis, to Rose Franken, April 16, 1943, Correspondence, box 1, Rose Franken Papers; Eleanor Roosevelt to Rose Franken, March 27, 1943, Correspondence, box 1, Rose Franken Papers.

3. Beasley and Gibbons, *Taking Their Place*, pp. 13, 15; Cairns, *Front-Page Women Journalists*, pp. 31–34.

4. Julie Des Jardins, "American Memories of Madame Curie: Prisms on the Gendered Culture of Science," in *Celebrating the 100th Anniversary of Madame Marie Sklodowska Curie's Nobel Prize in Chemistry,* eds. M.-H. Chiu, P. J. Gilmer, and D. F. Treagust (Boston: Sense Publishers, 2011), pp. 59–85.

5. Her decorations from European governments included the Médaille de Charleroi, Ordre de la Reine Élisabeth, and the Order of the Crown of Belgium (Belgium); Officier of the Legion of Honor, Médaille d'honneur des Assurances Sociales, and the Gold Medal for State Service (France); and the Order of Polonia Restituta (Poland). Memorandum dated June 30, 1941, "Mrs. William Brown Meloney Decoration: Elizabeth Medal, Decorations" Marie Mattingly Meloney folder, MMM manuscripts; Stéphane Lauzanne to MMM, July 9, 1921, November 11, 1921, December 2, 1921; MMM to Lauzanne, November 19, 1921, November 29, 1921; "French Arms Shield World, Says Briand," *New York Tribune,* November 25, 1921, p. 3; "World News About Women," *Woman's Journal,* December 3, 1921, p. 20; Elsa Maxwell's "Particles," Newark *Star Ledger,* October 24, 1942, Correspondence, box 40, Rose Franken Papers; George Palmer Putnam, *Wide Margins: The Autobiography of a Publisher* (New York: Harcourt, Brace, and Company, 1942), p. 175; "Noted Woman Editor."

6. MMM to Theodore Roosevelt Jr., August 12, 1938; Roosevelt Jr. to MMM, August 19, 1938; "Noted Woman Editor."

7. MMM to Eleanor Roosevelt, October 19, 1939.

8. See, for instance, Barbara Sicherman, "Working It Out: Gender, Profession, and Reform in the Career of Alice Hamilton," in *Gender, Class, Race and Reform in*

the Progressive Era, eds. Frankel and Dye, pp. 128–129, 139; Perry, *Belle Moskowitz,* pp. xiii–xiv.

9. Reid, " 'Missy' Meloney," pp. 32–34; "Noted Woman Editor."

10. Reid, " 'Missy' Meloney," pp. 31–34.

11. "Elizabeth" to MMM, n.d., Marie Mattingly Meloney Clubs file, MMM manuscripts; "Sit on the Side-Lines and Watch YOURSELF Go By: MY IMPRESSIONS OF MARIE MELONEY," typed draft, n.d., MMM manuscripts.

12. MMM to Donald Jeffrey Hayes, June 27, 1939, August 30, 1939; Hayes to MMM, August 12, 1939.

INDEX

STEVE FOGEL

JULIE DES JARDINS has taught at Harvard, Macalester, and Brown and previously was professor of history at Baruch College. She currently sits on the Advisory Council of the National Women's History Museum in Washington, DC. Des Jardins lives in San Carlos, CA.